JOURNAL FOR THE STUDY OF THE NEW TESTAMENT
SUPPLEMENT SERIES

38

Executive Editor, Supplement Series
David Hill

Publishing Editor
David E Orton

JSOT Press
Sheffield

MATTHEW'S MISSIONARY DISCOURSE

A Literary Critical Analysis

Dorothy Jean Weaver

Journal for the Study of the New Testament
Supplement Series 38

Published by JSOT Press
JSOT Press is an imprint of
Sheffield Academic Press Ltd
The University of Sheffield
343 Fulwood Road
Sheffield S10 3BP
England

Typeset by Sheffield Academic Press
and
Printed in Great Britain
by Billing & Sons Ltd
Worcester

British Library Cataloguing in Publication Data

Weaver, Dorothy Jean
    Matthew's missionary discourse.
    1. Bible. N.T. Matthew—Critical studies
    I. Title   II. Series
    226.206

    ISSN 0143-5108
    ISBN 1-85075-232-X

CONTENTS

Acknowledgments   7
Abbreviations   9

Chapter 1
INTERPRETIVE APPROACHES TO MATTHEW 9.35–11.1:
FROM HISTORICAL CRITICISM TO LITERARY
CRITICISM   13
   Introduction   13
   Three Major Historical Critical Approaches to 9.35–11.1   17
   A Literary Critical Approach to 9.35–11.1   24

Chapter 2
ANALYSIS OF MATTHEW 1.1–9.34:
THE IMPLIED READER'S 'PRE-INFORMATION'   31
   The Role of the Narrator   31
   The Basic Elements of the Narrator's Story   57

Chapter 3
LITERARY CRITICAL ANALYSIS OF MATTHEW 9.35–11.1   71
   Overview of the Text   71
   Structure of the Text   73
   Analysis of the Text   74
      The narrative introduction: 9.35–10.5a   74
      The discourse: 10.5b-15   83
      The discourse: 10.16-23   90
      The discourse: 10.24-42   102
      The narrative conclusion: 11.1   124

Chapter 4
ANALYSIS OF MATTHEW 11.2-28.20: 'TO SEE THE END'   127
  Perspective of the Implied Reader at 11.2   127
  Jesus Continues His Ministry: 11.2-16.20   129
  The Tension Mounts: 16.21-25.46   135
  The Denouement: 26.1-28.20   143
  Perspective of the Implied and Real Readers at 28.20   152

Notes   155
Bibliography   223
Index of Biblical References   233
Index of Authors   247

ACKNOWLEDGMENTS

It is with deep gratitude and very great pleasure that I wish to acknowledge those many persons without whom this project would never have come to completion:

Dr Jack Dean Kingsbury, my advisor, who has opened up to me the world of Matthew's Gospel and passed on to me a deep love for the same; who has given assistance and counsel at every step of the way in my study of Matthew's Missionary Discourse and devoted countless hours to reading and responding to my document as it took shape; who has showed me by example the meaning of excellence and continually challenged me towards that same excellence; whose persistent and patient efforts have nurtured this project from 'idea' into 'reality'.

Dr Ulrich Luz, Professor of New Testament at the University of Berne, Switzerland, who graciously 'adopted' me as a doctoral student during the year which I spent at the University of Berne and gave me generously of his time for discussions of Matthean theology.

Drs Paul J. Achtemeier and Matthias Rissi, who have assisted me in the completion of my program by reading my exams and my dissertations.

Martha Aycock, Reference Librarian, who has given invaluable assistance with the numerous details involved in formatting a dissertation.

Cecelia Clark, Assistant Reference Librarian, whose technical assistance has supplied me with numerous items in my bibliography; who because of her daily presence in the UTS library has 'been there' at those times when I most needed someone; whose generous friendship and constant moral support have replenished my courage all along the way.

Dr Esther K. Lehman, my aunt, who has patiently read my entire document with pencil in hand and spent long hours and late nights 'haggling' with me over words, phrases, and punctuation in an effort to improve the dissertation stylistically.

Myra K. Lehman, my grandmother, whose prayers have supported me through every day of the past ten years and whose frequent reminders of this fact have been a constant source of encouragement to me.

Miriam L. Weaver, my mother, who has 'hung in there' with me through all the joys and the agonies of my doctoral career; who throughout the past ten years has unceasingly 'supported the cause' in ways large and small, tangible and intangible; who knows perhaps better than any other person what this achievement represents to me.

Those many others—family members, friends, teaching colleagues, students—who have inquired frequently, listened patiently, cared deeply, encouraged persistently, supported creatively, believed in me always.

DJW
May, 1989

ABBREVIATIONS

AB	Anchor Bible
AssSeign	*Assemblées du Seigneur*
BAG	Bauer, Walter; Arndt, William F.; Gingrich, F. Wilbur. *A Greek-English Lexicon of the NT and Other Early Christian Literature* (Chicago: University of Chicago Press, 1957)
BBB	Bonner biblische Beiträge
BDF	Blass, F.; Debrunner, A.; Funk, Robert W. *A Greek Grammar of the NT and Other Early Christian Literature* (Chicago: University of Chicago Press, 1961)
BZNW	Beiheft zur Zeitschrift für die neutestamentliche Wissenschaft und die Kunde der älteren Kirche
BasMiss	Basler Missionsstudien
BeiEvTh	*Beiträge zur evangelischen Theologie*
Bib	*Biblica*
BibLeb	*Bibel und Leben*
BibRes	*Biblical Research*
Biblebh	*Biblebashyam: An Indian Biblical Quarterly*
CBNTS	Coniectanea Biblica, New Testament Series
CBQ	*Catholic Biblical Quarterly*
CBQMS	Catholic Biblical Quarterly Monograph Series
CNT	Commentaire du nouveau testament
CThM	Calwer theologische Monographien
Dia	*Diakonia*
EtBib	Études bibliques
ETL	*Ephemerides Theologicae Lovanienses*
ExpTim	*Expository Times*
FB	Forschung zur Bibel
FoiVie	*Foi et vie*
GBSNT	Guides to Biblical Scholarship, New Testament Series

GrOrthTR	*Greek Orthodox Theological Review*
HNT	Handbuch zum Neuen Testament
HNTC	Harper's New Testament Commentaries
ICC	International Critical Commentary
IDB	*Interpreter's Dictionary of the Bible* (ed. George Arthur Buttrick; Nashville: Abingdon Press, 1962-1976, 5 vols.)
IntRMiss	*International Review of Mission*
Interp	*Interpretation*
JAAR	*Journal of the American Academy of Religion*
JBL	*Journal of Biblical Literature*
JETS	*Journal of the Evangelical Theological Society*
JLSM	Janua Linguarum, Series Maior
JRel	*Journal of Religion*
JSNT	*Journal for the Study of the New Testament*
JSNTSup	Journal for the Study of the New Testament Supplement Series
JTS	*Journal of Theological Studies*
JTSA	*Journal of Theology for Southern Africa*
KKNT	Kritisch-exegetischer Kommentar über das Neue Testament
LXX	*Septuagint*
LingBib	*Linguistica Biblica*
MNTC	Moffatt New Testament Commentary
MissFor	Missionswissenschaftliche Forschungen
NCB	New Century Bible
NEB	*New English Bible*
NIV	*Holy Bible, New International Version*
NLH	*New Literary History*
NTL	New Testament Library
NTM	New Testament Message: A Biblical Theological Commentary
NTS	*New Testament Studies*
Neo	Neotestamentica
NovT	*Novum Testamentum*
OrbBibOr	Orbis biblicus et orientalis
RSV	*Holy Bible, Revised Standard Version*
RThPh	*Revue de théologie et de philosophie*
RechBib	Recherches bibliques
RefTR	*Reformed Theological Review*
SBLDS	Society of Biblical Literature Dissertation Series

SBLSP	Society of Biblical Literature Seminar Paper Series
SBLSemSt	Society of Biblical Literature Semeia Studies
SBLSemSup	Society of Biblical Literature Semeia Supplements
SBT	Studies in Biblical Theology
SJT	*Scottish Journal of Theology*
SNTSMS	Society for New Testament Study Monograph Series
SciEsp	*Science et esprit: revue de philosophie et de théologie*
Scrip	*Scripture*
Sem	*Semeia*
Spir	*Spiritus*
StANT	Studien zum Alten und Neuen Testament
StBibSt	Stuttgarter Bibel-Studien
StTh	*Studia Theologica*
TD	*Theology Digest*
TDNT	*Theological Dictionary of the New Testament* (ed. Gerhard Kittel and Gerhard Friedrich, trans. Geoffrey W. Bromiley; Grand Rapids, Michigan: William B. Eerdmans, 1964-1976, 10 vols.)
TEV	*Good News Bible: The Bible in Today's English Version*
ThBei	*Theologische Beiträge*
ThHKNT	Theologischer Handkommentar zum Neuen Testament
TS	*Theological Studies*
TynBul	*Tyndale Bulletin*
ZMiss	*Zeitschrift für Mission*
ZNW	*Zeitschrift für die neutestamentliche Wissenschaft und die Kunde der älteren Kirche*
ZTK	*Zeitschrift für Theologie und Kirche*

All biblical citations are my translations unless otherwise indicated.

Chapter 1

INTERPRETIVE APPROACHES TO MATTHEW 9.35–11.1:
FROM HISTORICAL CRITICISM TO LITERARY CRITICISM

I. *Introduction: Description of the Problem*

From the standpoint of historical critical studies Mt. 9.35–11.1, the
so-called 'Missionary Discourse'[1] of Matthew's[2] Gospel, has long
proved problematic to scholars. This passage consists of a discourse
of Jesus (10.5b-42) enclosed within a narrative framework (9.35–
10.5a and 11.1) which designates the occasion of its delivery. But a
closer look at the actual contents of the discourse reveals that certain
elements within it do not appear congruent with the setting
designated by the narrative framework. A brief comparison of the
contents of the discourse with the designated setting will make clear
the exact nature of the problem.[3]

Matthew establishes the setting for the discourse of 10.5b-42 in
two ways. He designates the general setting by the position which he
gives to the discourse and its narrative framework within his overall
account of the life of Jesus. The position of 9.35–11.1 points to a
setting within Galilee, where Jesus began his public ministry (4.18,
23) and to which he has just returned following a trip to the other
side of the lake to the country of the Gadarenes (8.18, 23, 28; 9.1).

Matthew specifies the more immediate setting for the discourse in
the narrative introduction (9.35–10.5a) and the narrative conclusion
(11.1). In the narrative introduction he describes the specific events
which lead up to the delivery of the discourse: Jesus' own mission
tour through the cities and villages (9.35), his compassion for the
crowds whom he encounters (9.36), his plea that the disciples pray
for workers to be sent out into the 'great harvest' (9.37-38), and his
empowering of these same disciples with his own authority to cast
out unclean spirits and to heal the sick (10.1; cf. 9.35). Finally,
Matthew lists the names of Jesus' twelve 'apostles' (*apostolōn*), whose
designation as 'sent out ones' functions to foreshadow the climactic

announcement of 10.5a: 'These twelve Jesus sent out (*apesteilen*)...'
Matthew has thus identified the setting as a specific occasion during
the Galilean ministry of Jesus on which he sends out his twelve
disciples on a mission of their own.

Following the discourse of 10.5b-42 Matthew then restates in his
narrative conclusion (11.1) the basic elements of the previously
established setting. In language strongly reminiscent of 9.35 he gives
notice that 'when Jesus had finished instructing his twelve disciples,
he went on from there to teach and to proclaim in their cities'.[4] Thus
the two halves of the narrative framework (9.35–10.5a and 11.1)
together present a unified picture of the occasion on which Jesus
delivers the discourse of 10.5b-42.

The discourse itself is a three part speech[5] in which Jesus instructs
his twelve disciples concerning the mission on which he is sending
them. The first section (10.5b-15) lays out the specifics of the
disciples' mission in terms which appear fully congruent with the
setting designated in the narrative introduction (9.35–10.5a). The
section opens in 10.5b-6 with the command: 'Do not go out among
the Gentiles and do not enter any city of the Samaritans, but go
rather to the lost sheep of the house of Israel'. The mission on which
Jesus is sending his twelve disciples is thus defined as a mission *to
Israel* (i.e., the Jewish nation)[6] *at the specific exclusion of both the
Gentiles and the Samaritans*. The following verses (10.7-14) clarify in
detail how this mission to the Jews is to be carried out: the disciples
are instructed concerning their proclamation (10.7), their healing
ministry (10.8), their means of support for the mission (10.9-10),
their strategy for finding lodging along the way (10.11-13), and the
steps to be taken in case of rejection in any given town (10.14).
Finally, 10.15 concludes this section of the discourse with a solemn
warning of what those who reject the disciples and their message can
expect on the 'day of judgment'. Nowhere in these verses are there
elements out of keeping with the idea of a mission by the twelve
disciples during the time of Jesus' own Galilean ministry.

The second section (10.16-23), however, presents a more complicated
picture. Here different portions of the text offer conflicting evidence
concerning the relationship of this section to the setting established
in the narrative framework and reinforced in 10.5b-15.

In certain respects 10.16-23 appears to agree with its setting. Verse
16a introduces the section with a repetition of the 'sending' motif of
10.2 and 10.5a, this time as a first-person declaration by Jesus:

'Behold, I send you out (*apostellō*) as sheep in the midst of wolves'. This opening line thus performs the same function as the opening line of the previous section (10.5b-6), namely, that of linking the verses which follow to the act of 'sending' described in 10.5a.

Further, the theme of 10.16-23 can be viewed as a logical—if somewhat startling[7]—followup to the theme of 10.5b-15. If 10.5b-15 defines the disciples' mission in terms of the task to be accomplished, 10.16-23 defines that mission in terms of the persecution which the disciples will be certain to face as a result.[8] And even the language used to describe this persecution points back to the mission defined in 10.5b-15: in 10.17b Jesus warns that the disciples will be handed over 'to the [Jewish] councils'[9] and flogged 'in their [i.e., the Jewish] synagogues', a warning fully in keeping with the Jewishness of the designated setting.

In other respects, however, 10.16-23 appears not to agree with its setting. Following the warning of 10.17b there comes an additional and unexpected prediction (10.18): 'And you will be led before governors and kings on my account, as a witness to them and to the Gentiles'. In the present setting this reference to 'governors', 'kings', and 'the Gentiles' seems out of place. The prediction that the disciples will be led before an indeterminate number of 'governors and kings' points to a mission apparently broader in scope than the present one, which prohibits the disciples from 'going out among the Gentiles' and from 'entering any city of the Samaritans' (10.5b). The further indication that the disciples will bear witness to 'the Gentiles' stands in direct conflict with the absolute prohibition (10.6) against going to any but 'the lost sheep of the house of Israel'. Thus the prediction of 10.18 effectively bursts the geographical boundaries of the mission initiated in 10.5a and described in 10.5b-15.

And if the prediction of 10.18 is problematic geographically, there are other predictions in this section which are problematic from the standpoint of time. Following a further warning of persecution and hatred for the disciples (10.21-22a), 10.22b offers the promise that salvation awaits the one who perseveres 'to the end' (*eis telos*), an apparent reference to 'the end of the age'.[10] And following a command to the disciples to flee from one city to the next when they are persecuted (10.23a), Jesus provides the reason for this action (10.23b): 'For truly, I say to you, you will not have completed the cities of Israel before the Son of man comes'.[11] Thus 10.22b and 10.23b support each other in bursting the time boundaries of the mission previously described: a mission which extends 'until the end of the age' and will not reach its completion 'before the Son of man comes' does not coincide chronologically with a mission which occurs within the framework of Jesus' Galilean ministry.[12]

In spite of the introduction and the theme of this section, therefore, 10.16-23 does not fit readily into its designated setting. Rather, it seems to depict a mission with considerably broader horizons.

The final section, 10.24-42, paints a similar picture. This section combines the 'mission' theme of 10.5b-15 and the 'persecution' theme of 10.16-23 by calling for 'fearless confession' of Jesus in the face of life-threatening persecution. In doing so, however, it omits any concrete references to the 'sending' act described in 10.5a. Instead of opening with the command to 'go' (10.6) or with the declaration 'I send you' (10.16), this section opens with a generalized definition of the relationship between the 'disciple' and the 'teacher', the 'slave' and the 'master' (10.24-25a). Further, while the form of address continues to be that of the second person plural in certain passages (10.26-31, 34, 40), the referents of 10.32-42 are for the most part designated in the third person and in general terms: 'everyone who ...' (*pas hostis* + finite verb),[13] 'whoever ...' (*hos/hostis* ... [*an*] + finite verb),[14] and 'the one who ...' (*ho* + present/aorist participle).[15] Finally, there is no further mention of the original geographical setting (10.6; cf. 10.23), the original time frame (10.5a), or the original recipients of the mission (10.5b-6). As a result, there are no elements in 10.24-42 which specifically link this section to the clearly delineated mission of 10.5a, 5b-15. Rather, the overall generality of this section seems to point toward the broader mission hinted at in 10.16-23.

In light of the above evidence it is clear that 9.35–11.1 presents some difficult questions for its interpreters. Does 10.5b-42 represent a unified discourse which can be interpreted solely in terms of the setting provided by its narrative framework, 9.35–10.5a and 11.1? Or does 10.5b-42 in fact require the assumption of two settings, only one of which is the setting provided by the narrative framework? And if this is so, what then is the second setting?

II. *Three Major Historical Critical Approaches to 9.35–11.1:*
Presentation and Critique

Three major approaches have been taken to the resolution of these questions. But while they differ significantly from each other, these three approaches nevertheless share a basic historical orientation. In each case an attempt is made to interpret 10.5b-42 in terms of an actual historical setting or sequence of settings, i.e., in terms of the life of Jesus and/or of the Matthean church.

The 'Galilean' approach
The first approach assumes for the entire discourse a setting within the Galilean ministry of Jesus. H.A.W. Meyer, for example, resolves the apparent contradiction between 10.5b-6 and 10.18 by referring the 'witness' of 10.18 not only to the 'governors' (*hēgemonas*) and 'kings' (*basileis*) of the same verse but also to the Jews who are the implicit subjects of the previous verse.[16] Accordingly, the disciples' witness 'to them and to the Gentiles' no longer refers to the 'governors and kings' of 10.18 on the one hand and to unspecified 'Gentiles' on the other. Instead, the witness 'to them' is now a witness to the Jews of 10.17, while the witness 'to the Gentiles' is a witness to 'the *hēgemonas* and *basileis* and their Gentile environment'.[17] Meyer's tacit assumption appears to be that if he can establish the identity of the 'Gentiles' of 10.18 with the 'governors and kings' of the same verse, then there will no longer be a contradiction in terms between 10.5b-6 and 10.18. Rather, the reference to 'Gentiles' will then be primarily a reference to the secular officials in Palestine before whom Jesus' disciples will be led as a result of their mission work within Israel.[18]

J. Lange takes this argumentation one step further by making concrete what Meyer leaves unspecified, namely, the specific identity of these 'governors and kings'.[19] Judging on the basis of Matthean usage, Lange argues that *hēgemōn* is for Matthew none other than a reference to Pilate (cf. 27.2, 11, 14, 15, 21, 27; 28.14) and that *basileus* refers to such figures as Herod the Great (cf. 2.1, 3, 9), Archelaus (cf. 2.22), and Herod Antipas (cf. 14.9). He therefore concludes that just as Jesus was vulnerable to 'kings' (2.13, 22; 14.13), 'Gentiles' (20.19), and 'governors' (27.11) on Palestinian soil, so also Jesus' disciples can be brought before 'governors' and 'kings' even while they are still in Israel.[20]

Meyer and Lange, accordingly, interpret 10.5b-42 in terms of a single setting within the Galilean ministry of Jesus. And they arrive at their conclusion by arguing that 10.18 is a prediction *which found its fulfilment* in a one-time mission to Israel by the twelve disciples of Jesus.

But the most well-known attempt to explain 10.5b-42 in terms of a setting within the ministry of Jesus argues in opposite fashion to Meyer and Lange. A. Schweitzer, in his polemic for the eschatological interpretation of 10.23b ('For truly, I say to you, you will not have completed the cities of Israel before the Son of man comes'),[21] starts with the same assumptions as the above scholars: (1) Jesus delivered this entire discourse on a single historical occasion; and (2) this discourse pertained to an immediate mission which was then carried out by Jesus' twelve disciples. But while the above scholars assume the reliability of Jesus' prediction that the disciples will meet with persecution on this mission, Schweitzer argues on the basis of 10.23b that Jesus' predictions in this chapter are mistaken predictions and thus not reliable. Since the Son of man has not 'come'—as Jesus has predicted in 10.23b that he would - by the time the disciples have returned from their mission,[22] it follows that Jesus was mistaken in this prediction as well as in the prediction of the sufferings to befall the disciples.[23] Schweitzer thus argues that 10.18 (along with all the other verses which relate to the sufferings of the disciples) represents a prediction *which was not fulfilled*.[24] This line of argument ultimately leads Schweitzer to the conclusion that the discourse is 'historical as a whole and down to the smallest detail precisely because, according to the view of modern theology, it must be judged unhistorical'.[25]

Thus scholars use opposing lines of argument to support the conclusion that 10.5b-42 is to be interpreted in terms of a single setting within the Galilean ministry of Jesus. But the fact that Meyer can fit the discourse into that setting only by taking unwarranted liberties with the exegesis of 10.17-18[26] and the fact that Schweitzer can do the same only by classifying Jesus' predictions as mistaken point to the basic problem which the majority of scholars find with this approach: not all elements within 10.5b-42 fit readily with the assumption of a setting within the Galilean ministry of Jesus. In his *Introduction to the New Testament* T. Zahn reflects the basic thrust of scholarly consensus on this point:

> The connected and well-arranged discourse of chap. x., which is associated with a definite occasion, could not have been spoken on the occasion then indicated. While the *idou apostellō* (not *apostelō*) (x. 16) cannot be referred to any other sending out of the apostles than that which is narrated in x. 5, every intelligent reader [*sic!*] says to himself that on this preaching tour the apostles could not possibly have been in a position where they would be brought before kings and rulers, and where they would flee from city to city in expectation of Jesus' return (x. 16-23).[27]

But while there is general scholarly consensus on the problem of interpreting 10.5b-42 in terms of a setting within the Galilean ministry of Jesus, there is no such consensus on how to resolve the difficulties inherent in this approach. Here two basic schools of thought prevail.

The 'dual' approach
By far the most widely accepted approach to the interpretation of 10.5b-42 is one which views this discourse not in terms of a single setting but rather in terms of two separate, sequential settings. According to this approach, Matthew's designated setting (i.e., the Galilean ministry of Jesus) applies only to 10.5b-15, while the remainder of the discourse describes a mission which is to take place at a later time and in a broader setting.

But this approach raises several questions. Who is responsible for the divided focus within what is ostensibly a single, unified discourse (cf. 10.5a and 11.1)? Further, if this discourse requires the assumption of two separate settings, only the first of which is the Galilean ministry of Jesus, then what is the second setting? Here two pictures emerge.

There are scholars who attribute the divided focus of this discourse to Jesus, concluding that he is addressing on one and the same occasion two different situations, one of them immediate and the other long range. As R.C.H. Lenski explains it,

> Matthew ... records the complete charge as given by Jesus when the Twelve were first sent out. He is telling us, not like Mark and Luke, only of the mission to Galilee during the next days or weeks, but of the complete apostolic mission of the Twelve, into Galilee now, and then at last into all the world.[28]

According to this view, therefore, there are two major shifts from the first to the second half of the discourse, the one with reference to time frame and the other with reference to geographical boundaries. Thus in delivering the discourse of 10.5b-42 Jesus first describes the forthcoming Galilean mission of his twelve disciples (10.5b-15) and then shifts to a description of the ongoing worldwide mission which they are later to carry out.[29]

But the more prevalent view is one which attributes the divided focus of 10.5b-42 not to Jesus—who on one occasion is found to be addressing two different situations—but rather to Matthew—who has brought together a collection of sayings of Jesus which were originally spoken on different occasions and in regard to different situations.[30] Zahn once again reflects a widespread scholarly consensus when he concludes that '*Matthew connected the commission* which Jesus gave His disciples when He sent them out for the first time *with other sayings* relative to their later work, *weaving the whole into an ordered discourse*' (italics mine).[31]

Here, however, opinions vary as to the identity of the referents of the second half of the discourse. There are those who, like Zahn, hold that the entire discourse still refers to Jesus' twelve disciples. F.C. Grant, for example, who interprets both 10.18[32] and 10.23[33] in terms of post-Easter Palestine, comments that 10.23 serves to '[direct] the XII what to do in case the message met with hostility (vv. 14ff.)'.[34]

Others, however, pointedly distinguish between the referents of the two halves of the discourse: while in their view the first half refers to Jesus' twelve disciples, the second half refers instead to 'the Church' in general.[35] As Günther Bornkamm puts it, 'this last part of the missionary discourse [10.17-39] is no longer missionary instruction in the proper sense, but it gives directions to the Church as a whole and indicates what the disciples of Jesus as a whole must expect and endure'.[36] This distinction between the twelve disciples and 'the Church' represents a third major shift from the first to the second half of the discourse.

In his analysis of 10.16-39, B.W. Bacon then notes one further shift within the discourse. In addition to the shifts in time frame, geographical boundaries, and referents, there is also a shift in the intention of the text[37] from the reporting of history to preaching. In Bacon's words,

> The framer of this expanded form of the Markan Discourse (Rmt) has obviously lost sight of the situation with which he began (another indication of Mk's priority). The scenes are no longer those of hospitable Galilee, where a kindly reception could be anticipated and, according to Lk 22.35, was actually experienced.

Galilee and the mission to heal and proclaim the coming kingdom has faded out of the picture. In its place has come the world-wide persecution of the apostolic and post-apostolic age. *The compiler has ceased to be a historian, he is now a preacher addressing his own age under color of prediction by Jesus* (italics mine).[38]

According to the proponents of the 'dual' approach these four major shifts issue in a fundamentally divided discourse: the first half of the discourse refers back to a specific event during the lifetime of Jesus and his twelve disciples, while the second half refers to the situation of Matthew's own church. But there are several problems with this approach.

First of all, Matthew does not in any way announce his intention to shift from one setting to another. Instead, the reader is left to draw the necessary conclusions from the abrupt intrusion into the text of details or entire statements which appear irreconcilable with what has gone before. F. Filson finds, for example, that 'most of [10.17-22] *does not fit* a swift preaching tour in Galilee',[39] while M. Hooker comments conversely (p. 361) that 'much of this section [10.17-22] *seems more appropriate* to a later period than to a mission set in the course of Jesus' own lifetime'[40] (italics in both cases mine). Even Bacon, who appears to emphasize the intentionality of Matthew's shift from one situation to another,[41] nevertheless indicates that Matthew has '*obviously lost sight of* the situation with which he began'[42] (italics mine). Thus not only is the reader left to draw the necessary inferences from the text concerning the shift from one situation to another; but it also appears that not even the author responsible for this shift is consciously aware of what has taken place in his text.

Even more problematic for this approach is the fact that Matthew clearly presents 10.5b-42 as a unified discourse. The very fact that Matthew here brings together a collection of originally unconnected sayings of Jesus[43] and places them within a well-defined and unified framework (9.35-10.5a and 11.1) points to the conclusion that Matthew's purpose here is to create a unity where none had previously existed.

Thus while the 'dual' approach responds to the difficulties inherent in the 'Galilean' approach,[44] it nevertheless creates some difficulties of its own which call for resolution. Accordingly, the third major approach to the interpretation of 10.5b-42 attempts to resolve the difficulties inherent in both of the previous approaches, while at the same time retaining their respective strengths.

The 'Matthean' approach

This third approach finds it impossible to view the entirety of 10.5b-42 in terms of a setting within the Galilean ministry of Jesus. At the same time, however, it also recognizes the fallacy of positing a fundamental division within a discourse which is presented as a unity. As a result, this approach views 10.5b-42 as a unified discourse, not in terms of a setting within Jesus' Galilean ministry, but in terms of a setting within the life of Matthew's own church. It is only as Matthew has brought together these sayings of Jesus and has made them 'transparent' for the situation of his own church that they attain their unity as a discourse.

Here two complementary emphases, one negative and the other positive, come to the fore. On the negative side, the proponents of the 'Matthean' approach play down the significance for Matthew of an original historical event. W.C. Allen, for example, notes that 'to the editor of the first Gospel this mission of the Twelve during Christ's lifetime seems to have had little interest'.[45] F.W. Beare goes even further in this direction by discounting altogether the interest which Matthew might have had in an original historical event: 'At any rate it is clear that Matthew is not interested in [the disciples' mission] as an event which took place during the Galilean ministry of Jesus'.[46]

The positive conclusion, on the other hand, stresses Matthew's use of these sayings of Jesus to address directly the members of his own church. E. Schott finds the distinction between Matthew's discourse and the parallel discourses of Mark (6.6b-13) and Luke (9.1-6; 10.1-16) in the fact that Matthew addresses the words of Jesus directly to his readers in 'living and personal fashion' and not, as do Mark and Luke, in the form of 'historical recollection':

> Er [i.e., Matthew] erzählt nicht wie jene [i.e., Mark and Luke]; die gebotene Rede wird ihm unter der hand lebendig; was Jesus an seine Jünger geredet hat, redet er zu seinen Lesern, lebendig, persönlich, nicht in der Form geschichtlicher Erinnerung.[47]

It is F. Hahn, however, who introduces the terminology of 'transparence' to describe what Matthew is doing with 10.5b-42. Refuting the notion that Matthew is operating with the concept of a mission first exclusively to Jews (Mt. 10) and then exclusively to Gentiles (Mt. 24.14; 28.19), he observes:

> It is not an adequate explanation to say that whereas Matt. 10 refers only to the sending out of the disciples during Jesus' lifetime 24.14 and 28.19 refer to the period after Easter. For it is quite clear

that in chapter 10 the historical situation is *arranged* [*transparent gemacht*] for the disciples' mission in the time after Jesus' resurrection, as indeed all the longer discourses of the Gospel directly concern the Church.[48]

It appears, therefore, that while the 'Matthean' approach still views 10.5b-42 in terms of two settings, the second setting is no longer viewed as following the first but rather as superimposed on top of it. The resulting effect is that of a 'double exposure': underneath lies Matthew's historicizing account of an event in the life of Jesus and his twelve disciples,[49] while on the surface there is a sermon (in the words of Jesus) which Matthew has aimed at the members of his own church. S. Brown stresses this 'double exposure' effect in his analysis of the discourse:

In Mt 9.35-11.1 the evangelist has Jesus address his community in the person of the twelve disciples, and in the point-for-point assimilation of their missionary functions with those of Jesus, who sends them out, the Matthean community must be able to see the delineation of its own missionary task.[50]

But in the final analysis this approach virtually loses sight of the first half of the 'double exposure' in its emphasis on the second half. As H. Frankemölle sees it, 10.5b-42 is no longer in any real sense the account of an historical event in the life of Jesus and his disciples, but rather a 'literary fiction' of Matthew's own composition. In his view Matthew offers in ch. 10

... keine 'Aussendungsrede' im engen Sinn ... sondern eine reflektierende, geschichtstheologisch orientierte Anweisung für seine Gemeinde in der literarischen Fiktion, wodurch die vorausgesetzte Situation 'ent-historisiert' wird.[51]

But it is at this point that the problem with the 'Matthean' approach becomes most obvious. In order to accord primary significance to the 'transparent' or 'literary fictional' level of the discourse, it is necessary to remove the discourse from its narrative framework, 9.35-10.5a and 11.1. And to do this is to disregard Matthew's own clue to the interpretation of the discourse. The very fact that Matthew has connected disparate sayings of Jesus into a discourse and set them into this framework means that the framework itself is of primary significance in interpreting the discourse.[52] As a result, in downplaying the significance of the narrative framework, the 'Matthean' approach ultimately does violence to Matthew's own intentions.[53]

Summary critique

It has now become clear that none of the three major approaches to the interpretation of 9.35–11.1 has fully succeeded in its attempt to explain the apparent incongruities of the text. The 'Galilean' approach fails because it cannot convincingly fit all the details of 10.5b-42 into the setting of Jesus' Galilean ministry.[54] As a result, this approach arrives at a unified interpretation of 9.35–11.1 by denying some elements of the text their rightful significance.

The 'dual' approach, on the contrary, does not disregard or manipulate any elements of 10.5b-42. Rather, it carefully points out four major shifts from the first half of the discourse (10.5b-15) to the second half (10.16-42) and explains these shifts by assigning the first half of the discourse to one setting and the second half to a separate setting. Nevertheless, this approach fails because it cannot deal adequately with the unity which Matthew has imposed upon the sayings of 10.5b-42 by placing them within a unified framework. In assigning to two settings what Matthew himself has assigned to one, this approach does not do justice to Matthew's intentions in creating the discourse and placing it where he does.

The 'Matthean' approach fails for the same reason that the 'Galilean' approach fails: it can relate the entire discourse (10.5b-42) to a single historical setting only by disregarding part of the text. In this case, however, it is not details of the discourse but rather the narrative framework (9.35–10.5a and 11.1) which must be disregarded in order to place the discourse into the setting of Matthew's own church.

Consequently, none of the above three approaches has demonstrated that it can deal adequately both with Matthew's text and with a given historical setting or sequence of settings. Either elements of the text must be disregarded in order to fit the discourse into a single historical setting; or the unity of the Matthean text must be violated in order to allow for several historical settings. It appears that any new treatment of 9.35–11.1 will have to abandon the historical question as a central concern, if it intends to do justice to Matthew's text as that text now stands.

III. *A Literary Critical Approach to 9.35–11.1*

Rephrasing of the basic question

The approach of the present study has as its starting point not the historical critical questions of the above three approaches but rather the literary critical question.[55] This approach views the Gospels as 'stories' which are therefore to be analyzed as other 'stories' are analyzed.[56] According to this approach the Gospel of Matthew functions above all as a 'narrative' (i.e., as a literary work 'distinguished by two characteristics: the presence of a story and a story-teller').[57] Consequently, in order to do justice to the intention of Matthew's text, it is necessary to approach the analysis of that text as one would approach the analysis of any narrative.

This understanding has three important implications for the interpretation of the Gospel of Matthew, either as a whole or in part (as with the present study of 9.35–11.1). In the first place, viewing Matthew's text as a narrative is to assume a unity for that text which in the past has generally been ignored. In his discussion of narrative criticism as it relates to the Gospel of Mark, D. Rhoads makes an observation which is equally valid for the Gospel of Matthew:

> Redaction criticism, form criticism, source criticism, and even composition criticism break up the narrative in order to get at the questions they pursue. Distinctions between redaction and tradition, between history and tradition, naturally fragment the text, a tendency which is reinforced by the designation of chapters, verses, and pericopae. By contrast, literary questions about narrative features tend to reveal Mark's Gospel as whole cloth ... One can discover the unity of this Gospel in terms of the remarkable integrity of the 'story' which it tells, and come to trust that many apparent enigmas and discrepancies may be satisfactorily solved within the larger whole of the story. We know how to take the text apart to analyze it; adding narrative criticism to our study is an opportunity to reaffirm the original achievement of Mark in creating a unified story.[58]

Secondly, if Matthew's Gospel represents a unified story narrated by a storyteller, then the primary key to the interpretation of that story lies in the text of the story itself and not in the historical situation in which the story took shape or in the historical situation to which the story itself points. In other words, to view Matthew's Gospel as 'narrative' is to focus above all on the 'narrative world' of people, places and events which is found directly in the text and which is in the end the literary creation of the author.[59]

The third major implication which the literary critical approach has for the interpretation of the Gospel of Matthew grows logically out of the first two. If Matthew's Gospel represents a unified story with its own internal narrative world of people, places, and events;

then it is necessary to look at any given section or element of that story above all in terms of its relationship to the whole. In his 1972 appeal for the adoption of a literary critical approach to the study of the Synoptic Gospels and Acts, N. Perrin notes 'the growing recognition of the necessity to interpret any part of one of these works in terms of its function within the structure of the work as a whole'.[60] As he explains it,

> The fact to be recognized is that the [Synoptic Gospels and Acts] are carefully structured works within which the authors have given indications of their intended structures by means of various literary devices. It follows, therefore, that no interpretation of any pericope within, or section of, these works can be adequate which does not raise questions about the place and function of that pericope or section within the structure of the work as a whole.[61]

In light of these implications, 9.35–11.1 is seen to be an integral element of a larger narrative, Matthew's account of the life, death, and resurrection of Jesus. Consequently, the basic question to be asked of this text is literary critical in nature: what role does 9.35–11.1 play within Matthew's overall narrative?

Definition of literary critical terminology
In order to explain the role of 9.35–11.1 within Matthew's overall narrative, however, it will first be necessary to define the literary critical categories essential to such a study.[62] These categories will then determine the specific methodology to be used in the following study of 9.35–11.1, i.e., the specific questions to be asked of Matthew's text.

The fundamental category here is that of 'communication'. To look at the Gospel of Matthew as 'narrative' is to look at it above all as a 'communication' between a 'sender' and a 'receiver'.[63] The sender is the author of the narrative, i.e., Matthew,[64] while the receiver is the person who reads the narrative.

But the person who reads the narrative is not in fact confronted with the real flesh-and-blood 'Matthew' who is the author of the narrative. Rather, the reader is confronted with the 'implied author', that version of himself which Matthew 'implies' through the narrative he has written. As W. Booth explains it,

> As [an author] writes, he creates not simply an ideal, impersonal 'man in general' but an implied version of 'himself' that is different from the implied authors we meet in other men's works... Whether

we call this implied author an 'official scribe', or adopt the term recently revived by Kathleen Tillotson—the author's 'second self'—it is clear that the picture the reader gets of this presence is one of the author's most important effects. However impersonal he may try to be, his reader will inevitably construct a picture of the official scribe who writes in this manner.[65]

But if Matthew 'implies' a version of himself through his narrative, he likewise 'implies' a version of the reader. This 'implied reader' is thus 'an imaginary reader with the ideal responses implied or suggested by the narrative, experiencing suspense or feeling amazement or sympathizing with a character at the appropriate times'.[66]

Consequently, the Gospel of Matthew represents a communicational transaction between the implied author (Matthew) and the implied reader of the narrative: Matthew has a message to communicate and the implied reader has the task of responding to that message.[67] But in order to understand how this communicational transaction takes place, it is necessary to identify the means by which Matthew the implied author communicates with the implied reader of his Gospel.

Matthew communicates, first of all, through the voice of the narrator, the storyteller of Matthew's story.[68] As the spokesperson for Matthew, the narrator is thus the central figure in the communicational transaction, since it is the narrator's voice which directly confronts the implied reader of Matthew's narrative.[69] Accordingly, an examination of the characteristics of the narrator— his identity as a 'reliable' or 'unreliable' narrator,[70] the literary techniques by which he tells his story, and the point of view from which he tells his story—is the necessary starting point for a literary critical analysis of Matthew's Gospel. What Matthew communicates to the implied reader of his Gospel depends entirely on how that reader evaluates Matthew's narrator.

But the major focus of attention in such a study must obviously be the story which the narrator tells. This story can be viewed in terms of three basic elements: characters (the actors in the story), plot (the sequence of events within the story), and setting (the designated location or surroundings within which any given event of the story takes place).[71]

Thus far, therefore, there are two basic questions to be asked of Matthew's narrative: (1) what are the characteristics of Matthew's narrator? and (2) what is the story which that narrator tells? These are both questions which must be asked directly of or about the narrator, since it is the narrator who is telling the story under consideration in his own way and from his own point of view.

But the ultimate question to be asked of Matthew's narrative lies beyond the questions of narrator and story, questions which are objective in nature. This ultimate question is evaluative in nature, one which assesses the 'evidence' derived from the study of 'narrator' and 'story' in order to determine the effect of the narrator's story. And to ask this question is to point beyond the narrator to the implied author of the narrative, since it is the implied author who has 'invented the narrator, along with everything else in the narrative, . . . stacked the cards in this particular way, had these things happen to these characters, in these words or images'.[72] At the same time this question also implicates the implied reader, since the implied reader is the second partner in the communicational transaction. Accordingly, the ultimate question is the following: what does Matthew, the implied author of the Gospel, communicate to the implied reader of that Gospel?

There are thus three questions essential to the literary critical analysis of Matthew's Gospel: (1) the role of the narrator in telling the story; (2) the content of the story (i.e., the characters, plot, and setting); and (3) the effect of the narrative, or in other words, that which the implied author communicates to the implied reader. The specific task of the present study, therefore, is to utilize these questions in the search to discover the role of Mt. 9.35–11.1 within Matthew's overall narrative.

In addition, it is crucial to note that the object of the present study, Mt. 9.35–11.1, is simply one piece of a larger whole, one single segment within the 'sequential composite'[73] of events which constitutes Matthew's overall narrative. The text of 9.35–11.1 thus derives its significance not simply from its content as such but from its relationship to the other 'events' in the unfolding narrative of Matthew's Gospel. Accordingly, it is essential that the question of sequence be kept in mind at all times and that this passage be analyzed strictly in terms of its position within the Gospel.

Structure of the present analysis

In line with the above considerations I shall adopt the following three-step approach to the analysis of 9.35–11.1. The first step (Chapter 2) will be to examine Mt. 1.1–9.34 in order to discover the prior knowledge or 'pre-information' which the implied reader has concerning the narrator, characters, and setting of 9.35–11.1 and the plot of the story up to that point. The second step (Chapter 3) will be to examine 9.35–11.1 itself to determine what this passage communicates to the implied reader who encounters it within the sequence of Matthew's Gospel. The third step (Chapter 4) will be to examine the remainder of the Gospel, 11.2–28.20, with two questions in mind: (1) how does 11.2–28.20 respond to the unresolved tensions of 9.35–11.1? and (2) how does 9.35–11.1 inform the implied reader's understanding of the remainder of the Gospel? At the conclusion of Chapter 4 I shall analyze the evidence derived from this literary analysis of 9.35–11.1 in order to assess the role of this passage in Matthew's overall narrative.

Chapter 2

ANALYSIS OF MATTHEW 1.1-9.34:
THE IMPLIED READER'S 'PRE-INFORMATION'

The first step in my literary critical analysis of Mt. 9.35-11.1 is to examine Mt. 1.1-9.34 in order to discover what the implied reader[1] of Matthew's Gospel knows about the narrator, characters, plot, and setting of the narrative prior to 9.35. Since the act of reading is inherently a 'linear activity' in which the reader moves sequentially from beginning to end of a text,[2] it follows that the implied reader of Matthew's Gospel will interpret 9.35-11.1 according to the 'pre-information' received from reading the prior section of the Gospel.[3] Therefore it is essential that an examination of 1.1-9.34 be the starting point for a study which seeks to interpret 9.35-11.1 from the standpoint of the implied reader of Matthew's Gospel. Accordingly, I shall examine 1.1-9.34 first of all to analyze the role of the narrator in telling the story and then to assess the content of the story—characters, plot, and setting—up to 9.35.

I. *The Role of the Narrator*

Susan S. Lanser in *The Narrative Act: Point of View in Prose Fiction* has worked out a detailed system for the analysis of the narrator's point of view in a narrative,[4] a system which draws heavily on Boris Uspensky's designation of five 'planes' on which point of view occurs.[5] In the following discussion of the role of Matthew's narrator I will apply the basic categories of Lanser's system to Matthew 1.1-9.34.[6]

Lanser bases her 'descriptive poetics of point of view'[7] on the relationship between the author and the reader of a narrative. As she explains it,

> The degree of consent a reader gives [to a text] is a function of the authority which the fictional world holds for this reader, and this authority, in turn, is a manifestation of the novelist's authority. As

> whatever a reader knows of the author is brought to the reading of a text, the writer's and the text's authority are dynamically intertwined; either is capable of enhancing or diminishing the other.[8]

Lanser then defines the relationship between author and reader of a text in terms of 'a complex of factors involving the speaker's relationship to the listener, the message and the verbal act'.[9] This 'complex of factors' consists of three elements: the 'status' which the narrator has in the eyes of the implied reader, the 'contact' which the narrator establishes with the implied reader, and the 'stance' which the narrator assumes in telling the story.[10]

The status of the narrator
In Lanser's words, status

> ... concerns the relationship of the speaker to the speech act: the authority, competence, and credibility which the communicator is conventionally and personally allowed... The individual's status as communicator depends on a number of factors—on his or her identity, credibility with respect to the verbal act in question, apparent sincerity, and skill in conveying the message.[11]

The factors which determine the status of the narrator, therefore, relate both to the 'diegetic authority' of the narrator, the authority granted the narrator to assume the role of storyteller in the first place, and to the 'mimetic authority' of the narrator, that authority granted the narrator by virtue of his skill in telling the story.[12] As a result the first questions to be asked concerning Matthew's narrator deal with his diegetic and mimetic authority.

The diegetic authority of the narrator. Lanser distinguishes a variety of factors which together establish the diegetic authority of a narrator. The first of these is 'authorial equivalence', the extent to which the implied reader is willing to identify the narrator of a text with the implied author of that text. As Lanser views it,

> Ordinarily, the unmarked case of narration for public narrators is that the narrating voice is equated with the textual author (the extrafictional voice or 'implied author') unless a different case is marked—signaled—by the text. In other words, in the absence of direct markings which separate the public narrator from the extrafictional voice, so long as it is possible to give meaning to the text within the equation author=narrator, readers will conventionally make this equation.[13]

Lanser then goes on to posit an 'inverse relationship' between the equation of narrator and implied author and the extent to which the narrator functions as a character within the story itself. The narrator who does not participate as a character in his own story is normally identified with the implied author, while the narrator who functions as a character in the story he tells is generally distinguished from the implied author.[14]

To speak of the narrator's involvement/non-involvement as a character in the story which he narrates, then, is to speak of his 'representation' of himself in the story.[15] Lanser views the possible representation of the narrator in terms of a spectrum moving from 'sole protagonist' on the one end through 'co-protagonist', 'minor character', 'witness participant', and 'uninvolved eyewitness' to 'uninvolved narrator' on the other end.[16]

An examination of 1.1–9.34 makes it clear that Matthew's narrator represents himself as an uninvolved narrator rather than as a character of either greater or lesser importance. All of the verbs which constitute the narrative framework of the story[17] from 1.1 through 9.34 are in the third person,[18] with the result that the narrator in no instance directly identifies himself with the events of the story by means of first person verbs. Further, the presence in 1.1–9.34 of six 'formula quotations',[19] in which the narrator identifies certain events of the story as the 'fulfilment' of Jewish prophecy, would appear to indicate that the narrator stands at a great enough distance from the events of the story that he has had time to reflect on and evaluate their significance. While this evaluative stance in and of itself does not indicate that the narrator stands outside the events of the story,[20] the coincidence of this stance with the total absence of first person verbs within the narrative framework of the text builds a strong case for viewing Matthew's storyteller as an uninvolved narrator. According to Lanser's theory of the relationship between the representation of the narrator and authorial equivalence, therefore, the implied reader of 1.1–9.34 will be encouraged to identify the narrator with Matthew, the implied author.[21]

A third factor which helps to determine the diegetic authority of a narrator is that of 'privilege', the extent of the narrator's knowledge concerning the characters of the story.[22] If the narrator functions as a character in his own story, then the knowledge which he will have concerning the remaining characters will necessarily be limited to that which can be learned about others by natural means. If, however, the storyteller is an uninvolved narrator, then his privilege extends much further. Rhoads and Michie posit three levels of privilege which are available for the narrator who stands outside of his story:

> A narrator with 'objective omniscience' can tell everything which can be seen and heard, without showing what is in the minds of the characters... A narrator with 'limited omniscience', in addition to objective-style description, also tells thoughts and feelings, but only those in the mind of the protagonist. A narrator displaying 'unlimited omniscience' may tell anything about the story world, including what is in the mind of any character at any time and place.[23]

On the basis of this categorization it becomes evident that Matthew's narrator claims 'unlimited omniscience' for himself. In a variety of ways the narrator presents information which points to his unlimited access to the minds of his characters. He reports dreams which people have had,[24] feelings and thoughts of the characters,[25] and things which individuals or groups of people are saying privately.[26] He is aware of 'private' events which no outside party is present to witness.[27] And he relates that Jesus has the same ability to see inside other characters: what others say in private or merely think to themselves is known to Jesus, while Jesus' knowledge of their thoughts is, in turn, known to the narrator.[28]

Equally crucial to the omniscience of the narrator is his freedom to intrude his own ideas into the narrative in the form of direct commentary on the events being narrated or the characters involved in the action.[29] Here again Matthew's narrator claims unlimited omniscience for himself. Seven times within 1.1–9.34 he assumes the authority to interpret events in the lives of John the Baptist and Jesus as the 'fulfilment' of Jewish prophecy.[30] Such confidence on the part of Matthew's narrator indicates that he views himself as having 'the final word' on the life of Jesus, a stance possible only to one who has unlimited omniscience.

There is, however, one exception to the otherwise unlimited access which Matthew's narrator has to the minds of his characters and the private events in which they participate. The narrator has no access to the mind or thoughts either of God or Satan.[31] All that the implied reader learns about God in 1.1–9.34 is transmitted either by indirect means or by the voice of God emanating directly from heaven. God communicates by means of an angel or angels,[32] through the voices of the prophets,[33] by way of the 'written'/'spoken' words of the law,[34] and in his own voice directly from heaven (3.17). In addition, Jesus makes frequent references to God in his address of 5.3–7.27.[35] But at no point within 1.1–9.34 is there any hint that either Jesus or the narrator has 'inside' information concerning the motives which lie behind God's actions.[36] Nor does the narrator have access to the inner workings of Satan's mind. All that the implied reader learns about Satan is what he does.[37] Thus the omniscience of Matthew's narrator is truly unlimited only with regard to the 'human' characters of the story.

A fourth factor which helps to establish the diegetic authority of a narrator is what Lanser refers to as the narrator's 'referential claim',[38] that claim which the narrator himself makes as to the type of story being narrated. As Lanser puts it,

> Different kinds of privilege are implied by the claim of report and the claim of invention; if the narrator claims to be telling a true story, s/he is expected to account for information and to lay a plausible framework for the claim. Report commits the narrator in a way that invention does not, just as historical claim and obvious parody imply different relationships to the literary act.[39]

This means, in effect, that the implied reader enters into a 'contract' with the narrator in which the narrator proposes the genre of the text and the implied reader responds by reading the text 'as if it were' whatever the narrator claims it to be.[40] Such a contract lays an obligation on both of the parties. It is incumbent upon the implied reader to accept the narrator's claim for the story being told. Conversely, the narrator must 'keep faith' with the implied reader by respecting the conventional limitations of the genre which he himself has proposed.

Here there are two observations with regard to 1.1–9.34. The first of these is that Matthew's narrator is telling a story. This means that the narrator may assume the storyteller's freedom to tell his story in whatever way and by whatever means he chooses. As noted above (p. 33), Matthew's narrator chooses to tell his story as an uninvolved narrator with virtually unlimited access to the minds of his characters and the private events in which they participate. This does not mean, however, that the narrator has either participated in or received 'inside' information about the events of which he writes. Rather, his omniscience emerges simply from his prerogative as a storyteller to know and tell whatever he chooses about the characters

of his story.[41] Accordingly, the characters and events of which
Matthew's narrator speaks belong to the 'narrative world' which he
himself has created by the telling of his story and not *ipso facto* to the
'real world'.[42] To accept Matthew's narrator as a storyteller,
therefore, is to accept his text as a story peopled with story-
characters and moved along by story-events.[43]

But if Matthew's narrator is on the one hand to be viewed as a
storyteller plying his trade, there is a second observation which is
equally crucial to the interpretation of his story. The evidence from
1.1–9.34 indicates that the narrator is here claiming to present
'report' as compared to 'invention'. He pointedly locates the events of
his story in relationship to recognizable (and thus verifiable) figures
and/or events from Jewish and secular history: Abraham,[44] David,[45]
the Babylonian Exile,[46] Herod (the Great),[47] and Herod's son,
Archelaus.[48] He connects the events of his story directly to the entire
history of the Jewish people by way of a genealogy (1.2-16, 17) which
begins with Abraham, the recognized 'father' of the Jewish people,[49]
and ends with Joseph, 'the husband of Mary, of whom was begotten[50]
Jesus, who is called Messiah'. And he represents numerous events as
the 'fulfilment' of Jewish prophecy,[51] thus expressing strong confidence
in the story which he is telling.

It therefore appears that the implied reader's contract with
Matthew's narrator is to read the Gospel of Matthew as a story
which nevertheless 'insists on its historical truth by claiming to be a
factual document'.[52] Consequently, it is this understanding of
Matthew's Gospel which will inform all subsequent discussion of the
characters, events, and settings of the narrator's story.

In light of all four factors examined above[53]—authorial equivalence,
representation, privilege, and referential claim—the implied reader
of Matthew 1.1–9.34 now has the following picture of Matthew's
narrator: (1) he does not distinguish himself in any formal way from
the implied author of the text; (2) he recounts the story from the
vantage point of an uninvolved narrator; (3) he claims for himself
virtually unlimited access to the minds and private lives of his
characters; and (4) he makes a multi-faceted claim for the factuality
of the story he tells. All of these factors together lead the implied
reader not only to trust the reliability of Matthew's storyteller but
also to equate the storyteller with Matthew himself.

The mimetic authority of the narrator. Lanser defines the mimetic
authority of the narrator in terms of three factors: 'honesty',
'reliability', and 'competence'. She describes these factors as follows:

(1)　a belief that the narrator is honest and sincere; that is, that he or she will not dissimulate and will speak the truth as far as he or she perceives it; that the narrator will mean what he or she says; and that the narrator will not omit any information that is crucial to the meaning of the story;

(2)　a belief that the narrator is intellectually and morally trustworthy; that is, that his or her perceptions and mental capacities are at least acceptable, useful, and accurate, if not enlightening; and

(3)　evidence that he or she has sufficient competence as a storyteller to present the story in a manner that is coherent, complete, and skillful enough for it to remain 'tellable'.[54]

From an examination of 1.1–9.34 it is evident that Matthew's narrator represents the qualities of 'honesty' and 'reliability'.[55] This fact is apparent above all in the way in which all levels of the text— the events of the story, the direct commentary by Matthew's narrator, and the predictions found within the narrative—support each other by communicating the same messages to the implied reader.

Key examples of this corroboration of evidence lie in the various names and titles applied to Jesus: Jesus (1.1, 16, 18, 21, 25); Messiah (1.1, 16, 17, 18; 2.4); Son of David (1.1; 1.16 cf. 1.6; 1.17, 20, 25; 9.27); Son of Abraham (1.1; 1.16 cf. 1.2; 1.17). The implied reader also finds such multiple attestation elsewhere in the story: the facts that Mary 'bears a son' (1.21, 23, 25), that Jesus 'is born in Bethlehem of Judea' (2.1, 5, 6), that Jesus' life from conception on points to the presence of the Holy Spirit (1.18, 20; 3.11, 16; 4.1), and that Jesus is the 'Son of God' (1.22-23; 2.15; 3.17)[56] all receive verification from several sources. Similarly, both the narrator (2.3-4, 7-8, 16) and the 'angel of the Lord' (2.12) bear witness to Herod's treacherous actions in response to the birth of Jesus.

The use of this multiple attestation of names, titles, and events has two effects on the implied reader: it establishes the 'trustworthiness' of the story being told, and it points to the 'honesty' and 'reliability' of the story teller.[57] As a result, the implied reader is led to place implicit trust both in Matthew's narrator and in the story which he tells.

Matthew's narrator also proves himself 'competent' by the way in which he tells his story. A variety of literary devices point to his skillfulness as a storyteller.[58] Most obvious of these is that of parallelism—verbal, syntactical, and material—which occurs both in the narration and in the words of Jesus. Matthew's narrator pointedly establishes parallelisms within a variety of pericopes: the accounts of Joseph's three dreams (1.20-25; 2.13-15; 2.19-23), Satan's temptation of Jesus (4.1-11), the calling of four disciples (4.18-22), and Jesus' encounters with a scribe and a disciple (8.18-22) each have as their basis a sequence of carefully crafted parallel elements.[59]

In an even more pronounced way, however, the sayings of Jesus in the discourse of 5.3–7.27 reflect the narrator's liking for parallelisms of all types: verbal parallelisms built around the repetition of key vocabulary (5.19, 22, 29-30; 6.14-15, 19-20, 22-23; 7.7-8, 9-10, 13-14, 17, 18, 24-27); syntactical parallelisms created by identical syntax (5.34-36; 7.2) or similar sentence structures (5.32; 7.16, 22); and material parallelisms built around parallel content (5.39-41, 42, 44, 45, 46-47; 6.24).[60] Further, the narrator uses such parallelisms to connect not only single phrases, clauses, and sentences, but even in some cases extended portions of text (5.3-10 [cf. v. 11], 21-48; 6.1-18).[61]

Matthew's narrator also makes use of formulaic phrases in texts which are not otherwise set up in parallel fashion. A prime example here is the 'fulfilment' formula (1.22; 2.15, 17, 23; 4.13; 8.17)[62] which the narrator uses to link scriptural prophecies to the events which in his view represent their 'fulfilment'.[63]

Closely related to both the parallelism and the formulaic language of Matthew's narrator is his use of 'catchwords' within individual pericopes to connect the various sections of those pericopes verbally.[64] This device is especially prominent within the miracle stories of chapters eight and nine, where the request for healing, the healing saying, and the account of the actual healing are linked through the repetition of key vocabulary: to wish/to cleanse (8.2, 3a, 3b); to say/to be healed (8.8b, 13); to come (9.18b, 23); to save or heal (9.21, 22a, 22b); to believe/faith (9.28, 29).[65]

In addition, Matthew's narrator uses the related devices of 'inclusio' and 'chiasm' to structure both larger and smaller units of text.[66] Inclusio refers to 'the repetition of the same word or phrase at or near the beginning and ending of some unit, a sentence, a pericope, or a larger section'.[67] Chiasm, a term derived from the Greek letter *chi* (χ), refers to the 'crossing' or inversion of elements within a given unit of text.[68]

The text of 1.1–9.34 contains a variety of inclusios and chiasms, both in narrative material as well as in direct discourse and in the sayings of Jesus. The texts 5.3/10, 7.16/20, and 6.24a/24d represent simple (non-chiastic) inclusios, in which a similar or identical phrase is used to begin and end a unit of text. A slightly more complex construction can be seen in 1.1/17, where the two halves of the inclusio are set up in inverted (chiastic) fashion. And all types of chiastic constructions occur within 1.1-9.34: verbal chiasms (3.14b/ 14c); verbal-syntactical chiasms (6.34a/34b); syntactical chiasms (7.3a/3b); and material or content chiasms (7.6a/6b; 9.13b/13c; 9.15a/15b).

But while literary devices such as these assist the narrator in verbalizing the story, the ultimate test of his competence in storytelling lies in the overall power of the story itself to engage the attention of the implied reader. Here again, as will become evident below,[69] Matthew's narrator exhibits his competence by presenting a coherent and unified narrative.

The examination of 1.1-9.34 thus indicates that Matthew's narrator is a competent storyteller, who is not only conscious of his role in telling the story but who also appears to use literary techniques deliberately in the attempt to achieve certain results. Thus the implied reader of 1.1-9.34 is led to expect that the shape of the narrator's story throughout the remainder of the Gospel will likewise be highly intentional, both in its larger outlines and in its smaller details. In other words, by the time the implied reader reaches 9.35, he or she has developed a level of trust in the mimetic authority of the narrator's story equal to the level of trust developed in the diegetic authority of the narrator as storyteller.

The contact of the narrator

Lanser describes the psychological 'contact' between the narrator and the implied reader in terms of three factors: the 'mode' of address, the 'attitude' of the narrator, and the 'identity' of the implied reader.[70] As she puts it,

> ... in writing, the contact between author and audience is established through discourse register, tone, and other equivalents of visual/auditory contact. Contact may also be established in direct comments that call attention to the speaker's relationship to the audience; the speaker may even explicitly define his or her presumed readership.[71]

The mode of address. Lanser views the modes of address available to any given narrator as ranging from 'direct' (overt) address (in which an 'I-you' dialogue takes place between the narrator and the implied reader) to 'indirect' (covert) address (in which the intrusion of an 'I' would be totally unexpected and therefore confusing).[72] The mode of address which Matthew's narrator adopts in 1.1–9.34 lies on the indirect half of the spectrum. At no time does he refer to himself overtly, either by means of the first person pronoun or by means of first person singular or plural verbs. At the same time, however, the commentary which he offers on the events of the story (e.g., 1.22-24; 2.15, 17-18, 23; 3.3; 4.14-16; 8.17) points to the presence of a narrating 'I' whose direct intrusion into the fabric of the text in the form of personal references would create no great difficulty for the implied reader.[73] Matthew's narrator can thus be described as an indirect narrator who nevertheless stands immediately behind the written text.

The attitude of the narrator. Lanser measures the attitude of the narrator in reference both to the act of narrating itself and to the implied reader.[74] The narrator's attitude toward the act of narrating reveals itself in the relative 'self-consciousness' or 'unconsciousness' displayed by the narrator in regard to the writing of his text. Matthew's narrator makes no specific references within 1.1–9.34 to the act of narrating. But he makes it evident through his use of commentary that he is narrating his story in an attempt to communicate directly and convincingly with an implied readership.

A second index of the narrator's attitude toward the act of narrating itself lies in the relative 'confidence' or 'uncertainty' with which he goes about his task. On this scale Matthew's narrator rates an unqualified vote of 'confidence'. Nowhere does he hesitate with his facts or act defensive in regard to his opinions. Rather, he confidently narrates a sequence of events and unhesitatingly backs them up with his personal commentary on their significance. Accordingly, Matthew's narrator presents himself as one who has 'all the facts' concerning his story[75] and does not apologize for this stance.

The two factors which Lanser identifies as indices of the narrator's attitude toward the implied reader relate to the degree of 'deference' and 'formality' with which he addresses his implied readership. In each case Lanser defines a 'degree zero' point midway between the two ends of the spectrum. On the one hand, a 'relative equality between speaker and listener' serves as the 'degree zero' between the extremes of 'deference' and 'contempt'. On the other hand, a 'friendly but respectful' position stands midway between 'formality' and 'intimacy'. In light of the indirect approach of Matthew's narrator, no evidence is available to classify him in terms either of a 'deference/contempt' scale or of a 'formality/intimacy' scale. The single remaining option, therefore, is to place Matthew's narrator in the 'degree zero' position on both of these scales.

Taking all four indices into consideration the implied reader of 1.1–9.34 discovers that Matthew's narrator is (1) a non-pretentious storyteller who does not direct attention to himself or to his storytelling activity, (2) a confident storyteller who does not hesitate with his facts or his opinions, and (3) a respectful storyteller who does not attempt to manipulate his implied readership psychologically, either in a positive or in a negative fashion.

The identity of the implied reader. In an attempt to assess the identity of the implied reader on the basis of the written narrative, Lanser draws on the work of Mary Ann Piwowarczyk. In her study of 'The Narratee in Selected Fictional Works of Diderot',[76] Piwowarczyk defines what she terms the 'degree zero' narratee of any given narrative:

I.   The degree zero narratee has perfect knowledge of:
  (1)   the language of the narrator (limited by 4, 5, and 6)
  (2)   the referents of unmarked common nouns
  (3)   the grammar of a story (intuitive knowledge of what is a story)
II.   The degree zero narratee has no knowledge of:
  (4)   the referents of marked common nouns
  (5)   the referents of all proper nouns
  (6)   the meaning of some proper nouns
  (7)   any language other than that used to tell the story
  (8)   connotations/implications of either a sign or a situation
  (9)   other texts
  (10) the story prior to the telling, including
          (a) the events
          (b) the characters
          (c) the locations
          (d) the narrator
  (11) the details of social organization or of the customs/conventions associated with a particular group
III.   The degree zero narratee is:
  (12) able to reason logically
  (13) able to remember all that has been told

(14)   obliged to follow the linear and temporal progression of the
       text
(15)   a member of the same culture/civilization as the narrator
(16)   without any particularizing social, personal, or physiological
       characteristics which determine his/her identity
(17)   a participant in the situation of enunciation whose status
       and spatial-temporal location are undefined
(18)   a passive reader/listener whose presence is unemphasized[77]

On the basis of this description it becomes evident that Matthew's
narrator does not presuppose a 'degree zero' implied readership.
Within 1.1–9.34 there are a variety of unexplained references whose
full significance only a Jewish person (or a person acquainted with
Jewish history, life, and scriptures) would comprehend: the Babylonian
Exile (1.11, 12, 17); Joseph's 'naming' of the child born to Mary
(1.21, 25);[78] the clothing of John the Baptist (3.4);[79] the unexplained
mention of Moses (8.4);[80] unmarked citations of Jewish scriptures
(1.21; 8.13). At the same time, however, the narrator makes no
attempt to define his readership more narrowly.[81] The implied reader
is rather 'a passive reader/listener whose presence is unemphasized'.
Matthew's narrator, therefore, establishes only that the implied
reader of his story either comes out of the Jewish culture which his
text reflects or is acquainted with that culture.

The stance of the narrator
The third factor which is crucial in determining the relationship
between narrator and implied reader is what Lanser terms the
'stance' of the narrator, the point of view which the narrator adopts
toward the story narrated.[82] An analysis of the narrator's point of
view is essential to the study of any narrative, since it is the
narrator's point of view alone which determines how the story in
question is narrated. In the words of Robert Weimann,

> Since the act of narration involves selective communication more
> than mimetic participation, and since, therefore, the narrative is so
> obviously not identical with its subject, it already contains an
> unashamed element of perspective and evaluation. Without it, no
> narration is possible: how else could the narrator in real life hope to
> comprehend and arrange the multitude of details that he—in
> summary or silence—thinks fit to condense or pass over? But to
> achieve the necessary selection and evaluation is impossible
> without a point from which to select and evaluate, and this view

point (whether consciously or unconsciously taken) is indeed the absolute prerequisite of all narrative activity.[83]

In her examination of point of view Lanser adopts the fivefold methodological scheme introduced by Uspensky.[84] According to this scheme the narrator's point of view exhibits itself on five distinct and analyzable 'planes'—phraseological, spatial, temporal, psychological, and ideological or evaluative.[85]

The phraseological plane. Point of view as expressed on the phraseological plane has to do with the voice(s) through whom the narrator tells his story.[86] Lanser views the possibilities open to the narrator in terms of a spectrum ranging from 'diegetic discourse', discourse in the narrator's own voice and from his own perspective, to 'mimetic discourse', the narrator's use of direct speech or of written records such as letters and journals. Between these two extremes lie various levels of 'indirect discourse', discourse containing the speech of the characters but in the voice of the narrator. As Lanser notes, however,

> ... very few texts adopt a monolithic phraseology; in most instances there will at least be some purely narrative speech and some direct speech of characters. In describing an individual narrator's phraseological stance, or the phraseological stance of an entire text, one would therefore want to indicate dominant modes, relative proportions of the various forms, or the range of modes a text encompasses.[87]

From the standpoint of phraseology it becomes clear that Matthew's narrator is working with two basic modes of discourse, his own narration and the direct speech of Jesus. Of the 269 verses within 1.1-9.34, 113 verses (42%) contain nothing but the direct speech of Jesus; while an additional 26 verses (almost 10%) contain both the narrator's and Jesus' voices. Thus direct speech by Jesus occupies all or parts of 139 verses (almost 52%) of the text.[88] For his part, the narrator speaks alone (or in the voice of Scripture) in 92 verses (34%) and introduces the direct speech of other characters in an additional 56 (almost 21%). The narrator's voice is thus heard within 148 verses (55%) of the text. By contrast, the voices of all other characters or groups of characters constitute the sole contents of a mere 8 verses (almost 3%) and are found in conjunction with the voice of the narrator in an additional 30 (11%). The voices of the other characters thus comprise a total of 38 verses (14%) of the text.

Summarizing the above statistics yields the following phraseological profile of 1.1–9.34: the voices of Jesus and the narrator are the sole voices heard in almost 86% of the text, while the entire gamut of other voices (all the way from the heavenly voice of 3.17 to the voice of Satan in 4.3, 6, 9) together occupy only one fifth as many verses. Stated negatively, only eight verses of the entire text do not contain the voices of either Jesus or the narrator. As a result, the simple dominance of these two voices drives home to the implied reader the message that it is these two voices who have something significant to say.[89]

In addition, Matthew's narrator attaches great importance to the direct speech of Jesus. While he records the speech of Jesus directly in 139 verses, there are only 5 instances within 1.1–9.34 in which he transmits the speech of Jesus indirectly (4.21, 23; 8.16, 18, 26). Thus the direct speech of Jesus takes priority over the discourse of the narrator, and not the other way around.[90]

Further, very few characters in the story ever make a direct verbal response to what Jesus has said. Of twenty-seven instances of direct speech by Jesus,[91] only three are followed by a direct verbal response (8.7/8-9; 9.2/3, 28),[92] and an additional two by an indirect verbal response (9.24, 30/31).[93] Accordingly, while other characters frequently initiate encounters with Jesus (3.14; 4.3; 8.2, 5-6, 19, 21, 25, 28-31; 9.2, 10-11, 14, 18, 20-21, 27, 32), it is almost always Jesus who has 'the last word'. This communicates to the implied reader that once Jesus has spoken, that which is most significant has been said and the dialogue is over.

A third indication of the importance which the narrator attaches to the direct speech of Jesus lies in the fact that he allows Jesus to speak uninterruptedly for 107 verses, from 5.3 through 7.27. The sheer length of this speech dwarfs by comparison the longest uninterrupted discourse of the narrator (1.1-19) and the longest speech by any other character (John the Baptist's speech in 3.7-12).

Phraseologically, therefore, 1.1–9.34 represents first of all the viewpoint of Jesus and secondarily the viewpoint of the narrator himself. And this fact alone, aside from all reference to the respective world views of Jesus and the narrator, has a powerful impact on the implied reader. For the simple reason that he/she hears the greatest proportion of the story in the words of Jesus and the narrator, the implied reader will necessarily identify him/herself with the story precisely as the narrator sees it (i.e., in terms of the narrator's diegetic discourse) and as Jesus experiences it (i.e., in terms of Jesus' mimetic discourse).

The spatial plane. Point of view as expressed on the spatial plane has to do with the spatial position from which the narrator views the characters and events of the story. Lanser defines the spatial possibilities open to the narrator in terms of a continuum ranging from the 'panoramic overview' to the 'fixed suprapersonal' and the 'fixed intrapersonal' focus on a single character.[94]

The spatial point of view represented by Matthew's narrator most nearly fits Lanser's 'fixed suprapersonal' and/or 'fixed intrapersonal' categories.[95] From 3.13 on, the point at which Jesus appears on the scene as an adult, the narrator never leaves the vicinity of Jesus except to relate briefly Jesus' spreading reputation (4.24a; 8.33; 9.2b, 31). As a result, the entire story is told from the spatial viewpoint of someone who follows Jesus constantly and observes his encounters with others from a close but usually outside (suprapersonal) stance.[96]

In addition, several phraseological features also highlight the spatial centrality of Jesus within the story. The first of these features is the narrator's use of compound verbs beginning with *pros*, a preposition indicating 'direction toward'.

The most prominent of these verbs is *proserchomai*, 'to come to or approach'. This verb appears ten times throughout 1.1–9.34 (4.3, 11; 5.1; 8.2, 5, 19, 25; 9.14, 20, 28; but cf. 9.18) and in every instance describes the movement of another character or group of characters toward Jesus. This has the effect of placing Jesus in the center of the stage, while other characters—Satan, angels, sick persons and their relatives, disciples of John the Baptist, and Jesus' own disciples—approach him from all sides.

The narrator's use of *prospherō*, 'to bring [something] to [someone]', reinforces this picture. The verb *prospherō* occurs eight times within 1.1–9.34: five times within the discourse of the narrator (2.11; 4.24; 8.16; 9.2, 32) and three times in the words of Jesus (5.23, 24; 8.4). While Jesus uses *prospherō* to refer to the bringing of an offering/gift to the priest/altar, the narrator uses it in all five instances to describe what or whom people bring to Jesus: the magi bring gifts (2.11) and an anonymous 'they' bring all manner of sick persons to Jesus (4.24; 8.16; 9.2, 32). Once again Jesus stands in the center of the stage, while other characters gravitate towards him.[97]

The other prominent phraseological feature of 1.1–9.34 which highlights the spatial centrality of Jesus is the narrator's frequent use of the verb *akoloutheō*, 'to follow'.[98] This verb occurs twelve times prior to 9.35 (4.20, 22, 25; 8.1, 10, 19, 22, 23; 9.9—twice, 19, 27); and in eleven of these twelve instances it refers to persons or crowds who follow Jesus.[99]

The basic impression left with the implied reader is that all movement in the story flows toward Jesus, as if there were a great centripetal force at work drawing all the other characters into his presence. But since Jesus himself is moving, the spatial point of view adopted by Matthew's narrator can be described in terms of a moving spotlight which follows a single character across the stage. The light itself remains focused on Jesus as he moves from place to place. But it also illuminates, one by one or in groups, the other characters as they enter the spotlight briefly and then disappear from sight or follow along at the edge of the glow.

The temporal plane. Point of view as expressed on the temporal plane has to do with two time-related factors: (1) the 'pacing' of events within the story; and (2) the relationship between the time at which the narrating takes place and the time at which the events of the story take place.[100]

'Pacing' refers to the amount of space, and thus of detail, which the narrator uses to describe the various events of his story. Here the possibilities range from 'summary' on the one end of the spectrum to 'scene' on the other. According to Friedman's definitions of these extremes:

> . . . summary narrative is a generalized account or report of a series of events covering some extended period and a variety of locales, and seems to be the normal untutored mode of storytelling; immediate scene emerges as soon as the specific, continuous, and successive details of time, place, action, character, and dialogue begin to appear. Not dialogue alone but concrete detail within a specific time-place frame is the *sine qua non* of scene.[101]

The significance of the narrator's choice between summary and scene lies in the relative weight which this choice attaches to the various events of the story. As Lanser indicates, those events which the narrator summarizes often tend to serve as background material, while events presented 'scenically' normally constitute the central action of the story.

From the study of 1.1–9.34 it becomes clear that the lifetime of

Jesus and the events of Jesus' life constitute the focal point of the story in terms of time. While Matthew's narrator dispenses with the entire history (42 generations) of the Jewish people within a brief 17 verses (1.1-17), he spends a total of 252 verses on the events of Jesus' life (1.18–9.34). But even within 1.18–9.34, which is for the most part 'scenically' represented,[102] Matthew's narrator clearly paces the events of the story. In a total of 31 verses (1.18–2.23) he deals with Jesus' birth and early childhood. He then omits all mention of Jesus' later childhood and adolescence—Jesus is still described as a 'child' in 2.19, while 3.1 opens onto a scene in which Jesus appears as an adult—but takes 221 verses (3.1–9.34) to describe the beginnings of Jesus' public ministry. Thus within the life of Jesus the narrator gives most attention to the events of Jesus' public ministry.

The net effect which Matthew's narrator achieves by his pacing of the events of 1.1–9.34 is that of a temporal 'zoom lens'. Starting at a point far back in time, the narrator moves over hundreds of years of Jewish history (1.1-17) in order to 'zoom' in on the life of Jesus in general (1.18–9.34) and the public ministry of Jesus in specific (3.1–9.34).

The second factor which relates to temporal point of view within a narrative is the relationship between the time at which the narrating takes place and the time at which the events of the story themselves occur. The narrator can predict events which have not yet taken place (anterior or prior narration); he can narrate events at the moment of their occurrence (simultaneous narration); or he can recount events which have happened at some point in the past (posterior or subsequent narration).[103]

The basic stance adopted by Matthew's narrator is that of subsequent narration. The two main verb tenses used within the narrator's discourse are the aorist and the imperfect, both tenses which establish a distinct time-gap between the moment of narration and the moment of the event itself. But the narrator also uses the historic present tense at a number of points throughout his discourse. At these moments of simultaneous narration the narrator aligns himself temporally with the characters of the story. And in so doing he necessarily brings the implied reader along with him, since the implied reader is dependent on the narrator's perception of the events of the story. As a result, the use of the historic present has the effect of '[taking] the listener directly into the action of the narrative, and [putting] him into the same position as that occupied by the characters of the story'.[104]

With this effect in mind, it is instructive to note where Matthew's narrator uses the historic present. Of twenty-four historic presents found within the narrator's discourse of 1.1–5.2 and 7.28–9.34, half of them refer to the actions of various characters (2.13, 19, 22; 3.1, 13, 15; 4.5, 8—twice, 11; 9.14) or lie in the narrator's commentary (3.3). The other half refer to the act of speaking: once *legei* (= he says) refers to Satan (4.6); once *legousin* (= they say) refers to two blind men (9.28); ten times *legei* refers to Jesus (4.10, 19; 8.4, 7, 20, 22, 26; 9.6, 9, 28). Accordingly, the single most prominent function of the historic present tense within 1.1–9.34 is that of putting the words of Jesus into a framework of simultaneous narration.[105] Similarly, the narrator also makes use of the present participle of the verb *legō* (= saying) to link the words of Jesus to an action by Jesus described in the past tense (5.2; 8.3; 9.29, 30). Anderson assesses the effect of these present participles as follows:

> The action denoted by the present participle occurs at the same time as the action denoted by the main verb. The main verb freezes the moment of action and the participle indicates synchronically what was said at that moment as if it was [*sic*] being said in the present.[106]

A further technique which the narrator uses to surround the words of Jesus with an aura of 'presentness' is one already mentioned above (p. 44) in terms of phraseology. In the discourse of 5.3–7.27 Jesus is granted 107 verses of uninterrupted direct speech. This means that for 107 verses of mimetic discourse there are no indications which could remind the implied reader of the 'pastness' of these words or of the designated addressees. Rather, this long uninterrupted speech creates for the implied reader the impression that Jesus is saying these words directly to him or her in the present moment.[107]

But the most significant pointer to the 'presentness' of Jesus' speech comes from the words of Jesus himself: sixteen times within 1.1–9.34 Jesus reiterates the phrase, 'I say to you' (5.18, 20, 22, 26, 28, 32, 34, 39, 44; 6.2, 5, 16, 25, 29; 8.10, 11).[108] While this is ostensibly directed to the designated listeners, the sheer repetition of this phrase, especially when it occurs in the long uninterrupted discourse of 5.3–7.27, has the effect of bringing the implied reader directly into Jesus' audience.

Thus the temporal viewpoint of Matthew's narrator in 1.1–9.34 serves to focus the attention of the implied reader on the public ministry of Jesus and, within that ministry, on the words of Jesus.

And Jesus' frequently repeated 'I say to you' has the effect of bringing the implied reader directly into the presence of Jesus.

The psychological plane. Point of view as expressed on the psychological plane has to do with the 'distance' or 'affinity' which the narrator exhibits towards the characters of the story.[109] Lanser assesses this distance or affinity by means of three indices: 'information', 'focalization', and 'attitude'.

The 'information' which a narrator provides concerning the various characters of his story can be analyzed in terms of its quantity and its quality. The pertinent questions are thus the following: (1) how much information does the narrator provide concerning the various characters? and (2) does this information treat those characters as thinking, feeling, responding, acting 'subjects' or merely as 'objects' of the thoughts, words, or actions of others?[110]

Within 1.1–9.34 most characters appear as active subjects rather than as passive objects.[111] But the narrator's portrayal of Jesus is far more detailed than his portrayal of any other character or group: of twenty-six 'scenes' prior to 9.35,[112] the only one in which Jesus does not figure in some manner is 2.16-18. By contrast, the second most frequently cited group of characters, the crowds, are mentioned as such in a total of seven scenes;[113] while Jesus' closest associates, the disciples, are cited as a group in only six scenes.[114] All other characters or groups of characters figure five times or less within 1.1–9.34.[115]

In addition, the other characters who appear on the scene from 3.13 onward are pictured almost without exception in relationship to Jesus alone. While Jesus relates to all the other characters of the story, these characters do not relate to each other.[116] As a result, the implied reader sees a multi-faceted Jesus interacting with an entire spectrum of single-faceted characters. Within 1.1–9.34, therefore, Matthew's narrator provides a far greater quantity of information about Jesus than about any other single character or group of characters.

The second index of the narrator's affinity to or distance from the characters of his story is 'focalization'. Lanser defines the 'focalizer' of a text as 'the presence—the recorder, the camera, the consciousness— through whose spatial, temporal, and/or psychological position the textual events are perceived'.[117]

The narrator has three choices to make in determining how he will focalize his story.[118] First of all, he must determine the stance of the focalizer in relation to the characters of the story. The possibilities here range from totally 'external' vision (a stance in which the focalizer functions as a camera, describing events strictly on the basis of what can be seen and heard) to totally 'internal' vision (a stance in which the character involved is his/her own focalizer). Further, the narrator must determine the depth of vision which his story will reflect. On one end of the depth spectrum is 'surface' vision, the reporting of actual deeds and spoken words; on the other end is 'deep' vision, the reflecting of processes which lie altogether below the level of human consciousness. Finally, the narrator must determine whether to retain the same stance and depth of focalization throughout the story ('fixed' focalization), to alter the focalization from time to time ('multiple' or 'variable' focalization) or to operate without any distinct pattern of focalization ('free' focalization).

On each of the above three scales Matthew's narrator stands somewhere in the middle. In regard to the stance of the focalizer, he most frequently utilizes 'external' vision: 1.1–9.34 is primarily the record of the visible/audible ministry of Jesus, what Jesus does and says as it would be picked up by a movie camera with soundtrack. At the same time, however, Matthew's narrator occasionally employs 'internal' vision, which describes events in terms of what the characters themselves see, hear, think, and feel (1.19, 20; 2.3, 9, 10, 11, 12, 13, 16, 19, 22; 3.7, 16; 4.2, 18, 21; 5.1; 7.28; 8.10a, 14, 18, 34; 9.2, 4, 9, 11, 12, 21, 23).[119] And when he does provide such 'inside' perspectives, Matthew's narrator makes more frequent reference to Jesus' perceptions than to the perceptions of any other character or group of characters.[120] Further, of all the 'human' characters of the story, only Jesus shares the narrator's ability to 'read' the minds and hearts of the other characters.[121] Thus in terms of the stance of the focalizer, Matthew's narrator has greater affinity to Jesus than to any other character.

On the question of depth of vision, 1.1–9.34 reflects primarily 'surface' vision. By far the greatest proportion of the text consists of a recounting of visible deeds and audible words: Jesus goes places, encounters persons, heals them or responds to their questions or concerns. Nevertheless, the narrator also makes occasional reference to the feelings of the various characters: the implied reader learns that characters are reflective (1.20), disturbed (2.3), joyful (2.10), enraged (2.16), afraid (2.22; 9.8), hungry (4.2), amazed (8.10, 27;

9.33). Here it is significant to note that all of the feelings to which the narrator makes reference are either feelings which represent the responses of others to Jesus or the feelings of Jesus himself.

Two conclusions can be drawn from this treatment of depth of vision. In the first place, the deeds and the words of Jesus assume primary importance within the narrator's story, so that Jesus is in focus on the strictly 'surface' level of vision. In addition, whenever there is evidence of 'deeper' vision, that vision always relates in some way to Jesus. As a result, Matthew's narrator uses depth of vision above all as a technique to highlight Jesus.

On the question of 'fixed' or 'free' focalization 1.1–9.34 reflects variation. While the greatest proportion of the narrator's discourse has as its focalizer the omnipresent narrator himself, there are also moments when the focalizer becomes one of the characters in the story. Further, whenever a character speaks, he/she becomes the focalizer for the duration of his/her speech. As noted above, Jesus says far more than any other character in the story. As a result, Jesus stands second only to the narrator in his importance as a focalizer within the story.[122] Accordingly, on all three scales relative to focalization Matthew's narrator exhibits greater affinity to Jesus than to any other character in the story.

The third index of point of view as expressed on the psychological plane is 'attitude', the extent to which the narrator exhibits approval or disapproval of the characters within his story. While this question will be analyzed more extensively in the discussion of 'the ideological (evaluative) plane' below, it is nevertheless possible to draw some basic conclusions here concerning the attitude of Matthew's narrator toward the characters of his story.

On the basis of quantity of information alone, the narrator apparently approves both of what Jesus does and of what he says. Not only does Jesus receive by far the greatest amount of coverage of any character within the story; but this also means that no other character or group of characters has any comparable opportunity to discredit the deeds or rebut the words of Jesus.

The narrator also indicates his attitude toward the characters by the tone of the words used throughout the text to describe them. For the most part, words with positive connotations are used in connection with Jesus, while words with negative connotations are used in connection with those who oppose him.[123] The vocabulary surrounding Jesus and his ministry includes such words as the following: to save/heal (*sōzō*: 1.21; 8.25; 9.21, 22—twice); to heal (*therapeuō*: 4.23, 24; 8.7, 16; *iaomai*: 8.13); to cleanse (*katharizō*: 8.2, 3); to teach (*didaskō*: 4.23; 5.2; 7.29); to proclaim (*kēryssō*: 4.17, 23); to fulfill (*plēroō*: 1.22; 2.15, 23; 3.15; 4.14; 5.17; 8.17); authority (*exousia*: 7.29; 9.6, 8); to have mercy/mercy (*eleeō*: 9.27; *eleos*: 9.13); to forgive sins (*aphiēmi* + *hamartia*: 9.2, 5, 6; cf. 1.21). The vocabulary used in connection with Jesus' opponents, on the other hand, includes such words as the following: to be disturbed (*tarassō*: 2.3); to destroy (*apollymi*: 2.13); to kill (*anaireō*: 2.16); to be enraged (*thymoō* + *lian*: 2.16); to seek the life (*zēteō* + *psyche*: 2.20); to test/ tempt (*peirazō*: 4.1, 3); to think evil (*enthymeomai* + *poneros*: 9.4). The psychological picture thus drawn is of a powerful, authoritative and yet compassionate Jesus who is opposed in his infancy by persons who are angry and murderous and later on by persons who are either seductive or evil-thinking.[124] This picture leads the implied reader to approve of Jesus and disapprove of those who oppose him. Here again it is clear that Matthew's narrator has greatest affinity for Jesus and stands at the greatest distance from those who oppose him.

The ideological (evaluative) plane. Point of view as expressed on the ideological or evaluative plane has to do with the particular world view which the narrator sets forth by means of his story. As. R. Alan Culpepper notes, 'No narrator can be absolutely impartial; inevitably a narrator, especially an omniscient, omnipresent, omnicommunicative, and intrusive one, will prejudice the reader toward or away from certain characters, claims, or events and their implications'.[125] Simply by telling his story as he does, the narrator necessarily evaluates the characters and the events described. This leads to the question: which character(s) does the narrator evaluate positively, and which negatively? Or stated in terms of point of view, whose evaluative point of view does the narrator assume, and whose does he reject, in telling the story as he does?

In 1.1–9.34 it becomes evident that there are only two evaluative positions represented in the story. The one position is that represented by Jesus and those who respond positively to him, the other by all those who respond negatively to Jesus.[126] Characters either worship Jesus (2.2, 11) or plot to kill him (2.7-8, 13); they either submit to Jesus (3.15; 4.20, 22; 9.9) or try to seduce him (4.1, 3, 5-6, 8-9); they either cry out for Jesus to save them (8.25) or implore him to leave their region (8.34); they either respond to Jesus in faith (8.10; 9.2, 22,

29) or in disbelief and scorn (9.23-24). There appears to be no middle ground in the matter of responding to Jesus.

Further, it is clear that of these two positions Matthew's narrator holds Jesus' evaluative viewpoint to be the valid one. And, as Kingsbury rightly observes,

> ... if Matthew aligns his own evaluative point of view with that of Jesus, he does not stop there but goes on to align both his evaluative point of view and that of Jesus with the evaluative point of view of God. By authorial design, Matthew establishes God's conception of reality, his system of values or 'will', as being normative for the story he tells.[127]

Therefore, by making 'God's conception of reality' the final authority in the story while establishing Jesus as the protagonist, the narrator communicates to the implied reader (1) that it is Jesus of all the characters in the story who is the authoritative and reliable representative of the '[divine] conception of reality'; and (2) that Jesus is to be viewed as authoritative and reliable precisely because he represents that '[divine] conception of reality'.[128] It now remains to examine the way in which Matthew's narrator communicates this evaluative stance.

Lanser analyzes evaluative point of view in terms of three indices: 'expression', 'relation to the culture text', and 'authority'.[129] Expression has to do with the extent to which world view is 'explicit' or 'embedded' within a text. Within 1.1-9.34 Matthew's narrator communicates his evaluative stance in both ways. All evaluative statements made directly by the narrator or one of the characters constitute explicit statements of world view. All aspects of the story beyond those straighforward evaluative statements are in one way or another embedded statements of world view.

Matthew's narrator communicates his evaluative stance in explicit form first of all through his own direct commentary to the implied reader.[130] He opens the story (1.1) with an explicit evaluative statement which identifies the protagonist as Jesus *Messiah*, Son of David and Son of Abraham (1.1; cf. 1.16, 17).[131] Throughout 1.1-9.34 he communicates his evaluative stance explicitly through the repeated use of a 'fulfilment' formula (1.22; 2.15, 17, 23; 4.14; 8.17; cf. 3.3), in which he designates events in the lives of John the Baptist and Jesus as the 'fulfilment' of Jewish scriptures.[132] And he further verbalizes his world view by the way in which he speaks by extremes: Jesus goes through 'all' Galilee, healing 'every' disease and 'every' sickness (4.23); he casts out evil spirits 'by a word' and heals 'all' who are sick (8.16); the Gadarene demoniacs are so dangerous that 'no one' can pass that way (8.28).[133]

But it is the voice of God which utters the definitive word concerning the protagonist of the story: Jesus is none other than the Son of God. This evaluative statement is communicated in several different ways. In direct commentary to the implied reader[134] the narrator carefully identifies two Old Testament scriptures which make reference to 'a son/my son' (1.23; 2.15) as 'that which was spoken *by the Lord*' (1.22; 2.15).[135] But the first direct announcement of Jesus' identity comes in the scene which immediately follows Jesus' baptism. Here 'the heavens are opened to [Jesus]', he [sees] the Spirit of God descending like a dove and coming upon him', and a 'voice from heaven' announces: 'This is my beloved son, in whom I am well pleased' (3.16-17). As Kingsbury observes, 'With these events, God enters the world of Matthew's story as 'actor' and personally marks Jesus out to be his supreme agent'.[136] God's announcement in 3.17 is to be viewed as the definitive evaluative statement of 1.1–9.34, the authority according to which all other evaluative statements are to be evaluated.

Following Jesus' baptism it is the voice of Jesus himself which most conspicuously reinforces the definitive evaluative statement of 3.17.[137] While every word spoken by Jesus must, in light of 3.17, be viewed as an explicit statement of 'God's conception of reality', Jesus in fact makes a number of statements in which he specifically aligns himself with the pronouncement of 3.17: (1) he cites and/or interprets Scripture authoritatively in his interactions with Satan (4.4, 7, 10), the crowds and the disciples (5.21-48), and the Pharisees (9.13); (2) the pervasive and overarching theme of his entire proclamation is the 'kingdom of heaven' (4.17, 23; 5.3, 10, 19, 20; 6.9-10, 33; 7.21; 8.11); (3) he refers to God as 'my Father' (7.21), 'your [i.e., his disciples'] Father' (5.16, 45, 48; 6.1, 4, 6, 8, 14-15, 18, 26, 32; 7.11), and 'our [from the disciples' perspective] Father' (6.9); (4) he makes clear that he has come not to 'destroy' the law and the prophets, but rather to 'fulfill' them (5.17).[138]

But along with explicit evaluative statements, the narrator also communicates his evaluative stance in embedded fashion. All the observations made above concerning point of view on the phraseo-logical, spatial, temporal, and psychological planes are in fact none other than embedded reflections of the world view of Matthew's narrator.

On the phraseological plane it is significant that only the narrator and Jesus can cite Scripture authoritatively, while others cite Scripture without realizing the implications of what they are saying (2.5-6) or with 'perverse intent' (4.6).[139] It is likewise significant, as Anderson observes, that 'with rare exception [in the Gospel of Matthew] *only Jesus and the narrator ever narrate*' (italics mine).[140] In Anderson's words,

> ... the fact that the narrator and Jesus are the only storytellers is important. To tell a story is to have the opportunity to affect and perhaps persuade an audience to adopt a particular ideological point of view—at least while assuming the role of the reader or hearer in the text.[141]

By these methods the narrator not only highlights the validity of Jesus' evaluative viewpoint (and thus that of God himself), but also aligns himself phraseologically with that same viewpoint. The same type of effect obtains on the spatial, temporal, and psychological planes.[142] By placing Jesus physically at the center of the story, the narrator communicates that Jesus is the most important character in the story. By means of the genealogy (1.2-17) the narrator makes clear that Jesus' life represents the temporal climax of Jewish history, the point toward which everything has been moving since the time of Abraham.[143] And in a variety of ways—the amount of information provided concerning Jesus, the use of 'depth vision' to highlight Jesus, and the tone of the vocabulary used to describe Jesus and his opponents—the narrator places Jesus psychologically at the center of the story.

The second index of evaluative stance is what Lanser describes as 'relation to the culture text'.[144] Here there are two related factors: 'coincidence' and 'cruciality'. In Lanser's words,

> The axis of coincidence concerns whether a particular ideological stance taken by a narrator (or the textual ideology as a whole) coincides with or diverges from the culture text of the sending and/ or receiving groups. In other words, does the text uphold the cultural norms (the 'status quo') with respect to the issue in question?[145]

On the basis of 1.1-9.34 it is evident that the evaluative stance of Matthew's narrator opposes the apparent 'status quo' of the implied reader. At every step of the way Jesus' life, his ministry, and his words contradict conventional mores, wisdom, and expectations.

Even before the moment of birth, Jesus' existence creates an ethical problem for Joseph (1.19-20). The magi's announcement of Jesus' birth creates a political uproar in Jerusalem (2.1-3) which issues in an actual death-plot by the incumbent ruler (2.13, 20). Jesus himself disappoints all types of conventional social and religious expectations placed upon him by other characters: John the Baptist (3.14-15), 'would be' disciples (8.18-22), the Pharisees (9.10-13), and the disciples of John (9.14-17). By means of his deeds of power Jesus disproves such conventional wisdom as the following: 'no person on earth can control the winds and the sea' (cf. 8.23-27); 'only God can forgive sin' (9.1-8); 'death is final and unalterable' (cf. 9.18-19/23-26). And Jesus' teachings turn societal values upside down (e.g., 5.3-10; 6.19-21, 25-33). It therefore comes as no surprise to learn that the most frequently recorded response to Jesus by the crowds is that of 'amazement' (7.28-29; 8.27; 9.33; cf. 9.8).

The second factor impinging upon 'relation to the culture text' is 'cruciality': how trivial or significant does the culture text consider such evaluative opposition to be?[146] Two pairs of opposing responses to Jesus, one at the beginning of the section and the other at the end, illustrate the cruciality which the narrator's culture text accords to him. In 2.1-19 the narrator records two responses to the '[one] who has been born "King of the Jews"' (2.2). The magi consider this 'King' so crucial in a positive sense that they travel long distances for the privilege of kneeling before him and offering him costly gifts; while Herod considers this 'King' such a threat that he takes immediate steps to exterminate the child. In 9.32-34 the narrator records the responses of the crowds and the Pharisees to one of Jesus' miracles. The crowds acclaim this event as unique in the history of Israel (9.33); while the Pharisees attribute to Jesus the ultimate in sinister power, that which comes from the 'prince of demons' (9.34). Thus the culture text of Matthew's narrator considers Jesus of utmost cruciality, whether in a positive or a negative sense.

The third index of evaluative stance is that of 'authority'.[147] As Lanser defines it, this 'authority' depends on two related factors: 'the degree to which a given stance is reinforced, and the importance of the persona who takes the stance'.[148] On both of these counts it is clear that the evaluative stance represented by Jesus and the narrator in 1.1-9.34 is authoritative. On the one hand, this evaluative stance is reinforced both explicitly and in embedded form on the phraseological, spatial, temporal, and psychological planes.[149] On the other hand, the two primary voices which represent this ideology are the two dominant voices within the story.[150]

The resulting picture is unambiguous. By every means at his disposal Matthew's narrator has worked to create a picture of Jesus which shows him to be not only the central character in the story but also—with the exception of God himself—the one totally reliable and authoritative character in the story, the character whose authority and viewpoint are those of God himself. The narrator's 'Jesus' is, in short, none other than the Son of God.

II. *The Basic Elements of the Narrator's Story*

Now that the role played by Matthew's narrator in telling his story has been assessed, it remains to analyse the basic elements of the narrator's story—characters, plot, and setting. The primary questions to be resolved here are the following: (1) What does the implied reader learn from the text of 1.1–9.34 about the characters involved or mentioned in 9.35–11.1? (2) What is the plot of the story up to 9.35? (3) What does the implied reader know about the setting within which the scene depicted in 9.35–11.1 takes place? The ultimate question in each case, however, has to do with the way in which this 'pre-information' prepares the implied reader psychologically for what follows in 9.35–11.1: what understandings are established by the reading of 1.1–9.34 which will inform the implied reader's interpretation of 9.35–11.1?

Characters

The characters of the story are the 'actors' who make the story 'happen' by what they say and do. These characters, in turn, possess character. In the words of Abrams, they are 'interpreted by the reader as being endowed with moral and dispositional qualities that are expressed in what they say—the *dialogue*—and by what they do—the *action*'.[151]

There are two basic ways in which a narrator can present the characters of his story.[152] He can present them as persons with a single or dominant quality or trait, whose words and actions are generally predictable. Such 'flat' characters do not change or grow as the story progresses, but remain basically 'static' and 'typical' from their first appearance to their last. Or the narrator can present his characters as persons with a variety of qualities or traits, whose character unfolds step by step throughout the story. These 'round' or 'open-ended' characters develop as the story progresses, so that the implied reader must constantly add to or revise his/her understanding of who these persons 'are'. As a result of this differentiation between 'flat' and 'round' characters Scholes and Kellogg conclude:

> The ideal reader of narratives—ancient or modern—must be prepared to respond to the emphasis of the narrative with respect to character, placing individuality or 'typical' connections foremost to the extent which the narrative itself calls for such priority; but above all he must bring to his consideration of character a versatility of response commensurate with the infinite variety of narrative characterization.[153]

An examination of 1.1–9.34 leads to the conclusion that Jesus is the most nearly round character within the story. This stems in large part from the fact that Jesus alone is shown relating to a multiplicity of other characters, while all the other characters in the story (from 3.13 onward) are depicted solely in terms of their response to him.[154] As a result, it is Jesus alone who exhibits a variety of traits which come to the fore one by one. In his baptism (3.13-17), temptation (4.1-11), mountaintop address (cf. 5.17), and encounter with the Pharisees (9.10-13) Jesus evinces a strong sense of directedness, purpose, and calling: Jesus knows why he 'has come', whom he is to obey, and what he is to accomplish while on the scene. In a variety of settings Jesus shows himself to be a person of courage and determination: he stands up to Satan unflinchingly even at a time of physical weakness (4.1-11), takes on the elements in all their destructive fury (8.23-27), and faces violent demonic powers head on (8.28-34). Jesus exhibits an undeniable and virtually irresistible authority: when he calls, others drop whatever they are doing to follow (4.18-22; 9.9);[155] when he commands, people and powers of all types obey (3.15; 4.10-11; 8.26, 32; 9.6-7); when he teaches and does mighty acts, the crowds recognize that he does so with authority (7.28-29; 9.8). Jesus displays a personal magnetism which causes 'great crowds' to follow him about, listening to his words and seeking his healing (4.23-25; 5.1-2; 8.1, 16-17). And he responds to those around him in accordance with their actions. When sick or distressed persons come to him, whether in faith or desperation, and implore his assistance, Jesus responds with acts of power which represent healing and salvation for those involved (4.23-24; 8.1-4, 5-13, 14-15, 16-17, 23-27; 9.1-8, 18-19/23-26, 20-22, 27-31, 32-34). But when individuals or groups display lack of faith, hypocrisy, or evil intentions, Jesus responds with words of rebuke, warning, or judgment (4.1-11; 5.19, 20; 6.1-18; 7.15-20, 21-23, 24-27; 8.12, 20, 26; 9.4, 12-13).

Matthew's narrator draws successively less complex pictures of the disciples and the crowds, the other two groups of characters portrayed in 9.35–11.1. From the reading of 1.1–9.34 the implied reader learns the following facts about the disciples: (1) they are people caught up in a world of everyday pursuits (4.18, 21; 8.21; 9.9); (2) in response to the call of Jesus (4.19, 21; 9.9; cf. 8.22), they immediately and unhesitatingly leave their everyday world behind to 'follow' him (4.20, 22; 9.9; cf. 8.22); (3) they receive from Jesus the promise that he will make them 'fishermen for people' (4.19); (4) they stand in a 'learner-teacher' relationship to Jesus, listening to him teach (5.1-2) and following him about the countryside as he ministers to others (8.23; 9.10, 19); (5) in spite of Jesus' call and their own obedient response, they remain extremely human characters who display very normal emotions when faced with a crisis (8.23-27).

The picture which the narrator draws of the crowds is very simple. The crowds follow Jesus about (4.25; 8.1, 18), listen to Jesus teach (5.1-2; 7.28-29), bring their sick for Jesus to heal (4.24; 8.16) and exhibit amazement at what Jesus says (7.28-29) and does (8.27; 9.8, 33).

By the time the implied reader reaches 9.35, therefore, he/she has established that Jesus is a powerful and authoritative leader, the disciples obedient followers, and the crowds impressionable seekers. And it is against the backdrop of these understandings that the implied reader will evaluate what he/she encounters in 9.35–11.1.

Plot

The question of plot is one of sequential arrangement: in what order does the narrator relate the events of his story?[156] Since reading is itself a sequential act, the significance of plot is immediately evident: it is the plot of the story which engages the sustained attention of the implied reader and leads him/her from beginning to end of the story by arousing curiosity, dropping hints along the way, raising or shattering expectations, creating and resolving tensions. As Scholes and Kellogg observe,

> All plots depend on tension and resolution. In narrative the most common plots are the biographical (birth to death) and the

romantic (desire to consummation), because these are the most obvious correlatives for the tension and resolution which plot demands. One of the reasons stories have appealed to man for so long a time lies in their neatness. The reader of a narrative can expect to finish his reading having achieved a state of equilibrium— something approaching calm of mind, all passion spent. Insofar as the reader is left with this feeling by any narrative, that narrative can be said to have a plot.[157]

From the standpoint of plot, two questions need to be resolved with reference to 1.1–9.34: (1) What is the overall thread of the story onto which 9.35–11.1 is attached? and (2) What expectations or tensions are raised within 1.1–9.34 with regard to the remainder of the story?

The plot of 1.1–4.16. The plot of the narrator's story from 1.1–9.34 comprises two major 'movements' (1.1–4.16; 4.17–9.34).[158] The first of these opens in 1.1 with the heading, 'The book of the origin of Jesus Messiah, Son of David, Son of Abraham'.[159] By means of this heading the narrator establishes two points: (1) What follows this heading will be introductory material relative to the protagonist of the story;[160] and (2) The initial identification of the protagonist, Jesus, is that of 'Messiah', 'Son of David', and 'Son of Abraham'. In this way the narrator leads the implied reader to conclude that whatever this 'book of origin' has to say concerning the background of the protagonist, Jesus, will relate to his identity as 'Messiah', 'Son of David', and 'Son of Abraham'. And this is what the implied reader discovers as he/she moves through the subsequent text.

The narrator begins his story in 1.2-16 by reciting the family line of the Messiah from Abraham (1.2) through David (1.6) and the Babylonian Exile (1.11-12) on down to Joseph, 'the husband of Mary, of whom was begotten[161] Jesus, who is called Messiah' (1.16). And in 1.17 the narrator summarizes the genealogy by counting the number of generations from Abraham to David, from David to the Babylonian Exile, and from the Babylonian Exile to 'the Messiah'.

The narrator then picks up the action of the story in 1.18-25, which he links to the heading (1.1) by repeating the reference to 'the origin of Jesus Messiah' (1.18). Here the narrator explains how Jesus, who according to the genealogy itself (1.16) is not the biological son of Joseph, enters the messianic family line. This story proceeds as follows. While Mary is betrothed to Joseph but before they have 'come together' as husband and wife, she conceives Jesus through the agency of the Holy Spirit. Joseph responds to this apparently disgraceful situation by moving cautiously and yet deliberately to cut off his legal ties to Mary. But before he has acted on his decision, the 'angel of the Lord' appears to him in a dream. The angel explains Mary's extraordinary pregnancy, announces that she will give birth to a son, and commands Joseph to name the child 'Jesus' since 'he will save his people from their sins'. As the scene closes, Joseph takes Mary as his wife and names her son 'Jesus', in this way adopting him into the line of David and Abraham.[162]

But the fact that Jesus' birth and lineage have now been legitimized does not signal the end of tensions within the story. As 2.1-23 opens, the scene shifts to Jerusalem and an encounter between magi from the East (who have come to worship the '[one] who has been born "King of the Jews"') and Herod 'the King' (who senses an acute threat from this new-born rival). Herod hatches a sinister plot against the life of the child, a plot which involves the magi themselves as unwitting participants. But the magi, who by this time have found the child and worshipped him, are warned in a dream not to report back to Herod; and in this way they foil Herod's plot. At this point the 'angel of the Lord' again appears to Joseph and instructs him to take 'the child and his mother' to Egypt until he receives further notice, since Herod is plotting to 'destroy' the child. As a result, Joseph takes his family and flees to the safety of Egypt; while Herod, in a fit of rage, orders the massacre of all the children of Bethlehem two years of age and under. But once again Herod fails in his plot against the life of Jesus: as the scene progresses, it is Herod himself who dies; while the 'angel of the Lord' appears a third time to Joseph and assures him that the way is now clear for him to bring 'the child and his mother' back to the land of Israel. Accordingly, in 1.22-23 Joseph returns to Israel, passes by Judea out of fear of Herod's son Archelaus, comes instead to Nazareth in Galilee, and settles there with his family.

In 3.1-17 Jesus, now an adult, shows up at the Jordan River. Here John the Baptist is preaching a message of repentance, baptizing those who come confessing their sins, and announcing the mission of 'one coming after' him. Jesus requests baptism at the hands of John; and when John demurs, he inists that this is what the two of them must do 'to fulfill all righteousness'. Accordingly, John accedes to Jesus' request and baptizes him, thereby setting the stage for an extraordinary sequence of events: the heavens open to Jesus, he sees the Spirit of God descending upon him in the form of a dove, and a voice from heaven (i.e., the voice of God) announces, 'This is my beloved Son, in whom I am well pleased'. Thus the Jesus who has been introduced first as the 'Messiah' from the line of David and Abraham (1.1-25) and then as the true 'King of the Jews' (2.1-23) is now proclaimed by God himself to be 'Son of God'.

In the scene which follows, 4.1-11, Jesus is then led by the Spirit into a wilderness encounter with Satan, 'the Tempter', who attempts to seduce Jesus into using his 'sonship' for ulterior purposes.[163] Jesus, however, stands fast in his commitment to be obedient to God; and in the end it is Jesus who forces Satan from the scene. Jesus' 'sonship' has been put to the ultimate test; and Jesus has stood firm, exhibiting undeniable proof that he is the Son of God.

In a final brief scene, 4.12-16, Jesus learns that John the Baptist has been 'handed over' (arrested) and takes this opportunity to relocate from Nazareth to Capernaum. John the Baptist, who first announced the mission of the 'one coming after' and then baptized that one in preparation for that mission, has now been removed from the stage so that Jesus, the 'one coming after', can stand alone in the spotlight.

In analyzing the thread of the story thus far (1.1-4.16), it becomes clear that Matthew's narrator has accomplished that which he sets forth in 1.1. as his goal: namely, to describe 'the origin of Jesus Messiah, Son of David, Son of Abraham'. And in doing so he has made use of three motifs which tie this section of the story together and offer significant clues to the implied reader about the direction which the remainder of the story is to take.

The first of these motifs is that of 'preparation for messianic ministry'. In a step by step process the narrator demonstrates how Jesus is prepared by the events of his infancy and early manhood for the messianic ministry he is destined to undertake. In 1.1-25 the narrator establishes the fact that Jesus is the Messiah from the line of David and of Abraham. At the same time he announces the task which Jesus will accomplish and for which he is to receive the name 'Jesus', namely, that of 'saving his people from their sins' (1.21). In a skillful use of irony the narrator then confirms for the implied reader (2.1-23) that Jesus and not Herod is indeed the Messiah, the true 'King of the Jews'. In 3.1-17 Jesus appears on the scene as an adult to receive the 'ordination' for his messianic ministry. This 'ordination' comes first of all in Jesus' baptism at the hands of John the Baptist and, following that, in the proclamation of the 'voice from heaven' announcing that Jesus is the 'beloved Son' of God himself. In 4.1-11 Jesus' newly-proclaimed identity as Son of God is put to the ultimate test in a face to face encounter with Satan, 'the Tempter'. And in withstanding Satan's temptations and putting Satan himself to flight, Jesus establishes by his own actions that 'divine sonship' which has just been proclaimed by the 'voice from heaven'. Jesus Messiah, the Son of God, is now ready to embark on his mission of '[saving] his people from their sins'. The one thing which must yet take place before he can begin this mission, however, is for John the Baptist to leave the stage so that the 'one coming after' can take his place. In 4.12-16 the narrator removes John the Baptist from the action and deliberately relocates Jesus to a strategic position for the inauguration of his mission.[164]

Closely related to the motif of 'preparation for messianic ministry' is that of 'divinely ordained itinerary'.[165] Matthew's narrator takes great pains to establish that from the time of his birth in 'Bethlehem of Judea' (2.1) until his arrival in Capernaum in Galilee (4.12-16) Jesus is living out, step by step, a 'divinely ordained' journey which stands confirmed in the Scriptures. Jesus' point of origin, 'Bethlehem of Judea' (2.1), is identified by none other than the chief priests and scribes as the place from which the Messiah is to come. In response to Herod's inquiry as to the birthplace of the Messiah (2.4), they cite 'Bethlehem of Judea' (2.5) and base their answer on the word of 'the prophet' that 'a ruler who will shepherd [God's] people Israel' is to come from 'Bethlehem in the land of Judah' (2.6; cf. Mic. 5.1, 3).

From Bethlehem Joseph takes Jesus and his mother to Egypt (2.14), fleeing from Herod in obedience to a warning from the 'angel of the Lord', who has appeared to him in a dream (2.13). Joseph remains in Egypt with his family until the death of Herod, at which time the 'angel of the Lord' appears to him once again (2.19-20), reversing the command of 2.13 and instructing Joseph to bring Jesus and his mother back to Israel. Joseph again responds obediently, bringing his family back to Israel (2.21) and terminating Jesus' Egyptian sojourn. Joseph himself realizes only that he is acting as commanded in order to save Jesus from the evil designs of Herod. But the narrator points the implied reader to the ultimate significance of this event: Jesus' sojourn in Egypt brings to fulfilment 'that which was spoken by the Lord through the prophet, saying, "Out of Egypt I have called my son"' (2.15).

The next destination on the journey is Nazareth in Galilee. Upon returning to Israel, Joseph discovers that Herod's son Archelaus is now ruling in Judea. For this reason he is afraid to take up residence there; and in response to yet another dream (2.22), he takes his family to Galilee and settles down in Nazareth (2.22-23). Once again, Joseph knows only that he is acting on command in order to protect the life of Jesus. But just as before, the narrator points the implied reader to the ultimate significance of this event: Jesus must be taken to Nazareth in order that 'that which was spoken through the prophets might be fulfilled, "He shall be called a Nazarene"' (2.23).

But Nazareth is still not the final destination of this 'divinely ordained' journey. Following his baptism by John at the Jordan River (3.1-17) and his encounter with Satan in the wilderness (4.1-11), Jesus makes yet another significant move (4.12-16). Upon learning that John has been 'handed over' (4.12), he 'withdraws' into Galilee and relocates from Nazareth to Capernaum 'in the regions of Zebulon and Naphtali' (4.12-13). Here Jesus, acting apparently on his own counsel and not in obedience to a dream, responds to a perceived threat, just as Joseph before him (2.14, 22-23), by moving from one location to another. And here again the narrator clarifies for the implied reader the ultimate significance of this move: Jesus comes to Capernaum 'in the regions of Zebulon and Naphtali' in order to fulfill 'that which was spoken through Isaiah the prophet, saying, "The land of Zebulon and the land of Naphtali, the way of the sea, beyond the Jordan, Galilee of the Gentiles; the people who sat in darkness have seen a great light, and for those sitting in the land of the shadow of death light has dawned"' (4.15-16). Thus Jesus is now at the 'divinely ordained' location ('Galilee of the Gentiles') from which he is to launch his public ministry to the Jewish people ('the people sitting in darkness'; cf. 1.21 and 2.6).[166] Jesus' 'divinely ordained' journey, therefore, has prepared him, no less than the specific experiences he has encountered along the way, for the moment in which he is to assume publicly the messianic ministry to which he is destined.

The third motif which runs throughout 1.1-4.16 is that of 'recurring threat to Jesus' assumption of his messianic ministry'. This represents the 'counterpoint' to the first two motifs. If Jesus has been prepared, event by event and location by location, for the moment in which he is to assume his messianic ministry, this preparation has at the same time come about by means of a sequence of events in which the people around Jesus threaten either deliberately or unwittingly to prevent him from embarking on that ministry.

Both Jesus' supporters and his opponents play a role in the working out of this motif. In 1.18-25 it is Joseph, the 'righteous man' betrothed to Mary, who unwittingly poses a threat to Jesus' 'messiahship' by planning to divorce Mary (1.19-20), an act which would cut off the child she is to bear from the family line of David and Abraham. In 2.1-23 Herod makes a direct threat not against Jesus' messianic identity, which he has no power to alter (2.2, 4), but rather against the 'life' of Jesus (2.20), which he makes every effort to 'destroy' (2.13, 16). And even after Herod's death Jesus is not out of danger: judging from Joseph's 'fear' (2.22a) and the fact that he is 'warned' in a dream (2.22b), it is evident that Archelaus poses no less a threat to the life of Jesus than did Herod his father before him. In 3.1-17 it is none other than John the Baptist, whose very task is to 'prepare the way for the Lord' (3.3), who threatens instead to 'bar the way for the Lord' by declining initially to baptize him (3.14) in 'ordination' for his messianic ministry. In 4.1-11 Satan, 'the Tempter', sets out deliberately to jeopardize Jesus' ultimate identity as Son of God (4.3, 5; cf. 3.17) by attempting to seduce Jesus into disobeying the commands of God (4.3, 6, 9; cf. 4.4, 7, 10) and in this way denying his own 'sonship'.

Finally, in 4.12-16, after it has become evident that Jesus cannot be deflected from his course by any type of threatening situation (whether instigated by human beings or by Satan himself), the motif of 'threat' is transformed into one of 'warning'. By juxtaposing the announcement of Jesus' relocation from Nazareth to Capernaum (4.13) to the announcement that John has been 'handed over' (4.12), Matthew's narrator communicates an oblique warning: if John's mission (namely, to 'prepare the way' [3.3] for the 'one coming after' [3.11]) has ended in a violent manner, then Jesus' own mission (that towards which he has been moving from the beginning of the story and on which he is now ready to embark [4.15-16]) may likewise end in violence if he carries through with it.

The plot of 4.17–9.34. In 4.17 it becomes clear that Jesus does indeed intend to carry through with his messianic ministry. Here the narrator announces that Jesus is now 'beginning' his public ministry with the proclamation: 'Repent, for the Kingdom of heaven has come near'. This announcement by the narrator serves a double function: (1) it signals the opening of a new phase of the story, indicating in turn that 'the book of the origin of Jesus Messiah, Son of David, Son of Abraham' has come to its conclusion in 4.16;[167] and (2) it functions as the programmatic heading for this new phase of the story.[168]

Following the programmatic heading of 4.17, then, the first specific incident of Jesus' ministry which the narrator recounts is one in which Jesus calls four fishermen along the Sea of Galilee away from their nets, boats, and families with the words, 'Follow me, and I will make you fishermen for people' (4.19, cf. 21). While no hint is given that these men have ever heard of Jesus prior to this moment, their response is immediate and apparently unhesitating: 'and immediately they left their [nets/boat/father] and followed him' (4.20, 22). Striking here is the location of this account within the narrator's story. By placing the calling of the four disciples in this primary position within the overall account of Jesus' ministry, the narrator establishes not only that Jesus' disciples are present with him in his ministry from its very inception but also that their presence with Jesus is in some way crucial to the carrying out of his ministry.

In a second step the narrator presents a summary (4.23-25) of Jesus' ministry among the people and the people's response to Jesus. For his part, Jesus '[goes] about all Galilee teaching in their synagogues and proclaiming the gospel of the Kingdom and healing every disease and every sickness among the people (4.23). For their part, the people bring to Jesus all those who are sick; and he heals them (4.24). As a result of this, 'great crowds [follow] him from Galilee, the Decapolis, Jerusalem, Judea, and beyond the Jordan' (4.25). Of significance here is the fact that Jesus is carrying out the ministry predicted by the prophet Isaiah (4.15-16), namely, a ministry *in Galilee* and *to the people of Israel*.[169]

In these first two scenes from the ministry of Jesus (4.18-22 and 4.23-25) the narrator has thus brought on stage and established the roles of the two groups of characters directly related to Jesus' ministry. The role of the disciples is to follow Jesus about as he ministers to the people and, ultimately, to become themselves 'fishermen for people'. The role of the crowds is to flock after Jesus as he moves about the countryside and to bring him their sick for healing. With these two groups of characters in place, the narrator can now proceed with detailed recounting of Jesus' ministry.

In 5.1-7.29 the narrator depicts Jesus as teaching both his disciples (5.1-2) and the crowds (7.28-29; cf. 5.1): here in an extensive discourse of 107 verses (5.3–7.27), Jesus describes the lifestyle of the Kingdom of heaven. The function of this discourse is clear. In 4.17, the programmatic heading to this phase of the story, the narrator has indicated that the theme of Jesus' proclamation is 'the Kingdom of heaven'. In 5.3–7.27 Jesus now describes in detail the life of the Kingdom, a life characterized by 'righteousness [which] exceeds that of the scribes and Pharisees' (5.20) and by 'doing the will of God' (7.21).

Finally, in 8.1–9.34 the narrator presents a 'slice of life' view of Jesus' overall ministry.[170] Within this section Jesus heals people with all types of illnesses (8.1-4, 5-13, 14–15, 16–17, 28-34; 9.1-8, 18-19/ 23-26, 20-22, 27-31, 32-34), responds in unexpected fashion to an enthusiastic scribe and a reluctant disciple (8.18-22),[171] shows his authority over the elements (8.23-27) and the demons (8.28-34), assumes the divine prerogative to forgive sins (9.1-8), calls another person to follow him as a disciple (9.9), and fields controversial questions from other religious groups (9.10-13, 14-17). This section concludes with a scene (9.32-34) in which the crowds recognize in Jesus' ministry something unique in the history of Israel, while the Pharisees attribute Jesus' power and authority to Beelzebul, the 'prince of demons'.

The question now remains: what expectations has the narrator raised by means of his plot; and what tensions has he created in relation to Jesus, the disciples, and the crowds? Four observations are germane at this point.

As noted above, Jesus' ministry is defined as a messianic ministry to the Jewish people. At the same time, the narrator provides hints that this messianic ministry will be of significance to the Gentiles as well as to the Jewish people. The first of these hints lies in the reception accorded the infant Jesus: while King Herod 'and all Jerusalem with him' are 'disturbed' at the news of the '[one] who has been born "King of the Jews"', the (Gentile) magi come from a great distance to pay homage to this 'King'. It is thus evident that the Jewish leadership, headquartered in Jerusalem, is less ready to receive this 'King of the Jews' than are the Gentiles. A further hint concerning the ultimate significance of Jesus' messianic ministry lies in the account of his move to Capernaum (4.12-16): the fact that the point of departure for Jesus' ministry *to the Jewish people* is designated as 'Galilee *of the Gentiles*' hints that Jesus' ministry itself will likewise be of significance to these Gentiles. The implied reader is thus left with the question: when and how will the messianic ministry of Jesus Messiah, Son of David, Son of Abraham come to be of significance to the Gentiles?

Secondly, Jesus' ministry is defined in 4.23 as a ministry of teaching, proclamation, and healing; and in the scenes which follow (5.1–9.34) Jesus is depicted as carrying out all three aspects of his ministry with great effectiveness. By portraying Jesus in this way the narrator communicates to the implied reader that Jesus is fully capable of carrying out his own ministry in the power and authority which God has both visibly and audibly bestowed upon him at the time of his baptism. The implied reader is thus led to expect that Jesus will continue to function in this way throughout the remainder of the story. But this very expectation raises a question: what then is the significance of the calling of the disciples? If Jesus can carry out an effective ministry without assistance, what then is the need for disciples who will become 'fishermen for people'?

And this, in turn, leads to a third question: when and how will Jesus fulfill his promise to 'make' the disciples into 'fishermen for people'? As the story unfolds, the implied reader sees the disciples constantly in the presence of Jesus, but almost always playing a subordinate role in the action (5.1-2; 8.14, 23; 9.10, 11, 19).[172] But in assuming this subordinate role, the disciples are in fact fulfilling the condition laid down for them (4.19b), namely, that of 'following Jesus'. It is now, therefore, up to Jesus to carry out that which he has promised to do (4.19c), namely, to 'make' them into 'fishermen for people'. And since there has been no sign thus far that this has taken place, the implied reader is left at 9.34 with the question as to when and how this is going to happen.

Finally, the implied reader is also left with a growing sense of apprehension concerning the dangers which lie ahead both for Jesus and for his disciples. The narrator provides the first substantial hint of these coming dangers in 4.12-16, where he recounts the events which lead up to the beginning of Jesus' public ministry. By connecting the fate of John, Jesus' forerunner, to the final step in Jesus' preparation for his own ministry, the narrator offers the implied reader a clue that Jesus may encounter the same fate as John.

The next reference to impending danger is a straightforward warning: in his discourse of 5.3-7.27 Jesus indicates to his hearers that living the life of the Kingdom of heaven will inevitably lead them to 'persecution'. In 5.10, at the end of a list of 'beatitudes' addressed to those who espouse the values of the Kingdom of heaven (5.3-10), Jesus pronounces a blessing on 'those who are persecuted on account of righteousness'. In 5.11 he then reiterates: 'Blessed are you (pl.) when they revile you and persecute you and say all kinds of evil things against you falsely on my account'. In 5.12 Jesus calls his hearers to 'rejoice' in this persecution, since 'in this way they persecuted the prophets who were before you'. And finally, in another context altogether, Jesus enjoins his hearers to 'pray for those who persecute you' (5.44). A threefold message lies in these words of warning: (1) there will inevitably be persecution for those who live the life of the Kingdom of heaven; (2) this persecution will come to them on account of Jesus; and (3) experiencing this persecution will align them with 'the prophets who were before [them]', since those prophets were persecuted in the same way. The net effect of Jesus' message, therefore, is to forge for his hearers a link which connects them first to himself and then to 'the prophets who were before [them]', a link built of solidarity in persecution.

The implied reader thus stands warned at this early point in the story—while Jesus is receiving an enthusiastic reception from the crowds (4.23-25) and before the disciples have taken any initiatives at all—that times are going to change. The day will come when not only Jesus (cf. 4.12-16) but his followers in solidarity with him (cf. 5.10-12, 44) will face persecution from others.

Setting
The setting of the story from 4.12-16 through 9.34 has been, with one exception only (8.23–9.1), that of Galilee. The narrator indicates this by means of a variety of geographical 'markers' along the way (4.12-16, 18, 23, 25; 8.5; 9.1). In light of the close verbal relationship between 9.35 and 4.23[173] and in the absence of any indications to the contrary, the implied reader is left to assume that the setting for 9.35–11.1 is still Galilee. This raises the question: what does the implied reader know about Galilee which will influence his/her interpretation of any incident described as taking place there?

By the time he/she reaches 9.35, the implied reader understands the following about Galilee: (1) Galilee is the area indicated by divine revelation (2.22) as well as by the Scriptures themselves (2.23; 4.12-16) as the place in which Jesus is to live; (2) Jesus has apparently grown up in Galilee (2.22-23; 3.13), thus carrying out the divinely-written script concerning where he should live; (3) in the past (and also in the present?) Galilee has been a place of safety for Jesus (2.22-23; cf. 4.12); (4) Galilee is the place in which Jesus' presence represents a 'light' to the 'people who sat in darkness' (4.16), an apparent reference to the Jewish people; (5) at the same time Galilee, and along with it Jesus' own ministry, is identified with the Gentiles (4.15); (6) Galilee is the place in which Jesus calls his disciples, carries out his mission of teaching, proclaiming, and healing, and is followed about by the masses (4.18, 23, 25). The overall impression which the implied reader gains from this information about Galilee is positive: Galilee is the God-ordained place for Jesus to live and to carry out his messianic ministry.

Chapter 3

LITERARY CRITICAL ANALYSIS OF MATTHEW 9.35–11.1

I. *Overview of the Text*

Prior to 9.35 Matthew's narrator has depicted both the events leading up to Jesus' assumption of his messianic ministry (1.1–4.16) and the beginnings of that ministry (4.17–9.34). And in telling of the beginnings of Jesus' ministry the narrator has introduced two groups of characters directly related to that ministry: the disciples, whose task it is to 'follow' Jesus as he ministers; and the crowds, those to whom Jesus ministers.[1] But while it is clear to the implied reader that the crowds are essential to the story as the objects of Jesus' ministry, it is not yet clear what function Jesus' disciples serve.

On the one hand the narrator emphasizes the importance of the disciples for Jesus' ministry. He places the account of their 'calling' at the very beginning of his description of Jesus' public ministry (4.18-22) and describes that 'calling' in terms of Jesus' command and accompanying promise, 'Follow me, and I will make you fishermen for people' (4.19).

But the text which follows (4.23–9.34) shows the disciples assuming only the first half of this role: while they 'follow' Jesus (4.20, 22; 8.23; 9.9, 19), they give no indication that they are beginning to function as 'fishermen for people'. Nowhere throughout 4.23–9.34 do they take any initiatives towards the crowds in general or towards individuals out of the crowds. Instead they play a subordinate role in the story, remaining in Jesus' presence as those who are seen but seldom heard (but see 8.25). Further, Jesus does not appear to need their assistance. Instead he carries out his own ministry with great effectiveness in the authority bestowed on him by God at the time of his baptism.

At this point, therefore, two questions emerge for the implied reader with respect to Jesus' disciples. How will Jesus draw these disciples into the work which he has been doing singlehandedly? And when will the disciples fully 'realize' their calling and enter into the ministry of 'fishing for people'?

With 9.35 the narrator moves into a segment of the story in the course of which he begins to answer these questions. This segment opens in 9.35 with a virtually verbatim reprise of 4.23: 'And Jesus went about all the cities and villages teaching in their synagogues and proclaiming the gospel of the Kingdom and healing every disease and every sickness'.[2]

The obvious parallelism between 4.23(-25) and 9.35 functions in two ways. On the one hand it serves to place brackets around the intervening text (5.1–9.34), thus identifying this text as a unit and linking 5.1–7.29 and 8.1–9.34 thematically under the rubric, 'Jesus ministers to the people through teaching, proclaiming, and healing'.[3] Accordingly, the repetition of 4.23 in 9.35 points the implied reader backward in the text, establishing 9.35 as the second of a pair of brackets which surrounds and unifies 5.1–9.34.[4]

But what the implied reader discovers as the story progresses is that the summary statement of 9.35 also stands as the introduction to a new segment of text (9.35–11.1)[5] which parallels in basic content the segment introduced by 4.23-25. The narrator develops both segments in four stages. In an initial summary statement (4.23-25/9.35) he depicts Jesus as engaged in a ministry of teaching, proclaiming, and healing which takes him throughout the cities and villages of Galilee.[6] In a brief transitional statement (5.1a/9.36a) he notes that Jesus sees the crowds (which have gathered around him in response to this ministry; cf. 4.24-25).[7] He then describes in detailed fashion the ministry of proclamation and healing which issues as Jesus' response to the needs of the crowds. In the one case this is a ministry carried out by Jesus himself (5.1b–9.34); and in the other a ministry to which Jesus commissions his disciples (9.36b–10.42). He concludes the segment (9.35/11.1) with a repetition of his initial summary statement depicting Jesus as engaged in a peripatetic ministry within Galilee.[8]

But while 4.23–9.35 and 9.35–11.1 demonstrate a basic parallelism in content, it is only in 11.1 that the full significance of this parallelism becomes evident. The announcement that 'when Jesus finished instructing his disciples, he went on from there to teach and to proclaim in their cities' serves a twofold function with respect to the overall structure of 4.23–11.1.[9]

First of all, 11.1 marks the conclusion of the segment introduced by 9.35. By repeating the reference to Jesus' peripatetic ministry the narrator constructs a second 'bracketed text', 9.35–11.1, which not only follows but also interlocks with the first one, 4.23–9.35. And with the construction of this second 'bracketed text' the narrator establishes 9.35–11.1 as a distinct and clearly delimited segment of his story.

In addition, 11.1 points all the way back to 4.23, the first appearance of the 'ministry' motif, and in so doing creates a third and lengthier 'bracketed text', 4.23–11.1. Thus 4.23–11.1 forms a connected 'whole' which consists of two parallel and interlocking segments—4.23–9.35 and 9.35–11.1—linked by the 'hinge' verse, 9.35.[10]

As a result, the full significance of the parallelism between 4.23–9.35 and 9.35–11.1 lies in the fact that both segments fall under the rubric, 'Jesus ministers to the people of Galilee' (4.23; 9.35; 11.1). This rubric is what the implied reader would expect for the first segment (4.23–9.35), the one describing Jesus' ministry to the crowds. But it is clearly of strategic importance that the narrator uses this same rubric to bracket the second segment (9.35–11.1), since this one describes the ministry to which Jesus commissions his disciples.

In short, the narrator wishes the implied reader to interpret the ministry to which Jesus commissions his disciples (10.5b-42) as not merely parallel to, but rather an integral part of, the ministry of Jesus himself. It is for this reason that the narrator places the call of the disciples at the outset of Jesus' public ministry (4.18-22) and relates that call in terms of the words of Jesus, 'Follow me, and I will make you fishermen for people' (4.19). Jesus calls the disciples and promises them a new identity; and they, in turn, become part of his ministry. This, finally, is the import of 9.35–11.1.

II. *Structure of the Text*

Now that the limits, general content, and overall import of 9.35–11.1 have been established, the next task is to examine the text in detail. In order to do that, however, it is first necessary to outline the structure of the text. The analysis to follow will then deal with the text section by section, in accordance with the structural divisions thus established.

The basis for determining the structure of 9.35–11.1 is the formal characteristics of the text, that is, the rhetorical devices used by the narrator of the story.[11] The most prominent of these is the distinction between narrative material and discourse. According to this distinction 9.35–11.1 divides itself into three subsections: the narration of a sequence of events initiated by Jesus (9.35–10.5a); an extended and uninterrupted discourse by Jesus (10.5b–42); and the concluding announcement that following his discourse Jesus continues his ministry (11.1). On formal grounds, therefore, the overall structure of the text can be seen as the following: 9.35–10.5a and 11.1 form the narrative framework which surrounds an uninterrupted discourse by Jesus in 10.5b–42.[12]

But while the distinction between narrative and discourse dictates the overall structure of the text (9.35–10.5a; 10.5b–42; 11.1), another rhetorical device, the repeated formula, dictates the structure of the discourse itself. Jesus punctuates his discourse three times with the formulaic statement, 'Truly, I say to you . . . ' (10.15, 23, 42).[13] In each case this statement leads directly into a warning or promise which depicts in eschatological terms—'day of judgment' (10.15), 'coming of the Son of man' (10.23), 'reward' (10.42)[14]— the ultimate implications of the actions described or prescribed in the preceding verses. In light of its threefold repetition and its distinctly formal tone, this pattern (formulaic statement + eschatological warning or promise) serves to divide the discourse into three major sections: 10.5b–15, 16–23, and 24–42.[15]

On the basis of the formal characteristics thus observed in the text—distinction between narrative and discourse and use of a repeated formula—the passage 9.35–11.1 may be viewed as consisting of five sections: (1) the narrative introduction, 9.35–10.5a; (2, 3, 4) the discourse in three parts, 10.5b–15, 16–23, 24–42; (5) the narrative conclusion, 11.1. The following analysis of 9.35–11.1 will therefore be structured in accordance with these sectional divisions.

III. *Analysis of the Text*

The narrative introduction: 9.35–10.5a (text)

9.35   And Jesus went about all the cities and villages
           teaching in their synagogues
           and proclaiming the gospel of the Kingdom
           and healing every disease and every sickness.

9.36   And when he saw the crowds,
           he took compassion on them;

for they were harassed and helpless,
like sheep without a shepherd.

9.37   Then he says to his disciples:
The harvest is great,
but the laborers are few;

9.38   beseech, therefore, the lord of the harvest
that he send out laborers into his harvest.

10.1   And when he had called to him his twelve disciples,
he gave them authority
over unclean spirits—to cast them out—
and to heal every disease and every sickness.

10.2   (Now these are the names of the twelve apostles:
first Simon, the one who is called Peter,
and Andrew his brother,
James the son of Zebedee
and John his brother,

10.3   Philip
and Bartholomew,
Thomas
and Matthew the tax collector,
James the son of Alphaeus
and Thaddaeus,

10.4   Simon the Cananaean
and Judas Iscariot, the one who handed him over.)

10.5a   These twelve Jesus sent out, instructing them saying,

The narrative introduction: 9.35–10.5a (analysis)
The internal unity of this section of text is established by the sequence of finite verbs used to describe the actions of Jesus: Jesus goes about (9.35), takes compassion (9.36), speaks (9.37), gives authority (10.1), and sends out (10.5a). Into this sequence the narrator inserts an explanatory parenthesis (10.2-4) in which he introduces 'the twelve apostles' by name (and in some cases a descriptive qualifier). As a result, the narrative introduction consists of six distinct segments—9.35, 9.36, 9.37-38, 10.1, 10.2-4, and 10.5a—which together create a connected sequence of events.

To determine the literary significance of this narrative introduction as a whole, therefore, it will be useful to examine the text segment by segment, paying attention to the narrator's treatment of the three basic elements of his story—setting, plot, and characterization. On the basis of this analysis it will then be possible to assess the overall impact of the narrative introduction both in relation to what has preceded it and in anticipation of what is to follow.

Jesus goes about (9.35). In the opening segment (9.35) of the
narrative introduction, the narrator establishes the setting for the
following sequence of events in two ways. First, he depicts Jesus in
an ongoing ministry[16] which takes him to 'all the cities and villages'.
This serves to delimit the scope of Jesus' mission: the clear
parallelism with 4.23, where Jesus goes about 'all Galilee', strongly
suggests that the reference here is to 'all the cities and villages [of
Galilee]'.[17] In this way the narrator locates the remaining events of
this sequence (i.e., 9.36; 9.37-38; 10.1; 10.5a) within the same
geographical context as the ministry of Jesus detailed in 5.1-9.34, the
verses following the summary of 4.23-25.[18]

In addition, the narrator depicts Jesus as 'teaching in their
synagogues', 'proclaiming the gospel of the Kingdom', and 'healing
every diesease and every sickness'. This description, once again in
clear parallelism with 4.23,[19] establishes that Jesus' mission is the
same mission of teaching, proclaiming, and healing directed to the
Jewish people as the one described in 5.1-9.34.[20]

The parallelism between 9.35 and 4.23 in terms of geographical
context, recipients, and content of Jesus' ministry serves to remind
the implied reader of the specific events of Jesus' ministry as
described in 5.1-9.34. As a result, everything which the implied
reader has learned prior to 9.35 about the nature of Jesus' ministry to
the crowds of Galilee stands as the backdrop for that which is to take
place in the following verses, 9.36-10.5a.

In this regard two observations are germane. From the beginning
of Jesus' public ministry (4.17) up to this point in the story (9.35), the
implied reader has seen Jesus initiate and carry out his ministry
singlehandedly. In 9.35 this picture is reinforced: Jesus teaches,
proclaims, and heals on his own, while the disciples remain
unnoticed.[21] And from 4.17 on, the implied reader has observed as
the crowds flock after Jesus, listen to his words, and bring their sick
to be healed by him. This picture is also reinforced in 9.35: while the
narrator makes no explicit mention of the crowds, his announcement
that Jesus is teaching, proclaiming, and healing implies their
presence.[22]

According to 9.35, therefore, there has not yet been any change in
the lines of contact previously established between the various
characters of the story. While Jesus continues to relate both to his
disciples and to the crowds, these two groups are not portrayed as

relating to each other. And it is in light of this fact that the specific events which follow in 9.36–10.5a take on their real significance.

Jesus takes compassion (9.36). These specific events begin in 9.36[23] with the statement: 'And when he [i.e., Jesus] saw the crowds, he took compassion on them; for they were harassed and helpless, like sheep without a shepherd'. The reference here to the crowds provides a connecting link between the general setting described in 9.35 and the specific events of 9.36–10.5a. The participial phrase *idōn de tous ochlous* (= and when he saw the crowds) points backward to 9.35 by identifying the implicit object of Jesus' activities there.[24] This phrase also points forward to the initiatives taken by Jesus in the text which follows, since it is these same crowds on whom Jesus then 'takes compassion'. Thus the opening phrase of 9.36 provides the necessary transition from the summary statement of 9.35 to the specific events of 9.36–10.5a.[25]

The focus of 9.36 lies on Jesus' 'compassionate' response to the crowds,[26] a response which reflects Jesus' intense emotional identification with the plight of these crowds.[27] At the same time 9.36 also identifies the plight of the crowds which evokes that response: they are 'harassed and helpless, like sheep without a shepherd'. This picture has two facets. On the one hand, the crowds are depicted in terms which reflect vulnerability and weakness: they are not only 'harassed' but also 'helpless' to protect themselves from this 'harassment'. On the other hand, their condition is attributed to the fact that they are 'sheep without a shepherd', those who lack the leadership and protection which a shepherd provides for his flock.[28]

This description introduces a new element into the previous picture of enthusiastic and amazed crowds, who gather eagerly around Jesus to listen to his teachings and to bring him their sick for healing. Now the crowds are characterized as a helpless and leaderless group whose continued existence as a 'people' itself hangs in the balance.[29] An added note of distress has entered the picture.

But it is this note of distress vis-à-vis the crowds which draws the attention of the implied reader back to Jesus and his positive role with respect to these crowds. The reference here to 'sheep without a shepherd' points the implied reader back to the account of Herod's response to the birth of Jesus (2.1-8). When Herod asks the 'chief priests and scribes *of the people*' where the Messiah is to be born (2.4), they reply: 'In Bethlehem of Judea; for thus it was written by the prophet: "And you, Bethlehem, in the land of Judah, are by no means least among the rulers of Judah; for out of you will come a ruler *who will shepherd my people, Israel*"' (2.5-6; cf. Mic. 5.1, 3).

Ironically, the very ones who are themselves recognized as leaders 'of the people' (2.4; cf. 9.29) unwittingly connect the birth of Jesus with the prophetic prediction of a 'ruler' whose task will be that of 'shepherding [God's] people Israel'. But while the 'chief priests and scribes of the people' may not realize the true significance of what they are saying, the implied reader knows that the prophecy of 2.5-6 refers to Jesus, who has just been born in Bethlehem. Consequently, that reader knows that it is Jesus (and not the Jewish leaders) whose role is that of 'shepherding' the Jewish people.

As a result, when the narrator now describes Jesus' 'compassion' for the crowds, whom he sees as 'sheep without a shepherd',[30] the implied reader recognizes in this situation the outworking of that earlier prediction. While the Jewish leaders leave their own people floundering for lack of leadership, Jesus exhibits concern for them such as that of a shepherd for his sheep.

Jesus speaks to his disciples (9.37-38). In light of the narrator's portrayal of Jesus as 'shepherd', Jesus' next move (9.37-38) is surprising: 'Then he says to his disciples: "The harvest is great, but the laborers are few; beseech, therefore, the lord of the harvest that he send out laborers into his harvest"'. Just at the point where the implied reader expects Jesus to assume his own role as 'shepherd' vis-à-vis the 'harassed and helpless sheep' whom he encounters, he turns instead to his disciples and calls them into action.

This initiative constitutes a direct response to what has just taken place in 9.36. It is when Jesus sees the distressing condition of the crowds that he 'then' addresses himself to his disciples.[31] Consequently, that action to which Jesus calls his disciples represents his solution to the problem posed by the distress of the crowds. Thus it now remains to examine Jesus' message to his disciples to determine what that solution is.

In the first half of his saying (9.37b), Jesus draws a picture of a 'great harvest' for which there are 'few laborers'. The focus of this picture lies on the contrast between 'great' and 'few' and the tension created by this contrast. In and of itself, the reference to the 'great harvest' is positive: this language implies a crop which has produced well and now stands ready to be gathered in.[32] But the positive picture of the 'great harvest' is immediately clouded by the contrasting statement which follows,[33] namely that there are 'few laborers [available to harvest the crop]'. Accordingly, the weight of 9.37b falls not on the positive fact that the harvest is 'great', but rather on the negative fact that the laborers are 'few'.[34]

In the second half of the saying (9.38) Jesus enjoins his disciples to 'beseech . . . the lord of the harvest that he send out laborers into his harvest'. The disturbing picture of a 'great harvest' with 'few laborers' thus issues in the urgent command to pray for additional 'laborers'. As a result, it is evident that the question of 'laborers' provides the single element of movement within the saying: the lack of sufficient laborers (9.37b) creates the tension in the first half of the saying, and the despatching of additional laborers (9.38) is depicted as the solution to that tension.[35]

But two additional elements are likewise important to the thought of the saying. The 'laborers' to be 'sent out' do not act on their own initiative. Rather, they must be called into action by the 'lord of the harvest', the one in charge of the harvesting process[36] and as such the one 'responsible for hiring and dismissing harvest workers'.[37] Further, Jesus indicates that his disciples themselves have a significant role to play in all of this: their task is to 'beseech . . . the lord of the harvest' to 'send out' the requisite 'laborers'.

At this point, however, the question arises: How is Jesus' metaphor to be interpreted? For Jesus' disciples, the message is straightforward. For them as his followers, the 'great harvest' points to the size and the urgent need of the crowds, while the reference to the 'few laborers' points to Jesus' need for assistance in his ministry to these crowds.[38]

The second half of Jesus' saying (9.38), then, points the disciples to a new situation, one in which God will send out others to assist Jesus in his ministry to the crowds. Jesus' reference to the 'lord of the harvest' can only be a reference to God, since for Jesus and his disciples only God has such ultimate authority.[39] It is likewise clear that the 'laborers' to be sent out are to be associated with the work force already in the harvest (i.e., with Jesus himself) and identified with the task assigned to that work force (i.e, ministering to the crowds). For the disciples, therefore, the command of 9.38 calls them to pray that God will send out others to assist Jesus in his ministry to the crowds.[40]

The full significance of 9.37-38 is now evident. First of all, Jesus has made it clear to his disciples that he is not to complete his ministry to the crowds singlehandedly. Rather, his ministry is one which calls for additional laborers.[41] Secondly, he has for the first time in the story called his disciples to take specific and crucial action in regard to his ministry.[42] The ministry which previously was Jesus' concern alone has now become the concern of his disciples as well.[43] Thus a major shift is here taking place in terms of the lines of contact which exist between the characters of the story. No longer will it be Jesus alone who relates to the crowds. Rather, by turning to his disciples at this juncture and calling them into action, Jesus draws them also into a relationship with the crowds.

Jesus gives authority (10.1). It appears that the moment has arrived for which the implied reader has been waiting, the moment in which Jesus will begin to fulfill his promise (4.19) to make his disciples 'fishermen for people'.[44] And this is what the implied reader discovers in 10.1: 'And when he had called to him his twelve disciples, he gave them authority over unclean spirits—to cast them out—and to heal every disease and every sickness'. Here Jesus takes the initiative, first in gathering his twelve disciples about him[45] and then in giving them authority. Thus *Jesus' own actions* (10.1) constitute the direct response to the prayer which he has just instructed his disciples to pray (9.38), namely, that *God will act.* Accordingly, it is Jesus himself who implements the action of God described in 9.38, i.e., the sending out of laborers into the harvest. And this means that Jesus is acting not only with the authority of God (cf. 3.13-17; 7.29; 9.8) but in the very place of God: Jesus' initiative in calling together his disciples and giving them authority is no less than an action of God himself.[46]

This means, in turn, that Jesus' twelve disciples[47] are themselves the laborers to be sent out to assist Jesus in his ministry to the crowds. Further witness to this fact lies in the narrator's description of the authority which Jesus here gives to his disciples. The narrator speaks of 'authority over unclean spirits—to cast them out', the very authority which Jesus has previously demonstrated in ministering to the crowds (8.16, 28-34; 9.32-34). And he speaks of '[authority] to heal every disease and every sickness',[48] the very language used (9.35; cf. 4.23) to summarize Jesus' healing ministry. Thus when Jesus gives his disciples 'authority', it is evident that he is sharing with them his own authority so that they can enter into the ministry in which he himself is now active.[49]

The message is clear: Jesus' disciples do indeed have a crucial role to play in the story (cf. 4.19), a role which is not only thrust upon them by Jesus but also defined in terms of Jesus' own ministry. Jesus' ministry has become the mission of the disciples as well; and Jesus' authority for carrying out that ministry is now their authority likewise. The promised empowering of Jesus' disciples (4.19) is in progress.

Introduction of 'the twelve apostles' (10.2-4). Now that the narrator has moved the disciples out of the shadows (9.35) and (temporarily) onto center stage along with Jesus (10.1), he interrupts the flow of his narrative long enough to introduce them as a group of twelve to the implied reader (10.2-4). He opens this parenthetical explanation with the words, 'Now these are the names of the twelve apostles'; and he then lists in pairs the names of the twelve.[50]

This introduction serves a dual purpose. Here the narrator establishes the primary identity of Jesus' disciples as that of 'apostles', that is, 'those who are sent out'.[51] With this designation the narrator points the implied reader back to Jesus' saying of 9.38: it is because they themselves are the ones to be 'sent out' into God's harvest that Jesus' disciples are here identified as 'apostles'.[52] And this indicates that an act of 'sending' is about to take place which will warrant the use of that designation.

In addition the narrator introduces 'the twelve apostles' by name, and hints that two of them will have special roles to play as the story develops. Two apostles, alone of all the twelve, are introduced in 'verbal' language.[53] First on the list is Simon 'the one who is called Peter', and last is Judas Iscariot 'the one who handed him over'. These two descriptions, phrased in terms of the narrator's own temporal perspective,[54] serve to foreshadow future events in the story. The implied reader is alerted to the fact that there is significance in the epithet 'Peter' which is given to Simon,[55] even though that significance is not yet clear. And the implied reader is likewise alerted to the fact that Judas Iscariot is going to 'hand over' someone, a person who in the context of the story can only be Jesus himself.[56]

Jesus sends the disciples out (10.5a). Having introduced the 'apostles', the narrator moves back into his story with the announcement (10.5a): 'These twelve Jesus sent out, instructing them saying ... ' This event, which brings to its climax the sequence of events initiated in 9.35, has far-reaching implications for the narrator's story. In the first half of 10.5a the narrator forges the decisive link in the chain which connects the vocation of Jesus' disciples to the ministry of Jesus himself. If Jesus has initially 'called' his disciples (4.18-22; 8.21-22; 9.9) and subsequently 'authorized' them to carry out the same ministry as that in which he is now active (10.1), he now 'sends them out' to assume that ministry.[57]

It follows that the shape of Jesus' ministry (as the narrator has already described it in 4.23-9.35 and as he will describe it in the remainder of the story) has direct implications for the ministry of the disciples. In light of 10.5a, the narrator's depiction of Jesus' ministry to the crowds likewise serves to depict the shape which the disciples' own ministry is to assume. But the narrator does not leave the shape of the disciples' ministry solely up to the inference of the implied reader. Rather, in the second half of 10.5a he indicates that Jesus 'instructs' his disciples as he sends them out; and in 10.5b-42 the narrator then presents Jesus' words of instruction.

The implied reader thus has available to him/her two distinct sources of information concerning the shape and significance of the disciples' ministry: (1) Jesus' words of instruction to his disciples (10.5b-42) and (2) the narrator's depiction of Jesus' own ministry. The question at this point, therefore, has to do with the congruence of these two sources of information: how do the instructions which Jesus is about to give to his disciples correlate with the picture which the narrator has already drawn of Jesus' own ministry?

The overall impact (9.35-10.5a). The narrative introduction (9.35-10.5a) signals a significant turn in the story. Here Jesus begins to fulfil his longstanding promise to his disciples (4.19b) that he 'will make [them] fishermen for people'. A basic shift in characterization has thus taken place. No longer can the disciples be viewed as those who simply 'follow' Jesus, but rather as those who are also 'sent out' by Jesus into ministry.

Further, 9.35-10.5a establishes a fundamental parallelism between Jesus and his disciples in the fact that Jesus gives the disciples his own authority and sends them out into his own ministry. Thus not only does the narrator shift the characterization of the disciples, but he does so to make it conform to that of Jesus himself. And in establishing this parallelism between Jesus and his disciples, the narrator poses for the implied reader an overarching question which can only be answered as the story unfolds: what are the specific points of correlation between the ministry of Jesus and that of his disciples? It is therefore with this question in mind that the implied reader approaches Jesus' discourse in 10.5b-42.

The discourse: 10.5b-15 (text)

10.5b   Do not go out among[58] the Gentiles,
          and do not enter any city[59] of the Samaritans;
10.6   but go rather to the lost sheep of the house of Israel.
10.7   And as you go, proclaim, saying:
          'The Kingdom of heaven has come near'.
10.8   Heal the sick,
          raise the dead,
          cleanse lepers,
          cast out demons;
          you have received without payment;
          give without charge.[60]
10.9   Do not acquire gold or silver or copper for your belts,
10.10   or a traveler's bag for the road,
          or two tunics,
          or sandals,
          or a staff;
          for the laborer is worthy of his food.
10.11   And whatever city or village you enter,
          inquire who within it is worthy,
          and remain with that person[61]
          until you leave.
10.12   And as you enter the house, greet it.
10.13   And if the house is worthy,
          let your peace come upon it.
          But if it is not worthy,
          let your peace return to you.
10.14   And whoever does not receive you,
          nor hear your words,
          as you are leaving that house or that city,
          shake off the dust of your feet.
10.15   Truly, I say to you,
          it will be more tolerable
          for the land of Sodom and Gomorrah
          on the day of judgment,
          than for that city.

The discourse: 10.5b-15 (analysis)
Jesus opens the discourse to his disciples with a section (10.5b-15)
which paints them in a strongly active light. In a sequence of sixteen
imperative statements[62] Jesus tells his disciples what they are to do in
the ministry to which he sends them out. These actions fall into three
basic categories which together cover the entire scope of the

disciples' ministry: (1) where they are to go (10.5b-6); (2) what they are to do (10.7-10); and (3) how they are to deal with responses to their ministry (10.11-15).

The disciples' ministry: where to go (10.5b-6). In 10.5b-6 Jesus establishes the object of the disciples' ministry in emphatic fashion. Rather than beginning with a positive command, Jesus first specifies that his disciples are *not* to 'go out among the Gentiles' *nor* to 'enter any city of the Samaritans'. Only then does he indicate that they are to 'go rather to the lost sheep of the house of Israel', or in other words, to the Jewish people.[63]

The structure of this series of commands (i.e., two negative commands followed by a positive command) has the effect of placing heightened emphasis on the final element in the series, the command to 'go rather to the lost sheep of the house of Israel'.[64] This command points the implied reader back to the 'sheep without a shepherd' among whom Jesus has been ministering (9.36; cf. 9.35). And in this way the narrator links the ministry of the disciples with Jesus' own ministry by identifying the same group of people as the object of both ministries.[65]

Accordingly, the reason Jesus instructs his disciples to go neither to the Gentiles nor to the Samaritans but rather to the Jewish people is because that is what he himself has been doing. The disciples' ministry is to parallel Jesus' own ministry; and since Jesus' ministry is that of 'shepherding [God's] people Israel' (2.6), a people 'harassed and helpless, like sheep without a shepherd' (9.36), it follows that Jesus' disciples must likewise minister to these same people, 'the lost sheep of the house of Israel'.[66]

The disciples' ministry: what to do (10.7-10). Jesus' next directives (10.7-10) establish what the disciples are to do in their ministry to the Jewish people. And once again Jesus' words link the disciples' ministry integrally to his own.

First, Jesus instructs his disciples concerning the message they are to proclaim: 'And as you go, proclaim, saying, "The Kingdom of heaven has come near"' (10.7). This message is entirely appropriate in the present context, since it is 'the lost sheep of the house of Israel' who constitute the 'children' of this Kingdom (8.12) and for whom this reference to the Kingdom of heaven therefore has meaning. But the primary significance of the disciples' message lies in the fact that it parallels Jesus' own public proclamation (4.17; cf. 4.23 and 9.35),[67] the message that 'the Kingdom of heaven has come near', or in other words, 'the gospel of the Kingdom'.[68]

In addition, Jesus instructs his disciples concerning their ministry of healing. In 10.8a he indicates that their task is to 'heal the sick, raise the dead, cleanse lepers, [and] cast out demons'. Significantly, it is these very activities which have characterized Jesus' own ministry among the Jewish people. Jesus himself has healed many sick persons (4.23, 24; 8.7, 16; 9.35; cf. 8.5-13, 14-15; 9.2-8, 20-22, 27-31), raised a little girl from death (9.18-19/23-26), cleansed a leper (8.2-4), and cast out demons from possessed persons (8.28-34; 9.32-34).[69] Further, these activities are the very ones for which Jesus has already prepared his disciples by giving them his 'authority' (10.1; cf. 9.35). Thus in calling his disciples to the healing ministry described in 10.8a, Jesus links the disciples' ministry to his own as a ministry involving the same tasks and carried out in the same authority.[70]

In 10.8b Jesus establishes the basis on which the disciples are to carry out this ministry. In a statement which points back to the immediately preceding imperatives ('heal', 'raise', 'cleanse', 'cast out'), Jesus instructs his disciples: 'You have received without payment; give without charge'. The disciples have received their authority to minister as a gift from Jesus for which they have made no payment (cf. 10.1). Consequently, because Jesus has so 'gifted' them, they are to exercise this gift in a 'ministry without charge' among the Jewish crowds.[71]

Finally, in 10.9-10 Jesus spells out for his disciples what this 'ministry without charge' will mean in terms of their physical needs. In a lengthy list of items which a traveler would normally require for an extended journey (10.9-10a),[72] Jesus enumerates those things which his disciples are *not* to accept in payment for their ministry: 'Do not acquire gold or silver or copper for your belts, or a traveler's bag for the road, or two tunics, or sandals, or a staff'.

Here two emphases come to the fore. First, Jesus forbids his disciples to turn their ministry into an 'earning' proposition.[73] Not only does the immediate proximity of the two commands, 'give without charge' (10.8b) and 'do not acquire' (10.9), lead to this conclusion, but also the fact that money (gold, silver, copper) assumes the position of prominence at the head of the list.[74]

Secondly, Jesus intends the prohibition against 'earning' to be a prohibition for which there are no exceptions. He lists only items not to be acquired; and the items listed are specifically those useful for a traveler: money, a bag for carrying bread and other provisions, a change of clothing, the traveler's walking stick which could double as a defensive weapon against wild animals.[75]

But Jesus does not leave his disciples without resources for their journey. In 10.10b he indicates that the reason they are not to acquire money or material goods is because 'the laborer is worthy of his food'. In light of Jesus' previous identification of his disciples as 'laborers' for God himself (9.38), this means that the disciples are not to seek payment for their ministry because as God's laborers[76] they are to trust him to provide them with the necessities of life.[77]

At this point the reciprocal relationship between Jesus' two lists of commands is apparent. In 10.8a/b he instructs his disciples to minister freely to others because they have already received; in 10.9-10a/10b he forbids them to seek payment from others because they will in future receive. Jesus here makes it clear to his disciples that their entire ministry is to be viewed in terms of 'gift': as they have freely received, so they are to give; and as they freely give, so will they receive.[78]

The disciples' ministry: outcomes (10.11-15). In 10.11-15 Jesus goes on to instruct his disciples concerning their entrance into a given town, their search for lodging, and their departure from that town. But the emphasis in this passage lies on the reception which the disciples will encounter and the response which they are to make.

In 10.11 the movement is into the 'city or village' and the tone is positive: 'And whatever city or village you enter,[79] inquire who within it is worthy, and remain with that person until you leave'. Here Jesus explains the means by which his disciples' daily needs will be met (cf. 10.10b).[80] In each city or village they are to select a host and to lodge with that person as long as they remain there. Thus their physical needs, which are not to be met through payment for services (10.9-10a), will be met through the hospitality of the selected hosts in whose homes they find lodging. Further, Jesus makes clear that his disciples are to initiate a careful search in each town for someone who is 'worthy' and to take up lodging with that person; thus those who themselves are 'worthy' (10.10b) are to take up lodging with others who are likewise 'worthy'.[81]

The picture at this point is accordingly a positive one. Jesus' statement of 10.11 simply assumes that there will be a 'worthy person' in each city or village to which the disciples come[82] and enjoins the disciples to seek out and take up lodging with that person.

In 10.12-13, however, the picture shifts. Here Jesus describes the procedure which the disciples are to follow in their search for lodging:[83] 'And as you enter the house, greet it. And if the house is worthy, let your peace come upon it. But if it is not worthy, let your peace return to you'. Here what was merely implicit in the previous statement becomes explicit: if there are those in each town who are 'worthy', then there are likewise others who are 'not worthy'. In addition, Jesus hints at an explanation of these qualities. By indicating that 'worthiness' will become apparent only after the disciples have 'greeted' a house, he implies that this quality relates to the reception of the disciples in that house.[84]

Consequently, Jesus' message in 10.12-13 is that the disciples can expect one of two possible receptions and that they must therefore be prepared to make one of two possible responses. If the house is 'worthy'—and here the word 'house' stands as a cipher for the occupants of the building[85]—the disciples are to 'let [their] peace come upon it', an action which puts into effect the initial greeting they have extended, namely, 'Peace be to this house'.[86] If, however, the house is 'not worthy', the disciples are to 'let [their] peace return to [them]', an action which effectively revokes that initial greeting.

But if 10.12-13 points to a situation in which the disciples can expect either a positive or a negative reception, 10.14-15 depicts a situation which is totally negative in character. Here Jesus brings the threefold movement of 10.11-15, (10.11, 12-13, 14-15) to its climax in a graphic depiction of the certain rejection which the disciples will encounter and the certain consequences which that rejection will bring with it: 'And whoever does not receive you, nor hear your words, as you are leaving that house or that city, shake off the dust of your feet. Truly, I say to you, it will be more tolerable for the land of Sodom and Gomorrah, on the day of judgment, than for that city'.

With these words Jesus states directly that which was left unexplained in 10.11 and merely hinted at in 10.12-13: 'worthiness' hinges directly on the reception accorded the disciples' ministry. It is in receiving or not receiving the disciples themselves and in hearing or not hearing their words that persons reveal their worthiness or lack of it. Consequently the 'worthy person' whom the disciples are to seek out and with whom they are to lodge (10.11) is none other than that person who is willing to receive them into his or her home and to hear the message of the Kingdom which they bring with them.[87]

But here Jesus does not define 'worthiness' in terms of the person who will receive the disciples but rather in terms of the person who will not receive them. The climax toward which Jesus has been building since 10.11 is a negative climax: Jesus' disciples will encounter unqualified rejection in the form of persons who will neither 'receive [them]' nor 'hear [their] words'.

A further aspect of this negative climax lies in the consequences which rejection of the disciples will bring with it. These consequences are threefold. First, the disciples are to respond by 'leaving that house (cf. 10.12-13) or that city (cf. 10.11)' where they have encountered rejection,[88] thus terminating their ministry in that place and cutting off the occupants from the blessings conveyed by that ministry (cf. 10.7-8).[89]

But the disciples are not only to 'leave' the house or city in question. They are also to 'shake off the dust of [their] feet' as they do so. By this symbolic gesture, one of shaking from their garments the dust which their feet have stirred up in walking,[90] the disciples are to dissociate themselves totally from those who have rejected them.[91] The significance of this gesture will communicate itself readily to those against whom the disciples invoke it, since it is this ritual which the Jewish people perform in order to rid themselves of Gentile 'contamination' as they re-enter Jewish territory.[92]

But if the disciples are to dissociate themselves by means of this ritual from those who have rejected them and their ministry, they are not to do so in order to establish their own 'purity'. Rather, they are to carry out the ritual as a warning concerning the ultimate consequence, namely, the judgment of God.[93] In a deliberately formal pronouncement ('Truly, I say to you')[94] Jesus assures his disciples that the outcome on the 'day of judgment'[95] will be more tolerable for the proverbially wicked cities of Sodom and Gomorrah[96] than for that city which refuses to accept them and their ministry.[97]

The emphatic nature of this prediction becomes evident in a variety of ways. First of all, Jesus precedes his prediction with a formula ('Truly, I say to you') designed both to focus attention on what follows and to underline its significance.

Secondly, Jesus brings an eschatological dimension into the picture with his reference to the 'day of judgment'. The disciples' ministry is thus shown to have a significance which reaches far beyond the physical effects of their present ministry and which in turn magnifies to eschatological proportions the seriousness of rejecting that ministry.

Thirdly, the gravity of rejecting Jesus' disciples and their ministry is further underlined by way of the comparison with Sodom and Gomorrah, whose sole reputation in Jewish thinking is that of cities overthrown and utterly destroyed as a result of God's judgment against them. Jesus' use of this comparison thus highlights the seriousness of the situation for those who reject his disciples and the terrible fate which awaits them.[98]

Finally, however, the greatest impact of Jesus' prediction lies in the revelation that God himself is the ultimate authority behind the disciples' ministry. If it is Jesus, acting on the authority of God, who has given his disciples authority (10.1) and sent them (10.5a) into the ministry described in 10.5b-10, it is God himself who will ultimately confirm the authority of that ministry on the 'day of judgment'. The disciples' ministry, no less than that of Jesus himself, is one grounded in divine authority.

The disciples' ministry: overall impact (10.5b-15). In assessing the overall impact of 10.5b-15, three major emphases come to the fore. In the first place, Jesus here describes the ministry of his disciples in strongly active terms. It is the disciples themselves who are to take initiative, while those to whom they have gone in ministry merely respond to their initiatives.[99]

Further, the disciples' ministry is characterized by divine authority. The ministry of proclamation (10.7) and healing (10.8) to which Jesus here calls his disciples is not only a ministry parallel to his own (9.35; cf. 4.23-25) but also a ministry for which he shares with them his own authority (10.1). And it is God himself who will ultimately confirm the authority of this ministry through his actions on the 'day of judgment' (10.15).

The third major emphasis of this section, however, stands in sharp contrast to the first two. The disciples' ministry will meet primarily with rejection and not with acceptance. This fact becomes evident from the remarkable shift in tone which takes place from the beginning to the end of the section. In the beginning (10.7) Jesus is charging his disciples to proclaim that 'the Kingdom of heaven has come near', while by the end (10.15) Jesus is predicting a terrible fate on the 'day of judgment' for that city which rejects the disciples and their ministry.

Accordingly, the climax toward which the entire passage builds is negative. The disciples' ministry, one characterized by decisive activity and divine authority, will ultimately meet not with acceptance but with rejection.

The discourse: 10.16-23 (text)

10.16   Behold, I send you out like sheep in the midst of wolves;
        therefore, be wise as serpents and innocent as doves.
10.17   But beware of people.
        For they will hand you over to the councils;
        and in their synagogues they will flog you.
10.18   And you will be led before rulers as well as kings
        on my account
        as a witness to them and to the Gentiles.
10.19   But when they hand you over,
        do not worry about how or what you shall say;
        for it will be given you in that hour what you shall say.
10.20   For it is not you who are the ones speaking,
        but the Spirit of your Father which is speaking within
                you.
10.21   And brother will hand over brother to death, and father the
                child;
        and children will rise up against parents and put them to
                death.
10.22   And you will be hated by everyone
        for the sake of my name.
        But the one who remains steadfast to the end will be
                saved.
10.23   But when they persecute you in this city,
        flee to the next;
        for truly, I say to you,
        you will by no means complete the cities of Israel
        until[100] the Son of man comes.

The discourse: 10.16-23 (analysis)

In 10.16-23 the thrust of Jesus' instructions to his disciples shifts
significantly from that of the preceding verses. There the emphasis
lies on the initiatives to be taken by the disciples in their ministry to
'the lost sheep of the house of Israel'[101] and on the divine authority
with which they are to carry out these initiatives.[102] And while Jesus
indicates (10.12-15) that his disciples will meet with rejection, it is
nevertheless they who are still in control of the situation.

But in 10.16-23 it is no longer the disciples who initiate action.
Instead, those to whom the disciples have gone in ministry now
assume the active role, taking initiatives against the disciples
(10.17b-18, 21-22; cf. 10.19a, 23a); while the disciples' role becomes
one of response (10.16b, 17a, 19-20, 23).

The structure of 10.16-23 reflects this twofold emphasis on persecution and response. The opening verse (10.16) announces the two major themes of the section in a commissioning statement ('Behold, I send you out. . . ') which corresponds in function to the opening commands of the first section (10.5b-6: 'Do not go. . .; do not enter. . .; go rather. . . '). Then the general rubric 'But beware of people' (10.17a) introduces two parallel sequences (10.17b-18/19-20 and 10.21-22/23),[103] in which Jesus details the persecutions his disciples will face as the result of their ministry (10.17-18 and 10.21-22) and instructs them how to respond (10.19-20 and 10.23).

Persecution and response: announcement of themes (10.16). Jesus opens this section with a statement which builds on the previous section (10.5b-15) but also introduces a new element into the picture: 'Behold, I send you out like sheep in the midst of wolves; therefore, be wise as serpents and innocent as doves'. The presence here of the 'sending' motif ('Behold, I send you out') indicates that 10.16 corresponds in function to 10.5b-6: in both of these opening statements Jesus commissions his disciples for the ministry which they are to carry out. But it is this similarity in function which serves to highlight the difference between the two statements. In 10.5b-6 Jesus addresses the disciples with the command to 'go', an imperative which focuses on their initiative. In 10.16 Jesus announces 'Behold, I send you out', a statement which focuses not on the disciples' initiative but emphatically on his own.[104] It is no longer the disciples who act; rather they have been impelled into a situation by a force outside of themselves (i.e., Jesus). Consequently, the overall effect of the 'sending' motif in 10.16 is to shift the focus of attention from the active role of the disciples in 'going' to their passive role as those who are 'sent'.

But if 10.16 reflects a shift in the description of the disciples, it also reflects a shift in the description of those to whom the disciples are sent. In 10.5b-6 Jesus designates the object of the disciples' ministry as 'the lost sheep of the house of Israel'. In 10.16, however, it is the disciples themselves who are the 'sheep', while those to whom they are sent are depicted as 'wolves'. Jesus thus indicates to his disciples that those to whom they go in ministry will not merely reject them (a fact for which he has already prepared them in 10.13b-15) but will attack them violently, as wolves are known to attack defenseless sheep.[105] This means that a total reversal in descriptions has taken place. Those who were formerly depicted as 'harassed', 'helpless', and 'lost' have gone on the offensive; while those who formerly took the initiative are now depicted as vulnerable and defenseless.[106]

Further, the violent reception which the disciples will encounter is no incidental result of their activity. Rather, it belongs to the very essence of their ministry: Jesus sends them out *precisely as* 'sheep in the midst of wolves'.[107] The reception which the disciples will face is integrally related to their commissioning itself: mission entails certain persecution.

In light of this situation, 10.16b signals a corresponding shift in the substance of Jesus' directives. Here Jesus no longer instructs his disciples what initiatives to take in their ministry but rather what responses to make to the persecution which that ministry will arouse: 'Therefore, be wise as serpents and innocent as doves'.

The transitional conjunction 'therefore' identifies this command as a direct response to the preceding statement ('Behold, I send you out like sheep in the midst of wolves'). The disciples are called to respond not simply because they find themselves in a dangerous situation but, more specifically, because Jesus has sent them into that situation. Thus their response is to emerge not out of fear but rather out of obedience to Jesus.[108] And this means that the disciples' response to persecution, no less than their ministry of proclamation and healing itself, has its ultimate basis in the authority of Jesus. Every aspect of the disciples' life in ministry, response as well as initiative, is integrally linked to the authority of the one who has sent them into that ministry.

But Jesus' directive also delineates the nature of the disciples' response: they are to be 'wise (*phronimoi*) as serpents' and 'innocent (*akeraioi*) as doves'. This juxtaposition of 'serpent' and 'dove' points to a response comprised of seemingly contradictory actions.[109] On the one hand, the disciples are to respond to their precarious situation with the utmost in mental agility, that quality associated in Jewish thinking with the serpent, the 'most subtle' (*phronimōtatos*) of all the wild animals created by God (Gen. 3.1). In the present context, this call to 'be wise' implies the need for clear thinking as well as prudent actions.[110] But at the same time the disciples are to respond with the candor and simplicity symbolized by the dove.[111] The call to 'be innocent' thus represents the counterpart to the call to 'be wise': if the disciples are to exhibit an outstanding mental agility in facing persecution, they are likewise to exhibit an absolute simplicity which arises out of 'purity of intention'[112] and issues in transparent living.[113]

But Jesus does not stop with general language. Now that he has issued a general warning concerning the dangers which his disciples will face (10.16a) and a general command concerning how they are to respond (10.16b), he goes on to detail the nature of those dangers and the shape which the disciples' response is to take.

Persecution and response: superscript (10.17a). Jesus shifts from the general to the specific in 10.17a with the command, 'But beware of people', which serves as the superscript to 10.17b-20 and 10.21-23. Here Jesus restates in nonmetaphorical language the message which he has already conveyed in terms of 'sheep and wolves', 'serpents and doves': his disciples face a threat from 'people' in general, a situation which demands that they respond with an attitude of 'wariness'. Striking here is the openendedness of the designation 'people'. In contrast to the parallel command of 7.15, in which Jesus directs his hearers[114] to 'beware of false prophets', there is no closer identification here of the 'people' in question. It is thus apparent that no specific segment of the 'people' (its leadership, for example) is in focus. Rather, the threat seems to emerge generally from those to whom the disciples have gone in ministry. And having issued this warning, Jesus now turns to the details of what these 'people' will do to the disciples and how they are to respond.

Persecution and response: sequence one (10.17b-18/19-20). Sequence one opens with a threefold series of predictions which specifies why the disciples are to be 'wary': (1) (for they [i.e., the 'people' of 10.17a] will hand you over to the councils'; (2) 'and in their synagogues they will flog you'; and (3) 'and you will be led before rulers as well as kings on my account as a witness to them and to the Gentiles'. The first two predictions in this series form a clearly defined chiastic structure built around two third person plural verbs in the active voice: (a) for they will hand you over; (b) to the councils; (b') and in their synagogues; (a') they will flog you. These predictions reflect the reversal announced in 10.16a. In each case the subject of the action is the anonymous 'they' implied by the third person plural verbs, a reference which points back to the antecedent 'people' in 10.17a. And in each case the object of the action is the disciples themselves, here identified by means of the second person plural pronoun 'you' in the accusative case. Accordingly, the 'people' of 10.17a are now the actors, while the disciples have become those who are acted upon.

Further, these predictions point to violent, if not yet life-threatening, action which the 'people' in question will take against the disciples.

Jesus first warns his disciples that 'they will hand you over', an indication that the disciples can expect to be seized with force and turned over to those in authority. He then notifies his disciples that 'they will flog you', a warning that the disciples will suffer the standard legal punishment[115] meted out by both the Roman and the Jewish authorities of the day for disorderly conduct.[116] Thus the disciples can expect not only forcible arrest as the response to their ministry but also the brutal physical punishment decreed by law which accompanies such arrest.

Finally, Jesus' predictions of 10.17b indicate that the persecution in question comes from the Jews. In light of the chiastic structure of these predictions, it is evident that the phrase 'to the councils' stands parallel to the phrase 'in their [i.e., the Jewish] synagogues'. Consequently, the 'councils' to which Jesus refers are to be understood as Jewish institutions. It is to Jewish 'councils'[117] that the disciples will be handed over, just as it is in Jewish 'synagogues' that they will be flogged.

But while the two predictions of 10.17b form a carefully structured inverse parallelism depicting the persecution of Jesus' disciples by the Jews, the third prediction (10.18) breaks with the first two both in style and content. Here the disciples are no longer the object of active verbs specifying what 'they' (defined by the context as the Jewish people) will do but rather the subject of a passive verb ('you will be led') with no designated agent. Further, the setting is no longer that of Jewish institutions, i.e., the Jewish 'councils' and 'synagogues'; rather, Jesus warns his disciples that they will be led before 'rulers as well as kings', i.e., before the designated authorities of the Gentile world.[118] The prediction of 10.18 still portrays the disciples as subject to the action of others, but it now appears that the agents of that action are no longer the Jewish people implied by the verbs of 10.17b but rather the Gentiles.[119] Thus Jesus here warns his disciples that along with the Jewish persecution they will encounter (cf. 10.17b) they can also expect persecution both instigated by Gentiles ('and you will be led') and carried out in a Gentile setting ('before rulers as well as kings') which extends well beyond the boundaries of their present ministry.[120]

The prediction of 10.18 also includes two phrases not paralleled in the predictions of 10.17b. In the first of these Jesus establishes the ultimate reason for the persecution his disciples will face from the Gentiles: 'and you will be led before rulers as well as kings *on my account*'. Jesus' disciples will face persecution by the Gentiles because they are disciples of Jesus,[121] that is, because the ministry which leads them into that suffering (10.16a) is the continuation of Jesus' own ministry. Accordingly, that for which the disciples will suffer indicates the ultimate significance of their ministry.

But not only will the disciples suffer persecution 'on account of' Jesus. In addition, Jesus indicates that when they are 'led before rulers and kings', that will serve 'as a witness to them and to the Gentiles'.[122] The persecution which the disciples will face will not only grow out of their ministry; it will also lead them back into ministry by providing them with the opportunity to witness through their suffering itself[123] to the Gentile authorities and the Gentile community at large. If mission entails certain persecution (cf. 10.16a), then persecution, for its part, furthers mission. And in this very fact lies the paradox of the situation: the disciples' helplessness and vulnerability to persecution bring about the extension of their witness; while the initiatives taken by the persecutors serve in the final analysis only to further the cause of those whom they persecute. The last phrase of 10.18, therefore, stands as a promise which puts the three previous warnings into proper perspective: persecution represents not merely an evil to be faced but also an opportunity to be embraced.

It is now evident from both the structure and the content of 10.17b-18 that the point of emphasis within this threefold series of predictions is the third element in the series. In this case, just as with 10.5b-6, the first two elements of the series are tightly connected to each other in style and content, while the third element offers significant variations in both respects. Consequently, the pattern which has been established with the first two elements of the series is broken with the third; and the focus of attention is thus drawn to those features which distinguish that element from the first two. Accordingly, while the series opens on the note of 'persecution', the emphasis lies on the concluding motif of 'persecution with promise'.

This same motif is present in 10.19-20, where Jesus builds directly on the content of the previous predictions (10.17b-18). This section opens with the directive, 'But when they hand you over, do not worry about how or what you shall say' (10.19a). Here the note of 'persecution' is sounded in the temporal clause, 'but when they hand you over', a clause which substantially repeats the first prediction of 10.17b-18 ('For they will hand you over...'). Then the note of 'promise' is sounded in the reference to 'how or what you shall say', which picks up and elucidates the reference to 'witness' in 10.18. Accordingly, in 10.19a Jesus confirms what he has established in 10.17b-18: the disciples will meet with persecution; but this persecution will provide them with further opportunity for witness.

At the same time, however, the focus of 10.19a lies neither on the 'persecution' itself (which is simply assumed as the given state of affairs[124]) nor even on the 'promise' of an opportunity for witness (which is likewise assumed as the obvious result of the 'persecution'[125]). Rather, the focus of 10.19a lies on that 'response' which falls sequentially *between* the 'persecution' and the fulfilment of the 'promise': But when they hand you over, do not worry about how or what you shall say'. In other words, it is not the verbal witness itself which constitutes the subject of Jesus' call to action, but rather the prohibition against worrying. Jesus' disciples are to counter the violent actions taken against them not, in the first instance, with any corresponding action of their own but rather with the non-active response of 'not worrying'.

In 10.19b-20 Jesus sets forth the reason for this non-active response. In a two-part explanation related chastically to the 'how' and 'what' of 10.19a, he addresses the questions first of what the disciples shall say (10.19b) and then of how they shall say it (10.20). The disciples are not to worry about what they shall say for the reason that their words will come to them as a 'gift': 'for it will be given you in that hour what you shall say' (10.19b). The implication of this prediction is that in the very moment of their need God himself will provide the disciples with the words they are to speak.[126]

Nor are the disciples to worry about the means by which that witness will take place. Here again, the reason lies in the promise of divine action. In 10.20 Jesus explains that ultimately 'it is not you who are the ones speaking, but the Spirit of your Father which is speaking within you'. God will not simply provide the disciples with words which they then have to speak on their own power. Instead, when the disciples open their mouths to speak, it is the Spirit of God their Father whose voice will be heard speaking from within them.[127] Thus the disciples' witness, in terms both of its content and its delivery, points to the action of God on their behalf.

The message communicated here is clear: the consequences of the disciples' ministry lie altogether outside of their grasp. On the one hand, they are totally vulnerable to persecution, which will come to them both from the Jews and from the Gentiles. On the other hand, they are totally open to the power of God their Father, which will work through them to turn persecution itself into an occasion for further witness. Accordingly, the only appropriate response for the disciples is to 'not worry' but rather rest in the confidence that God their Father will take what appears to be the defeat of their ministry and turn it into what is instead the extension of their witness.

Persecution and response: sequence two (10.21–22/23). Sequence two, like sequence one, opens with a threefold series of predictions detailing the persecutions which the disciples will face: (1) 'And brother will hand over brother to death, and father the child'; (2) 'and children will rise up against parents and put them to death'; and (3) 'and you will be hated by everyone for the sake of my name. But the one who remains steadfast to the end will be saved'. And as with sequence one, the first two predictions (10.21) form a chiastic structure built around the verbal motif of 'handing over to death'/ 'killing': (a) And brother will hand over brother to death; (b) and father the child; (b') and children will rise up against parents; (a') and put them to death.[128]

But along with the similarities there are also differences between 10.21 (the first two predictions of sequence two) and 10.17b (the first two predictions of sequence one). The first difference relates to the identity of those who will persecute the disciples. In 10.17b the disciples face persecution from an anonymous Jewish source: it is simply 'they' (i.e., the 'people' of 10.17a) who will hand over and flog the disciples. But in 10.23 persecution has become a family affair which sets 'brother' against 'brother', 'father' against 'child', and 'children' against 'parents'. This picture thus contains a note of immediacy not found in 10.17b.

The predictions of 10.21 also have a more ominous tone than those of 10.17b. While the prior predictions point to persecution which is violent but not yet life-threatening, the predictions of 10.21 focus on the prospect of death itself for the disciples. The brother who 'hands over' his brother will 'hand him over *to death*'; and the children who 'rise up against' their parents will do so in order to *have them put to death*.[129]

The situation depicted in 10.21, therefore, represents a twofold intensification of that depicted in 10.17b. Not only has the persecution moved from anonymous sources into the immediate family circle, but it has also escalated from the level of brutal physical treatment (i.e., seizure and flogging) to the level of capital punishment.

But here again, as with sequence one, the emphasis lies on the third prediction in the series (10.22). This prediction, in parallelism with the prediction of 10.18, breaks with both style and content of the previous two predictions. In the first place, the disciples are no longer the object of active verbs describing what family member will 'do' to family member but rather the subject of a passive verb ('you will be hated') which describes what 'will be done' to them. Further, persecution no longer comes solely from within the family circle but rather from 'everyone'. The net effect of these shifts is to depersonalize ('and you will be hated') and to universalize ('by everyone') the source of the persecution which the disciples will face.

As with 10.18, the prediction of 10.22 then offers an explanation and a promise[130] which have no parallel in the previous two predictions. First, Jesus establishes a direct link between the persecution which the disciples will face and the cause which they represent: 'and you will be hated by everyone *for the sake of my name*'. It is because the disciples are identified with Jesus that they will face hatred on all sides. Here, as with 10.18, the cause of their suffering serves as a direct clue to the significance of their task.

Then Jesus offers a promise which puts a new perspective on the disciples' sufferings: 'But the one who remains steadfast to the end will be saved'. Jesus' statement depicts the disciples at a total disadvantage. Their situation demands of them not action but rather endurance in light of the actions of others. In the context of 10.21-22a the reference to 'the one who remains steadfast' designates that disciple who perseveres while experiencing persecution from all sides, from within the family circle (10.21) and from society in general (10.22a). Further, the disciples' situation demands of them not short-term heroics but rather long-term commitment. The persecution which they face requires no less than endurance 'to the end'. While Jesus does not here specify what 'end' is in view,[131] this reference depicts endurance which knows no time limits and reaches no breaking point. This implies that the persecution itself is neither short-lived nor temporary in duration. Rather, it has become a permanent element of the disciples' situation which provides them with a constant and ongoing challenge to 'steadfastness'. The resulting picture, therefore, shows the disciples as permanently vulnerable to persecution which comes to them from all sides.

But it is this very situation of disadvantage which works, paradoxically, for the ultimate good of the disciples. The promise of

10.22b is that 'the one who remains steadfast to the end will be saved'. Thus the disciple who perseveres in the face of overwhelming odds ends up in the position of ultimate advantage. Here it is clear that the 'salvation' in question represents no immediate reality but rather an eschatological reward. Jesus has already predicted 'persecution to the death' for the 'brother', the 'child', and the 'parents' of 10.21. In addition, the promise of 10.22b itself applies to none other than 'the one who remains steadfast to the end'. Accordingly, the 'salvation' of which Jesus speaks does not rescue the disciples from the onslaughts of those who persecute them (10.21-22a) but rewards them after they have endured the ultimate in persecution. It thus seems apparent that Jesus speaks of that eschatological salvation which the disciples will receive on the 'day of judgment' mentioned in 10.15.[132] As with 10.18, therefore, Jesus' promise communicates that persecution is not simply an evil to be endured but, more significantly, an opportunity to be embraced.

It is now evident that the motif which dominates 10.21-22 is that of 'persecution with promise', the same motif which dominates 10.17b-18. And it is this motif which sets the tone for the instructions to follow in 10.23. This verse opens with a formulation parallel to that of 10.19a: 'But when they persecute you in this city, flee to the next'. The temporal clause ('But when they persecute you in this city') picks up the motif of 'persecution' which characterizes the three predictions of 10.21-22a. And the imperative ('flee to the next [city]') alludes to the 'promise' of 10.22b: in a paradoxical way, it is by 'fleeing' from city to city that the disciples 'remain steadfast to the end'. Since 'this city' represents the location of the disciples' ministry (cf. 10.11-15), the reference to persecution 'in this city' implies that the disciples have been active there in ministry. As a result, Jesus' call for disciples to 'flee [from this city] to the next' implies that they will thereby extend their ministry into new territory. This, in turn, opens up the prospect of further persecution in that 'next [city]' to which they flee. And it is in this continuing cycle of persecution which leads to ministry and ministry which leads to persecution that the disciples are challenged to 'remain steadfast to the end', and promised ultimate 'salvation'.

But while 10.23a points back to the persecution and the promise of 10.21-22, the focus of attention lies on that response of the disciples which falls sequentially *between* the persecution and the realization of the promise: 'But when they persecute you in this city, flee to the

next'. Here, as in 10.19a, Jesus counsels his disciples to respond to
the brutal initiatives of those who oppose them with an action (in
10.19a a non-action) which merely acknowledges the dominant
position of the opponents and does nothing to correct the imbalance
in power.

In 10.23b, however, Jesus offers an explanation which provides the
basis for this course of action: 'for truly, I say to you, you will by no
means complete the cities of Israel until the Son of man comes'. This
prediction has two effects. First, it confirms the fact that Jesus' call to
'flee' implies primarily the continued ministry of the disciples[133] and
not their escape from persecution.[134] This becomes clear from the
causal link ('for') between the command to 'flee' and the predicted
failure of the disciples to 'complete the cities of Israel'. It is because
they will 'not complete the cities of Israel' until the designated
moment that Jesus calls them to 'flee' from one city to the next. The
phrasing of 10.23b thus points to three conclusions: (1) 'completing
the cities of Israel' is a specific task laid upon the disciples;[135] (2) the
size of this task is so great that it cannot be accomplished prior to the
designated moment;[136] and (3) the urgency of making progress on
this task demands that the disciples respond to persecution by fleeing
from one city to the next.[137] If these conclusions are correct, then the
reference to 'completing the cities of Israel' points to the ministry of
the disciples; since it is this task which Jesus has assigned to them.
Accordingly, the task of 'completing the cities of Israel' relates
directly to the call to 'go . . . to the lost sheep of the house of Israel'
(10.6).[138]

But 10.23b also establishes the termination point of the disciples'
ministry: 'for truly, I say to you, you will by no means complete the
cities of Israel *until the Son of man comes*'. The disciples' ministry
will not reach its conclusion until the 'coming of the Son of man', an
apparent reference to the triumphal appearance of Jesus himself at
'the end of the age' as the agent of God's judgment and salvation.[139]
And it is in light of this fact that the full import of 10.23b finally
becomes evident. When Jesus promises his disciples that they will 'by
no means complete the cities of Israel until the Son of man comes',
he is extending the termination point of their ministry to the
eschaton itself.[140] More significantly, he is defining that eschatological
termination point in terms of an event in which he himself will be the
chief actor. If Jesus' disciples are to acknowledge the dominant
position of those who take initiative against them ('But when they
persecute you in this city, flee. . . '), they are to do so because Jesus

himself will ultimately take initiative on their behalf.[141] As in 10.19-20, the disciples' response to persecution has its ultimate basis in the promise of divine action.

Persecution and response: overall impact (10.16-23). It is now possible to assess the overall impact of this section both within its immediate context (9.35–10.15) and within the wider context of the narrator's story. Three observations are pertinent. In the first place, it becomes clear from the immediate context of 10.16-23 that persecution is the direct result of the disciples' ministry. The detailed description of this ministry (10.5b-15) leads directly into a discussion not of how to proceed with those who welcome the disciples but rather of how to respond to persecution from those who reject them.[142] Thus when Jesus sends his disciples into ministry, he does so not because he assumes that this ministry will be successful but rather with the full awareness that they will meet above all with rejection.

This message is not a new one for Jesus' disciples. Already in the previous discourse (5.3–7.27) Jesus has warned of persecution to come for those who live the life of the Kingdom of heaven.[143] The parallels between these two sets of predictions are difficult to overlook. In both instances Jesus speaks of persecution as inevitable,[144] as taking place on his account,[145] and as directly related to the proclamation of the disciples.[146] Nor does Jesus' call to response strike a new note for his disciples. In 6.31-33 Jesus commands his hearers 'not to worry' about food and clothing for the reason that their 'heavenly Father' not only knows, but will also supply, that of which they have need.[147] And in 6.34 Jesus summarizes his concerns of the preceding section (6.25-33) with the command 'not to worry' about the next day.[148] In 10.16-23, therefore, Jesus introduces no new concepts to the disciples but builds on and clarifies that which has been a part of his message from the beginning. The prediction of persecution and the call to a response of 'not worrying' thus represent the normal and not the unusual within Jesus' teaching.

But the ultimate significance of the situation depicted in 10.16-23 lies in the fact that it parallels the experience of Jesus himself. Virtually every aspect of this situation has its counterpart in that which has already happened to Jesus or that which the narrator has predicted concerning Jesus' future. In the first place, the disciples' ministry, here described as 'completing the cities of Israel' (10.23), parallels Jesus' own ministry which has taken him to 'all the cities

and villages'.[149] Secondly, it is the Spirit of God, who came upon
Jesus at the time of his baptism (3.16), who empowers the disciples as
they stand trial because of their ministry (10.20).[150] Thirdly, Jesus'
call to flight, a call which implies the extension and not the
abandonment of the disciples' ministry, reflects the pattern of Jesus'
own ministry: when faced with opposition (9.34), he responds by
carrying forward his ministry just as before (9.35; cf. 4.23).[151]
Further, Jesus' call to flight directly evokes the memory of the flight
of Joseph and his family from the evil designs of Herod (2.13-18), a
flight which likewise serves to further the cause of ministry.[152] But
the most striking parallel between the situation of the disciples and
that of Jesus lies in the nature of the persecution which awaits them:
three times Jesus predicts that the disciples will be 'handed over'
(10.17b, 19a, 21), the very fate which has been predicted for Jesus
himself (10.4) and which has already overtaken Jesus' predecessor
John the Baptist (4.12).[153]

Thus 10.16-23 has the overall effect of establishing a correlation
between the ministry of Jesus and that of his disciples which extends
beyond the activities of proclamation and healing (cf. 10.5b-15) to
the persecution which these activities will arouse. If the disciples are
sent out to minister as Jesus is ministering, they are also sent out (cf.
10.16a) to suffer as Jesus will suffer.

But this raises some significant questions for the implied reader:
where and when will the ministry of the disciples take place? In 10.18
Jesus speaks of a situation in which the disciples will 'be led before
rulers as well as kings . . . as a witness to them and to the Gentiles'.
This situation does not appear to fit the circumstances of a ministry
directed exclusively to 'the lost sheep of the house of Israel'. Further,
in 10.23 Jesus speaks of a situation in which the disciples will carry
forward their ministry under persecution 'until the coming of the
Son of man', a situation which does not appear congruent with a
ministry carried out during the lifetime of Jesus. Accordingly, the
implied reader stands alerted to the fact that the ministry to which
Jesus sends his disciples out may not be limited either to Galilee or to
the time frame of Jesus' own ministry there.

The discourse: 10.24-42 (text)

    10.24   A disciple is not above the teacher,
             nor a slave above his lord.
    10.25   It is sufficient for the disciple that he be like the teacher,
             and the slave like his lord.

If they have called the master of the house Beelzebul,
how much more so the members of his household.

10.26 However, do not fear them;
for nothing is hidden which will not be revealed,
and secret which will not be made known.

10.27 What I tell you in the darkness, say in the light;
and what you hear [whispered] in your ear, proclaim upon
the housetops.

10.28 And do not fear
those who kill the body
but are not able to kill the soul.
But fear rather
the one who is able to destroy
both soul and body in Gehenna.

10.29 Are not two sparrows sold for a penny?
Yet not one of them will fall upon the ground without your
Father.

10.30 But as for you,
even the hairs of your head are all numbered.

10.31 Therefore, do not fear;
for you are worth more than many sparrows.

10.32 Therefore, everyone who acknowledges me before people
I will also acknowledge before my Father who is in
heaven.

10.33 But whoever denies me before people
I will also deny before my Father who is in heaven.

10.34 Do not think that I have come to bring peace upon the
earth.
I have not come to bring peace but a sword.

10.35 For I have come to sever
a man from his father,
a daughter from her mother,
and a daughter-in law from her mother-in-law.

10.36 And the enemies of a person [will be] the members of his
household.

10.37 The one who loves father or mother above me
is not worthy of me.
And the one who loves son or daughter above me
is not worthy of me.

10.38 And whoever does not take up his cross and follow me
is not worthy of me.

10.39 The one who finds his life
will lose it.
And the one who loses his life on my account
will find it.

10.40   The one who receives you
    receives me.
    And the one who receives me
    receives the one who sent me.

10.41   The one who receives a prophet
    because he is a prophet
    will receive the reward of a prophet.
    And the one who receives a righteous one
    because he is a righteous one
    will receive the reward of a righteous one.

10.42   And whoever gives one of these little ones a cup of cold
         water
    simply because he is a disciple—
    truly, I say to you—
    will by no means lose his reward.

The discourse: *10.24-42 (analysis)*

A new thrust characterizes the third section of the discourse. The previous section (10.16-23) shifted the focus of attention from the initiatives which the disciples are to take in their ministry (10.5b-15) to the violent persecution which others will initiate against them. This section (10.24-42) now shifts the focus of attention back to the initiatives of the disciples. But rather than focusing either on ministry (as in 10.5b-15) or on persecution (as in 10.16-23), 10.24-42 combines these two emphases within a discussion focusing on relationships.

The theme is announced in 10.24-25, a proverbial saying which defines the relationship of the disciples to Jesus. The section concludes in 10.40-42 with a sequence of verses which (1) establishes a bond linking the disciples to Jesus and to 'the one who sent [him]' (10.40) and (2) spells out the implications of that bond for all those who receive the disciples (10.41-42).

Between the introduction (10.24-25) and the conclusion (10.40-42) lie two internally connected sequences of sayings (10.26-33 and 10.34-39). Both sequences begin with a negative command based on an aorist subjunctive verb (10.26: *mē phobēthēte* = do not fear/10.34: *mē nomisēte* = do not think [that . . .]). Both conclude with a saying pointing to the eschatological consequences of the disciples' actions (10.32-33: 'acknowledgment' or 'denial' by Jesus before '[his] Father who is in heaven'/10.39: 'losing' or 'finding' life).

The first of these sequences (10.26-33) is structured around the threefold repetition of the formula 'do not fear' (10.26, 28, 31),[154] a formula which is then brought to completion in the reference of 10.32 to 'everyone who acknowledges [Jesus] before people'. The thrust of 10.26-33 is that of encouragement to 'fearless witness' concerning Jesus. The second sequence (10.34-39) details the personal consequences of that 'fearless witness' for all those who 'acknowledge [Jesus] before people'.

In both of these sequences, just as in the introduction (10.24-25) and the conclusion (10.40-42), the focus lies not simply on the disciples' action (cf. 10.5b-15) nor on their opponents' counter-action (cf. 10.16-23) but rather on the disciples' relationship to Jesus. In 10.26-33 it is Jesus himself whom the disciples are called to acknowledge; while in 10.34-39 it is those who love family members above Jesus whom he describes as 'not worthy of me'. Thus 10.24-42 restates the themes of the previous two sections of the discourse (i.e., 'ministry' in 10.5b-15 and 'persecution' in 10.16-23) in terms of 'the disciples' relationship to Jesus'.

The disciples' relationship to Jesus: announcement of theme (10.24-25). This section of the discourse opens with a threefold series of couplets which establishes the relationship of the disciples to Jesus (10.24-25a) and then draws from the nature of that relationship the inevitable consequences for the disciples (10.25b). The logic of this series of couplets unfolds one step at a time.

In the first couplet (10.24), which exhibits synonymous parallelism, Jesus speaks to his disciples in proverbial form of the self-evident relationship which exists between 'disciple' and 'teacher', 'slave' and 'lord': 'A disciple is not above the teacher, nor a slave above his lord'. In the context of Jesus' discourse it is evident that this proverbial saying is to be applied to the situation of Jesus and the twelve disciples (cf. 10.1, 2, 5a) to whom he is speaking. Thus it is Jesus who relates to his twelve followers both as 'teacher' to 'disciples' and as 'lord' to 'slaves'. And since no disciples ever surpasses his teacher, nor any slave his lord, it follows that Jesus' disciples in no way stand above Jesus.

In 10.25a the logic moves one step further. In a second proverbial saying, likewise in synonymous parallelism, Jesus establishes the positive side of the relationship between 'disciple' and 'teacher', 'slave' and 'lord': 'It is sufficient for the disciple that he be like the teacher, and the slave like his lord'. This saying provides the clue necessary for understanding the thrust of the previous saying. If

Jesus is concerned to establish the negative fact that no disciple ever *surpasses* his teacher, nor any slave his lord, he does so in order to highlight by contrast the positive fact that the disciple should simply be *like* his teacher, and the slave in the same way *like* his lord. The emphasis within 10.24-25a thus falls on the 'like'-ness which exists between disciple and teacher, slave and lord, and thus, in this context, between the disciples and Jesus.

Together the couplets of 10.24-25a make explicit that which has been implicit up to this point: if Jesus' disciples are to go out in ministry (9.35-10.5a, 5b-15) and to accept the persecution which that ministry will arouse (10.16-23), they are to do so in order to be 'like' Jesus.[155] But the point of emphasis toward which these couplets move, that is, the climax of the threefold series (10.24-25), lies in 10.25b. Here, in a couplet which draws attention to itself by breaking the pattern of synonymous parallelism established in 10.24-25a,[156] Jesus spells out the implications of this 'likeness': 'If they have called the master of the house Beelzebul, how much more so the members of his household'.

The thrust of this argumentation 'from the lesser to the greater' is not difficult to determine. While the saying is couched in metaphorical language ('master of the house', 'members of his household'), the context in which it appears indicates that 10.25b, just as 10.24 and 10.25a, refers to Jesus and his disciples. Jesus' message is thus the following: 'If they have called me Beelzebul, how much more [will they apply the same name to] you who are my disciples'.[157]

In addition, the assertions which Jesus makes also serve to link the negative consequences which Jesus and his disciples will experience to their respective ministries. Coming at this point in the story, Jesus' reference to the epithet 'Beelzebul' points back to the recent incident (9.32-34), in which the Pharisees accuse Jesus of casting out demons through 'the prince of demons', 'Beelzebul' by name.[158] And because the disciples are related to Jesus as 'members of [the] household' to 'master of the house', the second half of the saying warns them that they will encounter with certainty ('how much more so') that which Jesus has already encountered. Thus Jesus' message to his disciples in 10.25b is the following: 'If they have slandered [or in the broader sense, persecuted] me because of my ministry, they will surely do the same to you because of your ministry as my disciples'.[159]

The overall logic of 10.24-25 is now apparent. In a three-step argumentation (10.24, 25a, 25b) focused on the question of relationships, Jesus warns his disciples that they can expect persecution as the consequence of their ministry; and he links that persecution (and by implication, the ministry as well) to the disciples' status *as disciples of Jesus*. Thus every aspect of the disciples' commission stands firmly grounded in their relationship to Jesus. And it is this emphasis on relationship to Jesus which dominates throughout the remainder of the section (i.e., 10.26-42).

The disciples' relationship to Jesus: call to fearless witness (10.26-33). In 10.26-31 Jesus issues a threefold call to his disciples 'not to fear' (10.26, 28, 31) and supports this call by providing three reasons why the disciples should not fear. The section then closes in 10.32-33 with an eschatological promise for all those who 'acknowledge [Jesus] before people' and an eschatological warning for all those who 'deny [Jesus] before people'. This section is thus comprised of four segments: 10.26-27, 28, 29-31, 32-33. The first three of these contain the call, 'Do not fear', while the fourth completes the idea implicit in the first three: 'Do not fear *to acknowledge me before people*'. The focus of 10.26-33 thus lies on the call to 'fearless witness concerning Jesus'.

The section opens in 10.26 with the first of these calls 'not to fear': 'However, do not fear them'.[160] Both the transitional conjunction 'however' and the obtrusive reference to 'them' require that 10.26 be interpreted in light of what has preceded it.[161] Thus the reference to 'them' points back most directly to the implied subject ('they') of 10.25b[162] and beyond that, to the 'people' of 10.17(-23).[163] Jesus thus calls his disciples 'not to fear' those who will malign them (10.25b) and otherwise persecute them (10.17-23).

The explanation of this imperative, then, lies in the pair of synonymous parallelisms which follow in 10.26b-27. Here, in two couplets (10.26b, 27) which parallel each other, Jesus explains the basis for his call 'not to fear': (1a) 'for nothing is hidden which will not be revealed'; (1b) 'and secret which will not be made known'; (2a) 'What I tell you in the darkness, say in the light'; (2b) 'and what you hear [whispered] in your ear, proclaim upon the housetops'. Striking within this pair of parallelisms is the identical movement in all four lines from concealment to disclosure. But it is the distinctions between these two parallelisms which point to their real significance.

In the first parallelism (10.26b) Jesus indicates that God himself is going to make public that which currently is 'hidden' and 'secret': the two future passive verbs (*apokalyphthēsetai* = will be revealed/ *gnōsthēsetai* = will be made known) point to the agency of God in the actions of 'revealing' and 'making known'.[164] This means that Jesus bases his call 'not to fear' in the certain knowledge that God himself will take action to bring to light that which is now concealed.

But what it is that God will reveal and how he will reveal it become evident only in the second parallelism (10.27). Here Jesus identifies that which is 'hidden' and 'secret' with that which he himself says to his disciples in a private setting ('what I tell you in the darkness', 'what you hear [whispered] in your ear'[165]). That which is to be revealed is nothing other than that which Jesus himself has communicated orally to his disciples. God's revelation thus has to do with the message of Jesus.

Further, Jesus identifies the means by which this revelation will take place. In contrast to the two future passive verbs of 10.26b, which designate God as the actor, the two aorist active imperatives of 10.27 (*eipate* = say/*kēryxate* = proclaim) are directed at the disciples. That revelation which is first described in terms of the action of God is now described as the task of the disciples: they themselves are to bring into the open ('say in the light'/'proclaim upon the housetops') that which Jesus has spoken to them in private ('what I tell you in the darkness'/'what you hear [whispered] in your ear'). Thus it is Jesus' disciples through whom God's revelation is going to take place.

But if the disciples, in proclaiming the words of Jesus, are none other than the human agents through whom God himself is acting, then it is clear that no one will be able to hinder the forward progress of their proclamation.[166] And it is this message which provides the basis for Jesus' call to fearlessness in 10.26a: the disciples have no need to fear those who persecute them, not because those persecutors have no power to harm the disciples but rather because they ultimately have no power to impede the progress of the disciples' proclamation.

And if Jesus' first call 'not to fear' (10.26) has its basis in the power of God to ensure the proclamation of the disciples, Jesus' second call 'not to fear' (10.28) has its basis in the power of God to determine the destiny of the disciples. Here, in two imperative statements structured in antithetic parallelism,[167] Jesus draws a contrast between those who are/are not to be feared: 'And do not fear those who kill the body but are not able to kill the soul. But fear rather the one who is able to destroy both soul and body in Gehenna'.

Here Jesus reiterates his warning (cf. 10.21) that the disciples can expect life-threatening persecution as the result of their proclamation. The reference to 'those who kill the body' warns of persecution to the death for Jesus' disciples; and the fact that this reference immediately follows the commands to 'say in the light' and 'proclaim upon the housetops' links the persecution in question to the proclamation of the disciples.[168]

At the same time, however, Jesus indicates that those who persecute the disciples have only limited power at their disposal: they can 'kill the body', but they have no power to 'kill the soul'. Accordingly, they have no ultimate power over the totality of the human being, that unity comprised of both 'body' and 'soul'.[169] There is thus no reason to fear them.

By contrast Jesus commands his disciples to 'fear rather the one who is able to destroy both soul and body in Gehenna'.[170] Here Jesus refers to God, who alone has the power to determine the ultimate destiny of the total human being, i.e., 'both soul and body'.[171] The scene depicted is that of the 'day of judgment' (cf. 10.15) on which God will exercise his awesome prerogative to destroy those human beings on whom his judgment falls. The picture is one not only of totality but also of finality. This 'destruction of soul and body' will occur in 'Gehenna', that place known in Jewish thinking as the place of fiery torment[172] reserved for the eternal punishment of evildoers.[173] Jesus' reference to 'the destruction of soul and body in Gehenna' thus points to the total and ultimate destruction of the human being,[174] a fate incomparably worse than that physical death which the disciples face at the hands of their persecutors.[175] It is therefore God, that one who alone has jurisdiction over the ultimate fate of 'both soul and body', whom the disciples are to 'fear'.

But if Jesus' second call to 'fearlessness' (10.28) points the disciples to the fearsome and final judgment of God, his third call 'not to fear' (10.29-31) promises them the providential care of a loving Father who concerns himself with the fate of even the least significant of his creatures. This segment opens with a rhetorical question (10.29a) which contrasts sharply with the preceding verse: 'Are not two sparrows sold for a penny?' The abrupt switch from talk about the judgment of God to the mention of insignificant birds sold in the market at 'two for a penny' has a distinct startle effect which is heightened, in turn, by the assertion which follows: 'Yet not one of them will fall upon the ground without your Father' (10.29b). Here

Jesus asserts that the same God who has jurisdiction over the eternal destiny of the disciples, as of all humankind, nevertheless concerns himself with the death of creatures so insignificant that two of them can be bought for a single penny, that is, for the smallest price possible.[176] Further, Jesus asserts that the same God who is Judge over all humankind is in fact none other than Father to the disciples. The contrast between the imagery of 10.28 and 10.29 could scarcely be more pointed.

But only in 10.30-31, the second half of the segment, does the real significance of this contrast become apparent. Here, by means of an argument 'from the lesser to the greater', Jesus indicates that his primary concern is not with insignificant sparrows, but rather with infinitely more valuable disciples: 'But as for you, even the hairs of your head are all numbered. Therefore, do not fear; for you are worth more than many sparrows'. Jesus has made reference to God's concern for the most insignificant of creatures in order to highlight by contrast God's far greater concern for the disciples themselves.[177]

But if Jesus here offers his disciples the assurance of God's providential care in their lives, he does not equate this providential care with escape from persecution.[178] Rather, in 10.29-31 Jesus argues in striking fashion that God's providence is at work precisely in the death of each sparrow and thus, by analogy 'from the lesser to the greater', also in the death of each disciple martyred because of his proclamation. Thus the message for Jesus' disciples is not that God will protect them from the ultimate which their opponents can inflict upon them (cf. 10.28a)[179] but rather that God will be present with the disciples and sustain them as they experience persecution to the point of death.[180]

It is now evident that two emphases characterize each segment of Jesus' threefold call to 'fearlessness' (10.26-27, 28, 29-31). Each segment is built around the element of contrast: (1) concealment/ disclosure (10.26-27); (2) the limited power of humans/the ultimate power of God (10.28); (3) insignificant sparrows/infinitely more valuable human beings (10.29-31). And in each case the effect of the contrast is to reinforce the impact of the second element by means of the rapid movement from one extreme to the other. The thematic movement within these verses is thus from (1) 'disclosure' or 'proclamation' to (2) 'the power of God to pass eternal judgment on humankind' to (3) 'the providential care of God for the disciples'.

And it is this thematic movement which points to the second emphasis within these verses, the stress throughout on the power of

God as the ultimate basis of Jesus' appeal for 'fearlessness'. The appeal of 10.26-27 is grounded in God's power and his will to reveal, the appeal of 10.28 in God's power to determine the ultimate destiny of humans, and the appeal of 10.29-31 in God's power and his will to sustain his children even as they experience persecution to the point of death. The message conveyed by 10.26-31, accordingly, is 'Do not fear! God's power is the final word'.

And if 10.26-31 constitutes an appeal for 'fearlessness', 10.32-33 concludes the section (10.26-33) with an antithetical parallelism defining that 'fearlessness' and its opposite and pointing to the eschatological consequences of both: 'Therefore, everyone who acknowledges me before people I will also acknowledge before my Father who is in heaven. But whoever denies me before people I will also deny before my Father who is in heaven'. The first half of each of these statements has to do with the witness of the disciples: the designation of the setting as public ('before people') and the responses as verbal ('acknowledgment' or 'denial' of Jesus) point to this fact. Thus it is the call to witness which stands as the ultimate object of Jesus' threefold appeal for 'fearlessness' in 10.26-31. The message of 10.26-33 is none other than the command, 'Do not fear . . . to acknowledge me before people'.[181]

The second half of each statement, then, has to do with the ultimate power which God holds to determine the destiny of the disciples. Jesus' reference here to his 'confession' or 'denial' of people 'before my Father who is in heaven' is unambiguous in its intent. With this reference Jesus depicts that ultimate tribunal which God will hold on the 'day of judgment' (10.15), when humans will either be 'saved' (10.22) or consigned 'soul and body' to Gehenna (10.28).[182] Thus the message of 10.32-33, communicated first positively and then negatively, is that the disciples' acknowledgment of Jesus under persecution, i.e., their witness under fire, is the factor which will determine their eternal destiny.[183]

But the crucial element in 10.32-33 is neither the reference to the disciples' witness nor the reference to the judgment of God, but rather the fact that Jesus himself plays a central role in regard both to the disciples' witness and to the judgment of God. Jesus here indicates that the disciples' witness is not simply a witness based on what he has told them (cf. 10.27). In the final analysis the disciples' witness is identified as their public acknowledgment of Jesus himself.[184] The ultimate significance of the disciples' witness lies in the stance which they take toward Jesus, the one who has sent them out to proclaim. The call to 'fearless witness' is thus relational in its essence.

And if the disciples' witness has to do ultimately with the stance which they take toward Jesus, the judgment of God hinges in reciprocal fashion on the stance which Jesus takes toward them. Here it is Jesus' 'acknowledgment' or 'denial' of the disciples before God which serves as their defense or their condemnation on the 'day of judgment'. Therefore it is the relationship which exists between the disciples and Jesus which is crucial both to the witness of the disciples and to the eschatological consequences which that witness has for them.[185]

In 10.26-33, therefore, Jesus issues an appeal for 'fearless witness' which takes place in the context of life-threatening persecution, grows out of the disciples' relationship to Jesus himself, and ultimately determines their eternal destiny. And it is these same three emphases which come to the fore in the section which follows (10.34-39).

The disciples' relationship to Jesus: consequences of fearless witness (10.34-39). If 10.26-33 sounds a clear note of encouragement with its threefold call to 'fearless witness', 10.34-39 sounds the contrasting note of caution with a threefold warning about the consequences of that 'fearless witness'. The section opens in 10.34-36 with a startling declaration by Jesus which sets the tone for what is to follow: 'Do not think that I have come to bring peace upon the earth. I have not come to bring peace but a sword. For I have come to sever a man from his father, a daughter from her mother, and a daughter-in-law from her mother-in-law. And the enemies of a person [will be] the members of his household'.

Three elements combine here to give this segment its impact. The first of these is the negative imperative 'do not think [that . . .]'. Here Jesus engages the attention of his listeners by announcing that he is about to disavow a widely held viewpoint.[186] This use of the negative imperative has the effect of riveting the attention of the listeners on that which is to follow.

The second element which adds to the emphasis of this segment is the threefold repetition of the formulaic phrase 'I have come', followed in each instance by an infinitive defining that action which Jesus 'has come' to carry out. The fact that this formula dominates the entire segment indicates that Jesus' overriding concern here is to establish a crucial point regarding the purpose of his ministry.

But it is Jesus' message itself which provides the ultimate impact of the segment. In the first step of this message (10.34a) Jesus announces in startling fashion that the purpose of his coming is not that of bringing peace: 'Do not think that I have come to bring peace upon the earth'. This announcement stands in contrast to that which the disciples would expect. In his first discourse Jesus has pronounced a blessing (5.9) on those who are 'peacemakers'. And within the present discourse he has instructed his disciples (10.12) to 'let [their] peace come upon' those houses which are 'worthy' as they move about from place to place in ministry.[187] Accordingly, Jesus' words appear to contradict his previous message concerning peace and force the question, 'If Jesus has not come to bring peace, then what has he come to bring?'

This question finds its answer in the second step of Jesus' message (10.34b): 'I have not come to bring peace but a sword'. This deliberate juxtaposition of 'peace' and 'sword' shocks the listener with its brutality: Jesus has not come to bring the harmony and well-being associated with 'peace', but rather the violence associated with 'war'.[188]

Finally, in the third step of his message (10.35), Jesus restates the metaphorical language of 'peace' and 'sword' in concrete terms: 'For I have come to sever a man from his father, a daughter from her mother, and a daughter-in-law from her mother-in-law'. Here the general imagery of violence evoked by the contrast between 'peace' and 'sword' gives way to more specific imagery associated with the function of the sword as an instrument of violence.[189] The 'sword' which Jesus has come to bring is one characterized by the violent separation of individuals one from another.[190] But most striking here is the fact that it is none other than the closest human relationships which are split apart by the 'sword' which Jesus brings: the father/son, mother/daughter, mother-in-law/daughter-in-law relationships, and by implication, all other such intimate familial relationships.[191] The message of 10.35 is thus shocking in the extreme.

In a final summary statement (10.36) Jesus then rephrases and generalizes the message of the previous verse: 'And the enemies of a person [will be] the members of his household'. If 10.35 depicts the violent dismemberment of the family unit, relationship by relationship, 10.36 speaks in general terms of enmity which applies to all possible family relationships.

In 10.34-36, therefore, Jesus uses the language of warfare, violent cleavage, and enmity to depict the radical dissolution of the most fundamental of human ties, those of the family. In its present context this picture conveys a warning to the disciples: their 'fearless witness' concerning Jesus (10.26-33) will result not in familial peace and household harmony but rather in the violent severing of the strongest human ties and the breaking up of the closest human relationships.

But the significance which Jesus attaches to this harsh warning makes it harsher still. By linking this warning to the threefold formula 'I have come', Jesus indicates to his disciples that the situation which he here depicts is not simply the unfortunate, if inevitable, result of their ministry. Rather, the situation of sharp separation within the family and enmity within the household reflects one function of Jesus' ministry, something which he 'has come' specifically in order to bring about.[192] If the disciples experience the violent severing of familial ties, this is because Jesus himself has brought the 'sword' which effects that action.

In the following verses (10.37-38) Jesus then presents the converse of 10.34-36. In contrast to the positive formulation of 10.34-36 ('I have come to ... '), 10.37-38 consists of a threefold parallelism in negative formulation: 'The one who loves father or mother above me is not worthy of me. And the one who loves son or daughter above me is not worthy of me. And whoever does not take up his cross and follow me is not worthy of me'.

Here Jesus reformulates the message of 10.34-36 in terms of its point of view. If 10.34-36 speaks of that which Jesus has come to do, 10.37-38 speaks of what this will mean for the disciples.[193] For Jesus to say that he has come to sever the closest of human relationships means that for the disciples no relationships, not even those with father or mother, son or daughter, dare assume higher rank than their relationship with Jesus. And if they place other relationships above their relationship to Jesus, they will forfeit their status as disciples altogether (i.e., they will no longer be 'worthy' of Jesus).[194]

The third element of the parallelism of 10.37-38 introduces an even more personal note than the first two:[195] 'And whoever does not take up his cross and follow me is not worthy of me'. Here Jesus introduces an image which is as violent as the image of the 'sword' in 10.34-36. The reference to 'taking up one's cross' points to death by crucifixion, that form of execution widely recognized as the Roman method of punishing criminals.[196] Thus Jesus here as well as in 10.34-36 uses the imagery of death by brutality to depict what his disciples will experience as the consequences of their 'fearless witness'.

But what sets this image apart from the image of the 'sword' in 10.34-36 is the object against which the brutality in question is directed. If the imagery of the 'sword' in 10.34-36 points to death-dealing violence directed against close family *relationships*, the imagery of the 'cross' in 10.38 depicts death-dealing violence directed against *the individual disciple himself*. The 'cross' in question is specifically designated as one which belongs to the disciple: it is 'his cross' which the disciple needs to take up in order to be worthy of Jesus. Further, the 'cross' of 10.38 is something which the disciple must actively 'take up': just as the condemned criminal is forced to pick up the crossbar of that cross on which he is to be executed and carry it to the place of execution, so the disciple himself must assume an active role in accepting the death-dealing violence directed at him.

But most striking here is the significance which Jesus attaches to this 'cross'. For Jesus' disciples the act of 'taking up one's cross' has significance because it is in doing so that the disciple 'follows' Jesus. The obvious implication of this statement is that Jesus himself already faces the death-dealing violence described here in terms of the 'cross'. Accordingly, if the disciple is to 'follow' Jesus, he must face that same violence.[197] It is the disciples' relationship to Jesus which both necessitates and gives significance to the 'cross' which they are called to 'take up'. A solidarity in suffering thus exists between Jesus and his disciples:[198] the disciples must suffer that which Jesus has suffered before them, if they wish to remain his disciples.

It is this message which stands as the climax to the threefold parallelism of 10.37-38.[199] And this message concerning the solidarity in suffering between Jesus and his disciples obliquely introduces a new element into the picture. From 10.16 on, Jesus has indicated that his disciples face the prospect of death at the hands of their persecutors. The metaphorical language of 10.16 concerning 'sheep in the midst of wolves' gives way to the straightforward language of 10.21 ('And brother will hand over brother to death. . .') and 10.28 ('And do not fear those who kill the body. . .') which speaks directly of physical death. Thus the reference in 10.38 to 'taking up one's cross' introduces no new message for Jesus' disciples in regard to what they themselves can expect. But the fact that their future sufferings are here linked by implication to that which Jesus will suffer in advance of them means that Jesus is here hinting at his own death. It is this which constitutes the new element within the message of 10.38.[200]

The following verse (10.39) underlines the message of 10.38 and puts it in proper perspective. In an antithetical parallelism Jesus spells out the eschatological consequences first of 'finding' and then of 'losing' one's life: 'The one who finds his life will lose it. And the one who loses his life on my account will find it'. The contrast which Jesus sets up here is a contrast between physical life and physical death.[201] Within the context of the preceding verses (10.16-38) Jesus' reference to 'finding' one's life can only be a reference to preserving oneself from death at the hands of persecutors, while the reference to 'losing' one's life points, conversely, to that violent death for which Jesus has been preparing his disciples since 10.16. That the situation envisioned is one of persecution is further assured by the fact that Jesus qualifies his reference to 'the one who loses his life' by means of the phrase 'on my account'. In this way Jesus identifies 'the one who loses his life' as none other than that disciple who has 'taken up his cross' in order to 'follow' Jesus.

But if Jesus speaks of physical life and physical death, he likewise speaks of the eschatological consequences which will follow for those who 'find' their physical life and those who 'lose' it. The references in the future tense to 'losing' and 'finding' life respectively point to an eschatological 'losing' and 'finding' which will take place on the 'day of judgment' (10.15)[202] and for which God is ultimately responsible (cf. 10.15, 22, 28, 32-33).[203] Accordingly, the purpose of the two antithetically parallel statements of 10.39 is to link the present situation of the disciple of Jesus with his future situation on the 'day of judgment'.[204]

What is striking here, however, is not the fact that these two situations (the present and the eschatological) are linked to each other but rather the way in which they are linked to each other. Here Jesus announces a twofold paradox. That disciple who succeeds at the present time in preserving his life from death-dealing persecution by 'denying [Jesus] before people' (10.33) will preserve his life for the present only to forfeit it irretrievably on the 'day of judgment'. And that disciple who forfeits his present life altogether because he fearlessly 'acknowledges [Jesus] before people' (10.32) will give it up for the present only to recover it as an irrevocable inheritance on the 'day of judgment'.[205]

And now the logical connection between 10.38 and 10.39 is apparent. If the individual disciple is called to 'follow' Jesus by forfeiting his own life, he is called to this action so that he can ultimately recover that life which he has forfeited.[206] It is thus in the interest of life itself that the disciple must face the prospect of death.

And now, having sounded the call to 'fearless witness' (10.26-33) and spelled out the consequences of that witness (10.34-39) in terms of the disciples' relationship to himself (cf. 10.24-25), Jesus concludes the third section of his discourse by pointing out (10.40-42) the ultimate significance of this relationship. And while in 10.24-39 Jesus has focused attention on the persecution facing his disciples, he now formulates his closing message in terms of those who will receive them and their ministry.

The disciples' relationship to Jesus: ultimate significance (10.40-42). This section opens with a two part saying spelling out the truth which underlies the whole of Jesus' address to his disciples: 'The one who receives you receives me. And the one who receives me receives the one who sent me'. This message, presented in step-logic fashion, has four basic elements: Jesus here makes pronouncements concerning (1) the disciples, (2) himself, (3) God, and (4) those who receive the disciples.

Jesus first establishes an identity between the disciples and himself. To receive the disciples is none other than to receive Jesus himself. With this pronouncement Jesus underlines that which he has already made clear throughout his discourse: since the disciples have been authorized and sent out by Jesus, and thus represent Jesus himself to the crowds,[207] it follows that to receive the disciples is to receive Jesus himself and to reject them, conversely, is to reject Jesus. It is this awesome fact, both in its positive and its negative formulations, which gives ultimate significance to everything which the disciples do in their role as 'apostles', those 'sent out' by Jesus.[208]

Jesus likewise establishes an identity between himself and God: those who receive the disciples receive not only Jesus, the one who has sent the disciples, but also God himself, the one who sent Jesus. With this pronouncement Jesus gives straightforward expression to that which he has thus far stated only indirectly, namely, that he has been sent by God. It is this message which lies behind Jesus' references to his 'coming' (5.17; 9.13; 10.34-35): Jesus has 'come' because God has 'sent' him. It is this message which lies behind that 'authority' which the crowds and the narrator himself attribute to Jesus (7.29; 9.8), which Jesus claims for himself (9.6), and which he shares with his disciples (10.1). And it is this message which explains why Jesus can first call his disciples to pray that *God* send out laborers into his harvest (9.38) and then in the next moment take action *himself* to send out his disciples (10.1, 5a).[209] Thus Jesus here adds his voice to the voice of God, who has already proclaimed in reference to him, 'This is my beloved Son . . . ' (3.17).

Conversely, Jesus' reference to 'the one who has sent' him likewise represents a pronouncement concerning God. While Jesus now sends his disciples out into ministry, it is God who has acted first in sending out Jesus. Thus it is God who is the original actor in the situation depicted; and it is ultimately God who stands behind the ministry to which Jesus sends out his disciples.

Finally, Jesus' message of 10.40 contains a pronouncement concerning those who receive the disciples and their ministry. Since an identity exists between the disciples and Jesus on the one hand and between Jesus and God on the other, this means that the one who receives the disciples receives both Jesus, the one who sent the disciples, and God, the one who sent Jesus. The disciples' ministry carries the authority of God himself, and thus conveys the presence of God to those who receive the disciples. In this message lies the ultimate significance of the disciples' relationship to Jesus.

Having thus established the bond which links the disciples, himself, and God, Jesus then concludes the third section of the discourse with a threefold parallelism (10.41-42) spelling out the implications of this bond for those who receive the disciples: 'The one who receives a prophet because he is a prophet[210] will receive the reward of a prophet. And the one who receives a righteous one because he is a righteous one will receive the reward of a righteous one. And whoever gives one of these little ones a cup of cold water simply because he is a disciple—truly, I say to you—will by no means lose his reward'.

The context, language, and internal structure of 10.41-42 all indicate that this threefold prediction is to be interpreted in terms of the disciples and those who receive them. The structural parallelism between 10.40 ('the one who receives you') and 10.41a/b ('the one who receives a prophet/righteous one') suggests that the 'prophet' and the 'righteous one' of 10.41 stand parallel to the 'you' of 10.40, namely, to the twelve disciples whom Jesus has sent out in 10.5a and to whom he has addressed the entirety of the discourse (10.5a; 11.1).[211]

Further, while the parallelism between 10.40 and 10.41 implicitly identifies those to be received with the disciples, the language of 10.42 makes this identification explicit. Here Jesus speaks unambiguously of a service rendered to 'one of these little ones ... simply because he is a disciple'. It thus seems most plausible that the entire sequence (10.41a/41b/42) should be interpreted with reference to Jesus' disciples and those who receive them.

Finally, the internal structure of 10.41-42 makes it evident that the reference to 'disciple' in 10.42 constitutes not simply the third element in the sequence of those to be received ('prophet', 'righteous one', 'little one/disciple') but rather provides the concept which governs the entire sequence. Here Jesus again offers a threefold saying in which the third element breaks the pattern established by the first two and thus forms the climax to the saying as a whole.[212]

The simple formula of 10.41a/41b ('the one who receives a.../ because he is a.../will receive the reward of a...') gives way in 10.42 to a parallel but significantly more weighty formula ('and whoever gives... a cup of cold water/simply because he is a.../— truly, I say to you—will by no means lose his reward'). By drawing special attention to the minimal nature of the service rendered ('a cup of cold water'), the ultimate identity of the one received ('simply because he is...'), and the certainty of the reward to come ('truly, I say to you—will by no means lose ...'), Jesus establishes the importance of the third element in the series as the clue to the interpretation of the entire saying.

But of even more significance than the shift in formula is the shift in identification of the one to be received. While 10.41a/41b speak of receiving a 'prophet' and a 'righteous one' on the basis of their respective identities as 'prophet' and 'righteous one', 10.42 speaks of offering a cup of cold water to 'one of these little ones' not because he is a 'little one' but rather because he is a 'disciple'. By inserting the reference to 'disciple' where his listeners would expect a second reference to 'little one', Jesus not only underlines the climactic importance of the third element in the series[213] but also establishes that the key to the interpretation of the entire saying lies in the term 'disciple'.

In 10.41-42 Jesus then identifies the disciples in terms of their specific functions or characteristics. Jesus here refers to his disciples under the respective rubrics of 'prophet', 'righteous one', and 'little one'. Accordingly, Jesus indicates that there are no less than three distinct groups among his disciples, each with its own distinct function or characteristic.[214]

The first group to which Jesus makes reference is that of 'prophets'. In Jewish thinking this designation identifies those persons throughout history whose human utterance has been recognized as the voice of God himself (1.22; 2.15; cf. 2.17, 23; 3.3; 4.14; 8.17).[215] And it is this notion of 'prophet as proclaimer' which has informed the 'proclamation' motif throughout the present discourse (e.g., 10.7, 14, 18, 19-20, 26-27, 32-33). Accordingly, Jesus' reference to 'prophets' defines the task of these disciples first of all as proclamation and establishes their predecessors in this task as 'the prophets who were before you' (5.12).[216] And by linking these disciples to the prophets of Jewish history, Jesus speaks not only to the question of their vocation but also to the question of his own identity. If his disciples are 'prophets', who by definition proclaim 'the words of the Lord', then it is clear that Jesus himself is the Lord whose words they are to speak. Just as Yahweh spoke through the prophets of Jewish history, so now Jesus speaks through the 'prophets' among his disciples.[217] Jesus thus lays claim to that role of 'divine message giver' which until now has been associated with God alone.[218]

But if the designation 'prophet' associates a disciple first of all with proclamation, it likewise associates him with a ministry of healing. Not only does Jesus commission his disciples to a ministry of healing alongside their ministry of proclamation (10.8 cf. 10.7) but he has already warned them against a false 'prophetism' which 'prophesies, *casts out demons*, and *does acts of power* in [his] name' while failing to 'do the will of [his] Father who is in heaven' (7.21-22).[219] Thus the 'prophets' of whom Jesus speaks are those identified by their proclamation of the words of Jesus and by their healing ministry.

The second group to which Jesus refers are the 'righteous ones'. This title appears to designate those disciples identified in a special way with the 'righteousness' which Jesus has set forth as the essential mark of life within the Kingdom of heaven (3.15; 5.6, 10, 20; 6.33).[220] The structure of 10.41-42, built as it is on the distinction between designated titles, indicates that those known as 'righteous ones' constitute a group separate from that of the 'prophets'.[221] Accordingly, Jesus here speaks of a group of disciples known not for prophetic words or deeds of power but rather for that quality of 'righteousness' which is the primary distinguishing mark of the Kingdom of heaven.[222]

The final group to which Jesus refers is the group composed of 'little ones'. This designation stands at the opposite end of the spectrum from that of 'prophet'. If the title 'prophet' appears to denote a position of respect among the disciples, the designation 'little one' denotes a position which lacks any outward honor at all.[223] Not only does the use of the term 'little' point to that conclusion but also the fact that the sequence moves from 'prophet' on the one end to 'little one' on the other.[224] But it is the manner in which Jesus refers to these 'little ones' which assures that they stand at the opposite end of the spectrum from the 'prophets' in terms of the honor of their position. While the 'prophet' is described as being received because of the respect accorded him as a 'prophet' and the 'righteous one' because of his status as a 'righteous one', the 'little one' is depicted as being received 'simply because he is a disciple'. Thus the designation 'little ones' refers to that group of disciples whose sole identifying characteristic is their relationship to Jesus. As a result, the only compelling reason for receiving such a person lies in his status as a 'disciple'.[225] But it is this very distinction between the last group and the two previous groups which serves to focus attention on the end of the series and place the crucial weight of the saying on the description of the 'little ones'.

And here the paradoxical nature of Jesus' saying becomes evident. First, Jesus identifies three groups among his disciples, those of the 'prophets', the 'righteous ones', and the 'little ones'; and he lists these groups in an order apparently based on the outward honor associated with the respective designations.[226] But he then establishes that it is the last and least of these groupings (i.e., the 'little ones') whose position has most significance.[227] Jesus has moved from top to bottom of the social ladder specifically in order to break that 'hierarchy' by placing the crucial weight of the saying on the 'little ones' at the bottom of the list.[228]

There is yet a third function served by 10.41-42. In each of the three parallel formulations within this saying (10.41a, 41b, 42) Jesus promises a 'reward' to the one who receives the disciples. And the language used to describe these 'rewards' indicates that they are eschatological in nature[229] and not any type of immediate or physical remuneration.[230] The verb which stands in the second half of each formulation is a verb in the future tense ('will receive', 'will receive', 'will [by no means] lose'). The events depicted, therefore, lie within a future time frame. And from the specific phraseology of the text it becomes evident that this 'future' is not immediate but rather eschatological. The language used here is that of 'receiving' (or conversely, of 'not losing') a 'reward'. Such language, when projected into the future by the Jesus of Matthew's Gospel (6.1, 4, 6, 18) points to an eschatological reward to be received 'in heaven' (5.12; cf. 5.46) rather than an immediate reward to be received in this life (6.2, 5, 16).

Further, the double negative construction of 10.42, *ou mē apolesē* (= will by no means lose), lends an emphatic tone to the third element of the threefold saying. In this way Jesus underlines the significance of the reward by describing it as both certain and lasting.

But it is the parenthetical phrase, 'truly, I say to you', which finally establishes the eschatological nature of the rewards described in 10.41-42. Jesus has used this same phrase twice before within the present discourse (10.15, 23), both times to introduce a prediction pointing to the eschatological implications of the disciples' ministry.[231] Accordingly, the use of this phrase in 10.42 signals that the prediction to follow is one of eschatological and not merely temporal significance.[232]

This language of eschatological reward is no less than reference to the inheritance of the Kingdom of heaven, since for Jesus there is no other reality of ultimate importance. It is the Kingdom of heaven alone which Jesus proclaims (4.17, 23; 9.35) and which he calls his disciples likewise to proclaim (10.7). And in his proclamation Jesus consistently sets this Kingdom before his hearers as that all important goal which alone is worth striving for. Jesus' followers are to 'seek' the Kingdom of heaven above all physical concerns (6.33) and to 'pray' for its advent (6.10); they are to live 'righteously' (5.20) and 'do the will of [the] Father who is in heaven' (7.21) in order to 'enter' this Kingdom; they are to 'do the commandments' and 'teach' others the same to gain good standing in this Kingdom (5.19); and it is the assurance that this Kingdom belongs to them which is the ultimate basis of their 'blessedness' in the present life (5.3, 10). For Jesus there is no other eschatological reward than that of the Kingdom itself.[233]

The overall message of 10.41-42 can therefore be rephrased as follows: those who receive the disciples of Jesus—the 'prophets', the 'righteous ones', but above all those who are simply 'disciples'—will receive in return the only 'reward' which is both certain and lasting, that of the Kingdom of heaven. This message stands as the positive counterpart to the negative message of 10.15, in which Jesus predicts eschatological judgment for those who do not receive the disciples as they go about from town to town. And these two predictions counterbalance each other not only in terms of content but also in terms of tone. While 10.15 uses extreme language ('more tolerable for the land of Sodom and Gomorrah . . . than for that city') to describe the consequences for those who reject the disciples, 10.42 speaks in equally emphatic terms ('truly, I say to you—shall by no means lose his reward') of the consequences for those who receive them.

Accordingly, the final verses of Jesus' discourse (10.40-42) serve as a powerful word of encouragement for the disciples, reassuring them that there is no task of greater significance than the ministry to which Jesus has called them. This ministry identifies them not only with Jesus but through him with God himself, and means entrance into the Kingdom of heaven for all those who receive them.[234]

The disciples' relationship to Jesus: overall impact (10.24-42). It is now possible to assess the overall impact of this section both in its own right and as the conclusion to the entire discourse (10.5b-42). Within 10.24-42 Jesus lays out a threefold message. In 10.24-25 he establishes that his disciples will face persecution in response to their ministry because of their relationship to him. In 10.26-39 he challenges the disciples to persevere in their 'fearless witness' concerning him in spite of the persecution which that will entail. And in 10.40-42 he reassures his disciples that if they must make the ultimate sacrifice, it is because their ministry is one of ultimate significance not only for them but also for those who receive them.

In light of this message the structural and thematic movement of the discourse as a whole can be recognized as having an *a b a'* format.[235] The *a* theme is set forth in 10.5b-15, where Jesus describes the disciples' ministry in active terms by way of a sequence of sixteen imperative statements directed to the disciples. This section ends in 10.14-15, however, with the ominous warning that eschatological judgment lies ahead for those who will not receive the disciples.

The *b* theme is set forth in 10.16-23. Here Jesus reverses the tone of his address to the disciples, describing them not in active terms as agents of ministry but rather in passive terms as objects of the brutal persecution brought on by that ministry. This section ends, however, on a positive note (10.23). Far from being destroyed as the result of persecution, the disciples' ministry will contine on amidst persecution until that eschatological moment when Jesus himself will initiate ultimate and decisive action on behalf of the disciples at 'the coming of the Son of man'.

The *a'* theme is set forth in 10.24-42. Here Jesus reverts back to an 'active' mode of address, challenging the disciples to fearless witness in spite of persecution which they will experience. This section ends (10.40-42) on a positive note which counterbalances the negative note of the *a* ending in 10.14-15. Here Jesus assures the disciples that eschatological reward, i.e., the Kingdom of heaven itself, awaits those who receive them and their ministry.

The striking feature of the entire *a b a'* format of the discourse lies in the fact that from beginning to end Jesus describes the ministry of his disciples and the suffering which they will face as directly linked to his own ministry and to the suffering which he himself will face. Accordingly, the overall function of Jesus' discourse is to establish the integral relationship between Jesus and his disciples in terms both of their essential life tasks and the fate which awaits them for carrying out these tasks. And it is this integral link between Jesus and his disciples which the narrator reinforces by means of the narrative conclusion (11.1), that bridge which connects Jesus' discourse to the ongoing movement of the overall story.

The narrative conclusion: 11.1 (text)

> 11.1 And when Jesus had finished instructing his disciples,
>   he went on from there
>   to teach
>   and to proclaim
>   in their cities.

The narrative conclusion: 11.1 (analysis)
The narrator signals the conclusion of Jesus' discourse with a two part message: (1) 'Jesus [has] finished instructing his disciples', and (2) 'Jesus [goes] on from there to teach and to proclaim in their

cities'. Both of these statements are logical as descriptions of everyday events in the life of Jesus. But the immediate context of these statements and the fact that they are linked to each other sequentially create a logical difficulty for the implied reader.

Just prior to the discourse itself (10.5a) the narrator indicates that Jesus sends out his disciples, instructing them as he does so. The text which follows (10.5b–42) then constitutes the substance of Jesus' instructions to his disciples. Accordingly, when the narrator says that Jesus has now 'finished instructing his disciples', the implied reader expects to find them embarking on the mission to which Jesus has sent them out. Instead, that reader finds no further mention of the disciples nor of their ministry[236] but rather the indication that Jesus himself goes on to continue his ministry among the Jewish people.[237] This poses several questions for the implied reader: (1) why does the narrator omit any mention of the disciples' response to Jesus' commission at the very point where the logic of the story calls for such mention?[238] and (2) why does he instead move back into his narrative with the mention of Jesus and his continuing ministry? It is accordingly these two questions which must find answers, if the discourse of 10.5b–42 is to make ultimate sense within the overall story of Matthew's Gospel.

The text of 11.1 provides several clues to understanding the narrator's purpose in concluding the 'sending account' (9.35–11.1) as he does. First of all, the implied reader discovers that Jesus is the sole actor in 11.1, while the disciples are portrayed simply as the objects of Jesus' instruction. Accordingly, the narrative conclusion (11.1) completes the sequence begun in the narrative introduction (9.35–10.5a), a sequence which focuses throughout on the actions of Jesus and which describes the disciples as the objects of those actions. Jesus goes about the countryside teaching, proclaiming, and healing (9.35); he takes compassion on the crowds (9.36); he speaks to his disciples (9.37); he calls them to him and gives them authority (10.1); he sends them out with instructions (10.5a); and when he has finished instructing them, he goes on once again to teach and to proclaim (11.1).

Accordingly, the narrative framework is a tightly structured and strictly logical sequence of actions taken by Jesus, a sequence which the narrator has then 'broken open' expressly in order to insert Jesus' words of commissioning to his disciples. Thus while Jesus' words focus on that action to be undertaken by the disciples (10.5b–42), the only concrete example of action is that of Jesus himself (9.35–10.5a; 11.1). It is evident, therefore, that the narrator wishes the implied reader to interpret Jesus' words of commissioning to his disciples in the light of Jesus' actions. The example of Jesus' own life provides the necessary basis for interpreting the commission given to the disciples.

A further clue to the narrator's purpose in concluding the 'sending account' as he does lies in the specific language used within 11.1 to describe Jesus' actions. The 'sending account' ends exactly as it has opened in 9.35, i.e., with the reference to Jesus' peripatetic ministry of 'teaching' and 'proclaiming'.[239] The narrator has framed Jesus' words of commissioning to his disciples not simply by a sequence of actions taken by Jesus, but specifically by the twofold reference (9.35; 11.1) to Jesus' own ministry among the Jewish people.[240] Thus in concluding the 'sending account' as he does, the narrator establishes the strongest possible link between the task to which Jesus is commissioning his disciples and the task which Jesus himself is carrying out.

And if the narrator's concern in 11.1 is to focus on the ministering activity of Jesus in order to draw a parallel between Jesus' ministry and that of his disciples, it is clear by the same token that his concern is not that of describing any activity undertaken by the disciples. While Jesus has 'sent out' *the disciples* in 10.5a, the conclusion of the 'sending account' in 11.1 finds *Jesus himself* '[going] on from there', while the disciples fade out of the picture altogether. The implied reader is thus left with the task of reconciling the indication that Jesus has 'sent out' the disciples (10.5a) with the implication that the disciples have not yet 'gone' (11.1).[241]

If the implied reader is not to conclude that the narrator is telling an incoherent story, the only resolution to this predicament lies in projecting the fulfilment of the 'sending act' of 10.5a into a future which lies somewhere beyond the time frame of the present sequence of events. Thus Jesus' 'sending out' of the disciples in 10.5a is an act which will find its fulfilment only in that still future moment when the disciples 'go out'. Accordingly, as the implied reader moves on from 11.1 into the remainder of the story, he or she recognizes the 'sentness' of Jesus' disciples in the present tense of the story and at the same time anticipates that future moment when this 'sentness' will finally be translated into action, as the disciples fulfil their commission by 'going out' to minister.

Chapter 4

ANALYSIS OF MATTHEW 11.2–28.20:
'TO SEE THE END'

I. *Perspective of the Implied Reader at 11.2*

At 11.2 the implied reader of Matthew's Gospel finds him/herself
with an unresolved question. The notice that Jesus has 'sent out' the
disciples (10.5a) and the recounting of a detailed set of instructions
for their mission (10.5b-42) together lead the reader to expect a
journey, which is not however narrated, and a ministry, which is
likewise not fulfilled (cf. 11.1).[1] There is thus an apparent disjuncture
in the narrative with reference to the disciples' ministry. The
seeming illogic of this conclusion to the 'sending account' forces the
reader to an ongoing search for the 'expected but as yet suspended'
fulfilment of the missionary commission. This leads to two questions:
(1) What role do the disciples in fact play throughout the remainder
of the story: do their attitudes and actions relate positively or
negatively to the ministry depicted in 9.35–11.1? (2) If the portrayal
of the disciples throughout the remainder of the Gospel concurs with
the apparent message of 11.1 (namely, that the disciples have not yet
embarked on their minstry), then at what point will they do so?[2]

These questions can ultimately be answered only through analysis
of the remainder of the story. But the 'sending account' already
provides pointers toward those answers in the parallelism which it
establishes between Jesus' ministry and that of his disciples. These
pointers are twofold.

First, if the disciples are to carry out a ministry which parallels
Jesus' own, then Jesus must provide them in advance with an 'image'
which their own ministry can then 'reflect'. And as yet the 'image' of
Jesus' ministry is not complete. To be sure, he has already modelled
much of what he calls his disciples to parallel. He has granted them
the same authority as that which already empowers his own
ministry,[3] commissioned them to the tasks in which he himself is

already engaged,[4] and warned them to expect verbal abuse such as he himself has already encountered.[5] But elsewhere in the 'sending account' Jesus predicts for his disciples things which lie far beyond what he himself has yet experienced. At a point at which Jesus himself has not yet faced anything beyond verbal abuse (10.25 cf. 9.32-34),[6] he warns his disciples that they will be 'handed over' (10.17, 19, 21), 'flogged' (10.17), 'led before rulers [and] kings' to stand trial (10.18), and ultimately faced with death itself (10.21, 28, 38, 39). And since Jesus himself has not yet suffered such persecution, neither can his disciples: not until Jesus himself has suffered can his disciples 'reflect' that suffering in their own.[7] Literarily, therefore, it follows that at least the conclusion, if not the entirety,[8] of the disciples' ministry is one which must lie well beyond the scope of the problematic transitional verse, 11.1.[9]

Secondly, since the shape of the disciples' ministry is to 'reflect' the 'image' provided by the ministry of Jesus, the implied reader has a clear standard by which to assess their role throughout the remainder of the story. When the disciples assume that task to which Jesus has 'sent [them] out' in 10.5a, three things will be apparent in their portrayal as characters: (1) they will exhibit in their attitudes and actions the authority which Jesus has given to them; (2) they will carry out among the crowds the tasks of 'proclamation' and 'healing' to which Jesus has called them; and (3) they will encounter the intense persecution which Jesus has promised them. Conversely, as long as these characteristics do not show up in the portrayal of the disciples, the implied reader must assume that they have not yet embarked on their ministry.

In order to assess the role of the disciples in the remainder of the story, therefore, the implied reader must focus attention in two directions. On the one hand, the reader must focus on Jesus, the one whose 'image' the disciples are to 'reflect' in their ministry. The questions here are the following: (1) what is the overall complexion of Jesus' ministry throughout 11.2–28.20? and (2) when and how does Jesus complete the 'image' of his ministry by suffering as has been predicted (10.4, 38)? On the other hand, the focus must lie on the disciples. The questions here are the following: (1) what does Jesus have to say with regard to the disciples' ministry? and (2) what do the disciples themselves say and do?

These questions will serve as focal points for the remainder of the present study. But since the plot of the story from 11.2 through 28.20

falls into three sections (11.2-16.20; 16.21-25.46; 26.1-28.20),[10] the
following analysis will have a corresponding threefold structure.
Accordingly, each of these three sections will be analyzed in terms of
the focal points identified above: (1) the overall portrayal of Jesus
relative to his ongoing ministry and his upcoming suffering; and (2)
the overall portrayal of the disciples relative to their designated
ministry and their demonstrated attitudes and actions.

II. *Jesus Continues his Ministry: 11.2-16.20*

As the implied reader moves out of the 'sending account' (9.35–11.1)
and back into the flow of Matthew's narrative, he/she discovers that
no significant shift has yet taken place in terms of roles. While Jesus
has 'sent [the disciples] out' to assume a new role vis-à-vis the
crowds, the actual events of the story indicate that they have not yet
assumed their new role. This is evident both from the portrayal of
Jesus and from that of the disciples themselves.

The portrayal of Jesus in 11.2-16.20

What stands out as the implied reader moves through the text of
11.2-16.20 is that the focus on Jesus' life and ministry still dominates
the story. Here again, just as previously,[11] Jesus is spatially at the
center of the story. The only scene from which Jesus is absent is the
'flashback' scene of 14.3-12, in which the narrator describes the
circumstances surrounding the death of John the Baptist. And just as
before,[12] the language of the story positions Jesus at the center of a
great centripetal force which draws all the other characters 'toward'
him. People of all persuasions—the disciples (13.10, 36; 14.15; 15.12,
23), the crowds (15.30), the religious authorities (15.1; 16.1)—'come'
to Jesus;[13] sick persons are 'brought' to him (12.22; 14.35);[14] and
Jesus himself initiates this movement on occasion by 'calling' to him
the crowd (15.10) or his disciples (15.32).[15]
    Further, Jesus is the commanding figure of the story, whose
ministry among the crowds dominates the flow of events and in this
way forces the question as to his identity. The segment opens (11.2-6)
with an inquiry by John the Baptist concerning Jesus' 'messiahship'.
Having heard from prison about 'the deeds of the Messiah', John
sends his disciples to ask Jesus whether he is in fact 'the one who is to
come'. Jesus responds by sending John's disciples back to relate to
him that which they themselves have 'heard and seen' of Jesus'
ministry: 'The blind see again and the lame walk about, lepers are

cleansed and the deaf hear, and the dead are raised and the poor have good news proclaimed to them' (11.5).[16] The message contained within these words is that Jesus' messiahship makes itself known precisely by way of his ministry to the crowds.

Accordingly, the following verses depict Jesus as deeply involved in activity directed toward the crowds. While they 'follow' Jesus (12.15; 14.13), 'gather together' to him (13.2), 'come' to him (15.30), and 'bring' to him their sick (12.22; 14.35; cf. 15.30), Jesus responds with a multi-faceted ministry which grows out of his 'compassion' for them (14.14; 15.32). He speaks to the crowds, teaching them in straightforward language (11.7-19, 20-24; 12.22-45, 46-50; 13.53-58; 15.10-11) as well as in parables (13.1-33, 34-35). He moves among the crowds, healing large numbers of people (12.15-21; 14.13-14; 15.29-31; cf. 14.34-36); and he carries on a one-to-one healing ministry, responding case by case to the needs of individuals (12.9-14, 22-24; 15.21-28). On occasions when the crowds are gathered around him without an adequate supply of food, Jesus multiplies meager rations of bread and fish into meals which feed thousands (14.13-21; 15.32-39).[17] And throughout all this activity Jesus consistently relates to the crowds as one in a position of authority: he summons them (15.10), directs their movements when necessary (14.19; 15.35), and dismisses them at the appropriate times (13.36; 15.22-23 cf. 14.15; 15.39).

As a result of this multi-faceted ministry to the crowds Jesus is recognized on all sides[18] as one who does 'powerful deeds' (11.20-24; 13.53-58) by means of the 'powers at work within him' (14.1-2).[19] And this section of the story concludes (16.13-20) with a resounding response to the 'Jesus of powerful deeds' portrayed within the previous verses. In contrast to the crowds, who view Jesus merely as the reincarnation of one of their 'prophets' (16.14), Simon Peter proclaims on behalf of all of the disciples[20] that Jesus is 'the Messiah, the Son of the living God'.

The dramatic flow of 11.2–16.20 is now visible: (1) in light of reports which he has received concerning Jesus' ministry,[21] John the Baptist raises the question of Jesus' 'messiahship'; (2) Jesus responds by instructing John's disciples to report back to him what they themselves have 'heard and seen' of Jesus' ministry; (3) the narrator portrays Jesus as a man of 'powerful deeds' involved constantly and intensely in this ministry to the crowds; (4) in a pronouncement which provides the definitive answer to John the Baptist's question, the disciples proclaim Jesus' 'messiahship'. In light of this carefully constructed sequence of events, there can be no question as to the primary message of 11.2-16.20: Jesus is the Messiah, and his 'messiahship' proves itself in the ministry of 'powerful deeds' which he carries out among the crowds.

But there is also a secondary message conveyed by 11.2-16.20: many of those who witness Jesus' ministry fail to respond appropriately to 'what [they] hear and see'. Instead, these persons reject Jesus' ministry by failing to recognize in that ministry 'the deeds of the Messiah' and in Jesus 'the Messiah to whom such deeds belong'. Accordingly, a note of 'rejection' sounds repeatedly throughout 11.2-16.20, creating a persistent and negative 'counterpoint' to the positive tone provided by Jesus' ministry of 'powerful deeds'.

Jesus himself introduces this note of 'rejection' at the outset of the section. After giving John's disciples a detailed account of his ministry—'the blind see again and the lame walk about, lepers are cleansed and the deaf hear, and the dead are raised and the poor have good news proclaimed to them' (11.5)—he immediately adds, 'And blessed is the one who does not take offense at me' (11.6). The message of this 'beatitude' is twofold. In the first place, Jesus indicates that how people respond to his ministry is a matter of extreme consequence: to 'take offense' at Jesus is none other than to fail to recognize in Jesus' ministry to the sick and the poor (11.5) the ministry of 'the one who is to come' (11.3), the Messiah himself. Secondly, Jesus warns that his ministry will meet with a negative response: by pronouncing a blessing on those 'who do not take offense' at him, Jesus hints that there are others 'who do take offense' at him. Accordingly, the 'beatitude' of 11.6 functions less as a positive word of blessing on those who recognize Jesus' messianic ministry than as an ominous warning that others will reject both ministry and Messiah.

Throughout the following verses this note of 'rejection' sounds repeatedly, in sharp contrast to the otherwise positive tone of the narrative. While the crowds toy with the possibility of Jesus' 'messiahship' (12.23: 'This man can't be the Son of David, can he?')[22] and offer praise to 'the God of Israel' (15.31), there are persistent indications that not everyone is ready to accept Jesus' messianic ministry.

On the one hand, there is growing evidence of rejection on the part of the crowds themselves. In 11.16-19 Jesus laments openly that 'this generation' has been willing to receive neither John the Baptist, who came as an ascetic, nor the Son of man, who eats and drinks with questionable social groups. In 11.20-24 Jesus addresses sharp words to Chorazin, Bethsaida, and Capernaum, those cities in which he has done most of his 'powerful deeds': because they have not 'repented' in response to Jesus' ministry, they will meet a fate on the 'day of judgment' which will be worse than the fates of Tyre, Sidon, and the land of Sodom.[23] In 13.10-17 Jesus explains to his disciples that he teaches the crowd in parables because they are people 'who see but do not see, hear but do not hear, and do not understand'. And when Jesus returns to his hometown and teaches in the synagogue (13.53-58), he discovers that because of his origins the townspeople are not ready to accept his 'wisdom' and his 'powerful deeds'. Rather, they 'take offense' at him just as he has warned will happen (13.57 cf. 11.6); and in response to their 'unbelief' he 'does not do many powerful deeds' in their midst.

And on the other hand, the response of the religious leadership[24] is totally negative. This leadership watches Jesus and his disciples closely, questioning every move they make: 'Look! Your disciples are doing what is not lawful to do on the sabbath' (12.2); 'Is it lawful to heal on the sabbath?' (12.10); 'Why do your disciples transgress the tradition of the elders?' (15.2). They 'take offense' at Jesus' words (15.12). They misinterpret Jesus' acts of healing as acts carried out in the power of 'Beelzebul, the ruler of the demons' (12.24). And since they fail to identify that which they have already seen of Jesus' ministry as the work of the Holy Spirit (12.28), they continue to demand from Jesus 'signs' which prove his authority (12.38; 16.1).

Their sole purpose in all of this, according to the narrator, is to bring about Jesus' downfall. In their verbal sparring with Jesus, they intend to 'tempt' him (16.2) and to trick him into responses of which they can then 'accuse' him (12.10). To further these negative aims, they not only engage Jesus publicly in verbal skirmishes but likewise gather privately in a sinister council meeting to consider how they might 'destroy' him altogether (12.14).

But the most straightforward indication of what lies ahead emerges not from any reference to Jesus' opponents but rather from the reference to John the Baptist's fate. In 11.2-3 John, who was 'handed over' just prior to the beginning of Jesus' ministry (4.12 cf. 4.17), hears *from prison* about that ministry and sends an inquiry *from prison* with regard to Jesus' 'messiahship'. Here as before (11.2-

6 cf. 4.12-16) the narrator links the account of John's imprisonment to the account of Jesus' ministry, thus hinting that Jesus will eventually meet with the same fate as John his predecessor.[25]

And in 14.1-2 that which has been an oblique hint to the implied reader now becomes a direct warning. Herod the tetrarch, who hears about the ministry of Jesus and 'the powers at work within him', identifies Jesus as John the Baptist '[who] has been raised from the dead'. In the following verses (14.3-12) the narrator then 'flashes back' to the account of John's death at the hands of Herod. The implications are clear: John's death, which has come about as a result of his ministry, constitutes a preview of the fate which awaits Jesus as the result of his own ministry.

The overall portrayal of Jesus in 11.2-16.20 is thus a picture of contrasts. On the one hand, the narrator depicts Jesus as actively involved in an ongoing ministry to the crowds, who trail him eagerly about the countryside and bring him their sick to be healed. On the other hand, the narrator depicts Jesus as the object of a growing wave of rejection, both from among the crowds and from the religious leadership as a whole. And as a grim portent of what is to follow, the narrator relates in detail the events surrounding the death of John the Baptist, Jesus' predecessor in ministry.

But while the response to Jesus and his public ministry is mixed, the evidence on one other question is univocal: the focus of the narrative is on Jesus and his ministry and not on any ministry carried out by Jesus' disciples. An analysis of the narrator's portrayal of the disciples reinforces this point.

The portrayal of the disciples in 11.2-16.20
In moving through 11.2-16.20 the implied reader discovers that the disciples are still portrayed much as they were prior to the 'sending account': even though Jesus has now given them 'authority' (10.1) and 'sent [them] out' (10.5a), there are as yet no indications that they have undertaken an independent ministry of their own. All evidence here points rather to the fact that the disciples are still acting totally within the context of Jesus' ministry to the crowds.

To begin with, the disciples appear to be almost constantly in Jesus' presence. While there are numerous passages in which their presence is not explicitly stated (11.2-30; 12.9-45; 13.53-58; 14.1-12; 15.29-31; 16.1-4), the unobtrusive manner in which they are re-introduced into the remaining scenes (12.1-8, 46-50; 13.1-52; 14.13-

36; 15.1-20, 21-28, 32-38; 16.5-12, 13-20) carries with it the implication that the disciples have been present all the while.[26]

In addition, the disciples are portrayed as speaking to no one other than Jesus himself (13.10, 36, 51; 14.15, 17, 28, 30, 33; 15.12, 23, 33, 34; 16.14, 16; cf. 14.26 and 16.7-8).[27] Thus throughout this section the disciples address neither the crowds as a whole nor individuals out of the crowds. Rather, whenever they see the need for communication with others, they call on Jesus to act as their spokesperson (14.15; 15.23).[28]

Nor are the disciples reaching out on their own in any ministry of 'powerful deeds'. While they clearly pay attention both to the crowds (13.10; 14.15; 15.33; 16.14) and to the individuals (15.23) who follow Jesus, they do not at the same time exhibit an attitude of compassion for these people. Instead, when they are faced with the needs of those around Jesus, their first response is 'Send them away!' (14.15; 15.23).[29] And when Jesus not only refuses to send hungry crowds away but calls the disciples themselves to involvement in massive feeding ministries (14.16 cf 14.21; 15.32 cf. 15.38), they respond not with the self-assurance of those who know they have the 'authority' to carry out such 'deeds of power' but rather with the incredulity of those faced with an impossible task: 'We have nothing here except five loaves of bread and two fish' (14.17); 'Where can we find enough bread in the wilderness to feed such a crowd?' (15.33). Only the fact that they first give their meager rations of bread and fish to Jesus (14.17-19; 15.34-36) and then receive them back again from him after he has 'blessed' and 'broken' them (14.19; 15.36), enables the disciples to pass out food to the crowds until everyone is 'satisfied' and there is even food to spare (14.19-20; 15.36-37). Thus even here where the disciples parallel Jesus' own 'deed of power',[30] they do so only through the direct agency of Jesus and in Jesus' presence, not as those who on their own initiative exercise the 'authority' to carry out such 'deeds of power'.[31]

But if there is no evidence within 11.2–16.20 that the disciples have either gone out (10.5a, 5b-6) or embarked on a ministry of proclamation and healing (10.1, 7-8), there is likewise no evidence that they have faced the persecution which Jesus has predicted will follow such a ministry (10.16-23 cf. 10.24-39). Nowhere is there reference to any threat against the disciples. Rather, it is Jesus alone whose life appears to be threatened at this point in the story (12.14; 14.1-12).

Nor do the disciples exhibit the 'fearlessness' with which Jesus calls them to meet persecution (10.26-33). Faced with the genuine danger of a late night storm at sea compounded by the apparent danger of what they perceive to be a 'ghost' (14.24-26), they display not 'fearlessness' but 'terror' (14.26). And when they become aware of opposition to Jesus' ministry (15.12: 'Do you know that the Pharisees took offense when they heard this word?'), they display an anxiety which reveals that they are not yet prepared even to contemplate suffering on Jesus' account.[32]

Accordingly, the picture which the narrator draws in 11.2–16.20 still portrays the disciples as those who 'follow' Jesus as he ministers to the people and 'respond' to Jesus as he takes initiatives. There is no evidence here that the disciples have embarked on their own ministry to the crowds or faced persecution as the result. Rather, the only ministry in focus is Jesus' own ministry; and the only hint of suffering to come is that which relates to Jesus himself.[33]

III. *The Tension Mounts: 16.21–25.46*

A crucial turning point in the story comes in 16.21 with an announcement by Jesus of what lies ahead for him: 'From that time on Jesus began to show his disciples that he must go to Jerusalem and suffer many things from the elders and chief priests and scribes and be killed and on the third day rise'.[34] This announcement finally states in direct language that which thus far has been communicated only indirectly—by way of subtle connections (4.12a/4.12b; 11.2-3a/11.3b-6; 14.2/14.1), unexplained allusions (10.4b), and hints (12.14): Jesus is going to suffer and die at the hands of the religious leadership.

And the direct announcement of 16.21 sets the stage for the entire sequence of events which follows: from 16.21 to 25.46 the tension mounts steadily, as Jesus moves on an unalterable course toward Jerusalem and the fate which awaits him there. The mounting tension within the story is in fact reflected by the persistence of geographical 'signposts' along the way which signal Jesus' progress on his journey toward death: (1) 'From that time on Jesus began to show his disciples that he must go to Jerusalem . . . ' (16.21); (2) 'As they were gathering in Galilee . . . ' (17.22); (3) 'Now when they came to Capernaum . . . ' (17.24); (4) 'And when Jesus had finished these sayings, he went away from Galilee and came into the region of

Judea beyond the Jordan' (19.1); (5) 'And as Jesus was going up to Jerusalem ...' (20.17); (6) 'And as they were going out of Jericho ...' (20.29); (7) 'And when they came near to Jerusalem and came to Bethphage, to the Mount of Olives ...' (21.1); (8) 'And when he came into Jerusalem ...' (21.10). With Jesus finally in Jerusalem, the tension escalates almost to the breaking point as he enters the temple itself (21.12, 23) and then subsides as he leaves the temple and retreats with his disciples to the Mount of Olives (24.1, 3). Thus it is against the backdrop of 'tension moving swiftly toward climax' that the narrator portrays Jesus and his disciples throughout 16.21–25.46.

The portrayal of Jesus in 16.21–25.46
Throughout this section of the story Jesus remains the focus of attention. At no time does he leave the scene: while other characters enter and leave the spotlight,[35] Jesus is the sole character whose presence is explicitly identified in each individual pericope between 16.21 and 25.46.[36] In addition, the narrator's phraseology still depicts Jesus as the central figure toward whom all the other characters of the story gravitate. People of all types—the disciples (17.19; 18.1, 21; 20.20; 24.1, 3), the crowds (21.14), individuals (17.14; 19.16), and elements of the religious leadership (19.3; 21.23; 22.23)—'come' to Jesus.[37] Parents 'bring' him their children so that he can lay his hands on them in blessing (19.13), while opponents 'bring' him the Roman coin which lies at the heart of a current religious controversy over the payment of taxes (22.19).[38] And Jesus 'calls' to himself on one occasion a child (18.2) and on another occasion his disciples (20.25).[39]

Further, Jesus is still depicted as active in a multi-faceted ministry to the crowds. All the way along his route toward Jerusalem—in Galilee (17.14-20), in 'the region of Judea beyond the Jordan' (19.1-2), and on the outskirts of Jericho (20.29-34)—Jesus continues to heal the sick both in ones and twos (17.14-20; 20.29-34) and in masses (19.1-2). When children are brought to him, he shows his concern for them by laying his hands on them in blessing (19.13-15). And he engages in serious dialogue with a 'would-be' follower who approaches him with a question about 'gaining eternal life' (19.16-22).

Even after his arrival in Jerusalem (21.1-11) Jesus is still involved with the crowds. Not only does he heal the sick people—the blind and the lame—who come to him in the temple during his first appearance there (21.12-17); but he also returns to the temple the next day for the purpose of teaching the crowds (21.18, 23). Even when he is interrupted by the hostile questions of the religious authorities (21.23; 22.15-17, 23-28, 34-36) so that the teaching session turns into a public debate with his opponents (21.23–22.46), the crowds remain on the scene, listening to Jesus and 'amazed at his teaching' (22.33). And when Jesus finally 'silences' his opponents (22.46 cf. 22.34), he turns back once again to the crowds and his disciples and delivers to them his final address from the temple precincts (23.1-39).[40]

But even while the narrator depicts Jesus' ongoing involvement with the crowds, he begins to focus greater attention on Jesus' interactions with a second group, the religious authorities.[41] These characters have moved on and off the scene with regularity ever since the time of John the Baptist's ministry (3.7; 8.19; 9.3, 11, 34; 12.2, 14; 15.1; 16.1; cf. 12.10, 24, 38). And even when they themselves have not been directly on the scene, there has been recurring mention of them either by the other characters of the story (5.20; 9.14; 15.12; 16.6, 11, 12; cf. 6.2, 5, 16) or by the narrator (7.29). And while from 12.1 on they assume a more prominent (and more ominous; cf. 12.14) role in the story,[42] the religious authorities do not dominate the scene prior to 16.21. Nor does this picture change significantly as Jesus and his disciples travel toward Jerusalem. While Jesus repeatedly predicts that he will suffer at the hands of the religious leadership (16.21; 20.17-19; cf. 17.9-13, 22-23), only once does an element of that leadership (the Pharisees) actually come onto the scene and approach Jesus with a hostile question (19.3-9).

But as Jesus and his disciples enter Jerusalem (21.1-11), the picture shifts dramatically. Once inside the city, Jesus' first act is to enter the temple and forcibly disrupt the economic transactions taking place there (21.12). In his words, 'It is written, "My house shall be called a house of prayer, but you have made it a den of robbers"' (21.13). And from this point on until he leaves the city for the Mount of Olives (24.1, 3), the longstanding hostility of the religious leadership toward Jesus becomes the driving force of the story. Not only do they come to him and complain about the 'messianic' accolades which he is receiving from the children in the temple (21.14-17), but they themselves go on the offensive. On the following day, when he returns to the temple to teach (21.18, 23), they approach him with the demand that he reveal the nature and source of his authority (21.23). This request sets off an extended public debate between the religious leadership and Jesus (21.23–22.46) which comes to an end only when Jesus has finally 'silenced' his opponents (22.46). But even when Jesus turns back to the crowds and his own disciples, the focus of attention does not shift: as his last words from the temple precincts, Jesus delivers a scathing denunciation of the 'hypocritical' practices of the 'scribes and Pharisees' (23.2-36) and pronounces a lament over Jerusalem '[whose] house'—in this context a clear reference to the temple itself—'has been left desolate' (23.37-39). Only when Jesus leaves the temple and retreats with his disciples to the Mount of Olives (24.1, 3) does attention finally shift away from the intense controversy between Jesus and the religious leadership.

But the narrator's primary attention throughout 16.21–25.46 lies not on the interaction between Jesus and the crowds nor even on the controversy between Jesus and his opponents but rather on the increasingly private relationship developing between Jesus and his disciples. It is to them that Jesus announces that he 'must go to Jerusalem' to face suffering and death (16.21). And from this point on until they arrive in Jerusalem (21.1-11), Jesus and his disciples share the spotlight almost exclusively. The journey to Jerusalem is characterized by constant and intense interaction between Jesus and his disciples, interrupted only occasionally by the appearance of other characters on the scene. Much of the time Jesus and his disciples appear to be alone (16.21–17.13; 17.19-23; 17.25b–18.35; 19.10-12; 19.23–20.28).[43] And even when other characters occasionally move into the spotlight with Jesus and temporarily displace the disciples, the effect of these apparent 'interruptions' is most often to focus attention back onto the ongoing dialogue between Jesus and his disciples by raising issues which they then discuss at greater length (17.14-18 cf. 17.19-20; 17.24-25a cf. 17.25b-27; 19.3-9 cf. 19.10-12; 19.13 cf. 19.14-15; 19.16-22 cf. 19.23–20.16).[44]

As Jesus and the disciples approach the end of their journey (20.29-34) and finally enter Jerusalem itself (21.1-11), the focus of attention shifts abruptly from personal to public interaction. Here the disciples drop out of the spotlight almost entirely (but see 21.1-7, 18-22), while attention focuses first on the crowds (20.29-34; 21.8-11, 14-15) and then on Jesus' opponents (21.12-13, 15-17, 23-46; 22.1-14, 15-22, 23-33, 34-40, 41-46).

But group by group the other characters disappear from the scene, leaving the spotlight focused once again on Jesus and his disciples. After Jesus succeeds in 'silencing' his opponents (22.46), they move out of the spotlight, leaving only the crowds and the disciples as an audience for Jesus (23.1).[45] And when Jesus has concluded his address to this group (23.2-39), he leaves the crowds behind, departing from the temple in the company of his disciples (24.1-2) and retreating with them to the Mount of Olives (24.3). As this section of the story closes, Jesus and his disciples are once again alone in the spotlight, gathered in a private enclave on the Mount of Olives (24.4–25.46).

The portrayal of Jesus in 16.21–25.46 thus shows him less involved overall in ministering to the crowds and more involved in debating with his opponents (21.12-13; 21.23–22.46; 23.1-39) and teaching his disciples (24.1–25.46). As a result, the story takes on an increasingly threatening tone. Tension builds almost to the breaking point as Jesus debates with the religious authorities in the temple and finally succeeds in 'silencing' them.[46] The tension then subsides but does not disappear, as Jesus takes his disciples to the Mount of Olives and there warns them once again of the persecution which they will some day face from their own opponents (24.9-14; cf. 10.16-23).[47]

But in spite of the threat posed by the hostility of the religious leadership, it is nevertheless Jesus who retains the upper hand. Although his opponents attempt repeatedly to put him on the defensive (21.15-16, 23; 22.15-17, 23-28, 34-36) and force him to condemn or compromise himself by his own words (21.23; 22.15, 34-35), Jesus at no point becomes a victim of their designs. On his first entrance into the temple (21.12-17) he not only assumes physical command of the situation, overturning money tables and driving out merchants (21.12); but he also assumes verbal command of the situation, citing Scripture in support both of his own actions (21.13) and those of the children who have welcomed him to the temple (21.16b). He redirects a politically charged question back to the ones who have raised it, leaving them scrambling for an appropriate response (21.23-27). He forces his opponents to condemn themselves through their responses to the stories which he tells (21.28-32, 33-46). He leaves them speechless with amazement in the face of his profundity (22.22, 34). When he initiates a question, he intimidates his opponents to such an extent that they can neither respond to his question nor raise others of their own (22.41-46). And after he has silenced his opponents (22.46), Jesus himself goes on the offensive with a sharply worded broadside aimed at those he has just silenced (23.1-39).

The portrayal of the disciples in 16.21–25.46

In contrast to the developing portrayal of Jesus, the portrayal of the disciples throughout 16.21–25.46 remains consistent with their previous portrayal as characters. There is still no indication that they have undergone significant change in terms of their personal associations, their attitudes toward others, or their understanding of Jesus, his words, and his ministry.

Just as before, the disciples remain constantly in Jesus' presence. Prior to Jesus' arrival in Jerusalem there are only three scenes which do not explicitly mention the presence of the disciples (19.1-2, 3-9, 16-22); and in each of these cases the most natural reading of the text leads the implied reader to assume that the disciples are present, even though they are not mentioned.[48] And while the disciples are mentioned only once (21.18-22) throughout the account of Jesus' public debates in the temple (21.12-22.46), the implication of the immediately following text (23.1) is that they have nevertheless been present all the while.[49] At no point, therefore, do the disciples appear to have gone on the journey envisioned in 10.5b-42.

Nor are they depicted as ministering to the crowds. Rather, when the disciples are explicitly placed on the scene by the narrator, they are almost always shown in interaction with Jesus alone (16.21-23, 24-28; 17.1-8, 9-13, 19-20, 22-23, 24-27;[50] 18.1-35; 19.10-12 19.23-20.16; 20.17-19, 20-28;[51] 21.1-7, 18-22; 24.1-25.46). When the disciples do come into close contact with the crowds (17.14-20; 19.13-15; 21.1-11), it is most often simply because they are following Jesus, who himself is in the midst of the crowds.[52]

There appear to be two reasons for the disciples' failure to minister to the crowds. On the one hand, they are depicted as unable to carry out a ministry of 'powerful deeds' such as that of Jesus, even though Jesus expects this of them. When a father turns to the disciples to request healing for his son (17.14-18), he finds them unable to respond to his need. Accordingly, he then brings his plea for healing directly to Jesus along with the explanation, '. . . I brought [my son] to your disciples, and they did not have the power (*ouk ēdynēthēsan*) to heal him' (17.16). After Jesus has healed the child, the disciples themselves come to Jesus privately and acknowledge their own failure with the question, 'Why did we not have the power (*ouk ēdynēthēmen*) to cast out [the demon]?' (17.19). And in response Jesus chides them for being people of 'little faith' (17.20).

On the other hand, the disciples are depicted as unwilling to carry out a ministry of 'compassion' such as that carried out by Jesus. When people bring their children to Jesus with the request that he lay his hands on them (19.13-15), the disciples' response is one of 'rebuke'; so that Jesus himself has to speak up on behalf of the children in order to prevent the disciples from keeping them at a distance.[53]

Accordingly, the disciples exhibit neither the 'authority' nor the 'compassion' requisite to carry out a ministry such as that of Jesus among the crowds. Nor do they exhibit any genuine understanding of the inevitable consequences of such a ministry. When Jesus first announces his upcoming sufferings (16.21), Peter's immediate response is to 'rebuke' him for uttering that which 'shall never happen' to him (16.22). When Jesus later repeats his warnings about the sufferings which he faces (17.9-13, 22-23; 20.17-19), the disciples at one time register 'great distress' (17.23b) but at other times make no response to Jesus' prediction (17.13),[54] or change the subject altogether (20.20-21).[55] Accordingly, they appear basically unreceptive to Jesus' words concerning his fate.

And if they fail to comprehend what Jesus says about his future suffering, they appear totally oblivious to the implications of Jesus' words for their own situation. The disciples register no awareness of the fact that if Jesus faces suffering on account of his ministry (16.21-23; 17.9-13, 22-23; 20.17-19), they too will face suffering on account of their ministry. Even when James and John, the 'sons of Zebedee', profess their willingness to 'drink the cup' which Jesus will have to drink (20.22), it seems evident that they have no conception of what their words mean.[56] The disciples' minds seem rather to be firmly lodged on thoughts of glory both present and future: Peter wishes to build three tents on the mountain in order to preserve indefinitely the present moment of glory created by Jesus' transfiguration (17.4); while the disciples as a whole appear to be constantly concerned with their future status in the Kingdom of heaven (8.1; 19.27; 20.20-21, 24).

But in spite of their present lack of involvement in ministry and their apparent inability to deal with the notion of suffering, Jesus continues to predict both ministry and suffering for the disciples. To the Jewish authorities[57] he tells a parable (22.1-14) concerning a 'king' who 'sent out (*apesteilen*)[58] his servants (*tous doulous autou*)'[59] to call 'those invited' to the wedding feast for 'his son'.[60] And at the conclusion of his diatribe against the Jewish authorities (23.1-39) Jesus announces concerning Jerusalem: 'Therefore, I send out (*apostellō*) to you prophets and wise people and scribes' (23.34; cf. 10.16).[61] Jesus' words thus imply a ministry by his disciples to the Jewish people and their leadership.[62]

But Jesus' words also speak of a ministry to the Gentiles. When 'those invited' fail to come to the wedding feast for the son (22.3, 5), the king commands his servants to 'go to the roads leading out of the city[63] and call to the wedding whomever you find' (22.9).[64] And in his final address to his disciples (24.1-25.46) Jesus tells them that before 'the end [of the age]' arrives 'this gospel of the Kingdom will be proclaimed throughout the whole world as a witness to all the nations' (24.14).[65]

And just as Jesus speaks of the ministry of his disciples, he also speaks of the persecution which they will face. In language both direct and parabolic Jesus defines for his disciples the 'cup' which will in future be theirs to 'drink' (20.22, 23): they will be 'hated' (24.9, 10), 'handed over' (24.9, 10), 'flogged' (23.34), 'persecuted from town to town' (23.34), and 'crucified' (23.34; cf. 16.24). Put into basic terms, they will 'lose their lives' (16.25) or be 'killed' (22.6; 23.34; 24.9). And in predicting these sufferings Jesus makes it clear that they will come as the result of the disciples' ministry. Persecution and death come to the 'servants' who 'call those invited to the wedding feast' (22.1-6; cf. 21.33-36); to the 'prophets, wise people, and scribes' who are 'sent [to Jerusalem]' (23.34, 37); to those through whom '[the] gospel of the Kingdom will be proclaimed throughout the whole world' (24.9-14).

Accordingly, before the disciples have even left Jesus' presence, he speaks to them of a mission to the Jewish people (22.3-4; 23.34a) and beyond that a mission to 'all the nations' (24.14; cf. 22.8-10). And at a time when the disciples exhibit neither understanding of Jesus' future sufferings nor awareness of their own, Jesus warns them of persecution and violent death (22.6; 23.34b; 24.9-13). A major disparity thus exists between the narrator's portrayal of the present attitudes and actions of the disciples and Jesus' predictions concerning their future.

IV. *The Denouement*: 26.1–28.20

The final section of the story opens in 26.1-2 with the announcement that the climax is imminent: 'And it happened that when Jesus finished all these sayings, he said to his disciples, "You know that after two days it will be the Passover and the Son of man will be handed over to be crucified"'. The death of Jesus, toward which the tension has been steadily building (cf. esp. 16.21–25.46), is no longer simply inevitable (cf. 16.21; 17.12, 22-23; 20.17-19) but also immediate. And within the final three chapters of the Gospel (26.1–28.20) the circumstances which propel Jesus into and out of that death unfold in rapid succession in a moment-by-moment narration of events.

This section comprises three major 'acts', distinct from each other with reference to characters, setting, and focus of attention. In the first of these (26.1-56) the primary characters are Jesus and his disciples. Together they dominate the narrative flow of the story from the point of Jesus' announcement concerning his death (26.1-2) to the point of his arrest in the Garden of Gethsemane (26.47-56). The other major character groups within this act, the religious authorities,[66] appear on the scene only briefly near the beginning of the act, in order to plot against Jesus (26.3-5) and make a deal with Judas (26.14-16), and again at the end, in order to consummate their plot by arresting Jesus (26.47-56). In between these appearances attention lies focused on Jesus and his disciples as they sit together at a meal in the house of Simon the leper in Bethany (26.6-13),[67] make preparations (26.17-19) and share the passover meal (26.20-29), retreat to the Mount of Olives (26.30-35) and then to Gethsemane (26.36-46), the site of Jesus' arrest (26.47-56). The act ends abruptly following Jesus' arrest with the announcement (26.56): 'Then all the disciples left him and fled'.

The second act (26.57–27.66) deals with Jesus' arrest, his trials before the Sanhedrin and Pilate, his mockery by the soldiers, his execution, and his burial. The disciples as a group are totally absent from the scene.[68] In their place it is now Jesus' opponents on all levels—religious authorities, civil authorities, Jewish crowds, Roman soldiers—who interact with Jesus. And although Jesus is still at the center of the action, the action itself has changed hands: now it is those around Jesus who take the initiative, while Jesus becomes the passive object of their actions.

In 28.1-20, the final act of this section (26.1–28.20) and of the

Gospel itself, attention focuses on the events surrounding the resurrection of Jesus. The act opens with the arrival of the women at the tomb (28.1). It goes on to describe the 'descent' of an angel to the tomb (28.2-3) and the ensuing scene in which first the Jewish guard and then the women themselves encounter that angel (28.4-7). The scene at the tomb leads to a twofold result: (1) as the women set out to tell the disciples the message of the angel—that Jesus is risen and goes before them to Galilee (cf. 26.32)—they encounter the risen Jesus, who greets them and repeats the words of the angel (28.8-10); (2) as the women go to carry this word to the disciples, certain of the Jewish guard return to Jerusalem, report to the chief priests 'all the things that have happened', and are paid to spread the rumor that Jesus' disciples have stolen his body (28.11-15). Finally, the disciples, who have been absent as a group since the time of Jesus' arrest (26.56), reappear on the scene. In 28.16-20 they go to the appointed mountain in Galilee (28.7, 10; cf. 26.32), encounter there the risen Jesus, and receive from him a commission ('Go, therefore, and make disciples of all the nations . . . ') and a promise ('. . . and behold, I am with you always, until the consummation of the age'). And with these words from the risen Jesus, the story concludes.

Accordingly, it is against the backdrop of these three acts (26.1-56; 26.57-27.66; 28.1-20) that the narrator's final portrayals of Jesus and his disciples become visible. These portrayals reflect both continuity and discontinuity with what has gone before.

The portrayal of Jesus in 26.1-28.20

Throughout the first act of this section (26.1-56) the narrator once again portrays Jesus as the central actor in the story. Jesus is present on the scene for fifty out of fifty-six verses: only when the narrator depicts the plotting of the Jewish authorities among themselves (26.3-5) and with Judas (26.14-16) is Jesus absent from the scene. And here, as before, other characters gravitate toward Jesus. As he sits at table in the house of Simon the leper, a woman 'comes' to Jesus (26.7) in order to anoint his head with expensive perfume. On the first day of unleavened bread the disciples 'come' to Jesus (26.14) to ask for instructions about preparing the passover meal. And finally, Judas and a large group of religious authorities 'come' to Jesus in Gethsemane (26.49, 50) in order to arrest him.

But while characters as varied as the woman and Judas 'come' to Jesus on occasion, there is no mention at all of the crowds who formerly flocked to him (cf. 4.25; 8.1; 12.15; 13.2; 14.13; 15.30; 19.2; 20.29; 21.8-9).[69] With his departure from the temple in 24.1 Jesus' public ministry has come to an end. Now it is the disciples with whom Jesus interacts and who, conversely, act in conjunction with him (cf. 24.1–25.46). At the passover meal Jesus sits at table 'with the twelve' (26.20). It is 'as they are eating' (26.21, 26) that Jesus warns the disciples of his betrayal and then offers them bread and wine. It is 'after they have sung a hymn' that 'they go out to the Mount of Olives' (26.30). A short while later Jesus 'comes with [the disciples]' to Gethsemane (26.36), where he 'takes with him' Peter and the two sons of Zebedee (26.37). After sharing with them the agony of his soul, he asks them to stay there and 'watch with [him]' (26.38b). Jesus then goes on ahead to pray by himself, but leaves his solitary place of prayer three times to 'come' to the disciples (26.40, 43, 45).

But not only does Jesus relate almost exclusively to his disciples throughout 26.1-56; he also carries on a constant verbal interchange with them. In twenty-eight out of fifty-six verses Jesus addresses himself directly to his disciples: to the group as a whole (26.2, 10-13, 18, 21, 23-24, 25, 26, 27-29, 31-32, 36, 45-46); to Peter, James, and John (26.38); to Peter (26.34, 40-41); to 'one who was with him' in Gethsemane (26.52-54); to Judas (26.25, 50).[70] Thus Jesus no longer ministers to the crowds but is nevertheless still active and verbal vis-à-vis his disciples.

This situation changes abruptly at 26.57, the point at which Jesus is taken from the Garden of Gethsemane. Prior to that point Jesus moves about in Gethsemane at his own initiative (26.37, 39, 40, 42, 43, 44, 45) and addresses himself freely to his disciples (26.36, 38, 40-41, 45-46, 50, 52-54) and the 'great crowd' who comes to arrest him (26.55-56). But after the disciples flee (26.56) and Jesus is led to Caiaphas (26.57), the character of the action shifts. Now it is others who act and speak, while Jesus remains essentially passive and silent.

From 26.57 through 27.66 there are only four actions attributed to Jesus: he 'stands before the governor' (27.11); he 'tastes [the wine offered to him]' (27.34), but 'will not drink it' (27.34); and finally he 'gives up his spirit' (27.50).[71] Apart from these actions, Jesus does nothing.

Even more striking, however, is Jesus' silence. Throughout his trials before the Sanhedrin and Pilate Jesus speaks only twice, once in response to the high priest (26.64) and once in response to Pilate (27.11). Otherwise he maintains an absolute silence, even in the face of direct questions (26.63; 27.14) and accusations (27.12). Throughout the mockery by the soldiers and the crucifixion itself Jesus says nothing at all. Only as he hangs on the cross does Jesus finally break this silence, crying out to God in his dying moments (27.46; cf. 27.50).

By contrast Jesus' opponents now take the initiative and make him the object of their actions and their words. This role reversal, which has already begun to take shape within 26.1-56, becomes increasingly prominent as the story progresses. Jesus' opponents plot to 'seize' him (26.4), 'hand [him] over' (26.16), 'kill' him (26.4), 'put [him] to death' (26.59; 27.1), and 'destroy' him (27.20). And when Jesus is finally within their grasp, they take corresponding action against him singly or in groups: Judas 'kisses' Jesus in mock salute (26.49), others 'lay hands on him' (26.50), 'seize him' (26.50, 57), 'bind him' (27.2), 'lead him away' (26.57), 'take him along' (27.27), 'hand him over' (26.25, 48; 27.2, 3, 18, 26), 'spit on him' (26.67; 27.30), 'strike him with the fist' (26.67), 'strike him with a rod' (26.67), 'beat him on the head' (27.30), 'flog him' (27.26), 'strip him' (27.28, 31), 'dress him' (27.31), 'put [clothing] around him' (27.28), 'put [things] upon/over his head' (27.29, 37), 'kneel down before him' in mock homage (27.29), 'crucify him' (27.26, 31, 35), 'divide his garments' (27.35), 'guard him' (27.36, 54).[72]

And as these opponents take action against Jesus, they also attack him with their words. They speak against him as 'false witnesses' (26.59-61), 'question him' (27.11), 'adjure [him]' to respond (26.63), 'bring charges against [him]' (27.12), 'condemn him' (27.3), 'cry out' for his crucifixion (27.22-23), 'mock him' (27.29, 31, 41), 'revile him' (27.39), and 'reproach him' (27.44).

Within this act, therefore, Jesus moves from the role of 'actor' to that of 'object of the action'. And in so doing, he finally experiences the suffering at which the narrator has been hinting (10.4; cf. 4.12; 11.2; 14.1-12) and which he himself has been predicting (10.38-39; 16.21; 17.9, 12, 22-23; 20.18-19; 26.2, 20-25). Thus Jesus through his suffering has now completed that 'image' of which he has already painted the 'reflection' in 10.5b-42: just as the disciples' active ministry (10.5b-15) will eventually give way to their passive acceptance of suffering (10.16-23), so Jesus' active ministry (4.17–26.56) has now given way to his own passive suffering (26.57–27.66).

But it is not merely his suffering as such which completes the 'image' of Jesus' ministry. It is rather the fact that Jesus suffers the very things which he has warned his disciples to expect for themselves. Just as he has predicted for his disciples, Jesus himself has now been 'seized' (26.4, 48, 50, 57; cf. 22.6), 'handed over' (26.15, 16, 25, 48; 27.2, 3, 18, 26; cf. 10.17, 19, 21), 'flogged' (27.26; cf. 10.17; 23.34),[73] 'led away' to stand trial before rulers (26.57; cf. 10.18), and finally 'killed/put to death' (26.4, 59; 27.1; cf. 10.21, 28; 22.6; 23.34) by means of 'crucifixion' (27.22, 23, 26, 31, 35; cf. 10.38; 23.34). Accordingly, Jesus has finally experienced, detail for detail, the suffering which he previously predicted for his disciples; and as a result the disciples are for the first time in a position to 'reflect' fully that ministry which has now been fully 'imaged' for them.[74]

In the final act of the section and of the Gospel (28.1-20) it is the risen Jesus who once again assumes a commanding role in the action. As the act opens, the women who have come to 'look at the tomb' (28.1) arrive there only to witness the 'great earth-shaking event'[75] which takes place as the 'angel of the Lord descends from heaven, approaches, rolls back to stone [from the now-empty tomb], and sits down on it' (28.2). Jesus himself is not present on the scene. But when the 'angel of the Lord' addresses the women (28.5-7), it is clear that his message comes from the risen Jesus: 'Go quickly and say to his disciples that he is risen from the dead, and behold, he goes before you to Galilee. There you will see him'. In the following verses (28.8-10) Jesus himself appears on the scene, encounters the women, and confirms that the angel's words are indeed his own message for his disciples: 'Go, report to my brothers that they should go to Galilee and there they will see me'. And when the disciples finally reappear on the scene (28.16-20), they show up on the mountain in Galilee 'to which Jesus has directed them [to go]'. Thus it is the risen Jesus who initiates the events of 28.1-16, calling into action first the 'angel of the Lord' (28.2, 5-7), then the women at the tomb (28.8, 11a), and finally the disciples themselves (28.16).[76]

As the Gospel concludes, Jesus extends this authority out into the world beyond the story with an 'all-inclusive' message to the eleven disciples gathered on the mountain in Galilee: '*All authority* in heaven and on earth has been given to me. Go, therefore, and make disciples of *all nations*, baptizing them in the name of the Father and of the Son and of the Holy Spirit, and teaching them to observe *all those things* which I have commanded you. And behold, I am with

you *always*, until the consummation of the age'. As the Gospel comes
to its close, therefore, the risen Jesus not only assumes a commanding
role vis-à-vis his disciples and 'all the nations' but establishes this
role as one for all time.

The portrayal of the disciples in 26.1-28.20

In 26.1-56 the narrator portrays the disciples in much the same light
as before. When they appear on the scene as a group, it is always in
conjunction with Jesus (26.1-2, 6-13, 17-19, 20-56); and Jesus,
conversely, never appears on the scene without his disciples.[77] When
the disciples act as a group, it is either with reference to Jesus (26.8,
17, 19, 22, 40, 43, 56)[78] or in conjunction with him (26.21, 26, 30).
And when the disciples speak as a group, it is either to Jesus (26.8-9,
17, 22; cf. 35) or with reference to him (26.19a cf. 18). As a group,
therefore, the disciples are consistently in Jesus' presence and relate
to no one but him.[79] And at the very point where other characters
enter the scene and begin to interact with Jesus (26.47-56) the
disciples disappear altogether, 'fleeing' from the Garden of Gethsemane
en masse (26.56). Thus there is still no indication that the disciples as
a group are prepared either to minister to others or to face suffering
at their hands.

Nor is there yet evidence that the disciples even understand Jesus'
mission. While they exhibit faithfulness to Jesus in certain acts, they
fail him completely at other points. On the one hand, they prepare
the passover meal 'as Jesus has directed' (26.19), eat that meal
together with him (26.20-29), and accompany him to the Mount of
Olives (26.30-35) and the Garden of Gethsemane (26.36-46). But
when Jesus instructs them to 'keep watch' with him (26.38, 41), all
they can do in response is 'sleep' (26.40, 43; cf. 45). And when Jesus'
opponents come to the garden in force to arrest him, the disciples
desert Jesus altogether, 'leaving' him in order to 'flee' from the scene
(26.47-56).

In contrast to the group as a whole, individual disciples do make
contact with persons other than Jesus. But these contacts portray the
disciples in a negative rather than a positive light and confirm that
the disciples are prepared neither to minister nor to suffer. In 26.14-
16 Judas Iscariot goes to the chief priests on his own initiative and
makes a deal with them to 'hand over' Jesus, a plan which he then
carries out at the 'right opportunity' (26.47-56; cf. 26.16). And during
the arrest scene in the Garden of Gethsemane 'one of those with

Jesus' strikes out with his sword and injures the servant of the high priest (26.51), an act for which he is immediately rebuked by Jesus (26.52-54).

This negative portrayal of the disciples is heightened within the next act (26.57–27.66). Following their flight from the Garden of Gethsemane (26.56) the disciples as a group are absent from the scene altogether throughout the whole ordeal of Jesus' appearances before the Sanhedrin (26.57, 59-68) and Pilate (27.1-2, 11-26), his mockery by the soldiers (27.27-31), his crucifixion and death (27.32-56), and his burial (27.57-66).[80] Accordingly, it is evident that the disciples are no more prepared to deal with the reality of suffering than they have been to contemplate the prospect.[81]

The portrayal of the disciples throughout 26.57–27.66, therefore, is almost totally negative. Neither as a group nor as individuals do they give any indication that they are prepared to minister to others or to accept the suffering which will accompany such a ministry. Judas Iscariot takes himself permanently out of the story by committing suicide. Ten other disciples have disappeared from the scene for the time being; and only Jesus' earlier prediction—namely, that he will 'go before [them] to Galilee' following his resurrection (26.32)—provides any hint that they will reappear.

The one visible sign of hope with regard to the disciples, however, lies in the narrator's portrayal of Peter (26.58, 69-75). It is because Peter has 'followed [Jesus]' to the courtyard of the high priest and taken the risk of sitting down with the servants 'to see the end' (26.58) that he is then confronted with regard to his identity (26.69-74). And it is because Peter 'remembers the word which Jesus has said' (26.75a; cf. 26.32) that he finally recognizes what he has done and leaves the courtyard to 'weep bitterly' over his actions (26.75b). Accordingly, Peter is still active as a disciple, 'following [Jesus]' and reflecting on 'the words which Jesus has said'. As a result, Peter's 'bitter weeping' communicates an attitude of genuine repentance on his part and hints at a future of renewed discipleship for Peter beyond the present moment of failure.[82]

Thus in spite of the predominantly negative portrayal of the disciples throughout 26.57–27.66, Jesus' prediction of 26.32 and the narrator's portrayal of Peter (26.58, 69-75) lead the implied reader to expect that the disciples will reappear in 28.1-20 and follow the resurrected Jesus to Galilee. And the implied reader is not disappointed: the entirety of chapter 28 drives toward the fulfilment of this expectation. The ultimate concern of the 'angel of the Lord' (28.5-7) is not to convince the women of Jesus' resurrection but to send them to the disciples with the message that they must go to Galilee and there see Jesus. When the women meet Jesus himself, his primary concern (28.10) is likewise with the message they are to deliver: 'Go, report to my brothers that they should go to Galilee and there they will see me'. And it is 'as the women are going [to deliver this message]' that the narrator injects the account of the guard at the tomb and the 'counter-message' which they deliver to the chief priests (28.11-15). Thus the central motif running throughout 28.1-15 is the concern that word of Jesus' resurrection get back to his disciples and that they go to Galilee to see him there.

This concern communicates two messages to the implied reader. In the first place, it communicates that Jesus still views his erstwhile followers as 'disciples' in spite of their failures of the last days: in the eyes of the angel they are still '[Jesus'] disciples' (28.7) and in the eyes of Jesus himself 'my brothers' (28.10; cf. 12.48-50). And this awareness leads the implied reader to expect that in spite of their recent failures the disciples will once again respond to Jesus as 'disciples' to 'Lord' (cf. 4.18-22; 9.9; 21.6; 26.19) and make the trip to Galilee.

Secondly, the concern with regard to Jesus' disciples communicates that these eleven men,[83] as disciples of the risen Jesus, remain subject to Jesus' word of command after his resurrection just as they were before. And this raises for the implied reader the expectation that Jesus has more for his disciples to do than simply return to Galilee: the repetition of the message (26.32; 28.7, 10) and the urgency connected with it (28.7: 'Go quickly') hint that Jesus will have a further word of command for the disciples when they get there.

In 28.16-20 the expectations of the implied reader concerning the disciples are finally met. Here they reappear on the scene, making their way to Galilee (28.16): 'And the eleven disciples went to Galilee to the mountain to which Jesus had directed them'. Thus they once again respond as obedient 'disciples' who 'follow Jesus' when he calls.[84] To be sure, their 'discipleship' is no more perfect than before. Even as they meet the risen Jesus, they display contradictory responses to him (28.17): 'And when they saw him, they worshiped him but they doubted'. Nevertheless, the fact that they have come to Galilee in direct response to the command of Jesus re-establishes them in their role as 'obedient followers' (4.18-22; 9.9; 21.6; 26.19).

And this, in turn, leads the implied reader to expect that whatever command Jesus may yet issue to his disciples will likewise meet with an obedient response.

In 28.18-20 Jesus does indeed address a command to his disciples: 'And he approached and spoke to them saying, "All authority in heaven and on earth has been given to me. Go, therefore, and make disciples of all the nations, baptizing them in the name of the Father and of the Son and of the Holy Spirit, and teaching them to observe all those things which I have commanded you. And behold, I am with you always, until the consummation of the age"'.

In these words the implied reader finally discovers the answers to his/her questions concerning the disiciples. The reason for which Jesus has called the eleven to this mountain in Galilee is to send them out on an 'all-inclusive' mission which in effect extends to universal dimensions the commission of 10.5b-42. Thus only now at the conclusion of the text does the 'expected but thus far suspended' fulfilment of Jesus' commission come into view. The Galilean commission (10.5b-42) issued by the earthly Jesus is tranformed into a universal commission (28.18-20) issued by the risen Jesus. And as a result, the commission which has not found its fulfilment in the pre-Resurrection activity of Jesus' disciples in Galilee now finds its fulfilment projected literarily into a universal mission of Jesus' disciples which extends from the Resurrection to 'the consummation of the age'.

The character of this transformed mission (28.18-20; cf. 9.35-11.1) can be seen in the fourfold usage of the word 'all': all authority, all the nations, all those things which I have commanded you, always (=all the days). The mission has its basis in the absolute authority of the risen Jesus,[85] an authority granted to him by God himself.[86] Thus the 'authority' undergirding the disciples as they go has been extended from 'authority over unclean spirits—to cast them out—and to heal every disease and every sickness' (10.1) to 'all authority in heaven and on earth' (28.18).

The mission is universal in its scope. The command to avoid the Gentiles and the Samaritans (10.5b) and to 'go rather to the lost sheep of the house of Israel' (10.6) has now been replaced by the command to 'make disciples of all the nations'.[87] The mission has thus been extended from an exclusive mission to the Jewish nation to a mission inclusive of all nations—Jewish, Samaritan, and Gentile alike.

The content of the mission is all-inclusive. The task of proclaiming that 'the Kingdom of heaven has come near' (10.7) is now defined as the task of teaching the new disciples to observe 'all those things which I have commanded you'. Accordingly, the whole body of Jesus' teachings as recorded in the narrator's story is to be passed on by the eleven to those whom they in turn 'disciple'. And since the body of Jesus' teachings includes the commission of 10.5b-42 itself, the ministry to which that commission points is now definitively incorporated into the life of discipleship (the 'observing' of 'all those things which I have commanded you').

Finally, Jesus promises to be present with the missioners 'always, until the consummation of the age'. This means that the time frame of this promise—and thus of the mission itself—extends to the very end of human history.[88] Thus the commission of 28.18-20 commits 'the eleven disciples' to a task which is not only universal in its scope ('all the nations') but also eschatological in its time frame.

V. *Perspective of the Implied and Real Readers at 28.20*

The projection by Jesus of this universal/eschatological mission into the world beyond the story has crucial implications with reference to the implied reader. Since the mission of 'the eleven disciples' extends from the resurrection of Jesus to the end of human history, and since the temporal location of the implied reader likewise lies between those two points, it is now clear that the boundaries between the story world of the text and the real world of the implied reader have disappeared. The world into which 'the eleven' will go out to 'make disciples of all the nations' is also the world of the implied reader, located between the Resurrection and the Parousia. Accordingly, the implied reader recognizes him/herself as the object of the mission to 'all the nations'. It is the implied reader whom 'the eleven' are to 'disciple'; and it is the implied reader to whom 'the eleven' are to teach the observance of 'all those things that [Jesus] has commanded [them]'.

But even more significantly, the implied reader him/herself is drawn by this route into the ongoing mission of 'the eleven disciples'. As one who has been 'discipled' *by* 'the eleven' and is therefore now a 'disciple' *like* 'the eleven', the implied reader now finds that Jesus' words in 28.18-20 apply to him/her in the same way that they apply to 'the eleven disciples'. Thus when Jesus commissions 'the eleven disciples' in 28.18-20, the implied reader hears Jesus' words as his/her own commission to 'make disciples of all the nations'. And when Jesus promises 'the eleven' that he 'is with them always, until the comsummation of the age', the implied reader hears Jesus' words as a personal promise.

Thus the Galilean commission of 10.5b-42, which has not been carried out by 'the twelve disciples' within the framework of the story, finds its fulfilment projected literarily beyond the framework of the story into a mission of universal dimensions (28.16-20) to be carried out by 'the eleven disciples' *and the implied reader* in that world which they both share, between the Resurrection and the Parousia. As a result, the implied reader of 28.18-20 understands him/herself to be not only an essential participant in the fulfilment of Jesus' commission (10.5b-42; 28.16-20) but as such an actor in the ongoing 'afterlife' of the story itself.

Accordingly, the narrator's story—which delays the fulfilment of Jesus' commission from within the text (11.1) to a point beyond its boundaries (beyond 28.20)—elicits the positive response of the implied reader to the challenge set forth in 10.5b-42 and reissued in 28.18-20. Thus the implied reader of the Gospel of Matthew must view him/herself as an active participant in the completion of the story in order to fulfil his/her 'contract' with the narrator. The 'sending account' of 9.35–11.1, the 'unfinished agenda' of Matthew's story, thus functions to call forth the obedient response of the implied reader to the missionary challenge laid down but not fulfilled within the story (9.35–11.1; 28.16-20).

For the real reader, the flesh-and-blood person who encounters the text, this means that to read the Gospel of Matthew faithfully is, finally, to accept the call of the risen Jesus: 'All authority in heaven and on earth has been given to me. Go, therefore, and make disciples of all the nations, baptizing them in the name of the Father and of the Son and of the Holy Spirit, and teaching them to observe all those things which I have commanded you. And behold, I am with you always, to the consummation of the age'.

NOTES

Notes to Chapter 1

1. The discourse proper is found in 10.5b-42, while 9.35-10.5a and 11.1 serve as the narrative framework for the discourse. For my discussion of the boundaries of this passage, see Chapter 3 below.

2. Throughout this study I shall refer to the 'author—or, as explained below the 'implied author'—of the First Gospel as 'Matthew'. By using this designation I am not intending to identify the author of the Gospel with the 'Matthew' of 9.9. Rather, I am simply adopting the traditional designation for the sake of convenience. A discussion of the historical questions concerning the identity of the author of the First Gospel lies by definition outside the scope of the present literary critical treatment of 9.35-11.1. For a description of the present approach to the text, see section III of this chapter below.

3. This examination of 9.35-11.1 attempts to make coherent sense of the passage in its present form and without making prior assumptions concerning source or redaction of the material. The one conscious assumption concerning the text which informs not only this reading of the text but also the entire study is that the author (i.e., Matthew) is ultimately responsible for the present form of the text and thus ultimately responsible for its coherence or lack of coherence.

4. It is striking, however, that just at the point where one would expect Matthew to report that the disciples 'go out' as Jesus has 'sent' them, one finds instead a reference to *Jesus'* continued mission. The significance of this unexpected development is discussed in Chapter 3 below.

5. As I argue in detail in Chapter 3 below, 10.5b-42 is a discourse in three sections (10.5b-15, 16-23, 24-42), each of which is concluded with the formulaic assertion, 'Truly, I say to you ...' (10.15, 23, 42: *amēn gar legō hymin*).

6. See my discussion in Chapter 3 below. The genitive form *tou oikou Israēl* (= of the house of Israel) is an epexegetical genitive rather than a partitive genitive. The reference is thus to Israel as a whole and not to certain 'lost sheep' within the Jewish 'fold'. Cf. Joachim Jeremias, *Jesus' Promise to the Nations* SBT, 24, trans. S.H. Hooke (London: SCM, 1958), p. 26 n. 3; Paul Hoffmann, *Studien zur Theologie der Logienquelle* (Münster: Aschendorff, 1972), p. 256, n. 79; Hubert Frankemölle, *Jahwebund und Kirche Christi*

(Münster: Aschendorff, 1974), p. 128, n. 226; Rudolf Laufen, *Die Doppelüber-lieferungen der Logienquelle und des Markusevangeliums*, BBB, 54 (Bonn: Peter Hanstein, 1980), p. 528 n. 408; John P. Meier, *Matthew*, NTM 3 (Wilmington, DE: Michael Glazier, 1980), p. 107.

7. The 'startling' nature of the shift from 10.5b-15 to 10.16-23 becomes clear already in 10.16a. Here the 'lost sheep' of 10.5b-15 have suddenly been transformed into 'wolves' vis-à-vis the disciples, who are themselves now pictured as 'sheep'.

8. Here mission is viewed not as an activity which may result either in acceptance (10.11-13a) or in rejection (10.13b-15), but rather as an activity which will necessarily result in persecution. The comparison of those 'sent out' by Jesus with sheep sent into the midst of a wolf pack (10.16a) serves to evoke an image of certain and brutal physical attack upon those 'sent out' individuals. And the definitive tone of the future indicative verbs of 10.17-18 (*paradōsousin* = they will hand [you] over/*mastigōsousin* = they will flog [you] /*achthēsesthe* = you will be led) reinforces that image and spells it out in concrete terms.

9. The term 'councils' (*synedria*) here refers to 'the local Jewish courts before which Christians will be brought' (*TDNT, s.v. 'synedrion'*, by Eduard Lohse, 7.867).

10. While the precise meaning of *eis telos* in this context is not spelled out here, a comparison of 10.22b with the other usages of *telos* in Matthew's Gospel (24.6, 13, 14) makes it appear likely that *eis telos* here denotes 'until the end of the age'.

11. The 'coming of the Son of man' is, for Matthew, that event which will issue in the end of the age (16.27, 28; 24.30, 44; 25.31; 26.64). See Chapter 3, n. 139 below.

12. The time boundaries of the mission described in 10.5b-15 must be inferred from the fact that the act of 'sending' is described as an accomplished action (*apesteilen* = he sent, 10.5a) which is both preceded (9.35) and followed (11.1) by accounts of Jesus' Galilean ministry. Thus the act of 'sending' is intended to be viewed as taking place within the time frame of Jesus' Galilean ministry.

13. Thus 10.32

14. Thus 10.33, 38, 42.

15 Thus 10.37a, 37b, 39a, 39b, 40a, 40b, 41a, 41b.

16. Heinrich August Wilhelm Meyer, *Critical and Exegetical Hand-Book to the Gospel of Matthew*, trans. Peter Christie, trans. rev. Frederick Crombie and William Stewart (New York: Funk & Wagnalls, 1884), pp. 212-13.

17. Ibid., p. 213. Thus also Hoffmann, p. 257.

18. Cf. John Peter Lange, *The Gospel According to Matthew*, trans. Philip Schaff (New York: Scribner, Armstrong, 1873), pp. 188-89. Lange argues similarly to Meyer, while at the same time leaving room for a wider

interpretation of 'the Gentiles' by defining the 'governors' as 'the provincial authorities, consisting of the Propraetors, the Proconsuls, and the Procurators' and the 'kings' as 'the rulers of Palestine, *of other countries, and of the Roman Empire*' (italics mine).

19. Joachim Lange, *Das Erscheinen des Auferstandenen im Evangelium nach Matthäus: Eine traditions- und redaktionsgeschichtliche Untersuchung zu Mt 28, 16-20*, FB, 11 (Würzburg: Echter Verlag, 1973), p. 258.

20. Ibid. William G. Thompson ('An Historical Perspective in the Gospel of Matthew', *JBL* 93 [1974], p. 253) draws the same conclusions from the text, when he argues that *tois ethnesin* (= to the Gentiles) represents the 'distinctive viewpoint' of Matthew. As Thompson sees it, this phrase 'highlights the fact that when the disciples appear before non-Jewish officials in Palestine, they will be giving testimony not merely to the governors and kings, but also to the other non-Jews present at their trial'.

21. Albert Schweitzer, *The Quest of the Historical Jesus*, trans. W. Montgomery (New York: Macmillan, 1968), pp. 358-64.

22. Since Schweitzer assumes that the discourse of 10.5b-42 represents the actual discourse given on the occasion indicated in 9.35-10.5a, he cannot avoid the difficulty which this assumption creates. Werner Georg Kümmel (*Promise and Fulfilment: The Eschatological Message of Jesus*, SBT, 23, trans. Dorothea M. Barton [London: SCM, 1957], pp. 62-63), however, points out the logical fallacy of Schweitzer's argument: 'Now it is of course correct that it is possible for Schweitzer to explain Matt. 10.23 strictly within the situation when the discourse sending out the disciples was held as recorded by Matthew. But he makes this possible only by tacitly combining the circumstances of Matt. 10 with those of Mark 6. Thus Matthew does indeed presume as the occasion for his missionary charge the dispatch of the disciples on a mission (10.5ff.), but Schweitzer then transfers the charge at once to the situation described in Mark 6.6ff., so that now the return of the disciples and Jesus' endeavor to separate himself from the crowd (Mark 6.30ff.) appear as the sequel in time to the mission, although Matt. 14.13 paralleled in Mark 6.30 in fact omits the return of the disciples. This combination produces therefore an *artificial* connexion between the missionary discourse and the disciples' return; and to this it must be added that nothing in the sources affords grounds for the assertion that Jesus was disappointed that the disciples came back without the end of the world having appeared'.

23. Schweitzer, pp. 360-61: 'The prediction of the Parousia of the Son of Man is not the only one which remained unfulfilled. There is the prediction of sufferings which is connected with it. To put it more accurately, the prediction of the appearing of the Son of Man in Matt. x.23 runs up into a prediction of sufferings, which working up to a climax, forms the remainder of the discourse at the sending forth of the disciples. This prediction of sufferings has as little to do with objective history as the prediction of the Parousia'.

24. While Schweitzer specifically refers to the sufferings described in the verses following 10.23, his own logic (namely, that the sufferings of the disciples are unhistorical, just as the occurrence of the Parousia is unhistorical) would force him to conclude that 10.17-22 is to be considered in the same light as 10.23ff. However, since Schweitzer does not deal with the question of how to construe 10.18 within the context of the discourse as a whole, he leaves unanswered the question of what Jesus meant by the reference to 'the Gentiles', a question which must be resolved regardless whether one views the prediction as having been fulfilled.

25. Schweitzer, p. 363.

26. Meyer's exegesis of these verses is not convincing. 10.17b consists of a synonymous parallelism set up in chiastic form and built around two future indicative active verbs (*paradōsousin/mastigōsousin*): (A) for they will hand you over; (B) to the councils; (B') and in their synagogues; (A') they will flog you. 10.18 does not fit into this synonymous parallelism; and the verb here (*achthēsesthe* = you will be led) is a future indicative passive. Thus it is clear that 10.17b and 10.18 are syntactically independent statements which are merely connected to each other by the particle *kai* (= and). The *autois* (= to them) of 10.18, therefore, does not refer back to the implied subject ('they', i.e., the Jews) of 10.17b. Rather, *autois* refers back to the immediate antecedents, *hēgemonas* (= governors) and *basileis* (= kings), while *ethnesin* (= to the Gentiles) refers to a group distinct from the *hēgemonas* and *basileis*.

27. Theodor Zahn, *Introduction to the New Testament*, vol. 2. trans. from 3rd German edn, John Moore Trout, William Arnot Mather, Louis Hodous, Edward Strong Worcester, William Hoyt Worrell, Rowland Backus Dodge (Edinburgh: T & T Clark, 1909), p. 558.

28. R.C.H. Lenski, *Interpretation of St. Matthew's Gospel* (Columbus, Ohio: Lutheran Book Concern, 1932), p. 379. In a similar vein, A. Schlatter (*Der Evangelist Matthäus: Seine Sprache, sein Ziel, seine Selbständigkeit. Ein Kommentar zum ersten Evangelium* [Stuttgart: Calwer, 1957], p. 355) notes that 'von Vers 15 an die Sprüche nicht mehr bei derjenigen Lage verweilen, die durch die Entsendung der Zwölf in die galiläischen Dörfer entstand. Diese Worte überschauen *die ganze apostolische Wirksamkeit*' (italics mine).

29. Cf. the view of John A. Broadus (*Commentary on the Gospel of Matthew* [Philadelphia: American Baptist Pub. Society, 1886], p. 210) that Jesus is here giving his twelve disciples 'instruction not only for this mission, but for all their subsequent labors in his name'. Charles R. Erdman (*The Gospel of Matthew* [Philadelphia: Westminster, 1920], p. 77) explains that 'the present and the more distant needs were in [Jesus'?] mind at the same time'. By this Erdman means that 'some of the exhortations and warnings belong to the days of the earthly ministry of our Lord; and others have their

application to all the intervening ages and to the experiences of his followers even in years yet to come'.

30. On the composite nature of 10.5b-42, see, for example, the following: Alfred Edersheim, *The Life and Times of Jesus the Messiah*, vol. 1 (New York: E.R. Herrick, 1886), p. 640 (tentatively phrased); Alfred Plummer, *An Exegetical Commentary on the Gospel According to S.* [sic] *Matthew* (London: Robert Scott, 1915), p. 148; Zahn, p. 558; Alan Hugh McNeile, *The Gospel According to St. Matthew* (London: Macmillan, 1952), p. 139; Frederick C. Grant, 'The Mission of the Disciples, Mt 9.35-11.1 and Parallels', *JBL* 35 (1916), p. 305; Erich Klostermann, *Das Matthäusevangelium*, HNT, 4, 2nd edn (Tübingen: J.C.B. Mohr [Paul Siebeck], 1927), p. 89; M.-J. Lagrange, *Evangile selon Saint Matthieu*, EtBib (Paris: Librairie Lecoffre, 1948), p. 194; Benjamin W. Bacon *Studies in Matthew* (New York: Henry Holt, 1930), pp. 196-98; Petrus Dausch, *Die drei älteren Evangelien*, 4th edn, (Bonn: Peter Hanstein, 1932), p. 170; Floyd V. Filson, *The Gospel According to St. Matthew*, HNTC (New York: Harper & Row, 1960), p. 131; Georg Strecker, *Der Weg der Gerechtigkeit: Untersuchung zur Theologie des Matthäus* (Göttingen: Vandenhoeck & Ruprecht, 1962), p. 41; Paul Gaechter, *Das Matthäus-Evangelium* (Innsbruck: Tyrolia, 1964), p. 320; Francis Wright Beare, 'The Mission of the Disciples and the Charge: Matthew 10 and Parallels', *JBL* 89 (1970), p. 2; Morna D. Hooker, 'Uncomfortable Words: X. The Prohibition of Foreign Missions (Mt 10.5-6)', *ExpTim* 82 (1971), p. 361; David Hill, *The Gospel of Matthew*, NCB (London: Oliphants, 1972), p. 188; Eduard Schweizer, *The Good News According to Matthew*, trans. David E. Green (Atlanta: John Knox, 1977), p. 242; Robert E. Morosco, 'Redaction Criticism and the Evangelical: Matthew 10, a Test Case', *JETS* 22 (1979), p. 328; Meier, pp. 102-103; Robert H. Gundry, *Matthew: A Commentary on His Literary and Theological Art* (Grand Rapids, Michigan: William B. Eerdmans, 1982), p. 192; Karen A. Barta, 'Mission in Matthew: The Second Discourse as Narrative', in *SBL 1988 Seminar Papers*, SBLSP, 27 (Atlanta: Scholars, 1988), pp. 527, 534.

31. Zahn, p. 558. In this case it appears to make no difference whether one approaches the question from the standpoint of Matthean priority, as does Zahn (pp. 601-17), or from the standpoint of Markan priority, as does Plummer (p. ix). Plummer's conclusion (p. 148) that 'Mat. has combined the report in Mk., which is our best guide as to what was said on this occasion, with material which belongs to other occasions' does not differ in essence from Zahn's conclusion, since both Zahn and Plummer hold Matthew responsible for the compilation of originally disparate materials.

32. Grant, p. 306: 'V. 18, *kai tois ethnesin* (cf. 24.9-14) perhaps meant (as in Mk. 13.10, its parallel) the heathen world at large; but Mt., in view of vv. 5f., 23b, thinks only of the heathen military residents in Palestine'.

33. Ibid., pp. 306-307: 'Mt., in harmony with his general conception of the present discourse, ... may possibly think that it refers to the early

Palestinian Christian mission after the death of Jesus (i.e., in his own day)'.

34. Ibid., p. 306. Cf. Zahn, p. 558; Gaechter, p. 329; Hooker, p. 361.

35. See, for example, Edersheim, pp. 640-41; McNeile, p. 142; Bacon, p. 198; Günther Bornkamm, 'End-Expectation and Church in Matthew', in *Tradition and Interpretation in Matthew*, NTL, trans. Percy Scott (Philadelphia: Westminster, 1963), p. 18; Strecker, p. 41; Heinz Eduard Tödt, *The Son of Man in the Synoptic Tradition*, NTL, trans. Dorothea M. Barton (Philadelphia: Westminster, 1965), p. 91; Siegfried Schulz, *Die Stunde der Botschaft: Einführung in die Theologie der vier Evangelisten* (Hamburg: Furche, 1967), p. 231; Hill, p. 188; John Wilkinson, 'The Mission Charge to the Twelve and Modern Medical Missions', *SJT* 27 (1974), p. 314.

36. Bornkamm, p. 18, Cf. the virtually identical phrasing of Tödt (p. 91). But while Bornkamm and Tödt contrast the emphases on 'mission' and 'Church', the more common approach is to combine these emphases in order to speak of 'the Church's mission'. See, for example, Edersheim, p. 640; Schulz, p. 231; Hill. p. 188. Walter Grundmann (*Das Evangelium nach Matthäus* ThHKNT, 1 [Berlin: Evangelische Verlagsanstalt, 1968], p. 284) points in the same direction with his reference to the 'Sendung und Schicksal der Boten der Gemeinde Jesu schlechthin'.

37. By 'intention of the text' I mean that which the author of any given text intends that text to communicate to the reader.

38. Bacon, pp. 197-98.

39. Filson, p. 131. Cf. the comments of C.H. Giblin ('Theological Perspective and Mt 10, 23b', *TS* 29 [1968], p. 642), who observes that 'in the second major section (10.16-23), in which the Twelve are still being addressed, there are warnings and assurances which, even to the Evangelist's knowledge, go well beyond the temporal and spatial framework of the public life [of Jesus]'.

40. Hooker, p. 361.

41. Bacon, p. 198: 'the compiler has ceased to be a historian, he is now a preacher addressing his own age'.

42. Ibid., p. 197.

43. See n. 30 above.

44. See, for example, Zahn's well-reasoned (if somewhat blunt!) negative argumentation against the 'Galilean' approach (cited above) or Bacon's equally incisive positive argumentation to the same effect (p. 197): 'These two interjected paragraphs [10.16-39] carry the reader far beyond the situation contemplated in the Sending into Galilee. No return of the Twelve is contemplated, the horizon extends temporally to the second Coming (verse 23) geographically to the ends of the earth (verse 22). The persecutions to be suffered are at the hands of "governors and kings", before whom confessors will be brought to trial "for a witness to them and to the Gentiles"'.

45. Willoughby C. Allen, *A Critical and Exegetical Commentary on the Gospel According to St. Matthew*, ICC (New York: Charles Scribner's Sons, 1907), p. 101. Cf. Theodore H. Robinson, *The Gospel of Matthew*, MNTC (Garden City, New York: Doubleday, Doran & Co., 1928), p. 86; Morosco, p. 325.

46. Beare, p. 3.

47. E. Schott, 'Die Aussendungsrede Mt 10. Mc 6. Lc 9. 10.', *ZNW* 7 (1906), p. 144. Contrary to most scholars who take this approach, however, Schott operates on the assumption of Matthean priority. He thus attributes the more 'historical' approach of Mark and Luke to the fact that they stand at a *greater distance* from the event described than does Matthew. As he sees it, 'sie [i.e., Mark and Luke] zeigen bei diesem Stoffe nicht mehr und nicht weniger Interesse als bei jedem andern, sie referieren über die Tatsache der Aussendung der Zwölf, sie wollen ein Stück aus der Geschichte Jesu bieten'. Matthew, on the other hand, writes for a time in which 'die Gemeinde hat noch nicht begonnen, selbst produktiv tätig zu sein. Die Aufzeichnung der Herrnworte hat den Zweck, die Lehren und Grundsätze des Meisters in lebendiger Weise für das eigene Leben verwendbar zu machen'.

48. Ferdinand Hahn, *Mission in the New Testament*, SBT, no. 47, trans. Frank Clarke (London: SCM, 1965), pp. 124-25. Cf. Frankemölle, p. 143. Ulrich Luz ('Die Jünger im Matthäusevangelium', *ZNW* 62 [1971], pp. 145-46), who on the one hand recognizes a shift from the first to the second half of the discourse (pp. 145-46), nevertheless appears to give the upper hand to 'transparence' in his conclusion (p. 146) that 'ein formaler Bruch ist aber zwischen 10.16 und 17 nicht feststellbar. Die Gebote Jesu sind eben grundsätzlich für immer gültig'. Gerhard Barth ('Matthew's Understanding of the Law' in *Tradition and Interpretation in Matthew*, NTL, trans. Percy Scott [Philadelphia: Westminster, 1963], pp. 100-101), while he does not use the terminology of 'transparence', nevertheless analyzes Matthew's intentions in a similar fashion: '[Through Matthew's redaction of his sources] the situation of the historical "then" is left behind, and the missionary discourse now speaks simply of the sending forth of the disciples. Still more, it is not a matter of sending out special missionaries but sending forth and persecution are essential for discipleship as such (10.24f.). To be a Christian means to be sent forth. . .'

49. This underlying account concerning Jesus and his twelve disciples extends only through v. 16 at the most. Luz concludes (pp. 145-46) that 'in der Aussendungsrede keine konsequente Historisierung des Jüngerverständ-nisses festzustellen ist. Sie liesse sich ohnehin nur für 10. 1-16 mehr oder weniger überzeugend vertreten, spätestens in v. 17f. aber wird der transparente Charakter der Rede deutlich'. But while he works with the categories of 'historicism' and 'transparence', Luz recognizes (p. 146, n. 23a) the difficulty involved in attempting to distinguish between the 'historicistic' and the 'transparent' elements of the chapter. P. Ternant ('L'envoi des douze aux

brebis perdues (Mt 9-10)', *AssSeign* 42 [1970], p. 30), on the other hand, considers this distinction between the two types of elements within the chapter to be self-evident: he resolves the question of incongruent elements by remarking that 'Mt a jugé ses lecteurs assez intelligents [sic!] pour distinguer, dans sa compilation du ch. 10, ce qui ne valait que pour la mission galiléenne et ce qui est applicable à tout le temps de l'Église'.

50. Schuyler Brown, 'The Mission to Israel in Matthew's Central Section', *ZNW* 69 (1978), p. 80.

51. Frankemölle, p. 127 n. 222.

52. Cf. Brown's observation (p. 73 n. 1): 'To refer to the section as a "discourse" implies that the narrative subsections at the beginning (9.35-36 [sic]; 10.1-5a) and the end (11.1) are secondary and subordinate to the sayings material, whereas, in fact, they perform an essential function within the section as a whole'.

53. It is instructive to note that Schuyler Brown, while he does not downplay the significance of the narrative framework, nevertheless ends up with a somewhat confused interpretation of 10.5b-6. In 'The Mission to Israel in Matthew's Central Section' he posits (p. 80) a 'point-for-point' correlation between the ministry of the earthly Jesus and that of Matthew's church. Consequently, he is left with the necessary conclusion (pp. 89-90) that Matthew's church knows itself to be called to a mission among the Jews, while others have received a call to go to the Gentiles: 'If the Central Section [9.35-11.1] envisages gentiles coming to believe in Jesus through the witness given by the sufferings of his disciples, then it presupposes the *existence* of a gentile mission, even though Mark's explicit reference to this mission (Mk 13.10) has been dropped. That is to say, the Central Section excludes not the gentile mission as such but only the *participation* in this mission by the Matthean community, who are addressed through the transparency of the twelve disciples (Mt. 10.5b-6). There is, then, no contradiction between Mt. 10.18 and Mt. 10.23. The phrase *eis martyrion autois* (v. 18) implies a *separate* mission for Jews and gentiles, and, as far as the Central Section is concerned, the responsibility of Matthew's community is strictly limited to the former'. And in Brown's article 'The Two-fold Representation of the Mission in Matthew's Gospel' (*StTh* 31 [1977], pp. 21-32) he argues in similar fashion (p. 30): 'The Central Section implicitly recognizes the existence of the gentile mission, but at the same time it excludes this mission from the responsibility of the Matthean community, which is "sent", like Jesus himself (Mt. 15.24), only to the lost sheep of the house of Israel'. But he then concludes as follows (ibid., p. 30): 'This does not prevent gentiles from being positively influenced by the witness given by the persecuted Matthean disciples. *But any such coming to faith on the part of gentiles remains extrinsic to the missionary responsibility of the Matthean community—until Jesus' Final Mandate* [i.e., 28.18-20]' (italics mine). But at what point in the historical situation of the Matthean community does it know itself to be

called to an exclusively Jewish mission while it recognizes that others are called to a Gentile mission? Brown's proposal does not resolve this question. Instead Brown posits of the Matthean community that which can be posited only of the twelve disciples of Jesus: it is they alone for whom 'any such coming to faith on the part of gentiles remains extrinsic to [their] missionary responsibility . . . until Jesus' Final Mandate'. For the Matthean community, *that community which has in front of it both 10.5b-6 and 28.19*, the only point at which the Gentile mission 'remains extrinsic to [their] missionary responsibility' appears to be the 'literary moment' which lies *between the reading of 10.5b-6 and the reading of 28.19*. There is for them no other possible time frame within which 'Jesus' Final Mandate' still stands in the future. Accordingly, Brown's proposal turns out in the end to be no real solution after all.

54. For example, attempts to interpret the predictions of 10.18 and 10.23 in terms of such a setting appear forced rather than compelling. See above.

55. The present reference to 'the literary critical question' uses that terminology as do literary critics in general and not as has previously been customary among biblical scholars, who have used the term to refer to source and/or form criticism of the biblical texts. As Norman R. Petersen (*Literary Criticism for New Testament Critics*, GBSNT [Philadelphia: Fortress, 1978], p. 10 n. 4) explains, 'It should be noted that for most historical critics "literary criticism" refers to *source* criticism! Otherwise the adjective "literary" is used principally in connection with the notion of literary history which refers to the history of the form and style of the material used in the composition of biblical writings. As a result of this usage, biblical critics have until recently lacked an understanding of literature like that found among literary critics'.

56. Only very recently have New Testament scholars begun to use this approach in studying the Gospels. In the early 1970's Roland Mushat Frye ('A Literary Perspective for the Criticism of the Gospels', in *Jesus and Man's Hope*, v. 2, ed. Donald G. Miller and Dikran Y. Hadidian [Pittsburgh: Pittsburgh Theological Seminary, 1971], pp. 193-221) and Norman Perrin ('The Evangelist As Author: Reflections on Method in the Study and Interpretation of the Synoptic Gospels and Acts', *BibRes* 17 [1972], pp. 5-18) pointed Gospel scholarship in this new direction by calling for the application of literary critical categories to the study of the Gospels. Since that time extensive work has been done on the literary critical analysis of the Gospels, much of it focusing on the Gospel of Mark. See, for example, the following representative list of works: (Gospel of Mark) Robert C. Tannehill, 'The Disciples in Mark: the Function of a Narrative Role', *JRel* 57 (1977), pp. 386-405; Norman R. Petersen, '"Point of View" in Mark's Narrative', *Sem.* 12 (1978), pp. 97-121; Robert C. Tannehill, 'The Gospel of Mark as Narrative Christology', *Sem.* 16 (1979), pp. 57-95; Frank Kermode, *The*

Genesis of Secrecy: On the Interpretation of Narrative (Cambridge, Massachusetts: Harvard University, 1979); Willem S. Vorster, 'Mark: Collector, Redactor, Author, Narrator?', *JTSA* 31 (1980), pp. 46-61; Joanna Dewey, *Markan Public Debate: Literary Technique, Concentric Structure, and Theology in Mark 2.1–3.6*, SBLDS, 48 (Chico, California: Scholars Press, 1980); Thomas E. Boomershine and Gilbert Bartholomew, 'The Narrative Technique of Mark 16.8', *JBL* 100 (1981), pp. 213-23; Thomas E. Boomershine, 'Mark 16.8 and the Apostolic Commission', *JBL* 100 (1981), pp. 225-39; Robert M. Fowler, *Loaves and Fishes: The Function of the Feeding Stories in the Gospel of Mark*, SBLDS, 54 (Chico, California: Scholars Press, 1981); Joanna Dewey, 'Point of View and the Disciples in Mark', in *SBL 1982 Seminar Papers*, SBLSP, 21 (Chico, California: Scholars, 1982), pp. 97-106; David Rhoads, 'Narrative Criticism and the Gospel of Mark', *JAAR* 50 (1982), pp. 411-34; David Rhoads and Donald Michie, *Mark As Story: An Introduction to the Narrative of a Gospel* (Philadelphia: Fortress, 1982); Jack Dean Kingsbury, *The Christology of Mark's Gospel* (Philadelphia: Fortress, 1983); (Gospel of Matthew) D.L. Barr, 'The Drama of Matthew's Gospel: A Reconsideration of Its Structure and Purpose', *TD* 24 (1976), pp. 349-59; Janice Capel Anderson, 'Point of View in Matthew—Evidence', Paper presented to the SBL Symposium on Literary Analysis of the Gospels and Acts, December 1981; H.J.B. Combrink, 'The Macrostructure of the Gospel of Matthew', in *Structure and Meaning in Matthew 14-28*, Neo, 16 (Stellenbosch: New Testament Society of South Africa, 1983), pp. 1-20; idem, 'The Structure of the Gospel of Matthew as Narrative', *TynBul* 34 (1983), pp. 61-90; Jack Dean Kingsbury 'The Figure of Jesus in Matthew's Story: A Literary-Critical Probe', *JSNT* 21 (1984), pp. 3-36; idem, *Matthew As Story* (Philadelphia: Fortress, 1986); Daniel Patte, *The Gospel According to Matthew: A Structural Commentary on Matthew's Faith* (Philadelphia: Fortress, 1987).

57. Robert Scholes and Robert Kellogg, *The Nature of Narrative* (New York: Oxford University, 1966), p. 4. On the Gospel of Matthew as 'narrative', see Combrink, 'Macrostructure', p. 5; idem, 'Structure', p. 66.

58. Rhoads, 'Narrative Criticism', pp. 412-13. Cf. Frye, p. 220 n. 42; Dewey, *Markan Public Debate*, pp. 5-6; Vorster, p. 57; Fowler, pp. 40-41.

59. As Vorster explains it (p. 57), 'The focus is upon the text as a completed signifier, a text with its own literary world which should be read from the text itself and not from the historical situation out of which it arose or within which the author had worked... It is the written text itself, the world of the text and not the real world to which it refers or not refers [sic], that is of importance'. Cf. Rhoads, p. 413; Rhoads and Michie, pp. 3-4.

60. Perrin. p. 16. Cf. Dewey, *Markan Public Debate*, p. 10.

61. Perrin, p. 16.

62. The three major sources on which I draw in the following delineation of literary critical categories are Seymour Chatman's *Story and Discourse*:

Narrative Structure in Fiction and Film (Ithaca, New York: Cornell University, 1978), Susan Sniader Lanser's *The Narrative Act: Point of View in Prose Fiction* (Princeton: Princeton University, 1981), and Wayne Booth's *The Rhetoric of Fiction*, 2nd edn. (Chicago: University of Chicago, 1983).

63. Chatman, p. 28.

64. That the Gospel writers are, in fact, to be viewed as 'authors' becomes clear from the following observation by Perrin (pp. 9-10): 'The consequence of recent developments in the study of the [Synoptic Gospels and Acts] has been ... the recognition that the evangelists are genuinely authors, authors using traditional material but nonetheless authors: they write for a definite purpose, they give their work a distinct and individual structure, they have thematic concerns which they pursue, the characters in the story they each tell function as protagonists in a plot...' Cf. Fowler, p. 40. On the use of the designation 'Matthew' for the author of the First Gospel, see. n. 2 above.

65. Booth, pp. 70-71. Cf. Chatman, p. 148.

66. Rhoads and Michie, p. 137. Cf. Chatman, pp. 149-50; Lanser, p. 116.

67. In reality the communications transaction is ultimately carried out by the real author and the real reader. But since both of these 'real' people lie outside of the written text, this final level of communication cannot be analyzed by studying the written text. For that reason it is necessary to speak of the 'implied author' and the 'implied reader'. See Chatman, pp. 28, 31, 151; Lanser, pp. 117-18.

68. For discussions of the role of the narrator in narrative, see Booth, pp. 149-65; Chatman, pp. 147-51. In the interest of simplicity of expression within the present analysis I shall when necessary refer to both the 'narrator in general' and 'Matthew's narrator' as 'he'. I shall designate the 'implied reader' as 'he/she'.

69. Although Chatman (pp. 150-51) distinguishes between the 'implied reader' and the person to whom the narrator addresses the narrative, the 'narratee', I shall not maintain that distinction within this study. Since Matthew in no way distinguishes between the functions of 'implied reader' and 'narratee' in his Gospel, I shall simply dispense with the term 'narratee' altogether and speak only of the 'implied reader'.

70. Booth (pp. 158-59) defines 'reliability' as follows: 'For lack of better terms, I have called a narrator *reliable* when he speaks for or acts in accordance with the norms of the work (which is to say, the implied author's norms), *unreliable* when he does not'.

71. For further discussion of these basic elements of narrative, see Chapter 2 section II below.

72. Chatman, p. 148.

73. Ibid., p. 21.

Notes to Chapter 2

1. As I have noted in Chapter 1, I will refer throughout the present analysis not to the 'author' and 'reader' but rather to the 'implied author' and 'implied reader', since it is these alone which can be recovered through the analysis of the written text. However, where I cite other works (such as Lanser's for example) which refer to 'author' and 'reader' instead of 'implied author' and 'implied reader', I shall simply use the author's terminology without further clarification.

2. Lanser, p. 238.

3. As Lanser explains it (p. 238), 'linearity plays a major role in determining the way information about the narrative point of view is amassed by the reader of a text. In other words, because discourse is sequential, reading takes place in a temporal frame, and texts are decoded through a system of linear construction and revision. This does not, of course, mean that every piece of information is treated equally by a reader and is processed only in terms of its linear position, but it does mean that linearity cannot be overlooked'. See also M.H. Abrams, *A Glossary of Literary Terms*, 4th edn (New York: Holt, Rinehart and Winston, 1981), pp. 149-50; Fowler, pp. 152-53; Wolfgang Iser, *The Implied Reader: Patterns of Communication in Prose Fiction from Bunyan to Beckett* (Baltimore: Johns Hopkins University, 1978), pp. 280-81.

4. Lanser, pp. 85-225.

5. Boris Uspensky, *A Poetics of Composition: The Structure of the Artistic Text and Typology of a Compositional Form*, trans. Valentina Zavarin and Susan Wittig (Berkeley: University of California, 1973), pp. 8-100. According to Uspensky the point of view of a narrative text exists on five distinct but interrelated 'planes': ideological or evaluative, phraseological, spatial, temporal, and psychological. See Chapter 2 below for further clarification of Uspensky's categories.

6. The following analysis will be structured according to Lanser's summary chart (p. 224) entitled 'descriptive poetics of point of view'.

7. Ibid., p. 224.

8. Ibid., p. 85.

9. Ibid., p. 86. It is crucial to note at this point that Lanser in effect merges the concepts of 'author'/'implied author' and 'narrator' rather than clearly distinguishing between them. As her argument progresses, she shifts her terminology from 'author' (pp. 85-86) to 'speaker' (pp. 86-94) to '(public) narrator' (pp. 137-38). Lanser defines her position on the distinction between 'implied author' and 'narrator' as follows (pp. 131-32): 'When we enter the "story world" we do not leave behind the extrafictional voice or "implied author"; that voice remains a significant if hidden presence throughout our reading of the fictional discourse... Difficulties about the nature of the narrative voice begin to multiply, however, when we try to distinguish

between this extrafictional speaker and a narrator within the fictional discourse who seems indistinguishable from the authorial voice'. In contrast to Lanser I shall distinguish between 'implied author' and 'narrator' on the basis of their respective functions as identified in Chapter 1 above. Accordingly, I shall identify the storyteller as 'the narrator' or 'Matthew's (i.e., the implied author's) narrator'.

10. Ibid., p. 86. In light of Lanser's interchangeable usage of terminology (see n. 9 above), I have taken the liberty to interpret her reference to the 'speaker' in terms of the 'narrator'. Consequently, my entire application of Lanser's 'descriptive poetics of point of view' will be in reference to the narrator of Matthew's Gospel (i.e., to the 'literary voice' which tells the story) and not to either the implied author or the flesh-and-blood writer of the Gospel.

11. Ibid., p. 86.

12. Lanser (p. 142) defines 'diegetic authority' as the 'authority attached to an authorial voice' and 'mimetic authority' as the 'authority that attaches to the acting persona'.

13. Lanser, p. 151.

14. Ibid., pp. 153-54.

15. Ibid., p. 224.

16. Ibid., p. 160. See also Booth, pp. 151-54; Gérard Genette, *Narrative Discourse: An Essay in Method*, trans. Jane E. Lewin (Ithaca, New York: Cornell, 1980), p. 186; and, somewhat differently, Lubomir Dolezel, 'The Typology of the Narrator: Point of View in Fiction' in *To Honor Roman Jakobson: Essays on the Occasion of his Seventieth Birthday*, JLSM, 31 (The Hague: Mouton, 1967), pp. 548-51. Lanser uses the terms 'autodiegesis' and 'heterodiegesis' to refer to the 'narrator as sole protagonist' and the 'uninvolved narrator' respectively. I have chosen to disregard her terminology in the interest of simpler, less obscure language.

17. By 'narrative framework' I refer to all finite verbs except those located either within direct discourse or within one of Matthew's 'formula quotations' (see n. 19 below).

18. Of 190 finite verbs constituting the narrative framework of 1.1–9.34, 142 are in the third person singular and 48 in the third person plural.

19. 1.22-23; 2.15, 17-18, 23; 4.14-16; 8.17. Cf. 3.3.

20. The narrator could, to be sure, be evaluating events in which he was a participant or at least an eyewitness.

21. As noted above (n. 9), however, I shall continue to refer to the storyteller as 'the narrator' or 'Matthew's narrator' and not simply as 'Matthew'. For another approach to this question, see Kingsbury, 'Figure of Jesus', p. 3.

22. See, for example, the representative definitions of 'omniscience' found in Booth (p. 160), Genette (p. 189), and Scholes and Kellogg (p. 51).

23. Rhoads and Michie, p. 36.

24. 1.20; 2.12, 13, 19, 22.

25. The narrator reports that Joseph does not 'wish' to disgrace Mary (1.20); that he has come to an (apparently personal) decision to divorce her (1.19); that he is 'pondering' the matter (1.20); that Herod and the populace of Jerusalem are 'troubled' when the magi come searching for the newly-born 'King of the Jews' (2.3); that the magi 'rejoice' when they see the star (2.10); that Herod is 'very angry' when he learns what the magi have done (2.16); and that Joseph is 'afraid' to remain in Judea (2.22). Related to the above cases of 'mind-reading' are numerous instances in which the narrator reports the thoughts or feelings of a character directly in conjunction with that character's verbal response to a situation: 8.27 (the people); 9.8, 33; cf. 7.28 (the crowds); 8.10 and 9.30 (Jesus). In these cases, however, it could be argued that the narrator is simply extrapolating from the verbalization to the feeling.

26. The narrator knows what the scribes are saying in their private huddle (9.3) as well as what the woman with the hemorrhage is saying to herself (9.21).

27. Such 'private' events include the experience in which Jesus sees the heavens open and the Spirit of God descend upon him (3.16) and hears the voice from heaven pronounce him to be the Son of God (3.17; cf. Kingsbury, *Matthew as Story*, pp. 49-50) and the entire experience of Jesus' temptation, from the opening remark that he 'was led by the Spirit' into the wilderness to the closing comment that the angels 'came to him and served him' (4.1-11). The other notable piece of 'private' information to which the narrator has access is a non-event even more 'private' in nature than the first two, namely that Joseph does not 'know' (i.e., have sexual relations with) Mary before the birth of Jesus (1.25).

28. 9.2, 4, 22. In her discussion of the omniscience of Matthew's narrator, Anderson (pp. 18-22) distinguishes between what she terms 'simple inside views' and 'complex inside views', instances such as the above, in which the narrator 'implies or tells the reader that Jesus has an inside view of a third party' (p. 18). See Anderson's charts labelled 'Simple' and 'Complex' (pp. 19-20) for her categorization of the narrator's 'omniscient' statements.

29. Norman Friedman ('Point of View in Fiction: The Development of a Critical Concept' in *Approaches to the Novel: Materials for a Poetics*, ed. Robert Scholes [San Francisco: Chandler, 1961], pp. 113-42) distinguishes between what he terms 'neutral omniscience' and 'editorial omniscience'. 'Neutral omniscience' occurs when there is an 'absence of direct authorial intrusions' (p. 128), while 'editorial omniscience' is characterized by 'the presence of authorial intrusions and generalizations about life, manners, and morals, which may or may not be explicitly related to the story at hand' (p. 126).

30. 1.22-24; 2.15, 17-18, 23; 4.12-16 and 8.17 refer to events which happened in order to 'fulfil [*plēroō*] that which was spoken (by the Lord)

through the prophet(s)'. And although it does not make use of the verb *plēroō*, 3.3, achieves the same result (i.e., of linking 'fulfilment' to 'prediction') with the variant formula, 'This is that which was spoken through the prophet. . .'

31. Kingsbury ('Figure of Jesus', p. 4) makes this observation concerning the narrator's treatment of God as a character in his story. The same thing holds true in regard to Satan. I use the title 'Satan' (4.10) rather than the terms 'the devil' (4.1, 5, 8) or 'the tempter' (4.3), since 'Satan' appears to function as the proper name of the character in question.

32. 1.20; 2.13, 19. Cf. 2.12, 22.

33. 1.22; 2.15. Cf. 2.17, 23; 4.14; 8.17 as well as 3.3. Rudolf Pesch ('Der Gottessohn im matthäischen Evangelienprolog [Mt 1-2]: Beobachtungen zu den Zitationsformeln der Reflexionszitate', *Bib* 48 [1967], p. 406) considers it 'self-evident' for the evangelist 'dass alle Vorhersagen durch den Propheten, die Propheten oder die Schriften der Propheten auf Gott selbst zurückgehen, dessen Sprachrohr die Propheten sind; dies gibt der Evangelist schon durch Benutzung der Formel *to rhēthen* zu erkennen'. But if it is true that all the words of the prophets are ultimately words of God, then 2.5 and 9.13 must also be listed with the above citations from the prophets, even though they are not 'formula quotations'.

34. The words of the law are described as 'written' (*gegraptai*) in 4.4, 7, 10. Here it should be noted that the Scripture cited (and misused) by Satan in 4.6b (= Ps. 91.11-12, LXX = 90.11-12) is just as clearly identified as a word of the Lord as are the Scriptures cited by Jesus, since the formulaic *gegraptai* appears here as well. The words of the law are described as 'spoken' (*errethē*) in 5.21, 27, 31, 33, 38, 43.

35. Note the references to 'God' in 5.8, 9, 34; 6.24, 30, 33. In addition Jesus makes even more frequent references to God as 'Father': 5.16; 6.1, 4, 6, 8, 9, 14, 15, 18, 26, 32; 7.11, 21.

36. It should be noted here that God's messenger, the 'angel' of 1.20, 2.13 and 2.19, also lies outside the realm of the narrator's omniscience. No indication is given of what this angel thinks or feels.

37. See 4.3, 5-6, 8-9, 11.

38. Lanser, p. 164.

39. Ibid., p. 164. See also the continuum which Lanser sets up (p. 163) between the extremes of 'report' and 'invention'.

40. It is essential to note here that the narrator's 'claim' regarding the type of story being narrated is not to be equated with the 'historicity' of the story. Petersen ('"Point of View"', p. 113) rightly observes that 'no single narrative can demonstrate by itself, or out of itself alone, whether it is fictional or historically factual. To demonstrate the congruence of a narrator with a real-world author, or of a narrative world with the real world, requires information from other sources than the isolated narrative. These sources might be the authors themselves, the original readers, if they can verify the

narrator's claims, other texts which together suggest the factuality of a narrative, or the generic code by which fictions are in a given culture distinguished from non-fictions'.

41. See Petersen's discussion of the omniscience of Mark's narrator ('"Point of View"', pp. 114-15) in which he concludes that the presence of Mark's narrator in the story which he narrates is strictly 'an implication of his rhetoric'. The same conclusion holds true for Matthew's narrator.

42. What Rhoads and Michie (pp. 3-4) posit for the Gospel of Mark applies equally well to the Gospel of Matthew: 'Although the author of the Gospel of Mark certainly used sources rooted in the historical events surrounding the life of Jesus, the final text is a literary creation with an autonomous integrity, just as Leonardo's portrait of the Mona Lisa exists independently as a vision of life apart from a resemblance or non-resemblance to the person who posed for it or as a play of Shakespeare has integrity apart from reference to the historical characters depicted there. One can read and interpret Mark's gospel as a story independent from the real people and events upon which it is based... Thus, Mark's narrative contains a closed and self-sufficient world with its own integrity, its own imaginative past and future, its own sets of values, and its own universe of meanings. When viewed as a literary achievement the statements in Mark's narrative, rather than being a representation of historical events, refer to the people, places, and events *in the story*... It is this story world which the reader enters'. See also Petersen, *Literary Criticism*, p. 21.

43. To read the Gospel of Matthew as story, however, is not to conclude that there is no connection between the narrative world of Matthew's storyteller and the real world of first century Palestine. It is rather to separate the literary analysis of the narrative from the assessment of its 'historicity' and to grant priority to the literary analysis. As Petersen rightly remarks ('"Point of View"', p. 101), 'It is a literary problem to grasp the narrative's world and the events that transpire in it; it is an historical problem to determine the relationship, if any (cf. fairy tales and novels), between the narrative's world and the real-world events to which it may or may not refer. In either case, we must start with the narrative world, lest we lose it by assuming that it refers to real-world events we know about from other sources than the narrative we are trying to understand'.

44. 1.1, 2, 17, Cf. the additional references to Abraham in 3.9 and 8.11 which are not used to locate the events of Matthew's story temporally.

45. 1.1, 6, 17. Cf. 1.20 and 9.27.

46. 1.11, 12, 17.

47. 2.1, 15, 19. Cf. 2.3, 7, 12, 13, 16, 22.

48. 2.22.

49. This is evident not only from Abraham's position in the genealogy itself (1.2, 17) but also from the status granted him in 1.1. as the ultimate originator of the line from which Jesus has come. The implications of 1.1,

1.2, and 1.17, further, are stated directly in 3.9, where Abraham's status as 'father' is recognized by the Pharisees and Sadducees as well as John the Baptist.

50. Thus Pesch, pp. 417-19. Here Pesch argues convincingly (p. 417) that 1.16b refers not to the *birth* but rather to the *begetting* of Jesus: 'Hier ist noch nicht von der *Geburt Jesu* (diese wird erst V. 21 für die Zukunft in den Blick genommen), sondern von *Jesu Zeugung*, der Herkunft im Sinne der genealogischen Aussagen des Stammbaums . . . die Rede'. See also Raymond E. Brown, *The Birth of the Messiah: A Commentary on the Infancy Narratives in Matthew and Luke* (Garden City, New York: Image Books, 1979), pp. 61-62.

51. 1.22-23; 2.4-6 (in the words of the 'chief priests and scribes of the people'), 15, 17-18, 23; 3.3, 4.14-16; 8.17.

52. Lanser, p. 163. Cf. the classification worked out by Frye (p. 219), who suggests that the Gospels represent the genre of 'dramatic history', a type of narrative which 'presents a basically historical story with economy and narrative effectiveness, which remains essentially faithful to the historical tradition but which may alter elements of that tradition as appears necessary in order to represent *multum in parvo*, and which is designed to convey important insights and understandings (both factual and interpretative) to a wide audience'. The significant difference between Frye's classification and my own is that I make no attempt to address or resolve the 'historical' question within the scope of this study. Cf. n. 43 above.

53. In addition to 'authorial equivalence', 'representation', 'privilege', and 'referential claim', Lanser makes reference (p. 166) to 'social identity' as a contributing factor of the narrator's 'status'. I have chosen not to include this factor in my discussion for two reasons: (1) as I have noted above (n. 10), my interest here is in the 'literary voice' of the narrator and not in the flesh-and-blood author of the text; and (2) since there is no external evidence available as to the 'social identity' of the flesh-and-blood author of the text, the question is itself a moot point. It would be 'circular reasoning' to first derive a 'social identity' for the Gospel writer from the text itself and then use the 'social identity' thus derived to assess the 'status' of Matthew's narrator.

54. Lanser, pp. 170-71.

55. Since, as I see it, there is no clear point of distinction between 'honesty' and 'reliability' as Lanser has defined them, I shall treat the two categories as one.

56. 1.22-23 and 2.15 identify scriptural predictions referring to 'a/my son' as 'that which was said *by the Lord*', while 3.17 cites 'a voice from heaven' (i.e., the voice *of God*) as saying of Jesus: 'This is my beloved Son. . . ' See Pesch, pp. 397-98.

57. It should be noted here that Lanser's definition of 'reliability' is somewhat less precise, and accordingly less helpful, than that established by Booth (pp. 158-59) and adopted by both Chatman (pp. 149, 233) and Fowler

(p. 229, n. 23). According to Booth, a narrator is '*reliable* when he speaks for or acts in accordance with the norms of the work (which is to say, the implied author's norms), *unreliable* when he does not'. Or, as Chatman puts it (p. 233), 'In "unreliable narration" the narrator's account is at odds with the implied reader's surmises about the story's real intentions'. As will become evident below from the analysis of the narrator's point of view, Matthew's narrator is fully in line with the 'norms' of his story, and is thus a fully 'reliable' narrator.

58. Ernst von Dobschütz ('Matthäus als Rabbi und Katechet', *ZNW* 27 [1928], pp. 338-48) attributes such stylistic features as doubling and repetition to the fact that Matthew was a 'converted rabbi', while Heinz Joachim Held ('Matthew as Interpreter of the Miracle Stories', in *Tradition and Interpretation in Matthew*, NTL, trans. Percy Scott [Philadelphia: Westminster, 1963], pp. 165-299) attributes the style of the miracle stories in chapters eight and nine to Matthew's careful work in redacting the traditional material at his disposal. My stance is to approach the stylistic features of the Gospel of Matthew as the deliberate decisions made by a storyteller as to how best to communicate his story. The further question as to whether the literary devices of Matthew's Gospel pertain to oral or written literature does not require analysis here. As Joanna Dewey remarks in reference to the Gospel of Mark (*Markan Public Debate*, pp. 30-31), 'Unquestionably, many if not all [of the rhetorical devices used in the Gospel of Mark] have their origin in oral literatures. Even extended symmetrical patterns are well documented in oral composition. But they are also techniques which can be used in written composition. And to assert a clear difference between oral and written composition for popular literature in the first century C.E. seems out of place. For even if a work was written, it was meant to be read aloud and to be heard. . . Thus the distinction between oral and written techniques does not appear applicable from the point of view of the audience'. On the oral basis of the literary techniques used by Matthew's narrator, see Charles H. Lohr, 'Oral Techniques in the Gospel of Matthew', *CBQ* 23 (1961), pp. 403-35.

59. In addition, as Held has demonstrated (p. 241), Matthew's narrator has shaped the miracle stories of chapters eight and nine into formulaic accounts built around a single basic structure.

60. While it is impossible to draw absolute distinctions between the parallelisms within 5.3-7.27, I have categorized them according to that element which serves most directly as the basis of parallelism in any given text.

61. Cf. Paul Gaechter, *Die literarische Kunst im Matthäus-Evangelium* StBibSt (Stuttgart: Katholisches Bibelwerk, 1966), pp. 19-20.

62. It must be noted here that while the formula is not identical in all cases, the reason for the differences lies in the specific circumstances relating to each citation. See Pesch for a careful and convincing argument to this effect.

63. A further example of this device is the formulaic conclusion to several of the miracle stories of chapters eight and nine (8.13b; 9.22b; cf. 8.3b). See Held, pp. 230-32.

64. Ibid., p. 238. Held here specifically excludes the use of 'catchword' as a reference to the technique of linking up *separate pericopes* by mean of key words. William G. Thompson ('Reflections on the Composition of Mt 8.1–9.34', *CBQ* 33 [1971], pp. 365-88), in his treatment of chapters eight and nine, attempts to build a case for his structural division of this section by pointing to the 'verbal contacts' between the various pericopes (pp. 370, 377-78, 383-85). However, the 'verbal contacts' cited by Thompson are not in all cases convincing as evidence of a specific and intentional literary technique. It would rather appear that the multiple occurrences of such words or phrases as 'alone' (8.8, 13, 16), 'the other side' (8.18, 28; 9.1), or 'into the house' (9.23, 28) reflect an unintentional repetition of vocabulary which is necessitated simply by the events of the story itself.

65. Held, pp. 237-39. Catchwords also occur in texts other than those with the above formulaic structure. The passage 1.18-25 is linked by no less than three key phrases—to take you/his wife (1.20, 24), to bear a son (1.21, 23, 25), and to call his name (1.21, 23, 25); while 9.1-8 contains the prominent catchword 'authority' (9.6, 8).

66. On the definitions and the functions of 'inclusio' and 'chiasm', see Dewey, *Markan Public Debate*, pp. 31-37. On the use of inclusio and chiasm within the Gospel of Matthew, see B.C. Butler, *The Originality of St. Matthew* (Cambridge: University, 1951), pp. 150-51; Angelico Di Marco, 'Der Chiasmus in der Bibel: 3. Teil', trans. Wolfgang Meyer, *LingBib*, no. 39 (1976), pp. 37-85; J.C. Fenton, 'Inclusio and Chiasmus in Matthew' in *Studia Evangelica: Papers Presented to the International Congress on 'The Four Gospels in 1957' Held at Christ Church, Oxford, 1957* (Berlin: Akademie, 1959), pp. 174-79; Lagrange, p. lxxxi; and Nils Wilhelm Lund, *Chiasmus in the New Testament: A Study in Formgeschichte* (Chapel Hill, North Carolina: University of North Carolina, 1942), pp. 240-319.

67. Dewey, *Markan Public Debate*, p. 31. Cf. Fenton, p. 174.

68. In Dewey's analysis of the literary devices within Mark's Gospel (*Markan Public Debate*, pp. 32-33) she specifies three basic types of chiasms: 'In its narrowest sense, [chiasm] refers to repetition of words in inverted order: a b : b' a' . . . However, chiasm also refers to a broader range of literary devices in which crossing occurs. Syntactical chiasm—e.g., subject, verb:verb, subject—occurs frequently in Mark. A chiasm may also consist of content parallels in inverted order'.

69. The discussion of the plot of 1.1-9.34 will be taken up below under the heading of 'plot'.

70. Lanser, p. 224; cf. pp. 90-92, 174-85. Lanser likewise identifies physical 'contact', that which relates to 'the display of words on a page, the size of paragraphs, the arrangement of text, the typography, even the stock of

paper...' However, since there is no method of analyzing this contact on the basis of the text alone, I am forced to disregard this category.

71. Lanser, pp. 91-92.

72. Ibid., pp. 174-76.

73. This observation on the basis of 1.1–9.34 is later confirmed, when in 24.15 the narrator breaks out of his 'indirect' mode of address to exhort 'the reader' to 'understand' the metaphor which he has just used.

74. Lanser, pp. 176-79.

75. See above.

76. Ph.D. Dissertation, Wisconsin, 1978.

77. Ibid., pp. 33-34, cited by Lanser, pp. 180-81.

78. As Raymond Brown explains (p. 139), 'By naming the child, Joseph acknowledges him as his own. The Jewish position on this is lucidly clear and is dictated by the fact that sometimes it is difficult to determine who begot a child biologically. Since normally a man will not acknowledge and support a child unless it is his own, the law prefers to base paternity on the man's acknowledgment. The Mishna *Baba Bathra* 8.6 states the principle: 'If a man says, "This is my son", he is to be believed'. Joseph, by exercising the father's right to name the child (cf. Luke 1.60-63), acknowledges Jesus and thus becomes the legal father of the child.

79. John the Baptist is here described in terms intended to evoke an image of Elijah. See 2 Kgs 1.8 and Mt. 11.14.

80. All that Matthew's narrator indicates in regard to Moses is that he handed down a single commandment having to do with a particular offering to be brought to the priest.

81. The historical fact that Matthew's Gospel was written for the purposes of a Jewish-Christian church does not in and of itself effect the question of the narrator's implied readership. That question must be answered strictly on the basis of the written text; and there is nothing in the written text which limits the implied readership to Jewish Christians. The ideological (or evaluative) biases which Matthew's narrator reflects (see below) can be viewed as 'apologetic' in nature and do not necessarily serve as a limiting factor.

82. Lanser, pp. 92-94.

83. 'Structure and History in Narrative Perspective: The Problem of Point of View Reconsidered', in *Structure and Society in Literary History: Studies in the History and Theory of Historical Criticism* (Charlottesville: University of Virginia, 1976), p. 246. See also Friedman, pp. 137-38; Petersen, '"Point of View"', p. 118; and Rhoads and Michie, p. 39.

84. Uspensky, pp. 8-100; Lanser, pp. 184-225.

85. Lanser here adopts Uspensky's use of the terms 'ideological' and 'ideology' (Uspensky, pp. 8-16). In the interest of using more 'neutral' terminology I shall adopt Uspensky's alternative adjective 'evaluative' (Uspensky, p. 8) in place of 'ideological' and substitute the phrase 'world

view' for 'ideology'. Cf. Kingsbury, *Matthew as Story*, p. 32.

86. Lanser, pp. 187-91. See also Uspensky, pp. 17-56; Genette, pp. 171-73; Petersen, '"Point of View"', pp. 109-12. In her discussion of the phraseological plane (pp. 2-9), Anderson appears to merge what Uspensky (pp. 15-16) sees as two distinct functions of the phraseological features of a text: (1) characterizing the world view of the character involved and (2) simply indicating the identity of the voice who tells the story. Here I shall follow Uspensky and deal at this point only with the identification of the voice or voices which dominate phraseologically in the narrator's text. For a discussion of the evaluative question, see below.

87. Lanser, p. 191.

88. This observation is the more striking in light of the fact that Jesus plays an entirely silent role in the story up to 3.15, 63 verses into the text. Jesus' lengthy discourse of 107 verses (5.3-7.27), however, more than makes up for this fact.

89. What these voices have to say, the extent to which they agree with each other, and the evaluative viewpoint which informs their respective 'discourses' will be the subject of discussion below under 'the ideological (evaluative) plane'. See n. 86 above.

90. It must be kept in mind that the question here has to do strictly with the identification of 'literary voices' at the level of the story. Obviously, Matthew's narrator, *as narrator*, is just as responsible for the direct speech of Jesus as he is for his own discourse. What is significant here is that the narrator chooses to give the 'literary voice' of Jesus priority over his own 'literary voice'.

91. 3.15; 4.4, 7, 10, 17, 19; 5.3-7.27; 8.3, 4, 7, 10-12, 13, 20, 22, 26, 32; 9.2, 4-6a, 6b, 9, 12, 15, 22, 24, 28, 29, 30.

92. It must be noted here that while 9.2 is indeed followed by direct speech, that speech is apparently only a private muttering and is not spoken directly to Jesus. Thus there are in reality only two instances within 1.1-9.34 of direct verbal response to Jesus.

93. In 9.30-31 the response is, precisely speaking, not to Jesus but to the people of the region. Nevertheless, verse 31 reflects a verbal response to the words of Jesus in verse 30.

94. Lanser, pp. 191-98. Cf. Uspensky, pp. 58-65.

95. What Petersen says in regard to Mark's narrator ('"Point of View"', p. 112) also applies to Matthew's narrator: he 'spatially hovers over every episode, able to see them all from a distance, in both space and time, yet free to descend at will into the action of an episode, locating himself as an invisible observer even in the most private councils...'

96. Cf. Anderson, p. 14.

97. Cf. the similar use of the verb *proskyneō*, 'to kneel before or worship'. Matthew's narrator uses this verb seven times prior to 9.35 (2.2, 8, 11; 4.9, 10; 8.2; 9.18); and in five of these instances (all but 4.9, 10) *proskyneō* refers

to the physical stance and/or the attitude which other characters assume (or, as in 2.8, pretend to assume) toward Jesus.

98. Regardless of the theological significance which *akoloutheō* appears to develop within Matthew's Gospel, the point of departure for the present study is the examination of the text in terms of the story which is told. At the level of the story the implied reader simply absorbs the fact that Jesus is moving from place to place and that others are following after him. Cf. Jack Dean Kingsbury, 'The Verb *Akolouthein* ('to Follow') As an Index of Matthew's View of His Community', *JBL* 97 (1978), pp. 56-73.

99. Only in 9.19 does the narrator turn the tables by relating that Jesus follows another character.

100. Lanser, pp. 198-201. Lanser here draws on the work of Genette.

101. Friedman, pp. 124-25.

102. The text of 1.18–9.34 does in fact contain at least three passages which can be viewed as summaries: 3.1-6, 4.17, and 4.23-25. In each case the time designation is either indeterminate (3.1: 'in those days'; 4.17: 'from that time on') or nonexistent (4.23: 'and he was going about'). In addition, the situation or action in focus is in each case depicted as either ongoing or repetitive rather than as one single event: 'John *was wearing*' (3.4); 'then Jerusalem ... *was going out* to him' (3.5); 'and they *were being baptized*' (3.6); 'Jesus *began* to proclaim and to say' (4.17); 'and he *was going about*' (4.23). But while these three passages are indeed summaries, they do not serve the narrator as a means to pass quickly over events of secondary importance. Rather, they function as headings for the material which follows: 3.1-6 sets the stage for the scenes depicted in 3.7-12 and 3.13-17, while 4.17 and 4.23-25 together function as a heading for 5.1–9.34. See below.

103. Lanser, pp. 198-200; Genette, p. 217.

104. Uspensky, p. 71. See also Anderson, p. 12.

105. To be sure, the words of Jesus are even more frequently introduced by verbs in the past tense: 3.15; 4.4, 7; 8.10, 13, 32; 9.2, 4, 12, 15, 22, 24. But since the narrator's discourse is primarily subsequent narration, these past tense verbs are merely what one would expect. It is the historic presents which break the general pattern of subsequent narration and thus draw attention to themselves. Cf. Anderson, pp. 12-13.

106. Anderson, pp. 13-14. The same logic could also be applied to the infinitive *legein* (= to say) found in 4.17. Here the infinitive is preceded by the inceptive aorist *ērxato* (= began). The implication of this phrase is that an ongoing process is initiated.

107. Cf. Anderson. p. 13.

108. In all cases except 5.26 the formula is *legō hymin*, 'I say to you (pl.)'. In 5.26 Jesus says *legō soi*, 'I say to you (sg.)'.

109. Lanser, pp. 201-15. Cf. Uspensky, pp. 81-100.

110. Lanser defines this distinction as follows (p. 205): 'Subjective

information reveals the character (temperament, personality, beliefs, responses) of a perceiver; it is discourse about persons as subjects. Objective information consists of descriptions about objects or persons-as-objects'.

111. The only characters or groups of characters treated strictly objectively are Mary (1.1-17, 18-25; 2.1-12, 13-15, 19-23), the servant of the centurion (8.5-13), the ruler's daughter (9.18-19/23-26), the children of Bethlehem (2.16-18), and the crowds of sick people (4.23-25; 8.16-17).

112. Note the following 'scenes', set off from each other by the designation of either location, time, or characters: 1.1-17, 18-25; 2.1-12, 13-15, 16-18, 19-23; 3.1-17; 4.1-11, 12-16, 17-25; 5.1-7.29; 8.1-4, 5-13, 14-15, 16-17, 18-22, 23-27, 28-34; 9.1-8, 9, 10-13, 14-17, 18-19/23-26, 20-22, 27-31, 32-34.

113. The term *ochlos* (= crowd) appears in 4.17-25, 5.1-7.29—twice, 8.1-4, 8.18-22, 9.1-8, 9.18-19/23-26—twice, and 9.32-34. In addition, other (large?) groups of people are identified in more specific terms in 2.1-12, 2.16-18, 3.1-17, 4.17-25, 8.5-13, 8.16-17, 8.23-27, 8.28-34, 9.10-13.

114. 5.1-7.29; 8.18-22, 23-27; 9.10-13, 14-17, 18-19/23-26. As in the case of the crowds, however, the narrator also makes other, more specific reference to individuals who are disciples: 4.17-25; 8.14-15; 9.9.

115. Calculating on the basis of the above-listed twenty-six scenes, the remaining characters either appear or are mentioned in the following number of scenes: *five*: Mary (1.1-17, 18-25; 2.1-12, 13-15, 19-23), Pharisees (3.1-17; 5.1-7.29; 9.10-13, 14-17, 32-34); *four*: Joseph (1.1-17, 18-25; 2.13-15, 19-23), Herod (2.1-12, 13-15, 16-18, 19-23), scribes (2.1-12; 5.1-7.29; 8.18-22; 9.1-8); *three*: the angel of the Lord (1.18-25; 2.13-15, 19-23); *two*: the magi (2.1-12, 13-15), the priests/chief priests (2.1-12; 8.1-4), John the Baptist (3.1-17; 4.12-16); *one*: Archelaus (2.19-23), the Sadducees (3.1-17), Satan (4.1-11), the angels (of 4.11), the demons (of 8.31-32), the tax collectors and sinners (9.10-13), the sick persons/friends/relatives (of chapters 8 and 9). God/the Lord/your heavenly Father is cited as a character in his own right in five scenes (1.18-25; 2.13-15; 3.1-17; 4.1-11; 5.1-7.29). In addition, both the angel and Jesus are identified in terms of their relationship to God: the narrator makes three references to 'the angel *of the Lord*' (1.18-25; 2.13-15, 19-23); and in two scenes other characters refer to Jesus as 'Son *of God*' (4.1-11; 8.28-34).

116. The only interaction recounted in which characters relate to each other and not to Jesus is found in 8.33 (between the herd boys and the residents of the city). In 9.3 (where the Pharisees mutter to each other) and in 9.11 (where they address Jesus' disciples) the interactions in fact include Jesus, since Jesus himself responds to their objections.

117. Lanser, p. 141.

118. Lanser, pp. 209-14. Cf. Uspensky's somewhat simpler analysis, pp. 83-97.

119. Cf. the narrator's reference to the emotions displayed by the crowds (8.27; 9.8, 33) and by Jesus (8.10; 9.30). As noted above (n. 25), however, the

emotions displayed in these cases are directly linked to the speech of the person(s) involved. As a result, the most natural inference is that Matthew's narrator simply extrapolates from the words to the emotions.

120. Of the thirty-two passages cited in the text above and in n. 119, thirteen of them refer to Jesus (3.16; 4.2, 18, 21; 5.1; 8.10, 14, 18; 9.2, 4, 9, 12, 23), five to Joseph (1.19, 20; 2.13, 19, 22), four to the magi (2.9, 10, 11, 12), four to the crowds (7.28; 8.34; 9.8, 33), two to Herod (2.3, 16), and one each to John the Baptist (3.7), 'the people' (8.27), the Pharisees (9.11), and the woman with a flow of blood (9.21).

121. Cf. Anderson, pp. 17-22. That this statement holds true only for the 'human' characters in the story is a given for Matthew's narrator, who assumes as a matter of course that God (or, by proxy, his angels) can not only see secret thoughts and private intentions (2.13) but can also predict events which have not yet taken place (1.23; 2.6).

122. Cf. Anderson's reference (pp. 18-19) to the 'sustained inside view' of Jesus provided by the narrator whenever Jesus speaks.

123. At this point it is not necessary to distinguish between the characters to whom these words apply, since the present concern is with the overall psychological impact of the text.

124. This picture is further supported by the following: Joseph, the husband of Mary, is described as a 'righteous' (*dikaios*: 1.19) man, and the magi are said to 'rejoice' (*chairō*: 2.10) when they see the star which will take them to Jesus; while the magi, on the other hand, are 'warned' (*chrēmatizō*: 2.12) concerning Herod, and Joseph is likewise 'warned' (*chrēmatizō*: 2.22) in apparent connection with Herod's son, Archelaus.

125. R. Alan Culpepper, 'The Narrator in the Fourth Gospel: Intratextual Relationships', in *SBL 1982 Seminar Papers*, SBLSP 21 (Chico, California: Scholars, 1982), p. 85.

126. Cf. the similar conclusions by J.M. Lotman concerning the Gospel of John ('Point of View in a Text', trans. L.M. O'Toole, NLH 6 [1975], pp. 342-43) and by Petersen concerning the Gospel of Mark ('"Point of View"', p. 108).

127. Kingsbury, 'Figure of Jesus', p. 4.

128. Cf. Anderson's observation (p. 3) that Jesus 'is not only the protagonist, he is consistently the most reliable character'.

129. Lanser, pp. 215-22. See also Uspensky, pp. 8-16.

130. Cf. Anderson (p. 6) on the Gospel of Matthew and Petersen ('"Point of View"', p. 110) on the Gospel of Mark.

131. Cf. Kingsbury's observation ('Figure of Jesus', p. 8) that 'because the reader trusts Matthew to be a reliable narrator and Matthew does not betray that trust, the reader accepts [the designations 'Christ', 'Son of David', and 'Son of Abraham'] as correctly applying to Jesus and as constituting Matthew's initial description of him'.

132. Cf. Birger Gerhardsson, *The Mighty Acts of Jesus According to Matthew* (Lund, Sweden: CWK Gleerup, 1979), p. 89.

133. Cf. ibid., p. 24; Held, pp. 171-72. In a similar vein, note also the exclamation by the crowds (9.33): '*Never* has such a thing been seen in Israel'.

134. Thus Kingsbury, 'Figure of Jesus', p. 13.

135. Note here Pesch's argument (pp. 409-11) that the specific formula of 1.22 ('that which was spoken *by the Lord* through the prophet'), when taken in conjunction with the language of the prophecy ('and she will bear a *son*'), creates a subtle (verhüllt) reference to Jesus as *God's Son*. And as Pesch further observes (pp. 411-13), the formula which precedes the scriptural citation of 2.15 ('Out of Egypt have I called *my son*') also refers significantly to 'that which was spoken *by the Lord* through the prophet'.

136. Kingsbury, 'Figure of Jesus', p. 12.

137. Cf. Kingsbury's observations on this point (ibid., pp. 5-7).

138. Note also such explicit evaluative statements as those by the magi (2.2), John the Baptist (3.11-12), the crowds (7.28-29; 9.33; cf. 8.27), the leper (8.2), the centurion (8.8b), the ruler (9.18), and the woman suffering from a hemorrhage (9.21).

139. Kingsbury, 'Figure of Jesus', p. 6. See also Anderson, pp. 6-8.

140. Anderson, p. 8.

141. Ibid., p, 8; cf. p. 14.

142. See above.

143. Cf. Kingsbury, 'Figure of Jesus', p. 8; Gaechter, *Kunst*, p. 16.

144. Lanser, pp. 218-19.

145. Ibid., p. 218.

146. Ibid., p. 219.

147. Ibid., pp. 220-21.

148. Ibid., p. 220.

149. See above.

150. See above.

151. Abrams, p. 20. See also Chatman, pp. 125-27. Here Chatman defines 'character' as 'a paradigm of traits' (p. 126). A 'trait', in turn, is 'a narrative adjective out of the vernacular labeling a personal quality of a character, as it persists over part or whole of the story' (p. 125).

152. Cf. Chatman, pp. 119-20, 132; Scholes and Kellogg, pp. 164, 204-5.

153. Scholes and Kellogg, p. 206. See also Chatman, pp. 119-20.

154. See above.

155. Cf. the account in 8.18-22. While there is no direct statement regarding the responses of the 'scribe' and the 'disciple', the implications of the language used (scribe/'Teacher' and disciple/'Lord') are that Jesus turns down the offer of the scribe, while challenging the disciple to follow him. (Cf. Kingsbury, 'The Verb *Akolouthein*', pp. 58-60). On the analogy of 4.18-22,

the implied reader is justified in assuming that the disciple will in fact respond positively to Jesus' call.

156. See Chatman, p. 43; Scholes and Kellogg, p. 207.

157. Scholes and Kellogg, p. 212. Note, however, that plot does not relate merely to the overall shape of a narrative. It also relates to each 'separable element' of that narrative. As a result, each segment of the story has 'its own little system of tension and resolution' which 'contributes its bit to the general system' (ibid., p. 239). Thus plot is a function both of the narrative as a whole and of each individual segment.

158. Here I build on the structural division of the Gospel of Matthew propounded by Jack Dean Kingsbury (*Matthew: Structure, Christology, Kingdom* [Philadelphia: Fortress, 1978], pp. 7-39, *Matthew as Story* [pp. 4, 57-77]) and recently restated by David R. Bauer (*The Structure of Matthew's Gospel: A Study in Literary Design*, JSNTSup, 31 [Sheffield: Almond, 1988]). Accordingly, 1.1–4.16 forms the first major section of the Gospel, one which focuses on the person (or identity) of Jesus Christ. The second (4.17–16.20) and third (16.21–28.20) major sections both begin with the formulaic phrase, 'From that time on, Jesus began to . . .' The section 4.17–16.20 opens with the announcement of Jesus' ministry of teaching, proclaiming, and healing in Israel: 'From that time on, Jesus began to proclaim and to say, "Repent, for the Kingdom of heaven has come near"'. This section of the story then describes Jesus' public ministry to Israel (4.17–11.1) and Israel's subsequent repudiation of that ministry (11.2–16.20). The section 16.21–28.20 opens with the announcement of Jesus' suffering, death, and resurrection: 'From that time on, Jesus began to show his disciples that he must go to Jerusalem and suffer many things from the elders and chief priests and scribes and be killed and on the third day rise'. This section of the story thus describes Jesus' journey toward Jerusalem and the fate which awaits him there (16.21–25.46) and then the denouement, the climax of the story, in which all the predictions concerning Jesus' suffering, death, and resurrection finally reach their fulfilment (26.1–28.20). For a differing assessment of Matthean structure, see the recent proposals of Frank J. Matera ('The Plot of Matthew's Gospel', *CBQ* 49 [1987], pp. 233-53), and Frans Neirynck ('*Apo Tote Ērxato* and the Structure of Matthew', *ETL* 64.1 [1988], pp. 21-59). While not identical, these proposals both conclude (1) that 4.12-17 (and not 4.17) marks the beginning of Jesus' public ministry and (2) that 16.13-23 (and not 16.21-23) marks the beginning of Jesus' journey towards Jerusalem and death. See also David Hill, 'The Figure of Jesus in Matthew's Story: A Response to Professor Kingsbury's Literary-Critical Probe', *JSNT* 21 (1984), pp. 42-48.

159. Kingsbury, *Matthew: Structure, Christology, Kingdom*, pp. 9-11.

160. Ibid., pp. 12-17.

161. See n. 50 above.

162. See n. 78 above.

163. The reference here to the agency of the Spirit points unambiguously to the 'divine sonship' of Jesus. Thus it is precisely as the Son of God that Jesus is led into the wilderness; and the testing which he faces there has to do with nothing more or less than his recognized status as such (4.3, 5). There is no question raised here as to 'whether' Jesus is the Son of God. Rather, the translations of 4.3 and 4.5 should read, 'Since you are the Son of God . . . ' Satan is not questioning Jesus *as to* his identity but rather attempting to seduce Jesus *because of* his identity. For a detailed discussion of this pericope, see Birger Gerhardsson, *The Testing of God's Son (Mt 4.1-11 & Par)*, CBNTS, 2.1 (Lund, Sweden: CWK Gleerup, 1966).

164. Kingsbury, *Matthew: Structure, Christology, Kingdom*, pp. 15-16.

165. Cf. ibid., p. 16.

166. But the very fact that the point of departure for Jesus' ministry to the Jewish people is designated as 'Galilee *of the Gentiles*' provides a hint to the implied reader that Jesus' messianic ministry will be of significance not only to the Jewish people awaiting their 'messiah' but also to the Gentiles. Cf. Kingsbury, *Matthew: Structure, Christology, Kingdom*, pp. 23-24.

167. Ibid., pp. 16-17.

168. Ibid., pp. 17-21.

169. See Chapter 1 above.

170. For detailed discussion of 8.1-9.34 see the varying treatments offered by Held, Thompson ('Reflections'), Christoph Burger ('Jesu Taten nach Matthäus 8 und 9', *ZTK* 70 [1973], pp. 272-87), and Jack Dean Kingsbury ('Observations on the "Miracle Chapters" of Matthew 8-9', *CBQ* 40 [1978], pp. 559-73).

171. See n. 155 above.

172. Only in the desperate incident which takes place out on the lake (8.23-27) do they themselves initiate action.

173. See Chapter 3 below.

Notes to Chapter 3

1. The narrator has also introduced the group which I shall identify collectively as 'the religious authorities' (see 3.7; 8.19; 9.3, 11, 34; cf. 5.20; 9.14). But since this group assumes its greatest prominence only later in the story, I shall reserve mention of them until that point (see Chapter 4 below). For a helpful discussion of the role of the Jewish leaders as a character group within Matthew's Gospel, see Jack Dean Kingsbury, 'The Developing Conflict between Jesus and the Jewish Leaders in Matthew's Gospel: A Literary-Critcal Study', *CBQ* 49 (1987), pp. 57-73.

2. The only differences between 4.23 and 9.35 are the following: (1) in 9.35 the narrator substitutes 'all the cities and villages' for the phrase 'in all

Galilee'; (2) in 9.35 the narrator omits the phrase 'among the people' as the conclusion to 'healing every disease and every sickness'.

3. On the 'bracketing' effect—usually described as 'inclusio'—created by 4.23 and 9.35, see the following: J. Schniewind, *Das Evangelium nach Matthäus*, 11th edn (Göttingen: Vandenhoeck & Ruprecht, 1968), p. 125; Lucien Deiss, 'Le discours apostolique ou le discours de mission selon Matthieu x', *Spir* 12 (1962), p. 285; Held, p. 246; P. Ternant, 'L'évangile (Mt 9, 35-38): La mission, fruit de la compassion du maître et de la prière des disciples', *AssSeign* 98 (1967), p. 26; Frankemölle, p. 111; Schweizer, p. 233; Francis Wright Beare, *The Gospel According to Matthew* (San Francisco: Harper & Row, 1981), p. 237. I have chosen to use the term 'bracketing' to describe the relationship of 4.23 and 9.35 in order to facilitate the discussion of structure within 4.23-11.1. Here, as I shall argue, there is not a single 'inclusio' (4.23/9.35) but rather two 'bracketed texts' (4.23-9.35; 9.35-11.1) which interlock with each other and form a third 'bracketed text' (4.23-11.1). See below.

4. Cf. Lohr's observation (p. 409): 'Because *inclusio* forces the attention of the audience back from the conclusion of a passage to its beginning, it can be used to interconnect the parts of a story'.

5. On the role of 9.35 as the introduction to a new segment of text, see the following: Grant, p. 294; Klostermann, p. 85; Thompson, 'An Historical Perspective', p. 252, n. 22; Leopold Sabourin, *L'évangile selon Saint Matthieu et ses principaux parallèles* (Rome: Biblical Institute, 1978), p. 130. For my discussion of 11.1 as the conclusion to this segment, see below.

6. While 9.35 omits both the reference to 'Galilee' and the reference to 'the people', it is evident from the otherwise verbatim repetition of 4.23 that 9.35 depicts the same essential ministry as that described in 4.23.

7. These transitional statements ('And when he saw the crowds. . . ') serve to lead the implied reader from the generalized summary statements of 4.23-25 and 9.35 back into the narration of specific events in the chronology of Jesus' public ministry (5.1bff./9.36bff.) Cf. Thompson ('An Historical Perspective', p. 252, n. 22) and Jean Radermakers (*Au fil de l'évangile selon Saint Matthieu* [Heverlee-Louvain: Institut d'études théologiques, 1972], p. 134), both of whom view the descriptions of Jesus' ministry (4.23 and 9.35) and the mention of the crowds (5.1 and 9.36) as parallel elements with respect to the first two discourses of Matthew's Gospel. This observation, while it is accurate as far as it goes, does not deal adequately with the overall structure of 4.23-11.1 and thus does not recognize the way in which 4.23-25 serves as the introduction not only for 5.1-7.29 but also for 8.1-9.34.

8. In 11.1, just as in 9.35, the narrator omits a specific reference to 'Galilee'. But here again it is clear from the obvious parallelism with 4.23 that Galilee is the scene of the action.

9. In addition, 11.1 serves to establish a fundamental link between 10.5b-42 and 5.3-7.27. The repetition of the phrase 'and when Jesus finished. . . '

(11.1; 7.28) to mark the conclusion of both of these discourses identifies them as parallel to each other in format and function. The format in each case is that of an extended and uninterrupted address whose conclusion is marked by the phrase 'and when Jesus finished . . . ' The function of these discourses is that of highlighting the teachings of Jesus by setting them forth in prominent and thematically organized blocks. Accordingly, 10.5b-42 and 5.3-7.27 both represent major 'teaching sessions' in which Jesus addresses himself on a given topic to a designated audience: in the case of 5.3-7.27, the audience is the disciples (5.1-2) and the crowds (7.28-29; cf. 5.1); in the case of 10.5b-42, it is the disciples alone (10.5a; 11.1).

10. Thus Francis Martin, 'The Image of Shepherd in the Gospel of St. Matthew', *SciEsp* 27 (1975), p. 274; Ternant, 'L'évangile', p. 26. See also Ternant, 'L'envoi', p. 22.

11. As Perrin observes in his influential article introducing the concept of 'evangelist as author' (pp. 15-16), '. . . an ancient author simply did not have the modern method of giving a structure to his work by means of a table of contents, chapter divisions, headings, etc. The indications of the intended structure had therefore to be internal, presented within the text itself. But the point is that prior to the rise of redaction criticism we were not thinking seriously enough of the evangelists as authors and hence not looking seriously enough for internal indices of their authorial intent in the works which they wrote. All this has now changed and today we concern ourselves as never before with such literary devices as summary reports, geographical references, formula quotations, intercalation and tautologous repetition, as well as with statements of purpose on the part of the risen Lord. All of these and other literary devices have been used by the evangelists to give form and structure to their work, and we must pay careful attention to them if we are to see the [Synoptic Gospels and Acts] as their authors intended them to be seen'. See also Beare, *Gospel*, p. 237.

12. My approach to the structure of 9.35-11.1 differs strategically from the approach of those Matthean scholars who structure this passage on the basis of thematic rather than formal grounds. The majority of these scholars recognize 9.35-38 (or 9.36-38) as a distinct unit and view the next major segment of text as either 10.1-15 (thus Bacon, p. 197; W.F. Albright and C.S. Mann, *Matthew*, AB, vol. 26 [Garden City, New York: Doubleday, 1971], p. 116; Morosco, p. 324) or 10.1-16 (thus Schniewind, p. 126; Schweizer, p. 234; R. Riesner, 'Der Aufbau der Reden im Matthäus-Evangelium', *ThBei* 9 [1978], p. 176). Other scholars view the first major segment of text as beginning with 9.35 and continuing on into the discourse by Jesus. For George Mangatt ('Reflections on the Apostolic Discourse (Mt 10)', *Biblebh* 6 [1980], p. 198) this segment is 9.35-10.5 (i.e., both *5a* and *5b*); for Corina Combet-Galland ('Du champ des moissonneurs au chant des serviteurs: Matthieu 9.35—11.1', *FoiVie* 81 [1982], pp. 33-34) it is apparently 9.35-10.8a; and for Frankemölle (p. 132) it is 9.35-10.16. The basic

weakness in the above attempts to work at the structure of 9.35–11.1 from a thematic standpoint, however, is that they effectively ignore the narrator's own formal clues to the structure of the text. A second group of Matthean scholars does give basic credence to formal considerations by viewing 10.4 as the end of one segment of text and 10.5 (i.e., in its entirety) as the beginning of the next: thus Beare, *Gospel*, p. 237; Schuyler Brown, 'The Mission to Israel', pp. 76–77; Dausch, pp. 169–70; Filson, pp. 124–35; Grundmann, pp. 286, 288; Gundry, pp. 181, 183; Paul S. Minear, *Matthew: The Teacher's Gospel* (New York: Pilgrim, 1982), p. 68; Plummer, p. 148; Schott, p. 140. But even this approach does not do justice to the structure of the text, since 10.5a represents the last of a sequence of events initiated in 9.35; while the discourse of Jesus begins formally only in 10.5b. My approach lines up with that of a third group of scholars which pays attention to formal considerations, viewing 10.5a as the conclusion to one segment and 10.5b as the beginning of the next: thus Ernst Lohmeyer and Werner Schmauch, *Das Evangelium des Matthäus*, KKNT (Göttingen: Vandenhoeck & Ruprecht, 1956), p. 181; Gaechter, *Evangelium*, pp. 315, 320; Radermakers, p. 136; H.J.B. Combrink, 'Structural Analysis of Mt 9.35–11.1', in *The Structure of Matthew 1–13: An Exploration into Discourse Analysis*, Neo 11, 2nd edn (Pretoria: New Testament Society of South Africa, 1980), pp. 100, 102; Patte, pp. 138–39. A final group of scholars makes no apparent attempt to determine the inner structure of 9.35–11.1: thus Bernhard Weiss, *A Commentary on the New Testament*, vol. 1: *Matthew–Mark*, trans. George H. Schodde and Epiphanius Wilson (New York: Funk & Wagnalls, 1906), pp. 75–88; Schlatter, pp. 321–57; Allen, pp. 98–113; Klostermann, pp. 84–94; Meyer, pp. 204–18.

13. David E. Aune (*Prophecy in Early Christianity and the Ancient Mediterranean World* [Grand Rapids, Michigan: William B. Eerdmans, 1983], p. 164) identifies this expression as one with a 'consistent social function wherever it occurs in early Jewish, early Christian, and (very rarely) Greco-Roman sources: [it] is used only by one whose social status is superior to the individual or group being addressed'. Aune goes on (p. 164) to enumerate the social situations in which this expression is used: '(1) a father speaking to his son(s), (2) a teacher addressing his pupil(s), (3) a rabbi introducing a contrary halakhic opinion to his colleagues, (4) a magician addressing the supernatural powers under his control, (5) a preacher addressing a sermon of repentance or admonition to his audience, (6) an apostle speaking to a Christian community whom he wishes to influence, (7) two peers engaged in a dispute with each other, (8) an angel addressing a man, (9) God addressing an angel'. In light of the evidence, Aune concludes (p. 165) that 'I say [to you]' functions as 'a *legitimation formula* since it implicitly claims the authority of one of greater social status when addressing one(s) of lesser status'.

14. See below for further discussion of the eschatological nature of this terminology.

15. Cf. Schott, pp. 140-41; Morosco, p. 324; Giblin, p. 641 n.12; Combet-Galland, p. 34. Neither Schott nor Morosco explains his reasoning behind such a division of the text. Giblin and Combet-Galland, on the other hand, both draw attention to the phrase 'truly, I say to you' as a formal device used by Matthew's narrator to conclude each of the three sections of the discourse.

16. The imperfect tense of the verb *periēgen* (= went about) serves to emphasize the ongoing nature of Jesus' action. As Maximilian Zerwick indicates (*Biblical Greek*, trans. and rev. Joseph Smith [Rome: Scripta Pontificii Instituti Biblici, 1963], p. 91), 'The imperfect ... exhibits an action not simply as a historical fact (aorist) but as in progress or repeated or tending toward its end, or as this or that *kind* of activity or habit (descriptive)'. Cf. BDF, p. 169.

17. See n. 6. above. Cf. Dausch's observation (p. 168): 'Ist dort [4.23] Galiläa als Schauplatz der Tätigkeit genannt, so hier im Gegensatz zu Kapharnaum: alle Städte und Dörfer jenes Landes'. In spite of the parallelism between 4.23 and 9.35, however, Beda Rigaux (*The Testimony of St. Matthew*, trans. Paul Joseph Oligny [Chicago: Franciscan Herald, 1968], p. 79) concludes that Galilee is no longer specifically in view in 9.35; instead, the 'field of vision' has 'broadened' from that of 4.23.

18. Here it must be noted that while Galilee serves as the overarching geographical setting for 4.23-9.34, Jesus nevertheless does not remain strictly within the boundaries of that region, but crosses temporarily into 'the region of the Gadarenes' (cf. 8.18, 23, 28; 9.1).

19. See n. 2 above. the only distinction between 4.23b-d and 9.35b-d is that in 9.35d the narrator refers only to 'healing every disease and every sickness' and omits the qualifying phrase 'among the people' found in 4.23d. That the Jewish people are still the primary recipients of Jesus' ministry in 9.35, however, is evident from the fact that Jesus is here depicted as teaching 'in their synagogues'.

20. But just as Jesus does not remain strictly in Galilee throughout 5.1-9.34 (see 18 above), neither does he restrict his mission entirely to the Jewish people. In 8.5-13 Jesus heals the servant of a Roman centurion and in 8.28-9.1 he heals a demon-possessed Gadarene.

21. While it must be assumed that the disciples are still 'following' Jesus about Galilee (cf. 4.20, 22; 8.23; 9.9, 19), the narrator makes no mention of them in this verse. Cf. Combrink ('Structural Analysis', p. 101), who observes that the section 9.35-10.5a 'is circumscribed by the fact that its opening statement describes Jesus' preaching and healing activity—but alone' in direct contrast to the following section (10.5b-15), in which 'Matthew describes the disciples and their mission in terms remarkably reminiscent of Jesus' words and deeds'.

22. This implication becomes an explicit reference in the opening phrase of 9.36, 'And when he saw the crowds ...'

23. The shift in narration from a summary account which establishes setting (9.35) to the recounting of specific events (9.36–10.5a) is evident from the fact that the imperfect verb tense employed in 9.35 (*periēgen* = he went about) gives way to the aorist in 9.36 (*esplanchnisthē* = he took compassion), 10.1 (*edōken* = he gave [authority]), and 10.5a (*apesteilen* = he sent out [the disciples]). The narrator's use of the historic present tense in 9.37 (*legei* = he says) has the effect not of breaking the continuity of the sequence of events in question but rather of giving added weight to the words of Jesus in 9.37-38. See my discussion in Chapter 2 above concerning Matthew's use of the historic present tense.

24. Cf. Ternant's observation ('L'évangile', p. 27) that the crowds of 9.36 are none other than those to whom Jesus has been ministering in 9.35.

25. See n. 7 above.

26. Here the narrator makes explicit that which has been implicit in his portrayal of Jesus up to this point: Jesus' ministry to the crowds is an expression of 'compassion'. Prior to this point Jesus' attitude toward the crowds has been most directly expressed in 9.13. There Jesus responds to the Pharisees, who question his propriety in eating with 'tax collectors and sinners', by citing Hosea 6.6 ('I desire mercy and not sacrifice') as the Scripture which these Pharisees should take to heart. The implication is that Jesus' motivation in eating with the 'tax collectors and sinners' is one of 'mercy'.

27. The verb *splanchnizomai* (= to take compassion) is derived from the noun *splanchnon* (pl. = bowels, entrails), which refers to that part of the human anatomy which in the ancient world was considered to be the seat of emotions. Joseph Henry Thayer (*A Greek-English Lexicon of the New Testament* [New York: American Book Company, 1889], p. 584) observes that 'in the Grk. poets fr. Aeschyl. down the bowels were regarded as the seat of the more violent passions, such as anger and love; but by the Hebrews as the seat of the tenderer affections, esp. kindness, benevolence, compassion . . . '

28. As Martin observes (p. 275), 'The expression ['sheep without a shepherd'] is a literary commonplace, evoking immediately an image of the people scattered and disorganized, as a result of a defeat in war (1 Kgs 22, 17 [= 2 Chron. 18, 16]; Jdt 11, 19), or because of a lack of true leaders (Nm 27, 17; Ez 34, 5; Zech 10, 2)'. See also Jürgen Roloff, 'Stationen urchristlicher Missionserfahrung', *ZMiss* 4 (1978), p. 7; Gundry, p. 181.

29. As P. Bonnard observes (*L'évangile selon Saint Matthieu*, CNT, 1 [Neuchâtel: Delachaux & Niestlé, 1970], p. 142), it is not the 'distress of each sheep of the flock' which is in focus here, but rather the fact that the flock of sheep as a whole faces 'dispersion' (or in other words, the extinction of the flock as a flock). H.J. Venetz ('Bittet den Herrn der Ernte: Überlegungen zu Lk 10, 2/Mt 9, 37', *Dia* 11 [1980], p. 158), who argues that the focus of 9.36 lies on the miserable conditions of the sheep and not on their dispersion, fails to recognize that the miserable conditions of the sheep are in fact linked, as

symptom to cause, to the fact that the sheep have no shepherd.

30. While the voice in 9.36 is that of the narrator, it is evident that the description of the crowds as 'sheep without a shepherd' corresponds to that which Jesus 'sees' when he observes these crowds.

31. Cf. Venetz, p. 156. Note also the observation of Wolfgang Schenk ('Das Präsens Historicum als makrosyntaktische Gliederungssignal im Matthäus-evangelium', *NTS* 22 [1976], p. 465) that Matthew's use of *tote* (= then) + the historic present tense of the verb is a construction which clearly designates a 'temporal sequence'.

32. Cf. the 'harvest as blessing' motif found in such verses as Isa. 9.2; 16.8-10; 17.11; Jer. 5.17, 24. While many scholars (thus, for example, Bonnard, p. 143; M. Eugene Boring, *Sayings of the Risen Jesus: Christian Prophecy in the Synoptic Tradition* SNTSMS, 46 [Cambridge: Cambridge University, 1982], p. 142, n. 33; Patte, pp. 139, 142, 143; Schniewind, p. 125; Ternant, 'L'envoi', p. 24, and 'L'évangile', p. 37; Hoffmann, p. 289) relate Jesus' saying of 9.37-38 to the 'harvest as judgment' motif found in such verses as Isa. 27.11ff., Jer. 51.33 (LXX = 28.33), Hos. 6.11, and Joel 4.13ff., this connection is not only unnecessary but also unwarranted. Martin Hengel (*Nachfolge und Charisma: Eine exegetisch-religionsgeschichtliche Studie zu Mt 8.21f und Jesu Ruf in die Nachfolge*, BZNW, 34, ed. Eltester [Berlin: Alfred Töpelmann, 1968], pp. 83-84) recognizes this fact, interpreting Mt. 9.37f. (= Lk. 10.2) as a saying which relates to 'mission' rather than to 'judgment'. And while L. Legrand ('The Harvest is Plentiful (Mt. 9.37), *Scrip* 17 [1965], pp. 3-5), Beare (*Gospel*, pp. 238, 241; 'Mission', p. 7), and Laufen (pp. 270-72) each recognize the twofold connotations of the 'harvest' motif as it appears in 9.37-38, they all downplay the note of 'judgment' communicated by the saying and lay stress instead on the 'missionary' connotations of the 'harvest' described here.

33. The contrast in this sentence is provided by the parallel constructions, *ho men therismos* (= the harvest) and *ho de ergatai* (= but the laborers). Cf. BDF, pp. 231-32.

34. The reference to the 'few' laborers (9.38) serves to transform the 'great harvest' from cause for rejoicing into cause for concern: if there are not sufficient laborers to gather it in, the 'great harvest' presents more problem than promise. Cf. Schlatter, pp. 322-23.

35. By contrast, the 'harvest' remains a fixed entity throughout, the unchanging background against which the movement from 'tension' to 'solution' is highlighted.

36. Schlatter, pp. 323-24.

37. Albright and Mann observe (p. 114) that 'in Aramaic, the phrase *rab hesādā* means the person responsible for hiring and dismissing harvest workers'. Cf. Gundry, p. 181.

38. Cf. Combrink, 'Structural Analysis', p. 100; Klostermann, p. 85.

39. Cf. the way in which Jesus consistently refers to God in terms of his

authority over the whole created order, including humankind: heaven is God's 'throne' and the earth his 'footstool' (5.34-35); God's domain is therefore the 'Kingdom of heaven' (4.17; 5.3, 10, 19, 20; 6.10; 7.21) and God's relationship to humankind that of the 'Father who is in heaven' (5.16, 45; 6.1, 9; 7.11, 21) or the 'heavenly Father' (5.48; 6.14, 26, 32); it is God's perfection which is to be emulated (5.48) and God's will which sets the standards for entrance into the Kingdom of heaven (7.21); it is God who is sovereign over the elements of nature (5.45), and God who sustains all living things from the 'grass of the field' to human beings (6.25-33); it is God (and not other humans) from whom reward is to be sought (6.1, 2-4, 5-6, 16-18); it is God to whom prayers and requests are to be addressed (6.6, 8, 9-13; 7.7-11) and God who will respond to such prayers and requests (6.6; 7.11). Judging from the way in which Jesus simply assumes these attributes of God, making them in effect the premise underlying his own imperatives (5.34-35, 48), it is clear that God's ultimate authority over the whole created order is a self-evident 'fact' for both Jesus himself and his disciples.

40. For the implied reader, whose perspective is broader than that of the disciples, Jesus' message communicates itself with even greater clarity. While the disciples recognize Jesus' own ministry to the crowds in his reference to the 'few laborers', the implied reader knows that Jesus' ministry (4.17 and on) was in fact preceded by the ministry of John the Baptist (3.1-17). Further, the implied reader knows that God is the 'lord of the harvest' not only because he alone has the ultimate authority attributed to that figure, but also because it is he who has authorized and empowered Jesus, the current 'laborer' in the harvest (cf. 3.13-17). Accordingly, the implied reader recognizes in 9.37-38 the prayer that persons be sent out by God into a ministry directly aligned with the current ministry of Jesus and the prior ministry of John the Baptist.

41. Cf. Robinson, pp. 86-87; Gaechter, *Evangelium*, p. 315; Grundmann, p. 286; Dausch, p. 168; Held, p. 250; Ternant, 'L'évangile', p. 27; Patte, p. 142.

42. Cf. Combet-Galland, p. 33.

43. Cf. Venetz, pp. 159-60.

44. And this means, in turn, that what Jesus here describes in terms of God's action (i.e., the 'sending out of laborers into the harvest') is in fact to be identified with that which Jesus has earlier described as his own action ('I will make you fishermen for people'): it is Jesus himself who will implement God's action of 'sending out laborers into his harvest'. Cf. Deiss, pp. 288-89. Plummer, while he refers back to the call of the two pairs of brothers (4.18-22) and of Matthew (9.9) in connection with his discussion of the commissioning of the disciples in 10.1ff., does not seem to recognize that 4.19 points proleptically to that commissioning. To the contrary, he concludes (p. 146) that 'as yet [i.e., prior to 10.1] nothing has been said of their working with Him or for Him'.

45. While the disciples are obviously already in Jesus' presence in 9.37-38 (and thus would not need to be 'called to him' in 10.1; cf. Schweizer, p. 236; Laufen, p. 204; Morosco, p. 328), it appears that the narrator pointedly depicts Jesus as calling the disciples to himself in order to emphasize that physical proximity between Jesus and 'his twelve disciples' from which he then gives them 'authority'.

46. There is thus no discrepancy here (as Klostermann [p. 85] and Schweizer [pp. 235-36] argue) in the fact that Jesus first instructs his disciples to pray *that God will act* and then responds immediately with *his own initiatives*. Cf. n. 44 above.

47. Here it is significant that the narrator now speaks of Jesus' disciples not simply as 'his disciples' (thus 5.1; 8.21, 23; 9.10, 11, 14, 19) but rather as 'his twelve disciples'. The obvious implications here are that Jesus has by now finished the task of 'calling' disciples (cf. 4.18-20, 21-22; 9.9) and that he now has a fixed group of followers, twelve in number. As Kingsbury observes ('"Miracle Chapters "', p. 562), 'Until 10.1-5, Matthew thinks of Jesus as still gathering his circle of twelve disciples (cf., e.g., 9.9). This explains why he never describes the disciples as being twelve in number prior to ch. 10, but then suddenly makes mention of this fact three times in five verses (cf. 10.1, 2, 5)'. See also Grant, p. 296. That this group of 'twelve disciples' is to be viewed as a group which has already been established and is therefore now a fixed entity, further, is clear from the way in which Matthew simply makes reference to the group without any additional explanation. As Robinson notes (p. 87), 'The "twelve disciples" are introduced in a way which makes it clear that the reader is expected to be familiar with them and with the circumstances of their appointment'. See also Grundmann, p. 287; Luz, p. 143; Frankemölle, pp. 146-47; Plummer, p. 145.

48. The phrase 'to heal every disease and every sickness' describes an authority parallel (and thus not subordinate) to the 'authority over unclean spirits'. The phrase 'to cast them out' functions epexegetically with reference to the 'authority over unclean spirits', defining it more specifically as the 'authority *to cast out* unclean spirits'. Accordingly, it is apparent that the phrase 'and to heal every disease and every sickness' describes not an additional aspect of the 'authority over unclean spirits' but rather a second authority parallel to the first. Cf. Meyer, p. 206; Gaechter, *Evangelium*, p. 317.

49. Cf. Bonnard, pp. 140-41; Gaechter, *Evangelium*, p. 316; Grundmann, p. 287; Gundry, p. 182; Held, pp. 249-50; Luz, p. 144; Patte, p. 142; Sabourin, p. 132; Schniewind, p. 126; Schweizer, p. 233.

50. Here it is clear that the narrator is depicting neither the initial calling by Jesus of twelve individuals nor the appointment by Jesus of a special group of twelve close associates. On the one hand, the calling of disciples two by two (4.18-20, 21-22) or one by one (8.21-22, 9.9) has already taken place; and the narrator draws attention to that fact by putting Simon (Peter),

Andrew, James, and John, i.e., the first disciples to be called (4.18-22), at the head of the list and describing them in exactly the same way as before. (Cf. Jack Dean Kingsbury, 'The Figure of Peter in Matthew's Gospel As a Theological Problem', *JBL* 98 [1979], p. 70). And as noted above (n. 47), the narrator has already (10.1) introduced Jesus' disciples as a fixed group, namely 'his twelve disciples'. Accordingly, in 10.2-4 the narrator simply recognizes the existence of a group which has already been formed and identifies by name (and in most cases an additional qualifying phrase) the members of that group. Thus the emphasis falls not on the establishment of the group but rather on the identity of its membership.

51. That the narrator uses the term 'apostle' to refer above all to the 'sent-ness' of Jesus' disciples is established in the immediately following verse (10.5a), where the narrator indicates that Jesus now 'sends out' (*apesteilen*) 'these twelve' who have just been characterized as 'apostles' (*apostoloi*). Cf. Albright and Mann, p. 122; Karen A. Barta, *Mission and Discipleship in Matthew: A Redaction-Critical Study of Mt. 10.34* (Milwaukee: Marquette University, 1979), pp. 125-26; Beare, *Gospel*, pp. 238-39; Schuyler Brown, 'The Mission to Israel', pp. 75-76; Gundry, p. 182; Meyer, p. 206; Minear, p. 68; Alexander Sand, 'Propheten, Weise und Schriftkundige in der Gemeinde des Matthäus-Evangeliums', in *Kirche im Werden: Studien zum Thema Amt und Gemeinde im Neuen Testament*, ed. Josef Hainz (Munich: Schöningh, 1976), pp. 170-71.

52. While the term 'apostles' (*apostoloi*) in 10.2 derives from the verb 'to send out' (*apostellō*) used in 10.5a rather than from the verb 'to cast/send out' (*ekballō*) used in 9.38, it is nevertheless clear that a strong material connection exists between 10.2 and 9.38.

53. Only Simon and Judas are introduced by means of participial phrases: *ho legomenos Petros* (= the one who is called Peter) and *ho kai paradous auton* (= the one who handed him over). Two of the remaining ten 'apostles' are introduced by name and an appositive noun indicating social or political affiliation: Matthew 'the tax collector' and Simon 'the Cananaean', apparently the designation for a member of the Zealot party (thus Lk. 6.15 and Acts 1.13, where the term 'Zealot' is used in connection with the reference to 'Simon'; cf. BAG, p. 403). Four 'apostles' are introduced by name and an appositive noun indicating family relationship: Andrew 'his [i.e., Simon's] brother', James 'the son of Zebedee' and John 'his brother', James 'the son of Alphaeus'. The remaining four are introduced by name alone: Philip, Bartholomew, Thomas, Thadddaeus.

54. In both cases the narrator describes the action not from the standpoint of the characters involved but rather from the vantage point which he and the implied reader share, i.e., a vantage point which looks back on the entire story as completed action. It is in the 'present time' of the narrator and implied reader between the Resurrection and the Parousia that Simon is known as 'Peter'; and it is in relation to the 'present time' of the narrator and

the implied reader that Judas Iscariot has already 'handed over' another person.

55. Cf. 4.18, where Simon is introduced in exactly the same way.

56. In other words, the narrator now states directly that which he hinted at earlier (4.12-16) in juxtaposing the references to John the Baptist and Jesus: just as John the Baptist has already been 'handed over', so Jesus will be 'handed over' by Judas Iscariot. And in the juxtaposition of the positive ('sending out') and negative ('handing over') motifs in 10.2-4 lies a subtle hint for the implied reader. Since this scene has the same two elements which comprised the scene of 4.12-16, namely, the reference to the 'handing over' of one individual involved in ministry and the indication that a new ministry carried out by another or others is about to begin, the inferences to be drawn from 10.2-4 are the same as those to be drawn from 4.12-16. Just as 4.12-16 hints that Jesus' ministry may well end with his being 'handed over' (in parallelism with the experience of John the Baptist), so 10.2-4 hints that the ministry of Jesus' twelve disciples may likewise end with their being 'handed over' (in parallelism with the prediction concerning Jesus). See also Patte, p. 143.

57. Cf. Ternant, 'L'envoi', p. 29.

58. The phrase *eis hodon ethnōn mē apelthēte* (= do not go out in the way of the Gentiles) is usually interpreted in terms of direction toward the Gentiles (thus, for example, BDF, p. 92; Bonnard, p. 144; Klostermann, p. 86; Maximilian Zerwick and Mary Grosvenor, *A Grammatical Analysis of the Greek New Testament*, vol. 1: *Gospels—Acts* [Rome: Biblical Insititute, 1974], p. 29). But it is clear from the context that what is being prohibited here is not simply movement towards the Gentiles but rather movement which puts one directly in contact with the Gentiles. Only when the phrase is interpreted in this way does it constitute a genuine parallel to the two following commands, both of which point to movement into direct proximity to a group of people. Thus the emphasis in 10.5b-6 is not on movement which tends in a direction but rather on movement which brings one to a goal. Cf. the translation of BAG (p. 556): 'Do not turn to the Gentiles'.

59. Grant conjectures (p. 298, n. 2) that the anarthrous expressions *hodon ethnōn* (= the way of the Gentiles), *polin Samaritōn* (= the city of the Samaritans), and *oikou Israēl* (= the house of Israel) may have 'acquired, among Greek-speaking Jews (i.e., bilingualists), a grammatical character approximating to that of proper names, fixed "*idiōmata*"'.

60. While the identical adverb, *dōrean* (= freely) is used in both phrases to describe first the giving and then the receiving, the sense is that of receiving without giving payment for that which is received and giving without demanding payment for that which is given.

61. The *kakei meinate* (= and remain there) refers back to the *tis en autē axios estin* (= the one in [that town] who is worthy).

62. There are, in addition, three indicative statements within 10.5b-15:

10.8e ('you have received without payment'); 10.10e ('for the laborer is worthy of his food'); 10.15 ('Truly, I say to you, it will be more tolerable. . . '). But by providing the reasoning behind the preceding commands (10.8a-d; 10.9-10d; 10.14) and in this way establishing the significance of those commands, even these indicative statements serve to highlight the imperative tone of the section as a whole.

63. The fact that the command of 10.6 stands parallel to the two commands of 10.5b means that the phrase 'the lost sheep of the house of Israel' parallels the references to 'Gentiles' and 'Samaritans'. Consequently, the object of the disciples' ministry is seen to be the Jewish people as a whole, and not simply certain 'lost' elements among the Jewish people. The phrase 'of the house of Israel' thus functions epexegetically rather than partitively in relation to the phrase 'the lost sheep': the literal meaning of the entire phrase 'the lost sheep of the house of Israel' is therefore 'the lost sheep, i.e., those who constitute the house of Israel'. Cf. Jeremias, p. 26, n. 3; Hoffmann, p. 256, n. 79; Frankemölle, p. 128, n. 226; Laufen, p. 528, n. 408.

64. The two negative commands of 10.5b ('do not go out', 'do not enter') establish a definite pattern which is then altered by the positive command of 10.16 ('go rather'). This shifting of a fixed pattern draws the attention of the implied reader to those features which distinguish the third element in the series from the first two and thus establishes the third element as the crucial one. As Robert C. Tannehill notes in his discussion of the 'forceful and imaginative language' of Jesus' sayings in the Gospels (*The Sword of His Mouth: Forceful and Imaginative Language in Synoptic Sayings*, SBLSSemSup, 1, ed. William A. Beardslee [Missoula, Montana: Scholars, 1975], pp. 43-44), 'It is no accident that threefold repetition is common not only in the Gospels but also in nursery tales . . . Two instances are sufficient to establish a pattern firmly. We then approach the third instance with a definite expectation that it will conform to this pattern. To be sure, we may suspect that the pattern will be twisted in the third instance . . ., but there is an element of suspense in this anticipation, which is the result of the pattern established by the first two instances. The pattern of expectation may function in several ways, then. It points forward to the third instance, and the third instance may simply be a forceful example of this same pattern. In that case, it becomes the climax, for we approach it with the feelings and meanings gathered from the two previous instances. . . However, the third instance may contain an important difference. Then the difference stands out strongly. The first two instances serve as a foil for the third, our attention being attracted by the variation in the pattern. Contrast within a pattern is a way in which a skillful speaker points to what is crucial, for the contrast can be limited to a single dimension of entities which are otherwise similar'.

65. Cf. Hoffmann, pp. 260-61; Schuyler Brown, 'The Mission to Israel', p. 79; Schniewind, p. 128.

66. Contra Patte (p. 145), who seeks a reason for the mission to 'the lost

sheep' in that which is 'appropriate' to them and 'not appropriate' to the Gentiles and Samaritans. That the parallel between Jesus' task of 'shepherding [God's] people Israel' (2.6) and the disciples' commission to 'go to the lost sheep of the house of Israel' is intentional is confirmed in 15.24, where Jesus announces that he himself has been sent 'only to the lost sheep of the house of Israel'.

67. While the disciples' message likewise parallels the message of John the Baptist (3.3), Jesus' predecessor in the ministry to the Jewish people, it is the parallel with Jesus' own message which is in focus here.

68. Jesus does not include the call to 'repent' (cf. 4.17; 3.3) in his directive concerning the disciples' proclamation, a circumstance which scholars have interpreted variously: in terms of the disciples' own identification with sinners (thus Grundmann, p. 290; Schweizer, p. 238), in terms of the emphasis here on the offer of salvation (thus Schweizer, p. 238), or in terms of the pitiable condition of the crowds to be addressed (thus Gundry, p. 185). It is Schlatter (p. 330) whose explanation best accounts for the omission of the call to repentance, when he observes that Matthew has no intention of downplaying the concept of 'repentance' but simply assumes that the reader will, on the basis of previous reference, know what is expected of the one who wishes to attain to the Kingdom of heaven.

69. Cf. Held, p. 250; Laufen, p. 223; Patte, p. 146; Thompson, 'An Historical Perspective', p. 252, n. 23; Claus Westermann, *Der Segen in der Bibel und im Handeln der Kirche* (Munich: Chr. Kaiser, 1968), p. 92. As both Laufen and Held observe, the only healing activity carried out by Jesus which does not appear in this list is the healing of the blind (cf. 9.27-31). Hoffmann (p. 275) and Schweizer (p. 239), while they recognize the parallel which is being drawn between the ministries of Jesus and his disciples, look ahead to 11.2-6 for parallels to the raising of the dead and the cleansing of lepers and thus fail to see the parallels found in chapters eight and nine.

70. That the ministry to which Jesus calls his disciples is to be interpreted literally, i.e, in terms of bringing 'physical' healing, and not metaphorically, i.e., in terms of bringing 'spiritual' healing (thus John Fenton, 'Raise the Dead', *ExpTim* 80 [1968], pp. 50-51; [tentatively] Beare, 'Mission', p. 8), is evident from the fact that the disciples' ministry is patterned after the ministry of Jesus himself. Accordingly, unless one is prepared to argue that the 'healing' which Jesus carried out was only 'spiritual' in nature, it is impossible to avoid the conclusion that the disciples are here called to minister to 'physical' illness, just as Jesus has done.

71. Cf. Beare, 'Mission', p. 8; Broadus, p. 220; Grundmann, p. 290; Hoffmann, p. 264; Mangatt, p. 203; Meier, p. 107; Plummer, p. 149; Radermakers, p. 142.

72. The list found in 10.9-10a can best be interpreted as representative of 'all those things which a traveler would need for a journey'. As Tannehill observes (*Sword*, p. 42), '... a repetitive pattern embracing a series of

particulars can point us beyond the literal sense of the words by suggesting that a series is open ended, that the pattern extends to many situations which have not been named'. Accordingly, the pattern found in 10.9-10a leads the implied reader to the conclusion that if he or she could think of any other items necessary for a journey, those things would also belong on the list.

73. Cf. Bonnard, p. 145, n. 1; Meier, p. 107; Schlatter, p. 331.

74. Cf. Beare, 'Mission', pp. 9-10; Gundry, p. 186; Hoffmann, pp. 264-65; Laufen, pp. 209-10. Klostermann states his viewpoint on this question tentatively, observing (p. 87) that since vv. 9-10 ('don't acquire ...') immediately follow v. 8b ('you have received .../give ...') the meaning of vv. 9-10 could possibly be: 'Don't accept payment on your journey'.

75. Cf. Gundry, p. 186.

76. Cf. Gundry (p. 187) and Schniewind (p. 129), both of whom relate the reference to 'laborers' in 10.10b back to the previous references to 'laborers' in 9.37-38. In a similar vein, see also Patte, p. 147.

77. While Laufen objects (p. 208) that the use of the word *trophē* (= food) does not account for how the disciples are to receive staff and sandals, it is evident from the proverbial tone of 10.10b that this reference to 'food' functions literarily as a synedoche, in which a single item stands as a cipher for the entire class of items which it represents (see Richard N. Soulen, *Handbook of Biblical Criticism* [Atlanta: John Knox, 1981], p. 186). Understood in this way, the word 'food' thus stands as a cipher for 'all those things which are essential for daily living'. Accordingly, the command of 10.9-10a does not relate to the cultic prohibition against entering the temple with staff, shoes, bag, and dusty feet (thus Schniewind, p. 129; Schweizer, p. 239); nor does it relate to the urgency of the mission on which the disciples are sent (thus Boring, p. 145; Sabourin, p. 135). Rather, it relates simply to the attitude of total reliance on God which is supposed to characterize the disciples' ministry. Cf. Gaechter, *Evangelium*, p. 325; Meyer, p. 210; Hoffmann, p. 265. See also Schniewind (p. 129), who moves from the assumption of a cultic basis for the command of 10.9-10a to the conclusion that this command now focuses on God's providential care for his 'laborers'.

78. Jesus' concern here closely resembles the concern expressed in the previous discourse (6.25-34). There he instructs his listeners not to worry about food and clothing but to concern themselves about the Kingdom of God, with the result that 'all these things will be provided for you'. Cf. Hoffman, p. 265; Patte, pp. 146-47.

79. Here Jesus once again draws a parallel between his own ministry and that of his disciples: the disciples' ministry will take them into 'city [and] village', just as Jesus' ministry has taken him to 'all the cities and villages' (9.35). Cf. Gundry, p. 188; Hoffmann, p. 277.

80. Cf. Gaechter, *Evangelium*, p. 327.

81. It is not yet clear, however, what constitutes such 'worthiness'.

82. By the same token, however, the very fact that the disciples are to seek

out the 'worthy person' in any given city or village implies that there are others in that place who are 'not worthy', a circumstance which Jesus then addresses in the following verses (10.12-13).

83. Cf. Alan Hugh McNeile, 'Matthew X 11-15', *JTS* 11 (1910), p. 559.

84. But here again (see n. 81 above) Jesus does not explicitly clarify what he means by 'worthy' and 'not worthy'. Cf. Grundmann, p. 291.

85. The word 'house' thus functions as a second type of synedoche (see n. 77 above), in which a term designating the 'whole' stands as a cipher for 'the sum of the individual parts'. See Soulen, p. 186.

86. Through the act of 'letting [their] peace come upon [a house]' the disciples have in effect transformed the traditional Jewish salutation of peace, the 'wish that one might be blessed in every way' (Broadus, p. 222), into a 'gift' which does not simply wish the peace of God upon a house but itself conveys that peace to the house. See TDNT, *s.v.* '*eirēnē*, by Werner Foerster, 2.413; Grundmann, p. 291; Sabourin, p. 135; Wolfgang Schenk, *Der Segen im Neuen Testament: Eine begriffsanalytische Studie* (Berlin: Evangelische Verlagsanstalt, 1967), p. 177, n. 435. Cf. Gundry's assertion (p. 189) that the disciples 'control the coming and going of peace, i.e., of divine blessing' and Combrink's similar reference ('Structural Analysis', p. 102) to the '*shalom* of God' as that which is 'mediated by the apostles'.

87. Cf. Combrink's observation ('Structural Analysis', p. 102-3) that 'the *shalōm* of God, mediated by the apostle, will return when a house and its inhabitants are not *axia*, i.e., not willing to accept (*dechomai*) the messengers and their words. Being *axios* is therefore correlated to the *dechesthai* of the messengers and their Gospel of the Kingdom ... ' See also Patte, p. 147; Sabourin, p. 135; Schenk, *Segen*, pp. 93-94; Schlatter, p. 333; Schweizer, p. 239. The further question as to whether the 'worthy person' to be sought out by the disciples is to be considered a 'Christian' (thus Schenk, *Segen*, p. 94) or a 'fellow disciple' (thus Gundry, p. 188) is irrelevant in terms of the narrator's story, since according to that story Jesus now has only twelve disciples and he is sending them out for the very purpose of evangelizing others. Cf. the argument of Akira Ogawa (*L'histoire de Jésus chez Matthieu: La signification de l'histoire pour la théologie matthéenne* [Bern: Peter Lang, 1979], p. 235), who disputes the identification of the 'worthy person' as a 'Christian' by raising two pertinent questions: (1) Of what does the 'evangelistic mission' consist, if the disciples are in fact to go to the homes of [those who are already] Christians? and (2) If the disciples do in fact go to the homes of those whom they know to be Christians, why then is there fear that these Christians will not accept them (thus v. 14)? In light of these questions, Ogawa concludes that the 'missionaries' in question are seeking out Jewish homes which they might 'evangelize'.

88. While the only imperative in 10.14 ('shake off the dust') concerns what the disciples are to do as they leave the house or city, it is clear from the correlation between 10.11 and 10.14 that this 'leaving' is in fact directly

connected to the rejection which the disciples have experienced. When the disciples find a worthy person (10.11), they are to remain; when they encounter rejection (10.14), they are to leave.

89. Cf. n. 86 above.

90. Thus BAG, p. 245; Beare, *Gospel*, pp. 243-44; Gundry, p. 190; Schlatter, p. 334; Hoffmann (tentatively), p. 271. But see Henry J. Cadbury ('Dust and Garments', in *The Beginnings of Christianity*, vol. 5, ed. Kirsopp Lake and Henry J. Cadbury [London: Macmillan, 1933], p. 270) for the viewpoint that this gesture involved shaking the dust off of the shoes or the feet.

91. Thus BAG, p. 245; Cadbury, pp. 270-71; Dausch, p. 172; Grundmann, p. 291; Meier, p. 108; Schlatter, p. 335.

92. Thus Hermann L. Strack and Paul Billerbeck, *Kommentar zum Neuen Testament aus Talmud und Midrasch*, Bd. 1: *Das Evangelium nach Matthäus* (Munich: C.H. Beck'sche Verlagsbuchhandlung, 1922), p. 571. See also G.B. Caird, 'Uncomfortable Words: II. Shake Off the Dust from Your Feet (Mk 6.11)', *ExpTim* 81 (1969), p. 41; Gundry, p. 190; Meier, p. 108; Meyer, p. 211.

93. Cf. the comments of Beare (*Gospel*, pp. 243-44), Cadbury (p. 271), Meier (p. 108), Schlatter (p. 334), and Schniewind (p. 127), who relate the significance of this ritual to the status of the city in question as a city which is 'condemned' (thus Meier), 'doomed' (thus Cadbury), underneath a 'curse' (thus Schniewind), awaiting a threatening 'fate' (thus Beare, Meier, Schlatter). See also Boring, pp. 90-91, 146.

94. See the discussion above on the structure of the text.

95. The term 'day of judgment' is one current within the Jewish writings of the intertestamental period (Ps. Sol. 15.12; Jub. 4.19) as a reference to that day on which God will mete out punishment for the wicked and reward for the righteous.

96. In light of the fact that the reference to 'Sodom and Gomorrah' is a firmly fixed motif in the Jewish Scriptures (Gen. 10.19; 13.10; 14.10, 11; 18.20; 19.24, 28; Dt. 29.23; 32.32; Isa. 1.9, 10; 13.19; Jer. 23.14; 49.18; 50.40; Amos 4.11; Zeph. 2.9), it is evident that the present reference to these cities focuses on their reputation as evil cities which met with the judgment of God (thus Filson, p. 130; Hoffmann, pp. 283-84; Schweizer, p. 240; cf. Gundry, p. 190; Laufen, p. 227). Contra Klostermann (p. 88) and Meier (p. 108), it does not point to the specific reputation of Sodom as the city which refused hospitality to the messengers of God.

97. That the primary focus in 10.14 is on rejection by the city as a whole and on the consequent dissociation of the disciples from that entire city becomes clear in 10.15. Here the judgment depicted is judgment against 'that city', described as a collective unit parallel to 'the land of Sodom and Gomorrah'. Cf. Cadbury, p. 271.

98. Contra Caird (pp. 41-42), this prediction of judgment to come is a

reference to the eschatological 'day of judgment' and not to a prior judgment which will occur 'in the course of history'. This is evident, on the one hand, from the fact that the term 'day of judgment', as found in previous Jewish writings (see n. 95 above), serves to designate a specific moment at the end of history. It is evident, on the other hand, from the thrust of Jesus' words themselves. Even though the cities of Sodom and Gomorrah have long ago been destroyed by God as a sign of his judgment upon them, Jesus indicates that they still await a terrible fate on the 'day of judgment'. And it is this fate, rather than the physical destruction of the cities themselves, to which Jesus correlates the fate of 'that city' which does not receive his disciples and their ministry. Further, the severity of this judgment hinges on the significance of the ministry which is rejected: to turn down that which the disciples offer, the gift of the Kingdom of heaven itself (10.7), is to incur a guilt greater than any guilt previously incurred, since the gift is greater than any gift previously offered. Cf. Schlatter, p. 335. In a similar vein Meyer observes (p. 211) that 'the more fully the will of God is proclaimed . . ., the greater the guilt of those who resist it'.

99. Even in 10.14, where it appears that the initiative lies with the one who does not 'receive' the disciples nor 'hear [their] words', it is still clear that the disciples have acted first, both by coming and by proclaiming their message.

100. While the phrase *heōs an elthē ho huios tou anthrōpou* is sometimes translated as 'before the Son of man comes' (thus Albright and Mann, p. 123; Beare, *Gospel*, p. 244; Bonnard, p. 147; Filson, p. 128; Robinson, p. 91; Schweizer, p. 241; Zerwick and Grosvenor, p. 30), there is no apparent grammatical justification for shifting the translation of *heōs* from 'until' to 'before'. Cf. Allen, p. 106; BAG, p. 334; Broadus, p. 227; Dausch, p. 175; Gaechter, *Evangelium*, p. 335; Giblin, pp. 646-47; Grundmann, p. 292; Klostermann, p. 88; Bruce M. Metzger, *A Textual Commentary on the Greek New Testament*, 3rd edn (London: United Bible Societies, 1971), p. 28; Meyer, p. 214; Plummer, p. 153; Schniewind, p. 129; Herman C. Waetjen, *The Origin and Destiny of Humanness: An Interpretation of the Gospel According to Matthew* (San Rafael, California: Crystal, 1976), p. 135.

101. Cf. Plummer's observation (p. 151) that the emphasis in 10.5-15 is on 'the beneficent character of the Gospel which [the disciples] have to carry to the lost sheep of Israel . . . '

102. Cf. Bonnard, p. 146.

103. Cf. Combet-Galland, p. 36; Combrink, 'Structural Analysis', pp. 104-5; Thompson, 'An Historical Perspective', p. 253, n. 25. On the parallelism of 10.19 and 10.23, see also Grant (p. 306) and Waetjen (p. 135).

104. The emphatic nature of the statement *idou egō apostellō hymas* (= behold, I send you out) derives from the conjunction of the demonstrative particle *idou* (= behold) and the emphatic use of the personal pronoun *egō* (= I). Cf. BAG, p. 216; Broadus, p. 224; Gundry, p. 191; Hoffmann, p. 263; Meyer, p. 211; Plummer, p. 151.

105. Cf. 7.15, in which it is evident that such 'sheep/wolf' imagery carries with it the implication of violence done by the wolves to the sheep. There Jesus refers to 'false prophets' who dress 'in sheep's clothing' but are in reality 'ravenous wolves' (presumably ready to 'devour' those who are 'genuine sheep'). For a discussion of the prevalence of the 'vicious wolf' motif in Graeco-Roman literature as well as in the Old Testament, see *TDNT, s.v. 'lykos'*, by Günther Bornkamm, 4.308-9.

106. Contra Gundry (p. 191), who views 10.16 as an indication that the missionaries are now being threatened by the same 'wolflike leaders of the people' who have likewise oppressed the 'lost and shepherdless people of Israel' (9.36; 10.6), it is clear from Jesus' words that the disciples will face persecution from the very people to whom they have gone, and not simply from the leaders. Three clues point to this conclusion: (1) the warning of 10.17a is a general one to 'beware of *people*'; (2) in 10.21 Jesus depicts a situation in which *family members* will attack family members; and (3) in 10.22a Jesus underlines the broad base of this persecution with the warning that the disciples 'will be hated by *everyone*'. Cf. Boring, p. 144.

107. Cf. Hoffmann, p. 294.

108. Cf. Broadus, p. 224; Gundry, p. 191.

109. Cf. *TDNT, s.v. 'ophis'*, by Werner Foerster, 5.580. That the comparison of 'serpents' and 'doves' is one of intentional contrast is reinforced by a parallel usage found in the midrash on Song 2.14 (cited by Strack and Billerbeck, p. 574), where God refers to the Israelites as 'simple as doves' in his presence but 'crafty as serpents' among the nations of the world.

110. Cf. BAG, p. 874; Bonnard, p. 146; Dausch, p. 173; Gaechter, *Evangelium*, p. 330; Sabourin, p. 137.

111. Cf. Combet-Galland, pp. 35-36; *TDNT, s.v. 'peristera'*, by Heinrich Greeven, 6.70; Sabourin, p. 137.

112. Thus Bonnard, p. 146. As Gerhard Kittel explains (*TDNT, s.v. 'akeraios'*, 1.209), the term *akeraios*, a derivation from the verb *keraizō* (= to ravage or destroy), originally denoted 'unravaged' or 'unharmed'. Out of that literal meaning *akeraios* then developed the figurative meaning of 'that which is still in its original state of intactness, totality or moral innocence'. Finally, as it was applied to such words as *oinos* (= wine) and *chrysos* (= gold), *akeraios* acquired the meaning of 'pure'. Cf. BAG, p. 29. That *akeraios* here carries the connotation of 'purity' as opposed to that of 'safety from harm' (thus T.H. Weir ['Matthew x. 16, *ExpTim* 28 (1917), p. 186], who translates 10.16b as follows: 'If you are wise as serpents, then you shall be unharmed as doves') becomes clear in the immediately following verses (10.17-23), where Jesus details the persecutions which await the disciples. It is obvious from these verses that exhibiting the 'wisdom of serpents' will in no way protect the disciples from physical harm.

113. Cf. Schlatter, p. 338.

114. In this case both the disciples and the crowds. See n. 9 above.

115. As Douglas R.A. Hare observes (*The Theme of Jewish Persecution of Christians in the Gospel According to Saint Matthew* [Cambridge: Cambridge University, 1967], p. 104), the verb *mastigoō* (= to flog) carries the judicial connotation of 'legal punishment' in contrast to the more general verb *derō* (= to beat), which could imply 'mob violence'.

116. Under Roman jurisdiction flogging was used as the punishment meted out to those accused of disorderly conduct as well as to those condemned to death. The Jews, on the basis of Dt 25.1-3, maintained flogging as the official punishment handed down by the synagogue. See *IDB*, *s.v.* 'Crimes and Punishments', by M. Greenberg, 1.743; BAG, p. 496. Hare indicates (p. 43) that 'according to the Mishnah a flogging of thirty-nine stripes could be administered by a judiciary of three judges for the violation of a negative precept of the Mosaic law not coupled with a positive precept'. But he goes on to observe (pp. 45-46) that 'local councils [of elders] were in the Diaspora as in Palestine empowered to employ various sanctions, including corporal punishment, for the maintenance of public order among the members of the synagogue. The Mishnah provides evidence that the synagogue authorities could impose a "punishment for disobedience" in certain instances not involving the violation of a Mosaic commandment. Since the Mishnah nowhere defines the nature and application of this non-Mosaic punishment we must assume that considerable freedom was permitted in its use'.

117. Jesus' reference to 'councils' (lit., 'sanhedrins') constitutes in all likelihood a reference to the local Jewish councils of first century Palestine, legal bodies consisting of 23 members. (Thus Strack and Billerbeck, p. 575; Bonnard, p. 148; Broadus, p. 225). But see Hare's suggestion (pp. 102-3) that the reference to 'councils' in 10.17 might refer not to the 'Court of Twenty-Three', which tried primarily capital cases, but rather to a still smaller body, the 'Court of Three', which tried non-capital cases.

118. That the 'rulers' and 'kings' of 10.18 refer to Gentile rather than Jewish authorities becomes evident from the fact that they create the counterpart to the 'councils' and 'synagogues' of 10.17b. And since the 'councils' and 'synagogues' of 10.17b are depicted as the locus of Jewish jurisdiction, it stands to reason that the 'rulers' and 'kings' of 10.18 constitute the corresponding locus of Gentile jurisdiction.

119. Cf. Chapter 1, n. 26. As Hare observes (p. 108), 'As it stands, [10.18] refers primarily to Gentile persecution. Had Matthew wished to implicate Jews as the instigators of this Gentile persecution, he could easily have carried through the parallelism of the preceding clauses by substituting an active verb with *hymas* as object as he has done in verse 17. The fact that he chooses to substitute yet supplies a passive rather than an active form is surely sufficient evidence that Matthew had no intention of implicating the Jews in this reference to Gentile persecution'.

120. The reference to an indeterminate number of 'rulers' and 'kings'

demands a setting which extends beyond the boundaries of Galilee and even of Palestine itself out into the Gentile world of the day. See Chapter 1 above.

121. Cf. Bonnard, p. 148.

122. The phrase, 'to them' points back to the immediate antecedents, the 'rulers' and 'kings' of 10.18 and not to the Jews implied by the verbs of 10.17b (see Chapter 1, n. 26). The immediately following reference to 'the Gentiles' is, accordingly, a reference to Gentiles in general as opposed to Gentile authorities. Cf. Hare, pp. 106-8.

123. That the 'witness' to be given is to be interpreted in a positive sense and not as a testimony *against* the 'rulers', 'kings', and 'Gentiles' in question (thus Frankemölle, p. 120) is clear from the context in which this phrase appears. Since the disciples are on trial 'on [Jesus'] account', the 'witness' which they will bring is accordingly a witness *concerning Jesus*. Cf. Schuyler Brown, 'The Mission to Israel', pp. 85, 88; Patte, pp. 148-49; Schlatter, p. 339.

124. This becomes clear from the definite tone of the temporal clause 'but when they hand you over'. There is no question here as to *whether* persecution will come; rather, Jesus here prepares his disciples to face that which *will certainly* come.

125. Note that Jesus does not command his disciples to give a verbal witness before those to whom they have been handed over, but simply assumes that such a verbal witness will take place.

126. The passive verb 'it will be given' functions as a 'theological passive', which Zerwick defines (p. 76) as ' . . . the passive used in order to avoid directly naming God as agent'.

127. That this process is not envisioned as operating mechanically and thus bypassing the conscious participation of the disciples themselves is evident, as Bonnard observes (p. 148), from the twofold emphasis on the pronoun 'you' in 10.19b-20. Cf. Grundmann, p. 293.

128. That 10.21 is structured chiastically and not simply as a parallelism (thus Grundmann, p. 294) becomes clear from the inverse parallelism represented in the sequences death-father-child and children-parents-death.

129. In light of the fact that the verb 'put to death' stands parallel to the phrase 'hand over to death', it seems evident that the action of the children against their parents is essentially the same as that of brother against brother and father against child. Accordingly, the phrase 'put them to death' carries the meaning 'to hand them over to the officials or mob that will kill them' (Filson, p. 131).

130. This promise ('But the one who remains steadfast to the end will be saved'), while not syntactically linked to the prediction itself, is to be interpreted in light of that prediction. This is evident from the fact that this promise stands parallel to the final phrase of 10.18 ('as a witness to them and to the Gentiles'), which also functions as a promise.

131. But see Chapter 1, n. 10 above and n. 132 below.

132. Cf. Bonnard, p. 149. But this means, however, that it is not justified to restrict the interpretation of 'the end' to the death of the martyrs, as does Bonnard (ibid.). If the first two predictions (10.21) refer to martyrdom itself, the third prediction (10.22a) speaks of an ongoing situation which the disciples will have to face throughout their lives. In light of this and in line with the connection between 'end' and 'salvation', it seems most reasonable to interpret the 'end' of which Jesus speaks in terms of 'the end [of the age]'. See Chapter 1, n. 10. Cf. Albright and Mann, p. 125; Allen, p. 106; Gundry, pp. 193-94; Patte, pp. 150-51; Schweizer, p. 243.

133. Cf. on this point the discussions of Bonnard (p. 149), Frankemölle (pp. 133-34), Gundry (pp. 194-95), Meyer (p. 214), and Ogawa (p. 238), all of whom relate the 'completing [of] the cities of Israel', and thus by the same token the 'flight' which takes the disciples from one city to the next, to the missionary task of the disciples rather than to their escape from persecution. In addition, Georg Künzel (*Studien zum Gemeindeverständnis des Matthäusevangeliums* CThM, Reihe A. 10 [Stuttgart: Calwer, 1978], pp. 232-34), Schniewind (p. 131), H. Schürmann ('Zur Traditions- und Redaktionsgeschichte von Mt 10, 23', in *Traditionsgeschichtliche Untersuchungen zu den synoptischen Evangelien* [Düsseldorf: Patmos, 1968], pp. 153-54, n. 17) and Schweizer (p. 244) likewise relate 10.23b to the mission of the disciples, while at the same time emphasizing the rejection which will accompany that mission.

134. Thus, for example, Allen, p. 107; Ernst Bammel, 'Matthäus 10,23,' *StTh* 15 (961), pp. 91-92; Dausch, p. 174; André Feuillet, 'Les origines et la signification de Mt 10,23^b', *CBQ* 23 (1961), p. 186; Klostermann, p. 89; Martin Künzi, *Das Naherwartungslogion Matthäus 10,23: Geschichte seiner Auslegung* (Tübingen: J.C.B.Mohr [Paul Siebeck], 1970), pp. 177-79; Meier, p. 110; Schlatter, p. 342.

135. This conclusion is confirmed by the fact that the verb *teleō* (= to complete) generally connotes the completion of a task or an undertaking. See Kümmel, p. 62; Jacques Dupont, '"Vous n'aurez pas achevé les villes d'Israël avant que le fils de l'homme ne vienne" (Mat. X 23)', *NovT* 2 (1958), p. 231; Gaechter, *Evangelium*, p. 336. Note, however, BAG (p. 818), who define *teleō* as 'bring to an end', 'finish', or 'complete' but then indicate that 'completing the cities of Israel' means 'to finish (going through) them'.

136. Cf. Schuyler Brown ('The Mission to Israel', p. 87), who relates this verse back to the 'great harvest' of 9.37.

137. As Schuyler Brown observes (ibid., p. 86), 'The impossibility of completing the task is not an excuse for resignation but a stimulus to keep on the move'. Hare (pp. 110-112), who likewise relates 10.23b to 'the mission and its urgency', nevertheless concludes that Matthew makes use of 10.23 as a whole 'only in order to report the prediction [of 10.23a] that Jewish persecution will harry missionaries from town to town'. Cf. Boring, p. 211.

138. Cf. Dupont, pp. 236, 238. Grundmann (p. 294), who also relates 10.23 to 10.5b-6, nevertheless interprets 10.23 strictly in terms of flight and not in terms of ministry.

139. While there has been no previous mention of such a future event, the context of the designation points to the nature of this event. First, it is evident that in speaking of the 'Son of man' Jesus refers to himself: previously when Jesus has used this term (8.18-22; 9.2-8), it has stood as a self-reference, i.e., as a circumlocution for the personal pronoun 'I'. But if 'Son of man' denotes a self-reference to Jesus in 10.23, it also carries with it an eschatological connotation. Jesus elsewhere refers to his present ministry as a 'coming' which has already taken place (5.17; 9.13; cf. 8.29), an event of utmost significance: Jesus 'has come' to 'fulfill the law and the prophets', to 'call sinners', and to break the hold of the demonic powers. Thus when Jesus refers to 'the coming of the Son of man' as an event still to take place, he points to a second major event equal in significance to this first 'coming'. Further, the context of 10.23b identifies this event as eschatological in nature: the linkage of 10.23 with 10.22b, which points to 'the end of the age', makes it most reasonable to construe 'the coming of the Son of man' similarly as an eschatological event. Thus the term 'Son of man', which in 8.20 and 9.6 functions as a self-reference used by Jesus in describing his ministry, here functions together with the reference to 'coming' to identify Jesus as the chief actor in the events of 'the end of the age' (cf. 10.22b). This conclusion is then confirmed by succeeding references to 'the coming of the Son of man' (*erchomai*: 16.27, 28; 24.30, 44; 25.31; 26.64; cf. 24.42, 46; 25.10, 19, 27; *parousia*: 24.3, 27, 37, 39). Cf. Patte, p. 151. For a helpful discussion of the overall significance of 'Son of man' within the Gospel of Matthew, see Jack Dean Kingsbury, 'The Figure of Jesus in Matthew's Story: A Rejoinder to David Hill', *JSNT* 25 (1985), pp. 61-81. Here Kingsbury argues that the best 'translational equivalent' for the term 'Son of man' is the phrase 'this man' (pp. 73-74), a designation which serves within the framework of Matthew's story as '(a) a self-designation, i.e., a term by which Jesus distinguishes himself from others, (b) a term that occurs exclusively in Jesus' mouth and is thus indicative of his phraseological point of view (i.e. of his peculiar speech), and (c) a technical term, in the sense that Jesus employs it in such fashion as to associate it with himself (present work, suffering, and vindication) in a way in which it can be associated with no other human being' (p. 69).

140. Contra Schuyler Brown ('The Mission to Israel', pp. 85-86), who speaks of 'the brief interval until the coming of the Son of man', there is no indication in 10.23b as to when the Son of man will come. The only information offered here concerning the timing of events is that the flight of the disciples, and consequently their ministry itself, will extend 'until the coming of the Son of man'. As Gerhard Delling observes (*TDNT, s.v. 'teleō'*, 8.60, n. 20), 'The pt. of 10.23 is not the time of the *parousia* ... but the

promise to the afflicted'. Cf. the slightly different analysis of Aune (pp. 183-84).

141. Cf. Dausch, p. 174; Künzel, pp. 222-23.

142. As Hare observes (p. 98), 'it is important to note how large a proportion of the material in the chapter is concerned with the non-acceptance of the gospel and the hostility with which the missionaries are treated. There is no instruction regarding what is to be done with converts in a successful mission! Nor is there any suggestion concerning how long missionaries are to stay in an accepting community'.

143. See the discussion of plot in Chapter 2 above. Cf. Schniewind, p. 130.

144. Cf. 5.11 ('Blessed are you *when* people revile you and persecute you and utter all kinds of evil against you falsely .. ') and 10.19a/23a ('But *when* they hand you over/persecute you in this city ... ').

145. Cf. 5.11 ('Blessed are you when people [do evil things to you] *on my account*') and 10.18a/22a ('and you will be led before rulers as well as kings *on my account*'/and you will be hated by everyone *for the sake of my name*').

146. Cf. 5.12 ('Rejoice and be glad, for your reward is great in heaven; for in this way they persecuted *the prophets who were before you*') and 10.18-19a ('and you will be led before rulers as well as kings on my account *as a witness to them and to the Gentiles*. But when they hand you over, do not worry about *how or what you shall say*').

147. 'Therefore, do not worry, saying, "What shall we eat?" or "What shall we drink?" or "What shall we wear?". For the Gentiles seek all these things; for your heavenly Father knows that you have need of all these things. But seek first the Kingdom [of God] and his righteousness; and all these things will be provided for you'. Here it must be noted that the passive verb 'will be provided' serves to indicate divine action (see n. 126 above), just as does the passive verb within 10.19b ('for *it will be given* to you in that hour what you shall say'). Cf. Gundry, pp. 192-93.

148. 'Therefore, do not worry about tomorrow; for tomorrow will worry about itself. Sufficient for the day is the evil of it'.

149. As Giblin observes (p. 655), ' ... the task to be finished [in 10.23] is a movement in cities that reflects the work which Jesus Himself has been doing and continues to do. Along with other features already discussed, this association helps bring out the fact that the mission of the Twelve is conceived in terms of a mission to Israel's cities because such was the scope of Jesus' own mission'. Cf. Schuyler Brown, 'The Mission to Israel', pp. 86-87.

150. Cf. Radermakers, p. 143.

151. Cf. Schuyler Brown, 'The Mission to Israel', p. 87.

152. Cf. Barta (*Mission and Discipleship*, p. 90, n. 6) and Grundmann (p. 294), who nevertheless view the 'flight' motif of 2.13-18 strictly in terms

of escape and not in terms of the furtherance of ministry. See also the recurrence of the 'flight' motif in 12.14-15, 14.12-13, 15.21, and 16.1-4.

153. Cf. N. van Bohemen, 'L'institution des douze', in *La formation des évangiles: Problème synoptique et formgeschichte*, RechBib, 2 (Paris: Desclée de Brouwer, 1957), p. 136; Gaechter, *Evangelium*, pp. 332-33; Helga Rusche, 'Die Boten der neuen Welt', *BibLeb* 8 (1967), p. 211. See also Combet-Galland (p. 33), who in reverse fashion points ahead to the 'brother vs. brother' motif of 10.21 in commenting on the prediction in 10.4 that Judas will 'hand over' Jesus.

154. While the second command 'not to fear' (10.28a) is paralleled by the command 'but fear rather' (10.28b), it is nevertheless clear that the overall focus of 10.26-33 lies on the threefold call 'not to fear'.

155. Cf. Barta, *Mission and Discipleship*, p. 90; Patte, p. 151.

156. See the above discussion.

157. Here a note of irony is contained in Jesus' words. It is scarcely by chance that Jesus, who has just commissioned his disciples to go to 'the lost sheep of the house of Israel' (10.6), now speaks of himself as 'master of the house' and designates his disciples as 'the members of his household'. Thus it is sheer irony that the ones ('they') who should recognize Jesus as 'the master of the house [of Israel]' and respond to him accordingly, instead identify him as 'Beelzebul, the prince of demons' (cf. 9.34), whose name means none other than 'master of the house [of demons]'. Cf. Dausch, p. 175; Gaechter, *Evangelium*, pp. 340-41; Gundry, p. 195; Meyer, p. 215; E.C.B. Maclaurin, 'Beelzeboul', *NovT* 20 (1978), p. 156.

158. While no mention is made in 9.34 of the name 'Beelzebul', it is clear that the so-designated 'prince of demons' is in fact to be identified with the 'Beelzebul' of 10.25b. Cf. 12.24, 27.

159. Here again, as in the case of 10.16-23, Jesus points back to the prediction of persecution to come which is found in the previous discourse: 'Blessed are you when people revile you and persecute you and say all kinds of evil things about you falsely on my account' (5.11). Cf. Barta, *Mission and Discipleship*, pp. 105-106.

160. The *oun* of 10.26 appears to carry an adversative sense (= however) rather than an inferential sense (= therefore). Cf. BAG, p. 597. Meyer (p. 215), who views the *oun* of 10.26 as an 'inference' from 10.24-25 ('since, from the relation in which, as my disciples, you stand to me as your Master, it cannot surprise you, but must only appear as a necessary participation in the same fate, if they persecute you'; cf. Bonnard, p. 151), nevertheless does not explain why fearlessness is the *logical* response to the situation depicted in 10.24-25.

161. Contra Gaechter (*Evangelium*, p. 342), who views the *oun* as 'purely stylistic' and consequently considers the entirety of 10.26-31 as 'virtually unconnected' to 10.24-25.

162. Cf. Gundry, p. 196.

163. Cf. Grundmann (p. 296), Harry S. Pappas ('The "Exhortation to Fearless Confession"—Mt. 10.26-33', *GrOrthTR* 25 [1980], p. 240), and Wolfgang Trilling ('Confession sans crainte [Mt 10.26-33]', *AssSeign*, 2e série, 43 [1969], p. 21), none of whom, however, relates the pronoun 'them' of 10.26 to its most immediate antecedent, the implied subject ('they') of 10.25b.

164. Cf. Bonnard, p. 151; Combrink, 'Structural Analysis', p. 106; Laufen, pp. 159-60. That *gnōsthēsetai* is best translated as 'will be made known', (thus Beare, *Gospel*, p. 246; Filson, p. 132; TEV; NIV; NEB; Schweizer, p. 245) and not as 'will be known' (thus RSV) is evident from the fact that the second half of the parallelism demands a 'theological passive' (see n. 126 above) which in its force parallels *apokalyphthēsetai* (= will be revealed).

165. The parallelism of these two phrases in position and in function— both of them serve as the object of the imperative verb which follows— indicates that the phrase 'what you hear [whispered] in your ear' points to the action of Jesus himself no less than the phrase 'what I tell you in the darkness'.

166. Cf. Trilling, p. 22; Laufen, p. 165.

167. The parallel structures consist of a present imperative (*mē phobeisthe* = do not fear/*phobeisthe de* = but fear) followed by a participial phrase (= those who . . ./the one who . . .).

168. Cf. Barta, *Mission and Discipleship*, p. 113; Laufen, p. 163.

169. While it is difficult to establish to what extent the Greek concept of 'mortal body' and 'immortal soul' has influenced the present form of 10.28a (note, for example, the differing positions on this question taken by Schlatter [p. 345], G. Dautzenberg [*Sein Leben bewahren: Psychē in den Herrenworten der Evangelien* StANT, 14 (Munich: Kösel, 1966), p. 147], Schweizer [pp. 247-48], and Pappas [p. 242; cf. Dausch, p. 176]), it is widely recognized that within the Jewish thought world of the first century the reference to 'body and soul' constitutes a reference to the totality of the human being (thus Bonnard, p. 152; Dautzenberg, pp. 150-52; I. Howard Marshall, 'Uncomfortable Words: VI. "Fear him who can destroy both soul and body in hell" [Mt 10.28 R.S.V.]', *ExpTim* 81 [1970], pp. 277, 279; *TDNT* s.v. '*psychē*' by Eduard Schweizer, 9.646; Waetjen, p. 136).

170. But as Dautzenberg observes (p. 148), the focus of 10.28 lies not on any discussion of the nature of future existence but solely on 'the Judge and his judgment': 'Die in 10,28a liegende Möglichkeit, das Überleben der *psychē* als solches irgendwie positiv oder tröstlich zu deuten und dadurch das Bestehen des Todes zu erleichtern, diese Möglichkeit wird nicht genutzt, der Zwischenstand interessiert nicht, ebensowenig irgendein menschlicher Zustand; es kommt nur auf den Richter und sein Gericht an. So erreicht die Aussage des Logions ihr Ziel wirklich erst in der zweiten Hälfte, der erste Teil ist im Gegensatz zu ihr geformt und muss von ihr her interpretiert werden'.

171. There is virtually unanimous agreement by scholars that 'the one who is able to destroy both soul and body in Gehenna' is God and not Satan (thus, for example, Allen, p. 109; Beare, *Gospel*, p. 248; Bonnard, p. 152; Broadus, p. 230; Dausch, p. 176; Filson, p. 133; Gaechter, *Evangelium*, p. 343; Gundry, p. 197; Klostermann, pp. 90-91; Meyer, p. 216; Pappas, pp. 242-43; Patte, p. 152; Plummer, p. 155; Sabourin, p. 142; Schlatter, p. 345; Schniewind, p. 133; Schweizer, *Good News*, pp. 247-48; Strack and Billerbeck, p. 580; Waetjen, p. 136). Even Grundmann (p. 297), who views the destruction of 'soul and body' as the work of Satan, is forced to admit that Satan can carry this out only when the human being has been turned over to him (presumably by God). Robinson (p. 94) refuses to resolve the question in any fashion, observing only that 'we need not decide this question in order to appreciate Jesus' meaning. Whichever, whoever, whatever it may be that destroys the soul, it is there that the real danger lies'.

172. Thus, for example, 5.22; 13.42, 50; 18.8, 9; 25.41; cf. 3.10, 12; 7.19; 13.40.

173. Thus, for example, 18.8; 25.41, 46.

174. As Dautzenberg points out (p. 149), this warning does not deal with questions of detail concerning the outworking of this fate but instead depicts Gehenna as a place of 'death' in contrast to a place of 'life'. Cf. Marshall, p. 279; Sabourin, p. 142.

175. The prospect of Gehenna is such a fearsome one that Jesus elsewhere (5.29, 30; 18.8, 9) counsels his hearers to take extraordinary measures rather than run the risk of being thrown into Gehenna.

176. See, for example, Gaechter, *Evangelium*, p. 343; Meyer, p. 216; Strack and Billerbeck, p. 582.

177. Contra Dausch (pp. 176-77), who sees first a contrast between sparrows and human beings and then a contrast between the hairs of the head and the entirety of human life ('das ganze Leben der Menschen'), it is by means of his reference to 'the hairs of the head' that Jesus illustrates the vast distinction between sparrows and human beings. Cf. Plummer, p. 155; Sabourin, p. 142.

178. Contra Schlatter (p. 346), who speaks of the promise of God's protection (10.29-31) which stands directly next to the word of warning found in 10.28. Cf. Boring's observation (p. 167) that 'the words concerning God's care for sparrows and numbering the hairs of our heads represent prophetic exhortation with the motifs of persecution and eschatological judgment in the background, not a romanticist view of nature'.

179. Cf. Beare, *Gospel*, p. 248; Dausch, p. 177; Filson, p. 133. Waetjen, however, goes too far when he asserts (p. 136) that 'the divine jurisdiction *cannot* prevent sparrows from falling to the earth or the apostles from being killed' (italics mine).

180. Cf. Gaechter, *Evangelium*, p. 344; Grundmann, p. 298; Pappas,

pp. 244-45; Robinson, pp. 94-95. While Bonnard argues (p. 152) that the phrase 'without your Father' refers to the will of God (thus also Beare, *Gospel*, p. 248; Gundry, p. 198; Daniel O'Connor and Jacques Jimenez, *The Images of Jesus: Exploring the Metaphors in Matthew's Gospel* [Minneapolis, Minnesota: Winston, 1977], p. 105; Plummer, p. 155; Sabourin, p. 142), the force of the logic in 10.29-31 indicates rather that Jesus' emphasis here is on the presence of God, which supports and sustains the disciples throughout their sufferings, and not on God's will. The imagery of 10.29b is that of a God who notices and has concern for even the insignificant little sparrow who falls to the ground. The argument 'from the lesser to the greater', accordingly, is that God will likewise notice and concern himself with your fate when you are persecuted. Only when interpreted in this way, do these words of Jesus serve as a promise in regard both to sparrows and to the disciples.

181. Here it must be noted that the scenes depicted in 10.32a, 33a point to a witness carried out in the context of persecution generally or court trial specifically (cf. Hare, p. 101): (1) the 'people' of whom the disciples are to 'beware' (10.17a) and who are responsible for 'handing over' the disciples (10.17, 19, 21) are now depicted as the 'people' before whom the disciples are to acknowledge Jesus (10.32a; cf. Brown, 'The Mission to Israel', p. 83; Gundry, p. 192); (2) the witness through suffering depicted in 10.18b is here specified to be 'acknowledgment' of Jesus (10.32a); (3) the witness of 10.32-33 takes place in the context of that persecution to the death depicted in 10.26-31 (cf. Bonnard, p. 153). Nevertheless, the structure of the statements of 10.32-33 indicates that the focus here does not lie on the aspect of 'court trial' but simply on the disciples' witness to Jesus or their rejection of him. While the trial setting ('before people') simply provides the constant backdrop in both statements, it is the response of the disciples which provides the point of contrast between the two.

182. While Pappas (p. 246) seems uncertain that the reference here is to 'a forensic situation', the previous references to the 'day of judgment' (10.15) and the significance of that day (10.22, 28) point in that direction.

183. Jesus' reference to 'denial before people', however, points not to the mere failure to witness, but rather to the straightforward rejection of one's relationship to Jesus, that is, to open 'apostasy'.

184. Cf. Laufen, p. 462, n. 52.

185. Cf. Gaechter, *Evangelium*, pp. 345-46; Patte, p. 154.

186. The negative imperative implies that the disciples *do* hold that viewpoint which Jesus is about to repudiate.

187. Cf. Dausch, pp. 177-78.

188. In Tannehill's words (*Sword*, pp. 140-41), '[This] announcement stands out against its opposite, the peace for which men long and which they hope Jesus will bring. This is surely a legitimate hope; indeed, "peace" is one way of expressing the eschatological salvation which God will give at the

chosen time through Christ. Here this hope is brushed aside, and our attention is directed instead to that which replaces our hope, the "sword". In contrast to peace, we naturally think of the "sword" as a symbol of war, and that is indeed part of its meaning here (cf. BAG, p. 497). So something important is gained by this use of antithesis. The word "sword" is more forceful because of contrast with its opposite, part of its meaning is clarified by this antithetical setting, and the reader is immediately involved in what is being said because of the sharp rejection of his hope for peace'.

189. As Tannehill observes (ibid., pp. 141-42), 'Since [the infinitive *dichasai*] explains and develops the reference to a sword, it here refers to the cutting function of that sword, and we could also translate "to split", "to cleave", "to sever".... The connection between this infinitive and the noun "sword" contributes to the force of both. It suggests, on the one hand, that the separating is a violent act. On the other hand, it awakens further connotations of "sword". This "sword" not only suggests war in contrast to peace but is also an instrument which violently severs what naturally belongs together, hacking to pieces the living organism of the family'. Cf. Combet-Galland, p. 37; Gundry, p. 199.

190. Thus O. Lamar Cope (*Matthew: A Scribe Trained for the Kingdom of Heaven*, CBQMS, 5 [Washington, D.C.: Catholic Biblical Association of America, 1976], p. 79) in distinction to Schlatter (p. 350), Schniewind (p. 135), and Schweizer (*Good News*, p. 251), each of whom interprets the sword in literalistic fashion as persecution carried out against the disciples by opponents who wield the sword.

191. Tannehill (*Sword*, p. 142) classifies the list of family relationships found in 10.35 as 'a series of focal instances' and observes in this regard: '... there is no reference to father and daughter, mother and son, brother and brother, etc. These are unnecessary, if the mode of language is properly understood, for we have here a series of focal instances. As we saw above ..., the focal instance consists of a specific and extreme case which implies more than what is said explicity. The choice of an extreme instance gives it a broad range of implication, suggesting that what holds true even here may be true of other situations as well. As frequently, the focal instances are arranged in a series, an openended series, for the list could easily be continued by mention of other relationships. Indeed, the rhythmic effect of the threefold repetition of the same pattern invites additions, for a rhythm, once established, suggests its own continuance'.

192. Cf. the parallel references to the purpose of Jesus' 'coming' in 5.17 and 9.13. As Tannehill observes (ibid., p. 143), '[The division of the family] is presented not as an unfortunate side effect of Jesus' ministry but as the very purpose of his coming. Obviously this is not a general summary of Jesus' mission; it is not meant to be. But the choice of this manner of speech is significant. The text contradicts our desire to think of such family divisions as temporary and accidental, as problems which can be overcome with time

or better counseling techniques. It claims that such divisions are inherent in Jesus' mission and therefore a fate which we cannot avoid if we follow him. It speaks not of temporary personal problems but of the dark will of God, of a cup which we wish would pass from us but which we must drink'. See also Minear (p. 70), Patte (pp. 154-55), and (tentatively) Meyer (p. 217), in distinction to Eduardo Arens (*The Ēlthon-Sayings in the Synoptic Tradition: A Historico-Critical Investigation*, OrbBibOr, 10 [Göttingen: Vandenhoeck & Ruprecht, 1976], pp. 87-89), Beare (*Gospel*, p. 249), Broadus (p. 232), Filson (p. 134), and Gaechter (*Evangelium*, p. 347), who view the reference to the 'sword' as a reference not to the purpose but rather to the result of Jesus' 'coming'.

193. Cf. Gaechter, *Evangelium*, p. 348.

194. Cf. Barta, *Mission and Discipleship*, p. 77. Here it is clear that the phrase 'is not worthy of me' is applied to those who are already disciples of Jesus (cf. Gaechter, *Evangelium*, p. 349). Accordingly, the threefold parallelism of 10.37-38 can only be interpreted as a warning concerning the conditions under which one forfeits one's present status as 'disciple'.

195. Cf. Wolfgang Trilling, 'Disponibilité pour suivre le Christ (Mt 10, 37-42)', *AssSeign*, 2e série, 44 (1969), p. 16.

196. Thus Albright and Mann, p. 132; Broadus, p. 232; Dausch, p. 178; Filson, p. 134; D.R. Fletcher, 'Condemned to Die. The Logion on Cross-Bearing: What Does It Mean?' *Interp* 18 (1964), pp. 161-64; Laufen, pp. 313-14; Plummer, p. 156; Schniewind, p. 136. In a similar vein, Gaechter (*Evangelium*, p. 350), Schlatter (pp, 350-51), Hengel (pp. 64-65), and (tentatively) Laufen (p. 313) relate the reference to 'cross' to the death meted out to those who stood up against Rome as 'Zealots'. For a helpful analysis of other possible origins of the 'cross-bearing' motif, see Laufen, pp. 309-12.

197. Cf. the complementary observations of Schlatter (p. 351) concerning Jesus and of Bonnard (p. 157) concerning the disciples.

198. Cf. Bonnard, p. 157; Combet-Galland, p. 36.

199. The fact that the third element (10.38) breaks the pattern established by the first two (10.37a, 37b) indicates that the weight of the whole sequence lies on the final element. Accordingly, Jesus' primary concern in 10.37-38 is to establish that solidarity in suffering defined in 10.38.

200. While 10.38 provides the most direct clue thus far that Jesus will meet with a violent fate (cf. Patte, p. 139), there have already been three explicit clues to the same fact: (1) it is just as John the Baptist is 'handed over' that Jesus positions himself for the inauguration of his own ministry (4.12-16; see Chapter 2 above); (2) in 9.15 Jesus speaks of a time when the 'bridegroom' will be 'taken away', a time at which the 'wedding guests' will 'fast'; (3) in 10.4 the narrator introduces Judas Iscariot as 'the one who handed him [i.e., Jesus] over'.

201. Thus Bonnard (p. 158), Dautzenberg (p. 57), Hare (p. 101), and Klostermann (p. 92) in distinction to those who view 10.39 as a reference not

to physical death but rather to self-renunciation (thus Laufen, pp. 326-29) or self-giving service (thus Barta, *Mission and Discipleship*, p. 86).

202. Cf. Dautzenberg, pp. 58-59.

203. Cf. Laufen, p. 334.

204. Cf. Aune, pp. 166-67.

205. As Dautzenberg correctly argues (p. 58), the 'inner dynamic' of this saying demands that the term 'life' carry a unified meaning in both halves of the parallelism.

206. Cf. Trilling, 'Disponibilité', pp. 16-17.

207. Cf. Bonnard, p. 158.

208. Cf. Schlatter, pp. 351-52.

209. See the discussion of 10.1 above.

210. The phrase *eis onoma* (lit., 'in the name [of]') is best translated as 'because he is' (thus Allen, p. 112; Dausch, p. 179; J. Ramsey Michaels, 'Apostolic Hardships and Righteous Gentiles: A Study of Matthew 25.31-46', *JBL* 84 [1965] p. 28, n. 5; Schniewind, p. 137; Strack and Billerbeck, p. 590). Minear (p. 71), to the contrary, interprets the phrase 'in the name [of]' as a reference to the situation in which 'a host entertains as guest a prophet *who has been sent by another prophet*' (italics mine).

211. Cf. Beare, *Gospel*, p. 251.

212. See n. 64 above.

213. Cf. Frankemölle (pp. 147-48), Gaechter (*Evangelium*, p. 352), Rusche (p. 215), and Schniewind (p. 137), all of whom consider the threefold sequence of 10.41-42 to have reached its climax in the reference of 10.42 to the 'little one' who is a 'disciple'.

214. Cf. Allen (p. 112), Bonnard (pp. 158-59), Boring (p. 212), Dausch (p. 179), Filson (p. 134), Gundry (pp. 202-5), Klostermann (p. 93), Meyer (p. 218), Plummer (p. 157), Schniewind (p. 137), Schweizer (*Good News*, p. 253), Trilling ('Disponibilité', p. 19), Waetjen (p. 137), and (tentatively) Grundmann (pp. 301-2), and Sabourin (p. 144), all of whom relate the terms 'prophet' and 'righteous one' to those who are followers of Jesus rather than to Old Testament personages, the 'prophets' and 'righteous ones' out of Jewish history (thus, for example, Gaechter, *Evangelium*, p. 352; Schlatter, pp. 352-53).

215. As Gerhard Friedrich observes with reference to the Gospel of Matthew (*TDNT*, *s.v.* '*prophētēs*', 6.831), 'The OT prophets are [for Matthew] the mouth of God through which He speaks to men... The prophet is not the true speaker but God, who uses the prophet when He addresses the people'. Cf. Boring's parallel observation (p. 88) that 'The [early Christian] prophet speaks with a sense of immediate authority resulting from his conviction that he has been personally commissioned by the deity to deliver a message to the people'.

216. Cf. Boring, pp. 139-40. In addition, by linking his disciples to the 'prophets who were before [them]', Jesus alludes to another crucial aspect of

their situation. If the disciples stand in a line with the 'prophets' who have preceded them, it follows that they can also expect to meet the same fate as those earlier prophets, namely, persecution (5.12). And it is in order to make this very point that Jesus establishes this link between the disciples and their predecessors in 5.11-12. For further discussion of the 'suffering prophet' motif in Jewish and early Christian understanding, see Boring, pp. 114-17, and Friedrich, pp. 834-35.

217. Note the comments of Boring (p. 148; cf. p. 89), who observes with reference to 10.40: 'The speaker is the risen Jesus, who has his place in the revelatory "chain of command" second only to God. Even as the exalted one, he is still the "sent one", who now sends forth his own missioners to speak his word. The speaker is to declare his message with the *egō* of the exalted Lord, not reporting what Jesus once said but speaking the word of the Lord in the first person in the present, so that the hearer is addressed by the risen Jesus, who speaks in behalf of God'. That Jesus calls his disciples to proclaim his message is confirmed by the reference in 7.22 to those who 'prophesy in [Jesus'] name'. Cf. Sand, p. 175.

218. Cf. Boring's comments (p. 148) on 10.40.

219. Cf. ibid., p. 46.

220. Cf. Plummer's observation (p. 157) that '[missionaries] are "righteous", for they preach the righteousness which is set forth in the Sermon on the Mount, and it is assumed that they practice it'. In a similar vein, Gottlob Schrenk (*TDNT, s.v. 'dikaios'*, 2.190) notes that '*dikaios* can . . . be used of the disciple or the Christian as the one who truly fulfils the Law or the divine will. . . Thus the *dikaios* in Mt. 10.41, who is received *eis onoma dikaiou*, is pleasing to God'.

221. Cf. Boring, p. 212; Grundmann, pp. 301-2; Sabourin, p. 144; Sand, p. 177; Schweizer, *Good News*, p. 253; Trilling, 'Disponibilité', p. 19.

222. Thus, for example, 3.15; 5.20; 6.33. Sand suggests (p. 178) that the reference to 'righteous ones' designates persons who serve as 'witnesses to the secrets of the Kingdom of God, . . . to whom it is given to understand the truths of this Kingdom'.

223. This view appears to be confirmed in ch. 18, where Jesus exhorts his disciples not to 'offend' (18.6: *skandalizō*) or to 'despise' (18.10: *kataphroneō*) 'one of these little ones [who believe in me]' and concludes (18.14) that it is 'not the will of your Father in heaven that one of these little ones perish'.

224. Cf. the similar comments of Grundmann (pp. 301-2), Gundry (p. 203), Klostermann (p. 93), and Meier (p. 115), all of whom view 10.40-42 in terms of a 'hierarchical' listing from 'apostle' (10.40; but see n. 226 below) down to 'little ones' (10.42). Gaechter (*Evangelium*, p. 352), to the contrary, views the 'prophet' and 'righteous one' as OT figures and sees the series in 10.41-42 thus rising to its climax in the NT figure of the 'disciple'.

225. Cf. Trilling, 'Disponibilité', p. 19. See also Schlatter's related comments (p. 353) concerning the 'disciples' of 10.42 (whom he, however,

identifies as NT figures in contrast to the OT 'prophets' and 'righteous ones' of 10.41).

226. See n. 224. above. While the structure of the text makes it invalid to identify the sequence as beginning with the reference in 10.40 to 'apostle' (thus Grundmann, pp. 301-2; Gundry, p. 203; Meier, p. 115; Klostermann, p. 93), it is correct to observe that the ordering of the series in 10.41-42 moves from 'greater' to 'lesser' in terms of outward honor.

227. The shift in the description of those to be received draws attention to the last item in the series as does also the shift in the description of the reward to be granted those who receive. See n. 64 above.

228. Cf. the comments of Wolfgang Trilling, 'Amt und Amtsverständnis bei Mt', in *Mélanges bibliques en hommage au R.P. Béda Rigaux*, ed. Albert Descamps and André de Halleux (Gembloux: Duculot, 1969), p. 39.

229. Cf. Schlatter, p. 354.

230. Contra Helga Rusche, *Gastfreundschaft in der Verkündigung des Neuen Testaments und ihr Verhältnis zur Mission* (Münster: Aschendorff, 1958), p. 15.

231. See the discussions of 10.15 and 10.23 above.

232. Here again the paradoxical nature of Jesus' saying comes to the fore. The strongest assurance of future reward comes neither to those who receive 'prophets' nor to those who receive 'righteous ones' but rather to those who receive the humblest of them all, the 'little ones', whose only identifying characteristic is that they are 'disciples'.

233. Cf. the conclusions of Günther Bornkamm with reference to the concept of 'reward' in Jesus' proclamation of the Kingdom ('Der Lohngedanke im Neuen Testament' in *Gesammelte Aufsätze*, 2: *Studien zu Antike und Urchristentum*, BeiEvTh, 28, ed. E. Wolf [Munich: Chr. Kaiser, 1959], pp. 77-79).

234. Cf. Dausch, p. 179; Klostermann, p. 93; Laufen, p. 278.

235. The thematic movement of the discourse aligns itself with the threefold structure of the text identified on the basis of formal analysis (See section II of the present chapter.

236. Cf. the comments of Beare ('Mission', p. 3): 'We must repeat and emphasize that Matthew, although he tells us that Jesus sent his disciples out and gave them directions, says not a word about what they did, or where they went, nor does he even mention that they returned... They are simply allowed to appear again, without any reference to a brief or prolonged absence on mission, in the controversy-story at the beginning of chapter 12, where they are criticized for plucking grain on the sabbath; and there is never another word about their mission. So far as Matthew is concerned, it drops into limbo and is forgotten as if it had never taken place. Perhaps it never did'. Cf. the comments of Combrink ('Structural Analysis', p. 99) and Patte (p. 138).

237. The reference in 11.1 to 'their cities' is best understood as a reference

to 'cities inhabited by Jewish people', as the parallel reference in 9.35 to 'their synagogues' makes clear. Cf. Morosco, pp. 328-29. Gundry (p. 203), however, misses the force of this parallel altogether, interpreting 'their cities' as 'the very cities *where the disciples were to go*' (italics mine).

238. Cf. the observation of J. Lee Magness (*Sense and Absence: Structure and Suspension in the Ending of Mark's Gospel*, SBLSemSt [Atlanta, Georgia: Scholars, 1986], p. 67) that 'whether or not the author intends for his reader to think that the journey took place immediately, took place later in Jesus' ministry, or could only occur after the resurrection and commission (Matthew 28.18-20), the expectation and visualization of a missionary tour has been created in the mind of the reader apart from any narration of it'.

239. While the narrator makes no specific mention here of Jesus' 'healing' activities (cf. 9.35), it is nevertheless evident from the verbal parallels between 9.35 and 11.1 that the focus of 11.1 lies on the similarities with 9.35 and not on the differences between the two verses.

240. See n. 19 above.

241. Cf. Radermakers (p. 134) and Waetjen (pp. 132-33) in contrast to those who speak of the departure and return of the disciples as either clearly implied by the text (thus Barta, 'Mission in Matthew', pp. 529-31; Broadus, p. 233; Schweizer, *Good News*, pp. 253-54) or apparently implied by the text (thus Beare, *Gospel*, pp. 251-52; Dausch, p. 170; Dupont, p. 238; Grundmann, p. 303; Hare, p. 97; Klostermann, p. 93; Schlatter, p. 355).

Notes to Chapter 4

1. Cf. the observation of Magness (p. 67): 'Matthew 10 records elaborate instructions for an evangelistic journey which is not narrated. Whether or not the author intends for his reader to think that the journey took place immediately, took place later in Jesus' ministry, or could only occur after the resurrection and commission (Matthew 28.18-20), the expectation and visualization of a missionary tour has been created in the mind of the reader apart from any narration of it'.

2. Since the implied reader accepts the narrator as 'reliable', there is no question as to 'whether' the disciples will act but only 'when'.

3. See the discussion of 10.1 above.

4. See the discussion of 10.7-8 above.

5. See the discussion of 10.24-25 above.

6. The fact that the implied reader already knows that Jesus will be 'handed over' does not mean that Jesus himself has faced the threat of persecution at this point in the story.

7. Cf. Barta (*Mission and Discipleship*, p. 92), who suggests that by introducing the persecution texts of 10.16-23 into the discourse of 10.5b-42

Matthew 'has set down a *pattern* of mission-persecution, ministry-suffering, which has its basis ultimately in the life, death, and resurrection of Jesus'.

8. Already at this point in the story the disciples would theoretically be in a position to 'reflect' the 'proclaiming and healing' aspects of Jesus' ministry, since Jesus has 'imaged' that for them in 4.23–9.34.

9. Contra Barta (*Mission and Discipleship*, p. 92), who concludes that because the persecution texts occur within the discourse of 10.5b-42 this means that Matthew 'has "historicized" the persecutions by linking them to the first mission charge . . . '

10. The limits of these sections are determined by the related transitional verses, 16.21 and 26.1-2, both of which announce a turning point in the story. In 16.21 the narrator indicates that the focus of the story is now shifting from the ministry of Jesus (4.17–16.20) to his suffering, death, and resurrection (16.21–28.20): 'From that time on Jesus began to show his disciples that he must go to Jerusalem and suffer many things from the elders and chief priests and scribes and be killed and on the third day rise'. And in 26.1-2 the narrator indicates that the suffering, death, and resurrection of Jesus, those events towards which 16.21–25.46 (indeed the entire story) has been building, are finally about to transpire. See Chapter 2, n. 158 for a discussion of the overall structure of the Gospel of Matthew.

11. See the discussion of point of view in Chapter 2 above.

12. See the discussion of point of view in Chapter 2 above.

13. *proserchomai*. In addition, the crowds 'follow' Jesus (12.15; 14.13) and 'gather together' to him (13.2).

14. *prosphero*.

15. *proskaleo*.

16. Contra Gerhardsson (*The Mighty Acts*, pp. 31-32) and Held (pp. 251-52), this reference is to Jesus and not to the disciples. Jesus' response in 11.4-5 thus represents a christological affirmation which corresponds to John's christological question (11.3; cf. 11.2).

17. While the disciples are involved here, it is nevertheless Jesus who gives them the bread which they then distribute to the crowds.

18. Even those who do not accept his powers as coming from God (12.24; cf. 9.34) nevertheless recognize the powers themselves.

19. The term *dynameis* can point, on the one hand, to the 'powers' at work in a person and, on the other hand, to the resulting 'powerful deeds' done by that person.

20. When Jesus addresses his question to the disciples as a group (16.15), it is Peter who responds (16.16). Accordingly, Peter's answer appears to represent the viewpoint of the disciples as a group. Cf. 14.33.

21. The reference to 'the deeds of the messiah' is direct commentary from the narrator to the implied reader and does not constitute the phraseological point of view of John the Baptist himself.

22. The use of the negative *meti* implies a negative response to the question which is raised. Cf. BDF, p. 220.

23. For a discussion of the significance of 'Sodom [and Gomorrah]' in Jewish thinking, see Chapter 3, n. 96 above. The cities of Tyre and Sidon had a similar reputation as 'cities destroyed because of the judgment of God'. Cf. Isa. 23.1-18 and Joel 13.4-8.

24. The religious leadership is variously identified: as 'the Pharisees' (12.1-8, 9-14, 22ff., 38); as 'the Pharisees and the scribes' (15.1-20); as 'the Pharisees and the Sadducees' (16.1-4, 5-12). But since all these groups function uniformly to oppose Jesus' ministry, it is clear that they together constitute a single major character group within the story. Cf. Kingsbury, 'Developing Conflict', p. 58.

25. See the discussion of plot in Chapter 2 above.

26. 12.1b cf. 12.1a; 12.49 cf. 12.46; 13.10 cf. 13.1-3a; 14.15 cf. 14.13-14; 15.23 cf. 15.21; 15.32 cf. 15.29-31; 16.5 cf. 16.4b; 16.13b cf. 16.13a. The only exception in this respect is 15.12, where the narrator specifically notes that the disciples 'come to Jesus'.

27. The only exceptions are found in 14.26 (where the disciples cry out in fear at seeing a 'ghost') and 16.7 (where the disciples discuss among themselves their lack of bread; cf. 16.8).

28. Neither the negative nature of the disciples' requests in 14.15 and 15.23 nor the fact that Jesus does not comply with these requests is germane to the argument at this point. What is in focus here is the fact that the disciples are depicted as having no verbal contact of their own with the crowds.

29. Taken together, the facts (1) that in both cases Jesus' attitude toward the crowds is identified as that of 'taking compassion' (14.14; 15.32b) and (2) that in both cases the disciples' response to the situation of the crowds is contrasted with that of Jesus (14.15 cf. 14.16; 15.32b cf. 15.32c) strongly suggest that the attitude of the disciples falls short of 'compassion'.

30. Jesus 'gives' bread to the disciples and they 'give' it to the crowds (14.19; 15.36).

31. Cf. 14.28-32, where the same principle holds true for Peter when he walks on the water.

32. The disciples' question in 15.12 indicates their sensitivity to the public impact of Jesus' teachings and betrays their fear of 'offending' the religious leadership.

33. Even the sufferings of John the Baptist (14.3-12; cf. 17.9-13) serve to point prolepticallly toward Jesus' future sufferings.

34. See Chapter 2, n. 158 above.

35. The other characters of the story are explicitly mentioned in the following passages: *disciples*: 16.21-18.35; 19.10-15; 19.23-21.11; 21.18-22; 23.1-25.46; *crowds*: 17.14-20; 19.1-2, 13-15; 20.29-21.11; 21.14-17; 23.1-39; *individuals*: 17.14-20; 19.16-22; 20.29-34 (the child of 18.1-35 functions more nearly as a 'stage prop' than as a character in the story); *elements of the religious leadership*: 17.24-27; 19.3-9; 21.12-17; 21.23-22.46.

36. Note the references to Jesus in the following verses in which there is a change either of scene or of characters: 16.21; 17.1, 9, 14, 22; 18.1; 19.1, 3, 10, 13, 16, 23; 20.17, 20, 29; 21.1, 12, 14, 18, 23; 22.1, 23, 35, 41; 23.1; 24.1, 3. Twice there is reference to action which takes place outside of Jesus' presence: in 17.24 the collectors of the half-shekel tax engage Peter in conversation about Jesus; and in 22.15 the Pharisees take counsel among themselves about how to entrap Jesus. But in both of these instances Jesus is reintroduced onto the scene in the following verse (17.25; 22.16).

37. *proserchomai*. In a similar vein, the Pharisees first 'send' people to Jesus (22.16) and then themselves 'gather together' to him (22.34, 41).

38. *prospherō*. Cf. 17.16-17, where a father 'brings' his child to the disciples.

39. *proskaleō*.

40. While his speech is a scathing denunciation of the religious leadership (here identified as 'scribes and Pharisees': 23.2, 13, 15, 23, 25, 27, 29), Jesus nevertheless addresses his words to the crowds and his disciples (23.1).

41. Here as before (see n. 24 above) these authorities comprise a variety of groups: Pharisees (19.3; 21.45; 22.15, 34, 41; 23.2, 13, 15, 23, 25, 27, 29); scribes (16.21; 17.10; 20.18; 21.15; 23.2, 13, 15, 23, 25, 27, 29); chief priests (16.21; 20.18; 21.15, 23, 45); elders (16.21; 21.23); Sadducees (22.23); Herodians (22.15). But as indicated in n. 24 they together constitute a single major character group within the story whose role is that of opponents to Jesus'.

42. See Section II of the present Chapter.

43. The 'child' of 18.2 functions more nearly as a 'stage prop' than as a real character. The 'mother of the sons of Zebedee' (20.20-21) seems to disappear altogether from the scene after making her request: when Jesus responds (20.22), he speaks to the two brothers themselves.

44. The only exceptions to this pattern are found in 19.1-2 and 20.29-34.

45. While Jesus' opponents are still the focus of attention, the narrator implies in 23.1 that they have moved physically off center stage.

46. The implied reader knows that this outcome can only be temporary and that Jesus' opponents will return to take revenge on him for humiliating them in public debate.

47. The close verbal and material parallels between 24.9-13 and 10.16-23 are further evidence that the disciples have not yet embarked on their ministry. Since the persecutions which await them still lie in the future, it appears that the ministry which issues in such persecutions must itself still lie in the future.

48. The presence of the disciples in 19.1-2/3-9 and 19.16-22 is a natural inference in light of the following considerations: (1) the 'casual' manner in which the narrator introduces the disciples back into the text in 19.10 ('His disciples said to him . . . ') and 19.23 ('And Jesus said to his disciples . . '); and

(2) the fact that in 19.10-13 and 19.23-20.16 Jesus and the disciples discuss at greater length the topics introduced in the previous scenes.

49. As was the case with 19.1-2/3-9 and 19.16-22 the presence of the disciples in 21.23-22.46 can be inferred from the 'casual' manner in which the narrator reintroduces them onto the scene in 23.1 ('Then Jesus spoke to the crowds and his disciples, saying. . . ').

50. In 17.24-27 the brief dialogue between Peter and 'those who collect the two-drachma piece' functions not as a significant contact between the disciples and the other characters of the story but rather as a stage-setting device to introduce the ensuing dialogue between Jesus and Peter.

51. The 'mother of the sons of Zebedee' appears here less as a character in her own right than as an extension of the 'sons of Zebedee' themselves. After she has made her request, she disappears from the scene without any further mention, while Jesus addresses himself to the two 'sons of Zebedee'.

52. But cf. 17.14-20, where the (nine) disciples who have not gone up the mountain with Jesus (17.1) are depicted as being in close proximity to the crowds.

53. It is apparent that the disciples' lack of 'compassion' in this instance stems from their concern for 'rank' in the Kingdom of heaven and their corresponding disdain for children, who in societal terms were at the bottom of the social ladder (cf. 18.1-4).

54. In 17.9-13 the focus of attention lies on 'Elijah' (John the Baptist) rather than on Jesus himself. Judging both from their question (17.10) and their response to Jesus' answer (17.13), it appears that the disciples do not even notice that Jesus is also speaking about his own sufferings.

55. Following Jesus' announcement that he is going to suffer (20.17-19), the mother of the 'sons of Zebedee' comes to Jesus not with a response to his announcement but rather with a request for special privileges for her two sons (20.20-21).

56. The immediate response of James and John to the question posed by Jesus seems to indicate that they do not fully understand what Jesus has asked them.

57. Here identified as 'the chief priests and Pharisees' (cf. 21.45-46 and 22.15).

58. Cf. 10.5a, 16.

59. Cf. 10.24-25.

60. This parable appears to represent an elaborate allegory which describes a mission to the Jewish people ('those invited') and their rejection of Jesus (the 'son'). Cf. the similar subject matter of the parable in 21.33-43.

61. It is striking that the 'past tense' action (*apesteilen*) by which Jesus has already 'sent' the disciples into mission (10.5a) is here depicted in the present tense (*apostellō*; cf. 10.16) as Jesus now 'sends' his emissaries to Jerusalem. This appears to indicate once again (cf. the narrator's overall portrayal of the

disciples from 11.2 on) that the disciples have not yet embarked on the mission to which Jesus has already 'sent' (10.5a) but is nevertheless still in the process of 'sending' (23.34a) them. That the disciples' mission is here to be viewed as still in the future is further supported by the fact that the persecution of 23.34b which follows hard on the 'sending' of 23.34a is described in terms of future events and in language which clearly reflects that of 10.5b-42: 'and some of them you will kill (*apokteneite*; cf. 10.21, 28) and crucify (*staurōsete*; cf. 10.38), and some of them you will flog in your synagogues (*mastigōsete en tais synagōgaisin autōn*; cf. 10.17b) and persecute from town to town (*diōxete apo poleōs eis polin*; cf. 10.23)'. Cf. n. 47 above.

62. Since Jesus is speaking to 'the chief priests and the Pharisees' in 22.1-14 (cf. 21.45-46 and 22.15), the reference to 'those invited to the wedding feast' implies a reference to the Jewish people. The negative responses of 'those invited' (22.5-6) further support this reading of the text, since they agree with the actual responses of the Jewish people and their leadership to Jesus within the story itself. The 'you' of 23.34, the group to whom Jesus 'sends out prophets and wise people and scribes', is identified as the 'scribes and Pharisees' (23.29; cf. 23.2, 13, 15, 23, 25, 27), a designation which ultimately gives way to the metaphorical term 'Jerusalem' (23.37).

63. Cf. BAG, p. 193.

64. The careful distinction drawn in the parable between 'those invited' (22.3, 4, 8) and 'whomever you find' (22.9; cf. 22.10) seems to imply the distinction between the Jewish people (those who consider themselves 'invited' into the Kingdom of heaven because of their Jewish heritage; cf. 3.9a; 8.12) and the Gentiles (those viewed as 'outsiders' to the Kingdom; cf. 3.9b; 8.11).

65. In a similar vein, cf. Jesus' reference in 26.13 to 'the proclamation of this gospel in all the world'.

66. They are identified in 26.3 as 'the chief priests', 'the elders of the people', and 'the high priest Caiaphas'; in 26.14 as 'the chief priests'; and in 26.47 as 'a great crowd . . . from the chief priests and elders of the people'.

67. The attention of both Jesus and the disciples during this meal is drawn to the action of the woman who comes and anoints Jesus' head with expensive perfume. As observed above, however, this action has the primary effect of providing an 'object lesson' which Jesus and his disciples then discuss.

68. And even the two disciples who do appear on the scene distinguish themselves in negative rather than positive fashion. Peter follows Jesus to the courtyard of the high priest (26.58) only to end up denying repeatedly and with vehemence that he 'does not know' Jesus (26.70, 72, 74). Judas makes a final reappearance (27.3-10) in which he returns the money which he has received for 'handing over' Jesus and then goes out and hangs himself.

69. The 'great crowd' which comes to Gethsemane along with Judas to

arrest Jesus (26.47) is pointedly designated as 'from the chief priests and elders of the people'. Whether this refers to the chief priests and elders themselves or simply denotes those who have been delegated by the chief priests and elders, it is clear that this is in some sense a select 'crowd' to be distinguished from those other 'crowds' which have been following Jesus throughout the story.

70. There are only four other verses in this section in which direct speech is attributed to Jesus: in two of these Jesus addresses God in prayer (26.39, 42; cf. 26.26, 27, 44) and in two of them he addresses the crowd which has come to arrest him (26.55-56).

71. In addition, the narrator makes Jesus the subject of two passive verbs: he 'is condemned' (27.3) and he 'is accused' (27.12).

72. The only 'merciful' actions directed to Jesus throughout 26.57–27.66 other than those of Joseph of Arimathea are those of the soldiers, who offer Jesus 'wine mixed with gall' to cut the pain of the crucifixion (27.34), and the onlooker, who offers Jesus vinegar to drink as he hangs dying (27.48).

73. The verb used with reference to Jesus (27.26) is *phragellō*, which refers to flogging by means of the *phragellion* (Latin: *flagellum*). This punishment was meted out by the Romans to those condemned to be executed. Cf. BAG, p. 873. The verb used with reference to the disciples (10.17; 23.34) is *mastigoō* (Latin: *verberatio*), which refers to flogging by means of the *mastix*. Cf. BAG, p. 496.

74. Cf. Section I of the present Chapter.

75. The context of this statement makes it clear that the term *seismos* does not refer to a literal earthquake, but rather to an 'earth-shaking event' which is then described as the descent of the 'angel of the Lord' from heaven. Contrast with this scene the 'earth-shaking event' of 27.54, which is described as a literal 'earthquake' (cf. 27.51-53).

76. Even the scene in which the guard at the tomb returns to Jerusalem to report to the chief priests (28.11-15) points to the risen Jesus as the initiator of events, since it is 'all those things which have happened' at the tomb which motivate the actions not only of the guard but also of the chief priests.

77. Even the scene in Gethsemane in which Jesus 'goes on ahead' to pray by himself (26.36-46) is twice punctuated (26.40, 43) and then concluded (26.45) by Jesus' return to the disciples.

78. Even the fact that the disciples fall asleep in the Garden of Gethsemane is portrayed as an action which relates to Jesus: since he has specifically told them to 'keep watch with [him]' (26.38, 41), their act of 'sleeping' (26.40, 43; cf. 45) represents a failure to carry out his command.

79. The only instance in which the disciples take action outside of the presence of Jesus and speak to someone other than him is when they 'do as Jesus has directed them' (26.19a) and go into the city to a designated house to prepare the passover meal (26.18, 19b).

80. Even the two disciples who do appear on the scene individually distinguish themselves in negative rather than positive fashion. Peter follows Jesus to the courtyard of the high priest (26.58) only to end up insisting repeatedly and with vehemence that he 'does not know' Jesus (26.70, 72, 74). Judas makes a final reappearance (27.3-10) in which he returns the money he has received for 'handing over' Jesus and then goes out and hangs himself.

81. See the portrayals of the disciples above.

82. Cf. with this portrayal the desperate remorse of Judas which leads him to commit suicide (27.3-5).

83. Judas has by now taken himself out of the story definitively (27.5), so that only eleven of Jesus' 'twelve disciples/apostles' (10.1, 2, 5; 11.1; 20.17; 26.14, 20, 47; cf. 19.28) remain.

84. Even though the language of 'following' does not appear in any of the references to the disciples' trip to Galilee (26.32; 28.7, 10, 16), the imagery of 'following' is implicit in the wording of the texts. Since Jesus 'goes before' the disciples to Galilee (26.32; 28.7), their own 'going' (28.7, 10, 16) is nothing other than an act of 'following Jesus'.

85. Although Jesus does not 'give' this absolute authority to the disciples, there is nevertheless an immediate connection between the authority and the mission. It is because 'all authority in heaven and on earth' has been given to Jesus that he sends the eleven out to 'make disciples of all nations'.

86. The use of the passive verb *edothē* (= has been given) represents the Jewish circumlocution for the action of God. Further, it is clear that from the perspective of Jesus and his disciples there is only one source from which 'all authority' can come, namely, God.

87. The 'all-inclusive' character of the commission of 28.18-20 indicates that the phrase *panta ta ethnē* is to be interpreted as 'all the nations' (i.e., including Israel) and not 'all the Gentiles' (i.e., excluding Israel). Cf. Karl Barth, *Auslegung von Matthäus 28,16-20*, BasMiss, 17 (Basel: Basler Missionsbuchhandlung, 1945), p. 15; Jean Zumstein, 'Matthieu 28.16-20', *RThPh*, 3e série 22 (1972), pp. 26; Frankemölle, pp. 121-23; Barr, pp. 356-57; Peter O'Brien, 'The Great Commission of Matthew 28.18-20. A Missionary Mandate or Not?' *RefTR* 35 (1976), p. 74; Schuyler Brown, 'Two-fold Representation', p. 29; John P. Meier, 'Nations or Gentiles in Matthew 28.19?' *CBQ* 39 (1977), pp. 94-102; Ferdinand Hahn, 'Der Sendungsauftrag des Auferstandenen: Matthäus 28, 16.20', in *Fides pro mundi vita: Missionstheologie heute*, MissFor, 14, ed. Theo Sundermeier (Gütersloh: Gütersloher Verlagshaus Gerd Mohn, 1980), p. 35; Jacques Matthey, 'The Great Commission According to Matthew', *IntRMiss* 69 (1980), p. 168; David J. Bosch, 'The Structure of Mission: An Exposition of Matthew 28.16-20', in *Exploring Church Growth*, ed. Wilbert R. Shenk (Grand Rapids, Michigan: William B. Eerdmans, 1983), pp. 236-37. For a discussion of the 'exclusivistic' viewpoint, see Douglas R.A. Hare and Daniel J. Harrington, '"Make Disciples of All Gentiles" (Mt 28.19)', *CBQ* 37

(1975), pp. 359-69. In a similar vein, see Barta, *Mission in Matthew*, pp. 533-35.

88. This time frame thus coincides with the time frame of the mission to the 'cities of Israel' (10.23), which will not be concluded 'before the coming of the Son of man'. Cf. Patte, p. 145.

BIBLIOGRAPHY

Abrams, M.H., *A Glossary of Literary Terms*, 4th edn, New York: Holt, Rinehart and Winston, 1981.

Albright, W.F., and C.S. Mann, *Matthew*, Anchor Bible, 26; Garden City, New York: Doubleday, 1971.

Allen, Willoughby C., *A Critical and Exegetical Commentary on the Gospel According to St. Matthew*, International Critical Commentary, New York: Charles Scribner's Sons, 1907.

Anderson, Janice Capel, 'Point of View in Matthew—Evidence', Paper presented to the Society of Biblical Literature Symposium on Literary Analysis of the Gospels and Acts, December 1981.

Arens, Eduardo, *The Élthon-Sayings in the Synoptic Tradition: A Historico-Critical Investigation*, Orbis biblicus et orientalis, 10; Göttingen: Vandenhoeck & Ruprecht, 1976.

Aune, David E., *Prophecy in Early Christianity and the Ancient Mediterranean World*, Grand Rapids, Michigan: William B. Eerdmans, 1983.

Bacon, Benjamin W., *Studies in Matthew*, New York: Henry Holt, 1930.

Bammel, Ernst, 'Matthäus 10,23', *Studia Theologica* 15 (1961), pp. 79-92.

Barr, D.L. 'The Drama of Matthew's Gospel: A Reconsideration of its Structure and Purpose', *Theology Digest* 24 (1976), pp. 349-59.

Barta, Karen A., *Mission and Discipleship in Matthew: a Redaction-Critical Study of Mt. 10.34*, Milwaukee: Marquette University, 1979.

—'Mission in Matthew: The Second Discourse as Narrative', in *SBL 1988 Seminar Papers*, pp. 527-35. Society of Biblical Literature Seminar Paper Series, 227; Atlanta: Scholars Press, 1988.

Barth, Gerhard, 'Matthew's Understanding of the Law', in *Tradition and Interpretation in Matthew*, pp. 58-164. New Testament Library; trans. Percy Scott; Philadelphia: Westminster Press, 1963.

Barth, Karl, *Auslegung von Matthäus 28, 16-20*, Basler Missionsstudien, 17; Basel: Basler Missionsbuchhandlung, 1945.

Bauer, David R., *The Structure of Matthew's Gospel: A Study in Literary Design*, Journal for the Study of the New Testament Supplement Series, 31; Sheffield: Almond, 1988.

Bauer, Walter, William F. Arndt, and F. Wilbur Gingrich, *A Greek-English Lexicon of the New Testament and Other Early Christian Literature*, Chicago: University of Chicago Press, 1957.

Beare, Francis Wright, *The Gospel According to Matthew*, San Francisco: Harper & Row, 1981.

—'The Mission of the Disciples and the Charge: Matthew 10 and Parallels', *Journal of Biblical Literature* 89 (1970), pp. 1-13.

Blass, F., and A. DeBrunner, *A Greek Grammar of the New Testament and Other Early Christian Literature*, trans. and revised Robert W. Funk; Chicago: University of Chicago Press, 1961.

Bohemen, N. van, 'L'institution des douze', in *La formation des évangiles: Problème synoptique et formgeschichte*, pp. 116-51. Recherches bibliques, 2; Paris: Desclée de Brouwer, 1957.

Bonnard, P., *L'évangile selon Saint Matthieu*, Commentaire du nouveau testament, 1; Neuchâtel: Editions Delachaux & Niestlé, 1970.

Boomershine, Thomas E., 'Mark 16.8 and the Apostolic Commission', *Journal of Biblical Literature* 100 (1981), pp. 225-39.

Boomershine, Thomas E., and Gilbert Bartholomew, 'The Narrative Technique of Mark 16.8', *Journal of Biblical Literature* 100 (1981), pp. 213-23.

Booth, Wayne, *The Rhetoric of Fiction*, 2nd edn; Chicago: University of Chicago Press, 1983.

Boring, M. Eugene, *Sayings of the Risen Jesus: Christian Prophecy in the Synoptic Tradition*, Society for New Testament Study Monograph Series, 46; Cambridge: Cambridge University Press, 1982.

Bornkamm, Günther, 'End-Expectation and Church in Matthew', in *Tradition and Interpretation in Matthew*, pp. 15-51. New Testament Library; trans. Percy Scott; Philadelphia: Westminster Press, 1963.

—'Der Lohngedanke im Neuen Testament', in *Gesammelte Aufsätze*, 2: *Studien zu Antike und Urchristentum*, pp. 69-92. Beiträge zur evangelischen Theologie, 28; ed. E. Wolf; Munich: Chr. Kaiser, 1959.

—'lykos', in *Theological Dictionary of the New Testament* 4: 308-11, ed. Gerhard Kittel and Gerhard Friedrich; trans. Geoffrey W. Bromiley; Grand Rapids, Michigan: William B. Eerdmans, 1967.

Bosch, David J., 'The Structure of Mission: An Exposition of Matthew 28.16-20', in *Exploring Church Growth*, pp. 218-48. Ed. Wilbert R. Shenk; Grand Rapids, Michigan: William B. Eerdmans, 1983.

Broadus, John A., *Commentary on the Gospel of Matthew*, Philadelphia: American Baptist Publication Society, 1886.

Brown, Raymond E., *The Birth of the Messiah: A Commentary on the Infancy Narratives in Matthew and Luke*, Garden City, New York: Image Books, 1979.

Brown, Schuyler, 'The Mission to Israel in Matthew's Central Section', *Zeitschrift für die neutestamentliche Wissenschaft* 69 (1978), pp. 73-90.

—'The Two-fold Representation of the Mission in Matthew's Gospel', *Studia Theologica* 31 (1977), pp. 21-32.

Burger, Christoph, 'Jesu Taten nach Matthäus 8 und 9', *Zeitschrift für Theologie und Kirche* 70 (1973), pp. 272-87.

Butler, B.C., *The Originality of St. Matthew*, Cambridge: Cambridge University Press, 1951.

Cadbury, Henry J., 'Dust and Garments', in *The Beginnings of Christianity*, ed. Kirsopp Lake and Frederick John Foakes-Jackson; London: Macmillan, 1933.

Caird, G.B., 'Uncomfortable Words: II. Shake Off the Dust From Your Feet (Mk 6.11)', *Expository Times* 81 (1969), pp. 40-43.

Chatman, Seymour, *Story and Discourse: Narrative Structure in Fiction and Film*, Ithaca, New York: Cornell University Press, 1978.

Combet-Galland, Corina, 'Du champ des moissonneurs au chant des serviteurs: Matthieu 9,35-11,1', *Foi et Vie* 81 (1982), pp. 31-39.

Combrink, H.J.B., 'The Macrostructure of the Gospel of Matthew', in *Structure and Meaning in Matthew 14-28*, pp. 1-20. Neotestamentica, 16; Stellenbosch: New Testament Society of South Africa, 1983.

—'Structural Analysis of Mt 9.35-11.1', in *The Structure of Matthew 1-13: An*

Exploration into Discourse Analysis, pp. 98-114. Neotestamentica, 11, 2nd edn, Pretoria: New Testament Society of South Africa, 1980.

—'The Structure of the Gospel of Matthew as Narrative', *Tyndale Bulletin* 34 (1983), pp. 61-90.

Cope, O. Lamar, *Matthew: A Scribe Trained for the Kingdom of Heaven*, Catholic Biblical Quarterly Monograph Series, 5, Washington, D.C.: Catholic Biblical Association of America, 1976.

Culpepper, R. Alan, 'The Narrator in the Fourth Gospel: Intratextual Relationships', in *SBL 1982 Seminar Papers*, pp. 81-96. Society of Biblical Literature Seminar Paper Series, 21; Chico, California: Scholars Press, 1982.

Dausch, Petrus, *Die drei älteren Evangelien*, 4th edn, Bonn: Peter Hanstein, 1932.

Dautzenberg, G., *Sein Leben bewahren. Psychē in den Herrenworten der Evangelien*, Studien zum Alten und Neuen Testament, 14; Munich: Kösel Verlag, 1966.

Deiss, Lucien, 'Le discours apostolique ou le discours de mission selon Matthieu x', *Spiritus* 12 (1962), pp. 281-91.

Delling, Gerhard, *'teleō'* in *Theological Dictionary of the New Testament* 8.57-61. Ed. Gerhard Kittel and Gerhard Friedrich; trans. Geoffrey W. Bromiley; Grand Rapids, Michigan: William B. Eerdmans, 1972.

Dewey, Joanna, *Markan Public Debate: Literary Technique, Concentric Structure, and Theology in Mark 2.1–3.6*, Society of Biblical Literature Dissertation Series, 48; Chico, California: Scholars Press, 1980.

—'Point of View and the Disciples in Mark', in *SBL 1982 Seminar Papers*, pp. 97-106. Society of Biblical Literature Seminar Paper Series, 21; Chico, California: Scholars Press, 1982.

Di Marco, Angelico, 'Der Chiasmus in der Bibel: 3. Teil', trans. Wolfgang Meyer, *Linguistica Biblica* 39 (1976), pp. 37-85.

Dobschütz, Ernst von, 'Matthäus als Rabbi und Katechet', *Zeitschrift für die neutestamentliche Wissenschaft und die Kunde der älteren Kirche* 27 (1928), pp. 338-48.

Dolezel, Lubomir, 'The Typology of the Narrator: Point of View in Fiction', in *To Honor Roman Jakobson: Essays on the Occasion of His Seventieth Birthday*, Janua Linguarum, Series Maior, 31-33; The Hague: Mouton, 1967.

Dupont, Jacques, 'Vous n'aurez pas achevé les villes d'Israël avant que le fils de l'homme ne vienne' (Mat. X 23)', *Novum Testamentum* 2 (1958), pp. 228-44.

Edersheim, Alfred, *The Life and Times of Jesus the Messiah*, New York: E.R. Herrick, 1886.

Erdman, Charles R., *The Gospel of Matthew*, Philadelphia: Westminster Press, 1920.

Fenton, John C. 'Raise the Dead', *Expository Times* 80 (1968), pp. 50-51.

—'Inclusio and Chiasmus in Matthew', in *Studia Evangelica: Papers presented to the International Congress on 'The Four Gospels in 1957' held at Christ Church, Oxford, 1957*, pp. 174-79. Berlin: Akademie-Verlag, 1959.

Feuillet, André, 'Les origines et la signification de Mt 10.23[b]', *Catholic Biblical Quarterly* 23 (1961), pp. 182-98.

Filson, Floyd V., *The Gospel According to St. Matthew*, Harper's New Testament Commentaries, New York: Harper & Row, 1960.

Fletcher, D.R. 'Condemned to Die. The Logion on Cross-Bearing: What Does It Mean?', *Interpretation* 18 (1964), pp. 156-64.

Foerster, Werner, *'eirēnē'*, in *Theological Dictionary of the New Testament* 2.406-17. Ed. Gerhard Kittel and Gerhard Friedrich; trans. Geoffrey W. Bromiley; Grand Rapids, Michigan: William B. Eerdmans, 1964.

—'*ophis*', in *Theological Dictionary of the New Testament* 5: 566-82. Ed. Gerhard Kittel and Gerhard Friedrich; trans. Geoffrey W. Bromiley; Grand Rapids, Michigan: William B. Eerdmans, 1967.

Fowler, Robert M., *Loaves and Fishes: The Function of the Feeding Stories in the Gospel of Mark*, Society of Biblical Literature Dissertation Series, 54; Chico, California: Scholars Press, 1981.

Frankemölle, Hubert, *Jahwebund und Kirche Christi*, Münster: Aschendorff, 1974.

Friedman, Norman, 'Point of View in Fiction: The Development of a Critical Concept', in *Approaches to the Novel: Materials for a Poetics*, pp. 113-42. Ed. Robert Scholes; San Francisco: Chandler, 1961.

Friedrich, Gerhard, '*prophētēs*', in *Theological Dictionary of the New Testament* 6.828-61. Ed. Gerhard Kittel and Gerhard Friedrich; trans. Geoffrey W. Bromiley; Grand Rapids, Michigan: William B. Eerdmans, 1968.

Frye, Roland Mushat, 'A Literary Perspective for the Criticism of the Gospels', in *Jesus and Man's Hope*, ed. Donald G. Miller and Dikran Y. Hadidian; Pittsburgh: Pittsburgh Theological Seminary, 1970-71.

Gaechter, Paul, *Die literarische Kunst im Matthäus-Evangelium*. Stuttgarter Bibel-Studien, 7; Stuttgart: Katholisches Bibelwerk, 1966.

—*Das Matthäus Evangelium*, Innsbruck: Tyrolia, 1964.

Genette, Gerard, *Narrative Discourse: An Essay in Method*, trans. Jane E. Lewin; Ithaca, New York: Cornell University Press, 1980.

Gerhardsson, Birger, *The Mighty Acts of Jesus According to Matthew*, Lund, Sweden: CWK Gleerup, 1979.

—*The Testing of God's Son (Mt 4.1-11 & Par)*, Coniectanea Biblica, New Testament Series, 2.1; Lund, Sweden: CWK Gleerup, 1966.

Giblin, C.H., 'Theological Perspective and Mt 10,23b', *Theological Studies* 29 (1968), pp. 637-61.

Good News Bible: The Bible in Today's English Version, New York: American Bible Society, 1976.

Grant, Frederick, C., 'The Mission of the Disciples, Mt 9.35-11.1 and Parallels', *Journal of Biblical Literature* 35 (1916), pp. 293-314.

Greenberg, M., 'Crimes and Punishments', in *Interpreter's Dictionary of the Bible* 1.733-44. Ed. George Arthur Buttrick; Nashville: Abingdon, 1962.

Greeven, Heinrich, '*peristera*', in *Theological Dictionary of the New Testament* 6.63-72. Ed. Gerhard Kittel and Gerhard Friedrich; trans. Geoffrey W. Bromiley; Grand Rapids, Michigan: William B. Eerdmans, 1968.

Grundmann, Walter, *Das Evangelium nach Matthäus*, Theologischer Handkommentar zum Neuen Testament, 1; Berlin: Evangelische Verlagsanstalt, 1968.

Gundry, Robert H., *Matthew: A Commentary on His Literary and Theological Art*, Grand Rapids, Michigan: William B. Eerdmans, 1982.

Hahn, Ferdinand, *Mission in the New Testament*, Studies in Biblical Theology, 47; trans. Frank Clarke; London: SCM Press, 1965.

—'Der Sendungsauftrag des Auferstandenen: Matthäus 28, 16-20', in *Fides pro mundi vita: Missionstheologie heute*, pp. 28-43. Missionswissenschaftliche Forschungen, 14; ed. Theo Sundermeier; Gütersloh: Gütersloher Verlagshaus Gerd Mohn, 1980.

Hare, Douglas R.A., *The Theme of Jewish Persecution of Christians in the Gospel According to Saint Matthew*, Cambridge: Cambridge University Press, 1967.

Hare, Douglas, R.A. and Daniel J. Harrington, '"Make Disciples of All the Gentiles" (Mt 28.19)', *Catholic Biblical Quarterly* 37 (1975), pp. 359-69.

Held, Heinz Joachim, 'Matthew As Interpreter of the Miracle Stories', in *Tradition and Interpretation in Matthew*, pp. 165-299. New Testament Library; trans. Percy Scott; Philadelphia: Westminster, 1963.

Hengel, Martin, *Nachfolge und Charisma: Eine exegetisch-religionsgeschichtliche Studie zu Mt 8.21f und Jesu Ruf in die Nachfolge*, Beiheft zur Zeitschrift für die neutestamentliche Wissenschaft, 34; ed. Walther Eltester; Berlin: Alfred Töpelmann, 1968.

Hill, David, 'The Figure of Jesus in Matthew's Story: A Response to Professor Kingsbury's Literary-Critical Probe', *Journal for the Study of the New Testament* 21 (1984), pp. 37-52.

—*The Gospel of Matthew*, New Century Bible; London: Oliphants, 1972.

Hoffmann, Paul, *Studien zur Theologie der Logienquelle*, Münster: Aschendorff, 1972.

Hooker, Morna D., 'Uncomfortable Words: X. The Prohibition of Foreign Missions (Mt 10.5-6)', *Expository Times* 82 (1971), pp. 361-65.

Iser, Wolfgang, *The Implied Reader: Patterns of Communication in Prose Fiction from Bunyan to Beckett*, Baltimore: Johns Hopkins University Press, 1978.

Jeremias, Joachim, *Jesus' Promise to the Nations*, Studies in Biblical Theology, 24; trans. S.H. Hooke; London: SCM Press, 1958.

Kermode, Frank, *The Genesis of Secrecy: On the Interpretation of Narrative*, Cambridge, Massachusetts: Harvard University Press, 1979.

Kingsbury, Jack Dean, *The Christology of Mark's Gospel*, Philadelphia: Fortress, 1983.

—'The Developing Conflict between Jesus and the Jewish Leaders in Matthew's Gospel: A Literary-Critical Study', *Catholic Biblical Quarterly* 49.1 (1987), pp. 57-73.

—'The Figure of Jesus in Matthew's Story: A Literary-Critical Probe', *Journal for the Study of the New Testament* 21 (1984), pp. 3-36.

—'The Figure of Jesus in Matthew's Story: a Rejoinder to David Hill', *Journal for the Study of the New Testament* 25 (1985), pp. 61-81.

—'The Figure of Peter in Matthew's Gospel as a Theological Problem', *Journal of Biblical Literature* 98 (1979), pp. 67-83.

—*Matthew as Story*, Philadelphia: Fortress, 1986.

—*Matthew: Structure, Christology, Kingdom*, Philadelphia: Fortress, 1978.

—'Observations on the 'Miracle Chapters' of Matthew 8-9', *Catholic Biblical Quarterly* 40 (1978), pp. 559-73.

—'The Verb *Akolouthein* ('to Follow') as an Index of Matthew's View of His Community', *Journal of Biblical Literature* 97 (1978), pp. 56-73.

Kittel, Gerhard, '*akeraios*', in *Theological Dictionary of the New Testament* 1.209-10. Ed. Gerhard Kittel and Gerhard Friedrich; trans. Geoffrey W. Bromiley; Grand Rapids, Michigan: William B. Eerdmans, 1964.

Klostermann, Erich, *Das Matthäusevangelium*, Handbuch zum Neuen Testament, 4; 2nd edn, Tübingen: J.C.B. Mohr (Paul Siebeck), 1927.

Kümmel, Werner Georg, *Promise and Fulfilment: The Eschatological Message of Jesus*, Studies in Biblical Theology, 23; trans. Dorothea M. Barton; London: SCM Press, 1957.

Künzel, G., *Studien zum Gemeindeverständnis des Matthäusevangeliums*, Calwer theologische Monographien, 10; Stuttgart: Calwer, 1978.

Künzi, Martin, *Das Naherwartungslogion Matthäus 10, 23: Geschichte seiner Auslegung*, Tübingen: J.C.B. Mohr (Paul Siebeck), 1970.

Lagrange, M-J., *Évangile selon Saint Matthieu*, Études bibliques. Paris: Librairie Lecoffre, 1948.

Lange, Joachim, *Das Erscheinen des Auferstandenen im Evangelium nach Matthäus: Eine traditions- und redaktionsgeschichtliche Untersuchung zu Mt 28, 16-20*, Forschung zur Bibel, 11; Würzburg: Echter Verlag, 1973.

Lange, John Peter, *The Gospel According to Matthew*, trans. Philip Schaff; New York: Scribner, Armstrong, 1873.

Lanser, Susan Sniader, *The Narrative Act: Point of View in Prose Fiction*, Princeton: Princeton University Press, 1981.

Laufen, Rudolf, *Die Doppelüberlieferungen der Logienquelle und des Markusevangeliums*, Bonner biblische Beiträge, 54; Bonn: Peter Hanstein, 1980.

Legrand, L., 'The Harvest Is Plentiful (Mt 9.37)', *Scripture* 17 (1965), pp. 1-9.

Lenski, R.C.H., *Interpretation of St. Matthew's Gospel*, Columbus, Ohio: Lutheran Book Concern, 1932.

Lohmeyer, Ernst, and Werner Schmauch, *Das Evangelium des Matthäus*, Kritisch-exegetischer Kommentar über das Neue Testament, Göttingen: Vandenhoeck & Ruprecht, 1956.

Lohr, Charles H., 'Oral Techniques in the Gospel of Matthew', *Catholic Biblical Quarterly* 23 (1961), pp. 403-35.

Lohse, Eduard, 'synedrion', in *Theological Dictionary of the New Testament* 7.860-71. Ed. Gerhard Kittel and Gerhard Friedrich; trans. Geoffrey W. Bromiley; Grand Rapids, Michigan: William B. Eerdmans, 1971.

Lotman, J.M., 'Point of View in a Text', trans. L.M. O'Toole, *New Literary History* 6 (1975), pp. 339-52.

Lund, Nils Wilhelm, *Chiasmus in the New Testament: A Study in Formgeschichte*, Chapel Hill, North Carolina: University of North Carolina Press, 1942.

Luz, Ulrich, 'Die Jünger im Matthäusevangelium', *Zeitschrift für die neutestamentliche Wissenschaft* 62 (1971), pp. 141-71.

Maclaurin, E.C.B., 'Beelzeboul', *Novum Testamentum* 20 (1978), pp. 156-60.

McNeile, Alan Hugh, *The Gospel According to St. Matthew*, London: Macmillan, 1952.

—'Matthew X 11-15', *Journal of Theological Studies* 11 (1910), pp. 558-59.

Magness, J. Lee, *Sense and Absence: Structure and Suspension in the Ending of Mark's Gospel*, Society of Biblical Literature Semeia Studies; Atlanta, Georgia: Scholars Press, 1986.

Mangatt, George, 'Reflections on the Apostolic Discourse (Mt 10)', *Biblebhashyam: An Indian Biblical Quarterly* 6 (1980), pp. 196-206.

Marshall, I. Howard, 'Uncomfortable Words: VI. 'Fear him who can destroy both soul and body in hell' (Mt 10.28 R.S.V.)', *Expository Times* 81 (1970), pp. 276-80.

Martin, Francis, 'The Image of Shepherd in the Gospel of St. Matthew', *Science et esprit: revue de philosophie et de théologie* 27 (1975), pp. 261-301.

Matera, Frank J. 'The Plot of Matthew's Gospel', *Catholic Biblical Quarterly* 49 (1987), pp. 233-53.

Matthey, Jacques, 'The Great Commission According to Matthew', *International Review of Mission* 69 (1980), pp. 161-73.

Metzger, Bruce M., *A Textual Commentary on the Greek New Testament*, 3rd edn, London: United Bible Societies, 1971.

Meier, John P., *Matthew*, New Testament Message: A Biblical-Theological Commentary, 3; Wilmington, Delaware: Michael Glazier, 1980.

—'Nations or Gentiles in Matthew 28.19?', *Catholic Biblical Quarterly* 39 (1977), pp. 94-102.

Meyer, Heinrich August Wilhelm, *Critical and Exegetical Hand-Book to the Gospel of Matthew*, trans. Peter Christie, revised by Frederick Crombie and William Stewart; New York: Funk & Wagnalls, 1884.

Michaels, J. Ramsey, 'Apostolic Hardships and Righteous Gentiles: A Study of Matthew 25.31-46', *Journal of Biblical Literature* 84 (1965), pp. 27-37.

Minear, Paul S., *Matthew: The Teacher's Gospel*, New York: Pilgrim, 1982.

Morosco, Robert E., 'Redaction Criticism and the Evangelical: Matthew 10, a Test Case', *Journal of the Evangelical Theological Society* 22 (1979), pp. 323-31.

Moulton, William F., and Alfred S. Geden, eds, *A Concordance to the Greek Testament*, 3rd edn, Edinburgh: T. & T. Clark, 1953.

Neirynck, Frans, '*Apo Tote Érxato* and the Structure of Matthew'. *Ephemerides Theologicae Lovanienses* 64 (1988), pp. 21-59.

Nestle, Eberhard, and Kurt Aland, eds., *Novum Testamentum Graece*, 26th edn, Stuttgart: Deutsche Bibelstiftung Stuttgart, 1979,

O'Brien, Peter, 'The Great Commission of Matthew 28.18-20. A Missionary Mandate or Not?' *Reformed Theological Review* 35 (1976), pp. 66-78.

O'Connor, Daniel, and Jacques Jimenez, *The Images of Jesus: Exploring the Metaphors in Matthew's Gospel*, Minneapolis, Minnesota: Winston, 1977.

Ogawa, Akira, *L'histoire de Jésus chez Matthieu: La signification de l'histoire pour la théologie matthéenne*, Bern: Peter Lang, 1979.

Pappas, Harry S., 'The "Exhortation to Fearless Confession" - Mt. 10.26-33', *Greek Orthodox Theological Review* 25 (1980): 239-48.

Perrin, Norman, 'The Evangelist as Author: Reflections on Method in the Study and Interpretation of the Synoptic Gospels and Acts', *Biblical Research* 17 (1972), pp. 5-18.

Pesch, Rudolf, 'Der Gottessohn im matthäischen Evangelienprolog (Mt. 1-2): Beobachtungen zu den Zitationsformeln der Reflexionszitate', *Biblica* 48 (1967), pp. 395-420.

Petersen, Norman R., *Literary Criticism for New Testament Critics*, Guides to Biblical Scholarship, New Testament Series, Philadelphia: Fortress, 1978.

—'"Point of View" in Mark's Narrative', *Semeia* 12 (1978), pp. 97-121.

Plummer, Alfred, *An Exegetical Commentary on the Gospel According to S.* [sic] *Matthew*, London: Robert Scott, 1915.

Radermakers, Jean. *Au fil de l'évangile selon Saint Matthieu*, Heverlee-Louvain: Institut d'études théologiques, 1972.

Rahlfs, Alfred, ed. *Septuaginta*, 9th edn, Stuttgart: Deutsche Bibelstiftung Stuttgart, 1935.

Rhoads, David, 'Narrative Criticism and the Gospel of Mark', *Journal of the American Academy of Religion* 50 (1982), pp. 411-34.

Rhoads, David, and Donald Michie, *Mark As Story: An Introduction to the Narrative of a Gospel*, Philadelphia: Fortress, 1982.

Riesner, R., 'Der Aufbau der Reden im Matthäus-Evangelium', *Theologische Beiträge* 9 (1978), pp. 172-82.

Rigaux, Beda, *The Testimony of St Matthew*, trans. Paul Joseph Oligny; Chicago: Franciscan Herald, 1968.

Robinson, Theodore H., *The Gospel of Matthew*, Moffatt New Testament Commentary; Garden City, New York: Doubleday, Doran, 1928.

Roloff, Jürgen, 'Stationen urchristlicher Missionserfahrung', *Zeitschrift für Mission* 4 (1978), pp. 3-8.

Rusche, Helga, 'Die Boten der neuen Welt', *Bibel und Leben* 8 (1967), pp. 209-16.

—*Gastfreundschaft in der Verkündigung des Neuen Testaments und ihr Verhältnis zur Mission*, Münster: Aschendorff, 1958.

Sabourin, Leopold, *L'évangile selon Saint Matthieu et ses principaux parallèles*, Rome: Biblical Institute Press, 1978.

Sand, Alexander, 'Propheten, Weise und Schriftkundige in der Gemeinde des Matthäus-Evangeliums', in *Kirche im Werden: Studien zum Thema Amt und Gemeinde im Neuen Testament*, pp. 167-84. Ed. Josef Hainz; Munich: Schöningh, 1976.

Schenk, Wolfgang, 'Das Präsens Historicum als makrosyntaktische Gliederungssignal im Matthäusevangelium', *New Testament Studies* 22 (1976), pp. 464-75.

—*Der Segen im Neuen Testament: Eine begriffsanalytische Studie*, Berlin: Evangelische Verlagsanstalt, 1967.

Schlatter, A., *Der Evangelist Matthäus: Seine Sprache, sein Ziel, seine Selbständigkeit. Ein Kommentar zum ersten Evangelium*, Stuttgart: Calwer, 1957.

Schniewind, J., *Das Evangelium nach Matthäus*, 11th edn, Göttingen: Vandenhoeck & Ruprecht, 1968.

Scholes, Robert, and Robert Kellogg, *The Nature of Narrative*, New York: Oxford University Press, 1966.

Schott, E., 'Die Aussendungsrede Mt. 10. Mc 6. Lc 9. 10', *Zeitschrift für die neutestamentliche Wissenschaft* 7 (1906), pp. 140-50.

Schrenk, Gottlob, '*dikaios*', in *Theological Dictionary of the New Testament* 2.182-91. Ed. Gerhard Kittel and Gerhard Friedrich; trans. Geoffrey W. Bromiley; Grand Rapids, Michigan: William B. Eerdmans, 1964.

Schulz, Siegfried, *Die Stunde der Botschaft: Einführung in die Theologie der vier Evangelisten*, Hamburg: Furche, 1967.

Schürmann, H., 'Zur Traditions- und Redaktionsgeschichte von Mt. 10.23', in *Traditionsgeschichtliche Untersuchungen zu den synoptischen Evangelien*, pp. 150-56. Düsseldorf: Patmos, 1968.

Schweitzer, Albert, *The Quest of the Historical Jesus*, trans. W. Montgomery; New York: Macmillan, 1968.

Schweizer, Eduard, *The Good News according to Matthew*, trans. David E. Green; Atlanta: John Knox, 1977.

—'*psychē*', in *Theological Dictionary of the New Testament* 9.637-56. Ed. Gerhard Kittel and Gerhard Friedrich; trans. Geoffrey W. Bromiley; Grand Rapids, Michigan: William B. Eerdmans, 1974.

Soulen, Richard N., *Handbook of Biblical Criticism*, Atlanta: John Knox, 1981.

Strack, Hermann L., and Paul Billerbeck, *Kommentar zum Neuen Testament aus Talmud und Midrasch*. Vol. 1: *Das Evangelium nach Matthäus*, Munich: C.H. Beck, 1922.

Strecker, Georg, *Der Weg der Gerechtigkeit: Untersuchung zur Theologie des Matthäus*, Göttingen: Vandenhoeck & Ruprecht, 1962.

Tannehill, Robert C., 'The Disciples in Mark: The Function of a Narrative Role', *Journal of Religion* 57 (1977), pp. 386-405.

—'The Gospel of Mark as Narrative Christology', *Semeia* 16 (1979), pp. 57-95.

—*The Sword of His Mouth: Forceful and Imaginative Language in Synoptic Sayings*, Society of Biblical Literature Semeia Supplements, 1; ed. William A. Beardslee; Missoula, Montana: Scholars Press, 1975.

Ternant, P., 'L'envoi des douze aux brebis perdues (Mt. 9-10)', *Assemblées du Seigneur* 42 (1970), pp. 18-32.

—'L'évangile (Mt. 9.35-38): La mission, fruit de la compassion du maître et de la prière des disciples', *Assemblées du Seigneur* 98 (1967), pp. 25-41.

Thayer, Joseph Henry, *A Greek-English Lexicon of the New Testament*, New York: American Book Company, 1889.

Thompson, William G., 'An Historical Perspective in the Gospel of Matthew', *Journal of Biblical Literature* 93 (1974), pp. 243-62.

—'Reflections on the Composition of Mt. 8.1-9.34', *Catholic Biblical Quarterly* 33 (1971), pp. 365-88.

Tödt, Heinz Eduard, *The Son of Man in the Synoptic Tradition*. New Testament Library; trans. Dorothea M. Barton; Philadelphia: Westminster, 1965.

Trilling, Wolfgang, 'Amt und Amtsverständnis bei Mt.', in *Mélanges bibliques en hommage au R.P. Béda Rigaux*, pp. 29-44. Ed. Albert Descamps and André de Halleux; Gembloux: Duculot, 1969.

—'Confession sans crainte (Mt. 10.26-33)' *Assemblées du Seigneur* 43 (1969), pp. 19-24.

—'Disponibilité pour suivre le Christ (Mt. 10.37-42)', *Assemblées du Seigneur* 44 (1969), pp. 15-20.

Uspensky, Boris, *A Poetics of Composition: The Structure of the Artistic Text and Typology of a Compositional Form*, trans. Valentina Zavarin and Susan Wittig; Berkeley: University of California Press, 1973.

Venetz, H.J., 'Bittet den Herrn der Ernte: Überlegungen zu Lk 10, 2/Mt 9.37', *Diakonia* 11 (1980), pp. 148-61.

Vorster, Willem S., 'Mark: Collector, Redactor, Author, Narrator?' *Journal of Theology for Southern Africa* 31 (1980), pp. 46-61.

Waetjen, Herman C., *The Origin and Destiny of Humanness: An Interpretation of the Gospel According to Matthew*, San Rafael, California: Crystal, 1976.

Weimann, Robert, 'Structure and History in Narrative Perspective: The Problem of Point of View Reconsidered', in *Structure and Society in Literary History: Studies in the History and Theory of Historical Criticism*, pp. 234-66. Charlottesville: University Press of Virginia, 1976.

Weir, T.H., 'Matthew x. 16', *Expository Times* 28 (1917), p. 186.

Weiss, Bernhard, *A Commentary on the New Testament*. Vol. 1: *Matthew–Mark*, trans. George H. Schodde and Epiphanius Wilson; New York: Funk & Wagnalls, 1906.

Westermann, Claus, *Der Segen in der Bibel und im Handeln der Kirche*, Munich: Chr. Kaiser, 1968.

Wilkinson, John, 'The Mission Charge to the Twelve and Modern Medical Missions', *Scottish Journal of Theology* 27 (1974), pp. 313-28.

Zahn, Theodor, *Introduction to the New Testament*, trans. from 3rd German edn. by John Moore Trout, William Arnot Mather, Louis Hodous, Edward Strong Worcester, William Hoyt Worrell, Rowland Backus Dodge; Edinburgh: T. & T. Clark, 1909.

Zerwick, Maximilian, *Biblical Greek*, trans. and revised by Joseph Smith; Rome: Scripta Pontificii Instituti Biblici, 1963.

Zerwick, Maximilan, and Mary Grosvenor, *A Grammatical Analysis of the Greek New Testament*, Rome: Biblical Institute Press, 1974.

Zumstein, Jean, 'Matthieu 28.16-20', *Revue de théologie et de philosophie* 22 (1972), pp. 14-33.

INDEXES

INDEX OF BIBLICAL REFERENCES

OLD TESTAMENT

Genesis
3.1 — 92
10.19 — 196n96
13.10 — 196n96
14.10 — 196n96
14.11 — 196n96
18.20 — 196n96
19.24 — 196n96
19.28 — 196n96

Numbers
27.17 — 186n28

Deuteronomy
25.1-3 — 199n116
29.23 — 196n96
33.32 — 196n96

1 Kings
22.17 — 186n28

2 Kings
1.8 — 174n79

2 Chronicles
18.16 — 186n28

Psalms
91.11-12 — 169n34
(LXX 90.11,12)

Song of Solomon
2.14 — 198n109

Isaiah
1.9 — 196n96
1.10 — 196n96
9.2 — 187n32
13.19 — 196n96
16.8-10 — 187n32
17.11 — 187n32
23.1-18 — 215n23
27.11ff. — 187n32

Jeremiah
5.17 — 187n32
5.24 — 187n32
23.14 — 196n96
50.40 — 196n96
51.33 — 187n32
(LXX 28.33)

Ezekiel
34.5 — 186n28

Hosea
6.6 — 186n26
6.11 — 187n32

Joel
4.13ff. — 187n32
13.4-8 — 215n23

Amos
4.11 — 196n96

Micah
5.1 — 63, 78
5.3 — 63, 78

Zephaniah
2.9 — 196n96

Zechariah
10.2 — 186n28

Judith
11.19 — 186n28

NEW TESTAMENT

Matthew
1.1-9.34 — 28, 31, 33-60, 167n18, 173n69, 174n73, 175n92
1.1-5.2 — 48
1.1-4.16 — 60, 62, 64, 71, 180n158
1.1-25 — 62
1.1-19 — 44
1.1-17 — 47, 177nn 111,112,115
1.1/17 — 39
1.1 — 37, 53, 60, 62, 170nn44, 45,49
1.2-17 — 55
1.2-16 — 36, 60
1.2 — 37, 60, 170 nn44,49
1.6 — 37, 60, 170

Matthew (cont.)

	n45
1.11-12	60
1.11	42, 170n46
1.12	42, 170n46
1.16	37, 53, 60
1.16b	171n50
1.17	36, 37, 42, 53, 60, 170 nn44,45,46, 49
1.18–9.34	47, 176n102
1.18–2.23	47
1.18-25	60, 65, 173 n65, 177nn 111,112,115
1.18	37, 60
1.19-20	56, 65
1.19	50, 168n25 178nn120, 124
1.20-25	38
1.20	37, 50, 168 nn242,25,32, 36, 170n454, 173n65, 178 n120
1.21	37, 42, 52, 62, 64, 171 n50, 173n65
1.22-24	40, 168n30
1.22-23	37, 61, 167 n19, 171nn 51,56
1.22	38, 52-54, 120, 169n33, 179n135
1.23	37, 54, 173 n65, 178n121
1.24	173n65
1.25	37, 42, 168 n27, 173n65
2.1-23	61, 62, 65
2.1-19	56
2.1-12	177nn111, 112,113, 115
2.1-8	77
2.1-3	56
2.1	17, 37, 63, 170n47

2.2	52, 56, 65, 175n97, 179 n138
2.3-4	37
2.3	17, 50, 52, 168n25, 170 n47, 178n120
2.4-6	171n51
2.4	37, 63, 65, 77, 78
2.5-6	55, 78
2.5	37, 63, 169 n33
2.6	37, 63, 64, 84, 178n121, 193n66
2.7-8	37, 52
2.7	170n47
2.8	175n97
2.9	17, 50, 178 n120
2.10	50, 168n25, 178nn120, 124
2.11	45, 50, 52, 175n97, 178 n120
2.12	37, 50, 168 n24, 169n32, 170n47, 178 nn120,124
2.13-18	102, 203 n152
2.13-15	38, 177nn 111,112,115
2.13	17, 48, 50, 52, 56, 63, 65, 168n24, 169nn32,36, 170n47, 178 nn120,121
2.14	63, 64
2.15	37, 38, 40, 52-54, 63, 120, 167n19, 168n30, 169 n33, 170n47, 171nn51,56, 135
2.16-18	49, 177nn 111,112,113,

	115
2.16	37, 50, 52, 65, 168n25, 170n47, 178 n120
2.17-18	40, 167n19, 168n30, 171 n51
2.17	38, 53, 120, 169n33
2.19-23	38, 177nn 111,112,115
2.19-20	63
2.19	47, 48, 50, 168n24, 169 nn32,36, 170 n47, 178n120
2.20	52, 56, 65
2.21	63
2.22-23	64, 69, 70
2.22	17, 48, 50, 64, 69, 168 nn24,25, 169 n32, 170 nn47,48, 178 nn120,124
2.22a	65
2.22b	65
2.23	38, 40, 52, 53, 64, 69, 120, 167n19, 168n30, 169 n33, 171n51
3.1-9.34	47
3.1-17	61, 62, 64, 64, 117nn 112,113,115, 188n40
3.1-6	176n102
3.1	47, 48, 176 n102
3.3	40, 48, 53, 65, 120, 167 n19, 169 nn30,33, 171 n51, 193 nn67,68
3.4	42, 176n102
3.5	176n102
3.6	176n102
3.7-12	44, 176n102

Matthew (cont.)		4.7	54, 65, 169	4.18-20	189nn47,50
3.7	50, 137, 178		n34, 175n91,	4.18	13, 50, 59,
	n120, 181n1		176n105		69, 70, 178
3.9	170n44, 171	4.8-9	52, 169n37		n120, 191n55
	n49	4.8	48, 169n31	4.19	48, 59, 66,
3.9a	218n64	4.9	44, 65, 175		71, 73, 80,
3.9b	218n64		n97		81, 175n91,
3.10	206n172	4.10-11	58		188n44
3.11-12	179n138	4.10	48, 54, 65,	4.19a	68, 82
3.11	37, 65		169nn31,34,	4.19c	68
3.12	206n172		175nn91,97	4.20	46, 52, 59,
3.13ff.	45, 58	4.11	45, 48, 169		66, 71, 185
3.13-17	58, 80, 179		n37, 177n115		n21
	n102, 188	4.12-17	180n158	4.21-22	189nn47,50
	n40	4.12-16	62-65, 67-69,	4.21	44, 50, 59,
3.13	48, 49, 69		133, 168n30,		66, 178n120
3.14-15	56		177nn112,	4.22	46, 52, 59,
3.14	44, 65		115, 191n56,		66, 71, 185
3.14b/14c	39		209n200		n21
3.15	48, 52, 58,	4.12-13	64, 65, 70,	4.23–11.1	72, 73, 182
	121, 175		102, 132, 146		nn3,7
	nn88,91, 176	4.12a/12b	135	4.23–9.35	72, 73, 82,
	n105, 211	4.13	38, 65		182n3
	n222	4.14-16	40, 167n19,	4.23–9.34	71, 185n18,
3.16-17	54		171n51		214n8
3.16	37, 50, 102,	4.14	52, 53, 120,	4.23–25/9.35	72
	168n27, 178		169n33	4.23/9.35	182n3
	n120	4.15-16	64-66	4.23-25	58, 66, 69,
3.17	35, 37, 44,	4.15	70		72, 76, 89,
	54, 64, 118,	4.16	66, 70		176n102, 177
	168n27, 171	4.17ff.	188n40		n111, 182n7
	n56	4.17-26.56	146	4.23-24	58
4.1-11	38, 58, 59,	4.17-16.20	180n158,	4.23	13, 44, 52,
	62-65, 168		214n10		54, 56, 66,
	n27, 177	4.17-11.1	180n158		68-70, 72, 73,
	nn112,115	4.17-9.34	60, 65, 71		76, 80, 84,
4.1	37, 52, 169	4.17-25	177nn112,		85, 102, 122,
	n31		113,114		176n102, 181
4.2	50, 178n120	4.17	52, 54, 65-		n2, 182nn3,6,
4.3	44, 45, 52,		67, 76, 84,		7,8, 185n17
	65, 169nn31,		122, 132,	4.23b-d	185n19
	37, 181n163		175n91, 176	4.23d	185n19
4.4	54, 65, 169		nn102,106,	4.24-35	72
	n34, 175n91,		180	4.24	45, 52, 59,
	176n105		n158, 188n		66, 85
4.5-6	52, 169n37		39, 193n68	4.24a	45
4.5	48, 65, 169	4.18-22	38, 58, 66,	4.25	46, 59, 66,
	n31, 181n163		71, 73, 82,		69, 70, 145
4.6	44, 48, 55,		150, 179	5.1-9.34	68, 72, 76,
	65		n155, 188		176n102, 185
4.6b	169n34		n44, 190n50		n20

Matthew (cont.)		5.22	38, 48, 206 n172	6.18	54, 122, 169 n35
5.1-7.29	66, 72, 177nn 112,113,114, 115, 182n7	5.23	45	6.19-21	56
		5.24	45	6.19-20	38
5.1-2	58, 59, 66, 68, 183n9	5.26	48, 176n108	6.22-23	38
		5.27	169n34	6.24	38, 169n35
5.1	45, 50, 66, 178n120, 182 n7, 183n9, 189n47	5.28	48	6.24a/24d	39
		5.29-30	38	6.25-34	194n78
		5.29	52, 206n175	6.25-32	56, 101, 188 n39
5.1a/9.36a	72	5.30	206n175	6.25	48
5.1bff.	182n7	5.31	169n34	6.26	54, 169n35, 188n39
5.1b-9.34	72	5.32	38, 48		
5.2	48, 52	5.33	169n34	6.29	48
5.3-7.27	35, 38, 44, 48, 67, 68, 101, 172n60, 175nn88,91, 182n9	5.34-36	38	6.30	169n35
		5.34-35	188n39	6.31-32	101
		5.34	48, 169n35	6.32	54, 168n35, 188n39
		5.38	169n34		
		5.39-41	38	6.33	54, 121, 122, 169n35, 211 n222
5.3-10	38, 56, 69	5.39	48		
5.3/10	39	5.42	38		
5.3	54, 123, 188 n39	5.43	169n34	6.34	101
		5.44	38, 48, 69	6.34a/34b	39
5.6	121	5.45	38, 54, 188 n39	7.2	38
5.8	169n35			7.3a/3b	39
5.9	113, 169n35	5.46-47	38	7.6a/6b	39
5.10-12	69	5.46	122	7.7-11	188n39
5.10	54, 69, 121, 123, 188n39	5.48	54, 188n39	7.7-8	38
		6.1-18	38, 59	7.9-10	38
5.11-12	211n216	6.1	54, 122, 169 n35, 188n39	7.11	54, 169n35, 188n39
5.11	38, 69, 203 nn144,145, 204n159	6.2-4	188n39		
		6.2	48, 122, 137	7.13-14	38
		6.4	54, 122, 169 n35	7.15-20	59
5.12	69, 120, 122, 203n146, 211 n216	6.5-6	188n39	7.15	93, 198n105
		6.5	48, 122, 137	7.16	38
5.16	54, 169n35, 188n39	6.6	54, 122, 169 n35, 188n39	7.16/20	39
				7.17	38
5.17	52, 54, 58, 118, 202n139, 208n1192	6.8	54, 169n35, 188n39	7.18	38
		6.9-13	188n39	7.19	206n172
5.18	48	6.9-10	54	7.21-23	59
5.19	38, 54, 59, 122, 188n39	6.9	54, 169n35, 188n39	7.21-22	120
5.20	48, 54, 59, 66, 121, 122, 137, 181n1, 188n39, 211 n222	6.10	122, 188n39	7.21	54, 67, 122, 169n35, 188 n39
		6.14-15	38, 54		
		6.14	169n35, 188 n39		
				7.22	38, 211n217
		6.15	169n35	7.24-27	38, 59
5.21-48	38, 54	6.16-18	188n39	7.28-9.34	48
5.21	169n34	6.16	48, 122, 137	7.28-29	56, 58, 59, 66, 179n138, 183n9
				7.28	50, 168n25,

Matthew (cont.)			
	178n120, 183	177n112, 177	113,115
	n9	n114	8.28-31 44
7.29	52, 80, 118,	8.14 50, 68, 178	8.28 13, 54, 173
	137	n120	n64, 185n18
8-9	172nn58,59,	8.16-17 58, 67, 177	8.29 202n139
	173nn63,64,	nn111,112,113	8.31-32 177n115
	177n115, 193	8.16 44, 45, 54,	8.32 58, 175n91,
	n69	59, 80, 85,	176n105
8.1-9.34	62, 72, 181	173n64	8.33 45, 177n116
	n170, 182n7	8.17 38, 40, 52,	8.34 50, 52, 178
8.1-4	58, 67, 177	53, 120, 167	n120
	nn112,113,115	n19, 168n30,	9.1-8 56, 58, 67,
8.1	46, 58, 59,	168n33, 171	173n65, 177
	141, 145	n51	nn112,113,115
8.24	85	8.18-21 38, 56, 67,	9.1 13, 69, 173
8.2	38, 44, 45,	177nn112,113,	n64, 185n18
	52, 175n97,	114,115, 179	9.2-8 85, 202n139
	179n138	n155, 202	9.2/3 44
8.3	48, 52, 175	n139	9.2 44, 45, 50,
	n91	8.18 13, 44, 50,	50, 168n28,
8.3a	38	59, 173n64,	175nn91,92,
8.3b	38, 173n63	178n120, 185	176n105, 178
8.4	42, 45, 48,	n18	n120
	175n91	8.19 44-46, 137,	9.2b 45
8.5-13	58, 67, 85,	181n1	9.3 137, 168n26,
	177nn111,112,	8.20 48, 59, 175	177n116, 181
	113, 185n20	n91, 202n139	n1
8.5-6	44	8.21-22 82, 189n50	9.4-6a 175n91
8.5	45, 69	8.21 44, 59, 189n47	9.4 50, 52, 59,
8.7/8-9	44	8.22 46, 48, 59,	168n28, 176
8.7	48, 52, 85,	175n91	n105, 178
	175n91	8.23-9.1 69	n120
8.8	173n64	8.23-27 56, 58, 59,	9.5 52
8.8b	38, 179n138	67, 177nn112,	9.6-7 58
8.10-12	175n91	113,114, 181	9.6 48, 52, 118,
8.10	46, 48, 50,	n172	173n65, 202
	52, 168n25,	8.23 13, 46, 59,	n139
	176n105, 177	68, 71, 185	9.6b 175n91
	n119, 178	nn18,21, 189	9.8 50, 52, 56,
	n120	n47	58, 59, 80,
8.10a	50	8.25 44, 45, 52,	118, 168n25,
8.11	48, 54, 170	71	173n65, 177
	n44, 218n64	8.26 44, 48, 58,	n119, 178n120
8.12	59, 84, 218	59, 175n91	9.9 46, 48, 50,
	n64	8.27 50, 56, 59,	52, 58, 59,
8.13	38, 42, 52,	168n25, 177	67, 71, 82,
	173n64, 175	n119, 178	150, 155n2,
	n91, 176n105	n120, 179n138	175n91, 177
8.13b	173n63	185n20	nn112,114,
8.14-15	58, 67, 85,	8.28-9.1 185n20	178n120, 185
		8.28-34 58, 67, 80,	n21, 188n44,
		85, 177nn112,	

Matthew (cont.)
189n47,50
9.10-13   56, 58, 67,
177nn112,113,
114,115
9.10-11   44
9.10   59, 68, 189n47
9.11   50, 68, 137,
177n116, 178
n120, 181n1,
189n47
9.12-13   59
9.12   50, 175n91,
176n105, 178
n120
9.13   52, 54, 118,
169n33, 186
n26, 202n139,
208n192
9.13b/13c   39
9.14-17   56, 67, 177
nn112,114,115
9.14   44, 45, 48,
137, 181n1,
189n47
9.15   175n91, 176
n105, 209n200
9.15a/15b   39
9.18-19/23-26   56, 58, 67,
85, 177nn111,
112,113,114
9.18   44, 45, 175
nn97,138
9.18b   38
9.19   46, 59, 68,
71, 176n99,
185n21, 189
n47
9.20-22   58, 67, 85,
177n112
9.20-21   44
9.20   45
9.21   38, 50, 52,
168n26, 178
n120, 179n138
9.22   52, 168n28,
175n91, 176
n105
9.22a   38
9.22b   38, 173n 63
9.23-24   53

9.23   38, 50, 173
n64, 178n120
9.24   44, 175n91,
176n105
9.27-31   58, 67, 85,
177n112, 193
n69
9.27   3,7, 44, 46,
170n45
9.28   38, 44, 45,
48, 173n64,
175n91
9.29   38, 48, 52,
78 175n91
9.30-31   175n93
9.30/31   44
9.30   48, 168n25,
175nn91,93,
177n119
9.31   45, 175n93
9.32-34   56, 58, 67,
80, 85, 106,
128, 177
nn112,113,115
9.32   44, 45
9.33   51, 56, 59,
168n25, 177
n119, 178
n120, 179
nn133,138
9.34   56, 68, 69,
102, 137,
181n1, 204
nn157,158,
214n18
9.35-11.1   13, 16, 17,
23-26, 28, 29,
31, 57, 59,
60, 69, 71-
74, 125, 127,
129, 151, 153,
155nn23, 159
n30, 162n53,
182nn3,12
72
9.35/11.1   72
9.35-10.16   183n12
9.35-10.15   101
9.35-10.8a   183n12
9.35-10.5   183n12
9.35-10.5a   13, 14, 16,
21, 23, 24,

74, 82, 106,
125, 126, 155
n1, 157n22,
158n21
9.35-38   183n12
9.35-36   162n52
9.35   13, 14, 31,
39, 46, 49,
57, 59, 69,
71-77, 80, 81,
84, 85, 89,
102, 122, 125,
126, 156n12,
175n97, 181
n2, 182nn3,5,
6,7,8, 183n12,
185nn17,19,
186nn23,24,
194n79, 213
nn237,239
9.35b-d   185n19
9.35d   185n19
9.36-10.5a   76, 77, 186n23
9.36-38   183n12
9.36   13, 74-78, 84,
125, 182n7,
185n22, 186
nn23,24,29,
187n30, 198
n106
9.36bff.   182n7
9.36b-10.42   72
9.37-38   13, 75, 76,
78-80, 186n23,
187n32, 188
n40, 189n45,
194n76
9.37   75, 125, 186
n23, 201n136
9.37b   78, 79
9.38   75, 79, 80,
81, 86, 118,
187n34, 190
n52
10   19, 22, 23,
157n22, 162
n49, 189n47,
213n1
10.1ff.   188n44
10.1-16   161n49, 183
n12

Matthew (cont.)

10.1-15	183n12
10.1-5	189n47
10.1-5a	162n52
10.1	13, 75, 76, 80-82, 85, 89, 105, 118, 125, 133, 134, 151, 186n26, 188 n44, 189nn45, 47, 190n50, 210n209, 213 n3, 220n83
10.2-4	75, 81, 190 n50, 191n56
10.2	14, 75, 105, 189n47, 190 n52, 220n83
10.3	75
10.4	75, 102, 128, 146, 184n12, 204n153, 209 n200
10.4b	135
10.5ff.	157n22
10.5f.	159n32
10.5	19, 184n12, 189n47, 220 n83
10.5a	14-16, 19, 75, 76, 81, 82, 89, 105, 118, 119, 125-28, 133, 134, 156n12, 183 nn9,12, 186 n23, 190nn 51,52, 217 nn58,61
10.5b-42	13, 14, 16-24, 73, 74, 82, 123, 125, 127, 140, 146, 151-53, 155 n1,5, 157n22, 159n30, 182 n9, 213n7, 214 n9, 218 n61
10.5b-15	14-16, 19, 20, 24, 74, 83,

	89, 91, 101, 102, 104-106, 146, 155n5, 156nn7,12, 185n21, 191 n62, 197n101
10.5b-10	89
10.5b-6	14-17, 84, 91, 95, 134, 162 n53, 163n53, 191n58, 202 n138
10.5b	15, 83, 151, 183n12, 192 nn63,64
10.6	15, 16, 83, 100, 151, 192 n63, 198 n106, 204 n157
10.7-14	14
10.7-10	84-86
10.7-8	88, 134, 213n4
10.7	14, 83, 84, 89, 120, 122, 152, 197n98
10.8	14, 83, 89, 120
10.8a-d	192n62
10.8a/b	86
10.8a	85
10.8b	85, 194n74
10.8e	192n62
10.9-10	14, 85, 194 n74
10.9-10d	192n62
10.9-10a/10b	86
10.9-10a	85, 86, 193 n72, 194n77
10.9	83, 85
10.10	83
10.10b	86, 194nn76, 77
10.10e	192n62
10.11-15	84, 86-89, 99
10.11-13	14
10.11-13a	156n8
10.11	83, 86-88, 195n88
10.12-15	90

10.12-13	86-88, 195 n82
10.12	83, 113
10.13	83
10.13b-15	91, 156n8
10.14ff.	20
10.14-15	87, 123, 124
10.14	14, 83, 120, 192n62, 195 nn87,88, 196n97, 197 n99
10.15	14, 74, 83, 89, 99, 109, 111, 116, 122, 123, 155n5, 192n62, 196 n97, 207n182, 212n231
10.16-42	24
10.16-39	20, 160n44
10.16-38	116
10.16-23	14-16, 19, 74, 90, 91, 101, 102, 104-106, 124, 134, 139, 146, 155n5, 156n7, 160n39, 204 n159, 213n7, 216n47
10.16	16, 19, 90-93, 115, 116, 142, 161n48, 192n64, 198 n106, 217 nn58,61
10.16a	14, 93, 95, 102, 156nn 7,8
10.16b	20
10.17-23	107, 198n112
10.17-18	18, 91, 156n8
10.17	17, 90, 128, 147, 161n48, 199nn117, 119, 207 n181, 219n73
10.17a	90, 91, 93, 97, 198n106, 207n181

Matthew (cont.)

			201n132		205n163
10.17b-20	93	10.22b	15, 99, 156	10.26a	108
10.17b-18/	91, 93-97		n10, 202n139	10.26b-27	107
19-20		10.23ff.	158n24	10.26b	108
10.17b-18	90, 95, 96,	10.23	16, 20, 74,	10.7	103, 108, 111
	99		90, 91, 97,	10.28	103, 105, 107-
10.17b	15, 94, 97,		99, 101, 102,		11, 115, 116,
	102, 158n26,		122, 124,		128, 147, 205
	199n118, 200		155n5, 157		n170, 206
	n122, 218n61		nn23,24, 160		n178, 207
10.18-19a	203n146		n44, 162n53,		n182, 218n61
10.18	15, 17, 18,		163n54, 197	10.28a	110, 204n154,
	20, 90, 94-		n103, 201		205nn169,
	96, 98, 99,		n137, 202nn		170
	102, 120, 125,		138,139,140,	10.28b	204n154
	147, 158nn		203n149, 212	10.29-31	107, 109-11,
	24,26, 159		n231, 218n61		206n178, 207
	n32, 162n53,	10.23a	15, 90, 99,		n180
	163n54, 199		201n137	10.29	103, 110
	nn118,119,	10.23b	15, 18, 100,	10.29a	109
	200nn122,		159n32, 201	10.29b	109, 207n180
	130		n137, 202nn	10.30-31	110
10.18a/22a	203n145		139,140	10.30	103
10.18b	207n181	10.24-42	16, 74, 102,	10.31	103, 105, 107
10.19-20	90, 91, 95,		104, 105, 123,	10.32-42	16
	101, 120		124, 155n5	10.32-33	104, 107, 111,
10.19	90, 128, 147,	10.24-39	117, 134		116, 120, 207
	197n100, 207	10.24-25	104-107, 117,		n181
	n101		123, 161n48,	10.32	103, 105, 117,
10.19a/23a	203n144		204nn160,		156n13, 221
10.19a	90, 95, 96,		161, 213n5,		n88
	99, 100, 102		217n59	10.32a	207n181
10.19b-20	96, 200n127	10.24-25a	16, 105, 106	10.33	103, 116, 156
10.19a	96, 203n147	10.24	102, 105, 106		n14
10.20	90, 96, 102	10.25	102, 128	10.33a	207n181
10.21-23	93	10.25a	105, 106	10.34-39	104, 105,
10.21-22/23	91, 97-101	10.25b	105-107, 204		112-17
10.21-22	90, 91, 99		n158, 205	10.34-36	112, 114, 115
10.21-22a	15, 98, 99		n163	10.34-35	118
10.21	90, 97-99,	10.26-42	107	10.34	16, 103, 104
	102, 109,	10.26-39	123	10.34a	113
	115, 128,	10.26-33	104, 105, 107-	10.34b	113
	147, 198n106,		12, 114, 117,	10.35	103, 113,
	200n128, 201		135, 204n154		208n191
	n132, 204	10.26-31	16, 107, 111,		
	n153, 207		204n161, 207	10.36	103, 113
	n181, 218n61		n181	10.37-38	114, 115, 209
10.22	90, 98, 111,	10.26-27	107, 110, 111,		nn194,199
	116, 160n44,		120	10.37	103
	207n182	10.26	103-105, 107,	10.37a	156n15, 209
10.22a	98, 198n106,		108, 204n160,		n199

Matthew (cont.)		11.2-3a/3b-6	135	13.36	129, 130, 134
10.37b	156n15, 209 n199	11.2-3	132	13.40	206n172
10.38-39	146	11.2	127, 146, 214 n16, 218n61	13.42	206n172
10.38	103, 115-17, 128, 147, 156 n14, 209nn 199,200, 218 n61	11.3	131, 214n16	13.50	206n172
		11.4-5	214n16	13.51	134
		11.5	130, 131	13.53-58	130, 132, 133
10.39	103, 104, 116, 117, 128, 209 n201	11.6	131, 132	13.57	132
		11.7-19	130	14.1-12	133, 134, 146
		11.14	174n79	14.1-2	130, 133
10.39a	156n15	11.16-19	131	14.2/14.1	135
10.39b	156n15	11.20-24	130, 132	14.3-12	129, 133, 215 n33
10.40-42	104, 105, 117-24, 211n224	12	212n236	14.9	17
		12.1ff.	137	14.12-13	204n152
10.40	16, 104, 118, 119, 211nn217, 218,224, 212 n226	12.1-8	133, 215n24	14.13-36	133
		12.1a	215n26	14.13-21	130
		12.1b	215n26	14.13-14	130, 215n26
		12.2	132, 137	14.13	17, 130, 145, 157n22, 214 n13
10.40a	156n15	12.9-45	133		
10.40b	156n15	12.9-14	130, 215n24	14.14	130, 215n29
10.41-42	104, 118-23, 210n213, 211 n224, 212n226	12.10	132, 167	14.15	129, 130, 134, 215nn26,28,29
		12.14-15	204n152		
		12.14	132, 134, 135, 137	14.16	134, 215n29
10.41a/41b/42	119	12.15-21	130	14.17-19	134
10.41	104, 119, 211 n220, 212n225	12.15	130, 145, 214 n13	14.17	134
				14.19-20	134
10.41a/41b	119	12.22ff.	2515n24	14.19	130, 134, 215 n30
10.41a	122, 156n15	12.22-45	130		
10.41b	122, 156n15	12.22-24	130	14.21	134
10.42	74, 104, 119, 122, 123, 155 n5, 156n14, 210n213, 211 nn224,225	12.22	129, 130	14.24-26	135
		12.23	131	14.26	134, 135, 215 n27
		12.24	132, 137, 204 n58, 214n18		
				14.28-32	215n27
		12.27	204n158	14.28	134
11.1	13, 14, 16, 19, 21, 23, 24, 72-74, 119, 124-28, 153, 155n1,156n12, 162n52, 182 nn5,8,9, 212 n237,213n239, 220n83	12.28	132	14.30	134
		12.38	132, 137, 215 n24	14.33	134, 214n20
		12.46-50	130, 133	14.34-36	130
		12.46	215n26	14.35	129, 130
		12.48-50	150	15.1-20	134, 215n24
		12.49	215n26	15.1	129, 137
		13.1-52	133	15.2	132
		13.1-33	130	15.10-11	130
		13.1-3a	215n26	15.10	129, 130
11.2-28.20	29, 127, 128	13.2	130, 145, 214 n13	15.12	129, 132, 134, 135, 137, 215 nn26,32
11.2-16.20	129-35, 180 n158				
11.2-30	133	13.10-17	132	15.21-28	130, 134
11.2-6	129, 132, 193 n69	13.10	126, 134, 215 n26	15.21	204n152, 215 n26
		13.34-35	130	15.22-23	130

Matthew (cont.)

15.23	129, 134, 215 n26, 215n28
15.24	162n53, 193 n66
15.29-31	130, 133, 215 n26
15.30	129, 130, 145
15.31	131
15.32-39	130
15.32-38	134
15.32	129, 130, 134, 215n26
15.32b	215n29
15.32c	215n29
15.33	134
15.34-36	134
15.34	134
15.35	130
15.36-37	134
15.36	134, 215n30
15.38	134
15.39	130
16.1-4	133, 204n152, 215n24
16.1	129, 132, 137
16.2	132
16.4b	215n26
16.5-12	134, 215n24
16.5	215n26
16.6	137
16.7-8	134
16.7	215n27
16.8	215n27
16.11	137
16.12	137
16.13-23	180n158
16.13-20	130, 134
16.13a	215n26
16.13b	215n26
16.14	130, 134
16.15	214n20
16.16	134, 214n20
16.21–28.20	180n158, 214 n10
16.21–25.46	129, 135-43, 180n158, 214 n10
16.21–18.35	215n35
16.21–17.13	138
16.21-23	140, 141, 180

	n158
16.21	135, 137, 138, 141, 143, 146, 214n10, 216 nn36,41
16.22	141
16.24-28	140
16.24	142
16.25	142
16.27	156n11, 202 n139
16.28	156n11, 202 n139
17.1-8	140
17.1	216n36, 217 n52
17.4	141
17.9-13	137, 140, 141, 215n33, 217 n54
17.9	146, 216n36
17.10	216n41, 217 n54
17.12	143, 146
17.13	141, 217n54
17.14-20	136, 140, 215 n35, 217n52
17.14-18	138, 140
17.14	136, 216n36
17.16-17	216n38
17.16	140
17.19-23	138
17.19-20	138, 140
17.19	136, 141
17.20	141
17.22-23	137, 140, 141, 143, 146
17.22	135, 216n36
17.23b	141
17.24-27	140, 215n35, 217n50
17.24-25a	138
17.24	135, 216n36
17.25	216n36
17.25b–18.35	138
17.25b-27	138
18	211n223
18.1-35	140, 215n35
18.1-4	217n53
18.1	136, 216n36
18.2	136, 216n43

18.6	211n223
18.8	206nn172,173, 175
18.9	206nn172,175
18.10	211n223
18.14	211n223
18.21	136
19.1-2/3-9	216n48, 217 n49
19.1-2	136, 140, 215 n35, 216n44
19.1	136, 216n36
19.2	145
19.3-9	137, 138, 140, 215n35
19.3	136, 216nn36, 41
19.10-15	215n35
19.10-13	217n48
19.10-12	138, 140
19.10	216nn36,48
19.13-15	136, 140, 141, 215n35
19.13	136, 138, 216 n36
19.14-15	138
19.16-22	136, 138, 140, 215n35, 216 n48, 217n49
19.16	136, 216n36
19.23–21.11	215n35
19.23–20.28	138
19.23–20.16	138, 140, 217 n48
19.23	216nn36,48
19.27	141
19.28	220n83
20.17-19	137, 140, 141, 143, 217n55
20.17	136, 216n36, 220n83
20.18-19	146
20.18	216n41
20.19	17
20.20-28	140
20.20-21	141, 216n43, 217n55
20.20	136, 216n36
20.22	141, 142, 216 n43
20.23	142

Matthew (cont.)

20.24	141
20.25	136
20.29–21.11	215n35
20.29-34	136, 138, 215 n35, 216n44
20.29	136, 145, 216 n36
21.1-11	136-38, 140
21.1-7	138, 140
21.1	136, 216n36
21.6	150
21.8-11	138
21.8-9	145
21.10	136
21.12–22.46	140
21.12-17	137, 139, 215 n35
21.12-13	138, 139
21.12	136, 137, 139, 216n36
21.13	137, 139
21.14-17	137, 215n35
21.14-15	138
21.14	136, 216n36
21.15-17	138
21.15-16	139
21.15	216n41
21.16b	139
21.18-22	138, 140, 215 n35
21.18	137, 216n36
21.23–22.46	137-39, 215 n35, 217n49
21.23-46	138
21.23-27	139
21.23	136-39, 216 nn36,41
21.28-32	139
21.33-46	139
21.33-43	217n60
21.33-36	142
21.45-46	217n57, 218 n62
21.45	216n41
22.1-14	138, 141, 218 n62
22.1-6	142
22.1	216n36
22.3-4	142
22.3	142, 218n64

22.4	218n64
22.5-6	218n62
22.5	142
22.6	142, 147
22.8-10	142
22.8	218n64
22.9	142, 218n64
22.10	218n64
22.15-22	138
22.15-17	137, 139
22.15	139, 216nn36, 41, 217n57, 218n62
22.16	216nn36,37
22.19	136
22.22	139
22.23-33	138
22.23-28	137, 139
22.23	136, 216nn36, 41
22.33	137
22.34-40	138
22.34-36	137, 139
22.34-35	139
22.34	137, 139, 216 nn37,41
22.35	216n36
22.41-46	138, 139
22.41	216nn36,37,41
22.46	137-39
23.1–25.46	215n35
23.1-39	137, 139, 140, 142, 215n35
23.1	139, 140, 216 nn36,40,45, 217n49
23.2-39	139
23.2-36	138
23.2	216nn40,41, 218n62
23.13	216nn40,41, 218n62
23.15	216nn40,41, 218n62
23.23	216nn40,41, 218n62
23.24	216nn40,41, 218n62
23.27	216nn40,41, 218n62
23.29	216nn40,41,

	218n62
23.34	142, 147, 218 n62, 219n73
23.34a	142, 218n61
23.34b	142, 218n61
23.37-39	138
23.37	142, 218n62
24.1–25.46	139, 140, 142, 145
24.1-2	139
24.1	136-38, 145, 216n36
24.3	136-39, 202 n139, 216n36
24.4–25.46	139
24.6	156n10
24.9-14	139, 142, 159 n32
24.9-13	142, 216n47
24.9	142
24.10	142
24.13	156n10
24.14	22, 142, 156 n10
24.15	174n73
24.27	202n139
24.30	156n11, 202 n139
24.37	202n139
24.39	202n139
24.42	202n139
24.44	156n11, 202 n139
24.26	202n139
25.10	202n139
25.19	202n139
25.27	202n1396
25.31	156n11, 202 n139
25.41	206n172, 206 n173
25.46	206n173
26.1–28.20	129, 140-52, 180n158
26.1-56	143-46, 148
26.1-2	143, 148, 214 n10
26.2	145, 146
26.3-5	143, 144
26.3	218n66
26.4	146, 147

Matthew (cont.)

26.6-13	143, 148
26.7	144
26.8-9	148
26.8	148
26.10-13	145
26.13	218n65
26.14-16	143, 144, 148
26.14	144, 218n66, 220n83
26.15	147
26.16	146-48
26.17-19	143, 148
26.17	148
26.18	145, 148, 219 n79
26.19	148, 150
26.19a	148, 219n79
26.19b	219n19
26.19b	219n79
26.20-56	148
26.20-29	143, 148
26.20-25	146
26.20	145, 220n83
26.21	145, 148
26.22	148
26.23-24	145
26.25	145-47
26.26	145, 148, 219 n70
26.27-29	145
26.27	219n70
26.30-35	143, 148
26.30	145, 148
26.31-32	145
26.32	144, 149, 150, 220n84
26.34	145
26.35	145
26.38	148
26.36-46	143, 148, 219 n77
26.36	145
26.37	145
26.38	145, 148, 219 n78
26.38b	145
26.39	145, 219n70
26.40-41	145
26.40	145, 148, 219 nn77,78

26.41	148, 219n78
26.42	145, 219n70
26.43	145, 148, 219 nn77,78
26.44	145, 219n70
26.45-46	145
26.45	145, 148, 219 nn77,78
26.47-56	143, 148
26.47	218n66, 219 n69, 220n83
26.48	146, 147
26.49	144, 146
26.50	144-47
26.51	149
26.52-54	145, 149
26.55-56	145, 219n70
26.56	143-45, 148, 149
25.57-27.66	143-46, 149, 219n72
26.57	145-47, 149
26.58	149, 218n68, 220n80
26.59-68	149
26.59-61	146
26.59	146, 147
26.63	146
26.64	146, 156n11, 202n139
26.67	146
26.69-75	149
26.69-74	149
26.70	218n68, 220 n80
26.72	218n68, 220 n80
26.74	218n68, 220 n80
26.75a	149
26.75b	149
27.1-2	149
27.1	146, 147
27.2	17, 146, 147
27.3-10	218n68, 220 n80
27.3-5	220 82
27.3	146, 147, 219 n71
27.5	220n83
27.11-26	149

27.11	17, 145, 146
27.12	146, 219n71
27.14	17, 146
27.15	17
27.18	146, 147
27.20	146
27.21	17
27.22-23	146
27.22	147
27.23	147
27.26	146, 147, 219 n73
27.27-31	149
27.27	17, 146
27.28	146
27.29	146
27.30	146
27.31	146, 147
27.32-56	149
27.34	145, 219n72
27.35	146, 147
27.36	146
27.37	146
27.39	146
27.41	146
27.44	146
27.46	146
27.48	219n72
27.50	145, 146
27.51-53	219n75
27.54	146, 219n75
27.57-66	149
28	149
28.1-20	143, 144, 147, 149
28.1-16	147
28.1-15	150
28.1	144, 147
28.2-3	144
28.2	147
28.4-7	144
28.5-7	147, 150
28.7	144, 150, 220 n84
28.8-10	144, 147
28.8	147
28.10	144, 150, 220 n84
28.11-15	144, 150, 219

Matthew (cont.)		28.18	151	*Luke*	
	n76	28.19	22, 163n53	1.60–63	174n78
28.11a	147	28.20	152, 153	6.15	190n53
28.14	17			9.1-6	22
28.16-20	144, 147, 150,	*Mark*		10.1-16	22
	153, 157n19	6	157n22	10.2	187n32
28.16	147, 150, 220	6.6ff.	157n22	22.35	20
	n84	6.6b-13	22		
28.17	150	6.30ff.	157n22	*Acts*	
28.18-20	151-53, 162	6.30	157n22	1.13	190n53
	n53, 213	13.10	159n32, 162		
	nn238,1, 220		n53		
	n87				

INDEX OF AUTHORS

Abrams, M.H. 57, 166n3, 179n151
Albright, W.F., & C.S. Mann 183n12, 187n37, 190n51, 197n100, 201n132, 209n196
Allen, W.C. 22, 161n45, 184n12, 197n100, 201nn132,134, 206n171, 210nn210,214
Anderson, J.C. 48, 55, 164n56, 168n28, 175nn86,96, 176nn104,105,106,107, 178nn121,122,128,130, 179 nn139, 140,141, 209n192
Arens, E. 209n192
Aune, D.E. 184n13, 203n140, 210n204

Bacon, B.W. 20, 21, 159n30, 160nn35, 38,41,42,44, 183n12
Bammel, E. 201n134
Barr, D.L. 164n56, 220n87
Barta, K.A. 159n30, 190n51, 203n152, 204nn155,159, 205n168, 209n194, 210n201, 213nn241,7, 214n9, 220n87
Barth, G. 161n48
Barth, K. 220n87
Bauer, D.R. 180n158
Bauer, W., W.F. Arndt, & F.W. Gingrich 190n53, 191n58, 196nn90,91, 197 n100,104, 198nn110, 112, 199n116, 201n135, 204n160, 208n188, 218 n63, 219n73
Beare, F.W. 22, 159n30, 161n46, 182n3, 183n11, 184n12, 187n32, 190n51, 193nn70,71, 194n74, 196nn90,93, 197n100, 205n164, 206nn171,179, 207n180, 209n192, 210n211, 212 n236, 213n241
Blass, F., and A. DeBrunner 185n16, 187n33, 191n58, 214n22
Bohemen, N. van 204n153
Bonnard, P. 186n29, 187n32, 189n49, 191n58, 194n73, 197nn100,102, 198nn110,112, 199n117, 200n121, 127, 201nn132,133, 204n160, 205

nn164,169, 206n171, 207nn180,181, 209nn197,198,201, 210nn207,214
Boomershine, T. 164n56
Boomershine, T., & G. Bartholomew 164n56
Booth, W. 26, 165nn62,65,68,70, 167 nn16,22, 171n57
Boring, M.E. 187n32, 194n77, 196n93, 198n106, 201n137, 206n178, 210 nn214,215,216, 211nn217,218,219,221
Bornkamm, G. 20, 160nn35,36, 198 n105, 212n233
Bosch, D.J. 220n87
Broadus, J.A. 158n29, 193n71, 195n86, 197nn100,104, 198n108, 199n117, 206n171, 209nn192,196, 213n241
Brown, R.E. 171n50, 174n78
Brown, S. 23, 162nn50,52,53, 184n12, 190n51, 192n65, 200n123, 201 nn136,137, 202n140, 203nn149,151, 207n181, 220n87
Burger, C. 181n170
Butler, B.C. 173n66

Cadbury, H.J. 196nn90,91,93,97
Caird, G.B. 196nn92,98
Chatman, S. 164n62, 165nn63,65,66,67, 68,69,72,73, 171n57, 179nn151,152, 153, 180n156
Combet-Galland, C. 183n12, 185n15, 188n42, 197n103, 198n111, 204n153, 208n189, 209n198
Combrink, H.J.B. 164n56,57, 184n12, 185n21, 187n38, 195nn86,87, 197 n103, 205n164, 212n236
Cope, O.L. 208n190
Culpepper, R.A. 52, 178n125

Dausch, P. 159n30, 184n12, 185n17, 188n41, 196n91, 197n100, 198n110, 201n134, 203n141, 204n157, 205

n169, 206nn171,177,179, 207n187, 209n196, 210n210,214, 212n234, 213n241
Dautzenberg, G. 205nn169,170, 206n174, 209n201,210nn202,205
Deiss, L. 182n3, 188n44
Delling, G. 202n140
Dewey, J. 164nn56,58,60, 172n58, 173 nn66,67,68
Di Marco, A. 173n66
Dobschütz, E. von 172n58
Dolezel, L. 167n16
Dupont, J. 201n135, 202n138, 213n241

Edersheim, A. 159n30, 160nn35,36
Erdman, C.R. 158n29

Fenton, J.C. 173nn66,67, 193n70
Feuillet, A. 201n134
Filson, F. 21, 159n30, 160n39, 184n12, 196n96, 197n100, 200n129, 205n164, 206nn171,179, 209nn192,196, 210 n214
Fletcher, D.R. 209n196
Foerster, W. 195n86, 198n109
Fowler, R.M. 164nn56,58, 165n64, 166 n3, 171n57
Frankemölle, H. 23, 155n6, 161n48, 162n51, 182n3, 183n12, 189n47, 192n63, 200n123, 201n133, 210n213, 220n87
Friedman, N. 46, 168n29, 174n83, 176n101
Friedrich, G. 210n215, 211n216
Frye, R.M. 163n56, 164n58, 171n52

Gaechter, P. 159n30, 160n34, 172n61, 179n143, 184n12, 188n41, 189 nn48,49, 194nn77,80, 197n100, 198n110, 201n135, 204nn153,157, 161, 206nn171,176,180, 207n185, 209nn192,193,194,196, 210nn213, 214, 211n224
Genette, G. 167nn16,22, 175n86, 176 nn100,103
Gerhardsson, B. 179nn132,133, 181n163, 214n16
Giblin, C.H. 160n39, 185n15, 197n100, 203n149
Grant, F.C. 20, 159nn30,32,33, 160n34, 182n5, 189n47, 191n59, 197n103
Greenberg, M. 199n116

Greeven, H. 198n111
Grundmann, W. 160n36, 184n12, 188 n41, 189nn47,49, 193nn68,71, 195 nn84,86, 196n91, 197n100, 200 nn127,128, 202n138, 203n152, 205 n163, 206nn171,180, 210n214, 211 nn221,224, 212n226, 213n241
Gundry, R.H. 159n30, 184n12, 186n28, 187n37, 189n49, 190n51, 193n68, 194nn74,75,76,79, 195nn86,87, 196 nn90,92,96, 197n104, 198nn106,108, 201nn132,133, 203n147, 204nn157, 162, 206n171, 207nn180,181, 208 n189, 210n214, 211n224, 212n226, 213n237

Hahn, F. 22, 161n48, 220n87
Hare, D.R.A. 199nn115,116,117,119, 200n122, 201n137, 203n142, 207 n181, 209n201, 213n241
Hare, D.R.A., & J. Harrington 220n87
Held, H.J. 172nn58,59, 173nn63,64,65, 179n133, 181n170, 182n3, 188n41, 189n49, 193n69, 214n16
Hengel, M. 187n32, 209n196
Hill, D. 159n30, 160nn35,36, 180n158
Hoffmann, P. 155n6, 156n17, 187n32, 192nn32,63,65,193nn69,71, 194nn74, 77,78,79, 196nn90,96, 197n104, 198n107
Hooker, M.D. 21, 159n30, 160nn34,40

Iser, W. 166n3

Jeremias, J. 155n6, 192n63

Kermode, F. 163n56
Kingsbury, J.D. 53, 54, 164n56, 167n21, 168n27, 169n31, 175n85, 176n98, 178nn127,131, 179nn134,136,137, 139,143,155, 180nn158,159,160, 181 nn134,165,166,167,168,170,1, 189n47, 190n50, 202n139, 215n24
Kittel, G. 198n112
Klostermann, E. 159n30, 182n5, 184n12, 187n38, 189n46, 191n58, 194n74, 196n96, 197n100, 201n134, 206n171, 209n201, 210n214, 211n224, 212 nn226,234, 213n241
Kümmel, W.G. 157n22, 201n135
Künzel, G. 201n133, 203n141
Kunzi, M. 201n134

Lagrange, M-J. 159n30, 173n66
Lange, J. 17, 18, 157n19
Lange, P. 156n18
Lanser, S.S. 31-33, 35, 36, 39-43, 45,
46, 49, 53, 55, 56, 165nn62,66,
165n67, 166nn1,2,3,4,6,7,8,9, 167
nn10,11,12,13,14,15,16, 169nn38,39,
171nn52,53,54,55,57, 173n70, 174
nn71,72,74, 174nn77,82,84,85,86,87,
175n94, 176nn100,103,109,110, 177
n117,118, 178n129, 179nn144,145,
146,147,148
Laufen, R. 156n6, 187n32, 189n45, 192
n63, 193n69, 194nn74,77, 196n96,
205nn164,166,168, 207n184, 209
n196, 210nn201,203, 212n234
Legrand, L. 187n32
Lenski, R.C.H. 19, 158n28
Lohmeyer, E., & W. Schmauch 184n12
Lohr, C.H. 172n58, 182n4
Lohse, E. 156n9
Lotman, J.M. 178n126
Lund, N.W. 173n66
Luz, U. 161nn48,49, 189nn47,49

Maclaurin, E.C.B. 204n157
McNeile, A.H. 159n30, 165n35, 195n83
Magness, J.L. 213nn238,1
Mangatt, G. 183n12, 193n71
Marshall, I.H. 205n169, 206n174
Martin, F. 183n10, 186n28
Matera, F.J. 180n158
Matthey, J. 220n87
Meier, J.P. 156n6, 159n30, 193n71,
194n73, 196nn91,92,93,96, 201n134,
211n224, 212n226, 220n87
Metzger, B.M. 197n100
Meyer, H.A.W. 17, 18, 156nn16,17,18,
158n26, 184n12, 189n48, 190n51,
194n77, 196n92, 197nn98,100,104,
201n133, 204nn157,160, 206nn171,
176, 209n192, 210n214
Michaels, J.R. 210n210
Minear, P.S. 184n12, 190n51, 209n192,
210n210
Morosco, R.E. 159n30, 161n45, 183n12,
185n15, 189n45, 213n237

Neirynck, F. 180n158

O'Brien, P. 220n87

O'Connor, D., and J. Jimenez 207n80
Ogawa, A. 195n87, 201n133

Pappas, H.S. 205nn163,169, 206nn171,
180, 207n182
Patte, D. 164n56, 184n12, 187n32, 188
n41, 189n49, 191n56, 192n66, 193
n69, 194nn76,78, 195n87, 200n123,
201n132, 202n139, 204n155, 206
n171, 207n185, 209nn192,200, 212
n236, 220n87
Perrin, N. 26, 163n56, 164nn60,61, 165
n64, 183n11
Pesch, R. 169n33, 171nn50,56, 172n62,
179n135
Petersen, N.R. 163nn55,56, 169n40, 170
n41, 174n83, 175nn86,95, 178
nn126,130
Piwowarczyk, M.A. 41, 174nn76,77
Plummer, A. 159nn30,31, 184n12, 188
n44, 189n47, 193n71, 197nn100,
101,104, 206nn171,177, 207n180,
209n196, 210n214, 211n220

Radermakers, J. 182n7, 184n12, 193n71,
203n150, 213n241
Rhoads, D. 25, 164nn56,58,59
Rhoads, D. & D. Michie 34, 164nn56,59,
165n66, 167n23, 170n41, 174n83
Riesner, R. 183n12
Rigaux, B. 185n17
Robinson, T.H. 161n45, 188n41, 189
n47, 197n100, 206n171, 207n180
Roloff, J. 186n28
Rusche, H. 204n153, 210n213, 212n230

Sabourin, L. 182n5, 189n49, 194n77,
195nn86,87,1981nn110,111, 206
nn171,174,177, 207n180, 210n214,
211n221
Sand, A. 190n51, 211nn217,221,222
Schenk, W. 187n31, 195nn86,87
Schlatter, A. 158n28, 184n12, 187nn34,
36, 193n68, 194n73, 195n87, 196
nn90,91,93, 197n98, 198n113, 200
n123, 201n134, 205n169, 206
nn171,178, 208n190, 209nn196,197,
210nn208,214, 211n225, 212n229,
213n241
Schniewind, J. 182n3, 183n12, 187n32,
189n49, 192n65, 194nn76,77, 196

n93, 197n100, 201n133, 203n143,
206nn171, 208n190, 209n196, 210
n210,213,214
Scholes, R., & R. Kellogg 58, 59,164n57,
167n22, 179nn152,153, 180nn156,157
Schott, E. 22, 161n47, 184n12, 185n15
Schrenk, G. 211n220
Schulz, S. 160nn35,36
Schürmann, H., 201n133
Schweitzer, A. 18, 157nn21,22,23, 158
nn24,25
Schweizer, E. 159n30, 182n3, 183n12,
189nn45,46,49, 193nn68,69, 194n77,
195n87, 196n96, 197n100, 201
nn132,133, 205nn164,169, 206n171,
208n190, 210n214, 211n221, 213n241
Soulen, R.N. 194n77, 195n85
Strack, H.L., & P. Billerbeck 196n92,
198n109, 199n117, 206nn171,176,
210n210
Strecker, G. 159n30, 160n35

Tannehill, R.C. 163n56, 192n64, 193n72,
207n188, 208nn188,189,191,192
Ternant, P. 161n49, 182n3, 183n10,
186n24, 187n32, 188n41, 191n57
Thayer, J.H. 186n27
Thompson, W.G. 157n20, 173n64, 181

n170, 182nn5,7, 193n69,197n103
Tödt, H.E. 160nn35,36
Trilling, W. 205nn163,166, 209n195,
210nn206,214, 211nn221,225, 212
n228

Uspensky, B. 31, 43, 166n5, 174nn84,85,
175nn86,94, 176nn104,109, 177
n118, 178n129

Venetz, H.J. 186n29, 187n31, 188n43
Vorster, W.S. 164nn56,58,59

Waetjen, H.C. 197nn100,103, 205n169,
206nn171,179, 210n214, 213n241
Weimann, R. 42, 174n83
Weir, T.H. 198n112
Weiss, B. 184n12
Westermann, C. 193n69
Wilkinson, J. 160n35

Zahn, T. 18, 20, 158n27, 159nn30,31,
160nn34,44
Zerwick, M. 185n16, 200n126
Zerwick, M., & M. Grosvenor 191n58,
197n100
Zumstein, J. 220n87

JOURNAL FOR THE STUDY OF THE NEW TESTAMENT
Supplement Series

1 THE BARREN TEMPLE AND THE WITHERED TREE
William R. Telford

2 STUDIA BIBLICA 1978
II. Papers on the Gospels
E.A. Livingstone (ed.)

3 STUDIA BIBLICA 1978
III. Papers on Paul and Other New Testament Authors
E.A. Livingstone (ed.)

4 FOLLOWING JESUS
Discipleship in Mark's Gospel
Ernest Best

5 THE PEOPLE OF GOD
Markus Barth

6 PERSECUTION AND MARTYRDOM IN THE
THEOLOGY OF PAUL
John S. Pobee

7 SYNOPTIC STUDIES
The Ampleforth Conferences 1982 and 1983
C.M. Tuckett (ed.)

8 JESUS ON THE MOUNTAIN
A Study in Matthean Theology
Terence L. Donaldson

9 THE HYMNS OF LUKE'S INFANCY NARRATIVES
Their Origin, Meaning and Significance
Stephen Farris

10 CHRIST THE END OF THE LAW
Romans 10.4 in Pauline Perspective
Robert Badenas

11 THE LETTERS TO THE SEVEN CHURCHES OF ASIA
IN THEIR LOCAL SETTING
Colin J. Hemer

12 PROCLAMATION FROM PROPHECY AND PATTERN
Lucan Old Testament Christology
Darrell L. Bock

13 JESUS AND THE LAWS OF PURITY
Tradition History and Legal History in Mark 7
Roger P. Booth

14 THE PASSION ACCORDING TO LUKE
    The Special Material of Luke 22
    Marion L. Soards

15 HOSTILITY TO WEALTH IN THE SYNOPTIC GOSPELS
    T.E. Schmidt

16 MATTHEW'S COMMUNITY
    The Evidence of his Special Sayings Material
    S.H. Brooks

17 THE PARADOX OF THE CROSS IN
    THE THOUGHT OF ST PAUL
    A.T. Hanson

18 HIDDEN WISDOM AND THE EASY YOKE
    Wisdom, Torah and Discipleship in Matthew 11.25-30
    C. Deutsch

19 JESUS AND GOD IN PAUL'S ESCHATOLOGY
    L.J. Kreitzer

20 LUKE: A NEW PARADIGM
    M.D. Goulder

21 THE DEPARTURE OF JESUS IN LUKE-ACTS
    The Ascension Narratives in Context
    M.C. Parsons

22 THE DEFEAT OF DEATH
    Apocalyptic Eschatology in 1 Corinthians 15 and Romans 5
    M.C. De Boer

23 PAUL THE LETTER-WRITER
    AND THE SECOND LETTER TO TIMOTHY
    M. Prior

24 APOCALYPTIC AND THE NEW TESTAMENT:
    Essays in Honor of J. Louis Martyn
    J. Marcus & M.L. Soards

25 THE UNDERSTANDING SCRIBE
    Matthew and the Apocalyptic Ideal
    D.E. Orton

26 WATCHWORDS:
    Mark 13 in Markan Eschatology
    T. Geddert

27 THE DISCIPLES ACCORDING TO MARK:
    Markan Redaction in Current Debate
    C.C. Black

28 THE NOBLE DEATH:
Greco-Roman Martyrology and Paul's Concept of Salvation
D. Seeley

29 ABRAHAM IN GALATIANS:
Epistolary and Rhetorical Contexts
G.W. Hansen

30 EARLY CHRISTIAN RHETORIC AND 2 THESSALONIANS
F.W. Hughes

31 THE STRUCTURE OF MATTHEW'S GOSPEL:
A Study in Literary Design
D.R. Bauer

32 PETER AND THE BELOVED DISCIPLE:
Figures for a Community in Crisis
K.B. Quast

33 MARK'S AUDIENCE:
The Literary and Social Setting of Mark 4.11-12
M.A. Beavis

34 THE GOAL OF OUR INSTRUCTION:
The Structure of Theology and Ethics in the Pastoral Epistles
P.H. Towner

35 THE PROVERBS OF JESUS:
Issues of History and Rhetoric
A.P. Winton

36 THE STORY OF CHRIST IN THE ETHICS OF PAUL:
An Analysis of the Function of the Hymnic Material in the Pauline
Corpus
S.E. Fowl

37 PAUL AND JESUS:
Collected Essays
A.J.M. Wedderburn

38 MATTHEW'S MISSIONARY DISCOURSE:
A Literary Critical Analysis
D.J. Weaver

39 FAITH AND OBEDIENCE IN ROMANS:
A Study in Romans 1-4
G.N. Davies

40 IDENTIFYING PAUL'S OPPONENTS:
The Question of Method in 2 Corinthians
J.L. Sumney

41 HUMAN AGENTS OF COSMIC POWER IN HELLENISTIC
   JUDAISM AND THE SYNOPTIC TRADITION
   M.E. Mills

42 MATTHEW'S INCLUSIVE STORY:
   A Study in the Narrative Rhetoric of the First Gospel
   D.B. Howell

43 JESUS, PAUL AND TORAH:
   Collected Essays
   H. Räisänen

44 THE NEW COVENANT IN HEBREWS
   S. Lehne